To Marsha,

I hope you enjoy reading and using this book as much as I have.

I don't think you'll you find one thing stoggy about Mr. Copley.

CLC
9-14-76

LATIN  LITERATURE
From the Beginnings to the
Close of the Second Century, A. D.

# LATIN LITERATURE
## From the Beginnings to the
## Close of the Second Century A.D.

By
FRANK O. COPLEY

*Ann Arbor*
THE UNIVERSITY OF MICHIGAN PRESS

*Copyright © by The University of Michigan 1969*
*All rights reserved*
*Library of Congress Catalog Card No. 76-90760*
*Published in the United States of America by*
*The University of Michigan Press and simultaneously*
*in Don Mills, Canada, by Longmans Canada Limited*
*Manufactured in the United States of America*

*Grateful acknowledgment is made to the following publishers*
*for permission to reprint materials:*

G. Bell & Sons, Ltd. for material from the Bohn Classical Library
edition of Suetonius, *The Lives of the Twelve Caesars*, translated by Alexander Tomson and revised by T. Forester.

The Bobbs-Merrill Company, Inc., for material from the plays of
Plautus and Terence, translated by Frank O. Copley; from
Vergil's *Aeneid*, translated by Frank O. Copley; and from
Moses Hadas's translation of Seneca in *Roman Drama
Anthology*, translated by Frank O. Copley and Moses Hadas.

Harvard University Press for material from Livy, translated by
B. O. Foster; Lucan, *The Civil War (Pharsalia)*, translated
by J. D. Duff; and Juvenal and Persius, translated by G. G.
Ramsay. Reprinted by permission of the publishers and The
Loeb Classical Library. Cambridge, Mass.: Harvard University
Press.

Holt, Rinehart and Winston, Inc., for "Diffugere Nives" from
*The Collected Poems* of A. E. Housman. Copyright 1936 by
Barclays Bank Ltd. Copyright © 1964 by Robert E. Symons.
Reprinted by permission of Holt, Rinehart and Winston, Inc.

The Society of Authors as the literary representative of the
Estate of A. E. Housman and Jonathan Cape Ltd. for "Diffugere Nives" from A. E. Housman's *Collected Poems*.

Little, Brown and Company for "Of all the souls that stand
creat" from *The Complete Poems of Emily Dickinson*, edited
by Thomas H. Johnson.

The University of Michigan Press for material from Petronius,
*The Satyricon*, translated by William Arrowsmith, Copyright
© by William Arrowsmith 1959; and from Catullus, *The
Complete Poetry*, translated by Frank O. Copley, Copyright
© 1957 by The University of Michigan.

John Murray (Publishers) Ltd. for material from *The Annals*
of Tacitus, translated by G. G. Ramsay.

Charles Scribner's Sons for material from J. W. Mackail, *Latin
Literature* and from *The Works of Robert Louis Stevenson*,
Vol. 8, edited by Lloyd Osborne.

A part of the chapter on Vergil's *Aeneid* appeared, in slightly
different form, in the *Newsletter* of the Classical Association
of Oregon, Nov. 9, 1967.

*To my wife*

# A Note on the Sources of this Book

Most of the factual information in this book came from J. Wight Duff's two volumes on the history of Latin literature. The interpretive material is more nearly my own, but Duff and many another scholar have had a hand here, too. This book is, in fact, the fruit of some thirty-five years of reading, teaching, writing, and talking about Roman literature. It was written from the heart, in every sense of the word. The appended bibliography is not intended as an indication of sources (although some of my sources are there) but as a list of suggestions for supplemental reading for anyone who feels impelled to read on for himself. The translations used in this book, except where otherwise noted, are my own.

*Ann Arbor, Michigan*
*October 1968*

# Contents

# Introduction

The emperor Augustus loved to boast that he had found Rome a city of brick and left it a city of marble. Rome, with considerable justification, might have boasted in somewhat parallel fashion that she found a world at war and left it a world at peace. For nearly 300 years—and some would say for 500—the Roman Empire embraced the whole known world in a realm of peace and stability under a remarkably responsible and conscientious government and a system of law that still remains a model of jurisprudence. The empire was of course far from perfect; its peace was maintained at the cost of endless wars along its borders, as the Roman armies fought doggedly down the years to hold back the hordes of barbarians to whom the Mediterranean, with its peace and prosperity, was an ever-tempting goal. Even within the Empire the peace was periodically troubled, if not shattered, by the marching and countermarching of armies that took place nearly every time an emperor was deposed or died. But it is fair to say that the border troubles and the armies of the kingmakers had little effect upon the lives of the peaceful populations that lived within Rome's world. That world was not the simple world of the Greek city-state; it was complex, confusing, and frightening; it was full of pressures and counter-pressures, both from national and ethnic groups and from individuals of stature and power. The problems that it raised were complex and difficult to answer; the answers that were found were frequently as puzzling as the questions themselves. In their struggle to keep the peace among the many peoples over whom they had extended their power, the Romans were not always sensible or even kind. They were sometimes arbitrary, sometimes stupid, sometimes too prone to take refuge in the letter of their laws. Conscious of the fact that the peace of the world was being maintained only by the power of their Empire, they were ruthless in their suppression of subversion, whether real or fancied: having brought a world to

1

heel as well as to peace, they were not about to see their hegemony contested.

It was to this kind of world that Rome's poets, orators, historians, and storytellers gave expression. Where Greece had gone before them in the literary arts, the Romans gladly followed, genuinely eager to learn from the masters who, because of a felicitous combination of luck and genius, could claim for themselves the honor of being the first discoverers of Western thought and civilization. From the Greeks the Romans learned all that was to be learned at that time about literary form, about artistic literary expression, about the meters of poetry, and the rhythm and balance of prose, and above all about that harmony of form and content which is the basis of all literary excellence. But the Roman authors also had the sense to see that slavish imitation is not only dull and tedious but dishonest, that a Greek literature in Roman dress, while it might have a certain piquant charm, could never speak for Rome or say what the Roman writers themselves wished to say. Above all, the simplistic view of the Greek was ill-adapted to the expression of the Roman's complex world; it could not comprehend his ideas, depict his life, or express his thoughts. For the Roman, Greek culture and Greek literature were the strong foundation stones on which he built his own superstructure. Like the world out of which it grew and of which it was the expression, that literary superstructure was complex, puzzling, full of unanswered questions and of unresolved stresses. It could hardly have been otherwise.

# CHAPTER I

# The Beginnings

The Romans were a workmanlike people, and it is perhaps because of this that historians of Latin literature have habitually set a specific date for the beginnings of Latin literature, as if the Romans, having reached a suitable point in the evolution of their culture, decided that it was about time they began creating a literature and promptly set about the task. Characteristically, and with the usual deferential bow in the direction of Greece, the historians tell us that it was a Greek who was responsible for the event: in the year 240 B.C., so Livy says, an emancipated Greek slave, Livius Andronicus, presented to the public at Rome two plays, a tragedy and a comedy, which he had translated from Greek into Latin; with this dramatic act, and in this dramatic way, Roman literature began. Whether Andronicus was really the first, or whether there had been others who preceded him only to be forgotten, how a foreigner, whose native language was Greek, could have mastered Latin well enough to perform such a feat, where he might have found examples of the specialized, artistic language that would have been necessary for such a translation, how he would have learned to write the necessary Latin verse—for it is unthinkable that these plays should have been composed in prose—these and a host of questions that really need to be answered before we can understand what Andronicus did, still remain to vex us. We dare not assume the advent in Italy of a genius so monumental that he could start his former masters out along the path of literature with nothing more for a base than everyday conversation, the wise saws of barnyard and battlefield, some lullabys and nursery rhymes, the curt language of tombstone inscriptions, and the repetitious verbiage of laws and treaties.

3

Yet, in the form of actual Latin texts before 240 B. C., this is about all we have. It is patent that there must have been more than this, and that the production in that year of the two Greek plays, presupposes a history—perhaps a very long history—of literary endeavor in the Latin language. Andronicus must have found something ready at hand to work with. We know from other passages in Livy that there were already in existence certain dramatic or semi-dramatic forms, perhaps no more than skits and energetically rendered folk songs, and that the Romans very early became adept in the art of speaking, this latter no doubt because of the heavy dependence of their governmental system on the debates of popular assembly and lawcourt. And Cicero tells us of a tradition still current in his own day and originally reported by Cato, to the effect that the ancient Romans, when gathered for an evening around their cooking-fires, used to tell tales and sing songs of the glorious deeds of their ancestors.

There is no reason whatever to doubt the existence and the active presence in Rome of the third century B.C. of all these forms of language use, and there is little reason to doubt that Andronicus knew them all. Except for some inscriptions on tombstones, pots, pins, and other household articles, and except for a few miscellaneous bits of early Latin that found their way in the form of quotations into the works of later authors, this whole body of linguistic endeavor is lost to us. Yet it must have been present; the early Italian must have shared the penchant, which we find even among the simplest and most primitive people, for making speeches, singing songs, and telling tales. Perhaps his speeches, songs, and stories, were amateurish; their total disappearance suggests that they were slight performances. Yet they must have been highly enough developed by the mid-third century B. C. to provide Andronicus with the models that he would have needed for his purposes. The fragments of Andronicus's work show that he could draw a clear distinction between an epic and a dramatic style, the former grave, ponderous, and archaistic, the latter bright, easy-flowing, and colloquial. Andronicus's younger contemporary, Naevius, shows a similar consciousness of appropriate style; he also went on to compose comedies and tragedies of his own, not translated from the Greek but based on native legend and his own imagination. The stories must have been there for him to use, in a form sufficiently developed to be adaptable for literature; the early books of Livy give us a host of colorful legends, the like of which must have found expression in Italy long before the days of Andronicus and Naevius.

What then became of all this literature? Why has not a single line of it been preserved? Paucity and expensiveness of writing materials may in part be responsible for the loss; the attrition of time will account for some of it. Responsible too would be the lack of repositories where literary materials could be safely stored; it is undoubtedly true, too, that later literature, more skillfully composed and with vastly greater artistic excellence, so overshadowed this earlier writing that it was lost from view. But probably the most important single cause of its loss was the fact that it was largely if not entirely oral; it had never been written down but had simply been passed along from person to person and generation to generation by word of mouth.

That a reasonably large volume of literature might have been preserved in this way need not tax our credulity. Before the art of writing became common and before writing materials onto which reasonably large texts might be transcribed could become readily available, men perforce memorized what they wished or needed to know; furthermore, it was incumbent upon them to memorize accurately, since in most cases they would be repeating songs and stories to an audience that had already heard them many times, was familiar with their content, and demanded that they be reproduced correctly. The literatures of illiterate peoples have always been preserved in this way; there is certainly no reason to think that the Italians should not have developed and preserved a sizeable body of oral literature, a body moreover sufficiently highly developed in content, form, and style, to provide Andronicus with the kinds of materials he needed to study and to know in order to turn out those first two plays. Roman literature did not begin in 240 B.C.; it had begun centuries earlier. It is appropriate to set the beginning of Roman literature in 240 only because before that date we have no names, whether of authors or of their works, around which to construct a history. After 240 we do; Andronicus stands at the head of a long list of Latin authors who were his heirs and successors, and whose names, works, and careers give us a consistent and coherent history of the rise, flowering, and decline of the literature of the Roman people.

The little that actually remains of written materials prior to the mid-third century B.C. is virtually useless to the historian of literature. The famous inscription on the brooch from Praeneste

(*Manios med fhefhaked Numasioi*) regularly cited as the earliest bit of Latin extant tells us nothing but that "Manius made me for Numerius," a line certainly without any pretense to literary excellence. It gives us no hint of the level of contemporary literary endeavor in Latin, and other than that it is inscribed in letters, has no claim whatever to inclusion in a history of literature. The same may be said of all the "remains" of early Latin, the *Duenos-Bowl*, the *Columna rostrata*, sundry dedicatory inscriptions, and the epitaphs of the Scipios. The statement that "everyone at Rome agrees that this man [Scipio] was one of their best" and the declaration that "the ladies of Pisaurum gave this [cup] to Queen Juno" fail somehow to shed much light on the kind of stories that were being told to children by their mothers, or were being repeated around the campfires by soldiers, on the skits and dramatic folk-songs performed and sung on festive occasions, or on the speeches delivered in Senate, assembly, or lawcourt. A little scrap of barn-yard song preserves some wisdom about the weather:

> Dusty winter, muddy spring, my good young friend,
>     good crops will bring.*

A riddle, too, shows that at least the Romans had a sense of humor, since the answer to the riddle, if it was ever known, cannot now be discovered:

> Shepherds found you; they picked you without hands;
> They cooked you without fire; they ate you without teeth.†

The fact that religious texts have a strong hold on men and are therefore less likely to be forgotten than others, has preserved for us, to be sure in garbled form, the ancient *Song of the Arval Brothers*, a hymn that seems to have formed some part of the worship of the god Mars; passing down through the centuries, its text had become so badly damaged that even the priests who sang

*Hiberno pulvere, verno luto
  grandia farra, camille, metes
     (E. Diehl, *Poetarum Romanorum veterum reliquiae*, 1935, frg. 8)
†Pastores te invenerunt
  sine manibus collegerunt
  sine foco coxerunt
  sine dentibus comederunt
    (*id.* 11)

it in antiquity did not fully understand it, but were content to sing it as they thought they had heard it from their predecessors. It ran something like this:

> Bless us, ye Lars! (Repeat three times)
> Mars, do not let death and destruction fall upon our people
>     (Repeat three times)
> Be sated, fierce Mars; leap the threshold! Stop!
>     Ply the lash! (Repeat three times)
> Pray, now one, now another, to all the demigods!
>     (Repeat three times)
> Bless us, Mars! (Repeat three times)
> Glory! Glory! Glory!*

In addition to these pitiful bits and scraps, we hear of an early verse form called the Saturnian. A good many lines of this supposed verse have been preserved, but the ancients themselves were not certain how to read it, and the texts of the lines themselves have probably been tampered with to make them fit one or another theory of how they should be read. To this day, scholars have been unable to determine whether they were accentual, quantitative, or syllabic in character; their existence proves very little beyond the fact that the early Italian peoples had some sort of metrical system.

In one of his early books (*History* 7.2) Livy gives an elaborate report on the development of a literary form that he calls a *satura*, telling how it had its origin in certain Etruscan dances that on one occasion were imported into Rome. His report is not at all clear; all that can be deduced from it is that this literary form was a kind of informal skit involving dancing, singing, and probably some dialogue. It had no relation whatever to the later literary satire, and dropped into oblivion once the Romans had learned to adapt Greek comedy to the Latin stage.

Livy and Horace (*Epistles* 2.1.139-55) also speak of an early form of verse which they call *Fescennines*, the salient characteristic

---

*Enos Lases iuvate (ter)
  Neve lue rue Marmor sins incurrere in pleores (ter)
  Satur fu, fere Mars; limen sali! sta! berber! (ter)
  Semunis alternei advocapit conctos (ter)
  Enos Marmor invato! (ter)
  Triumpe, triumpe, triumpe!
        (E.H. Warmington, *Remains of Old Latin*, Vol. IV, Cambridge, 1959, p. 250, no. 23)

of which appears to have been its broad humor. It seems to have been a feature of gay and festive occasions, presumably indulged in when the participants were well gone in drink; it also was used as an apotropaic, a form of ridicule directed at individuals who were experiencing particularly happy occasions, such as a triumph or a wedding; the aim of the song was to ward off the danger of hybris by making the celebrant feel embarrassed and foolish. Horace goes on to say that these verses became so offensive that they had to be restrained by law, and that they ended up by being nothing more than light, amusing verse. Nothing is left of the *satura*; such examples as we possess of *Fescennine* verses come from much later periods. All these phenomena put together seem to indicate the existence in Italy prior to the mid-third century B.C. of a fairly extensive body of literature and quasi-literature, showing a diversified character and a fairly well developed sense of style. It is not too much to say that by the time Andronicus came on the scene, Italy was ready to embark upon a more formal type of literature and had ready to hand the language, the devices, and the techniques which Andronicus would have needed to master in order to produce works of literary merit in the Latin language.

# CHAPTER II

# Andronicus, Naevius, and Ennius

Of the life of Livius Andronicus we know a little something. He appears to have lived in Tarentum, and when that city fell to the Romans in 272 B.C. he was brought to Rome where he became the slave of the senator Livius Salinator. In all probability Andronicus's education was superior to that of his owner; in any event, he ultimately became tutor to Salinator's children, and it may well have been for pedagogical purposes that he made a translation into Latin of Homer's *Odyssey*. As a meter for his Latin version, he chose the old Saturnian, probably for no other reason than that no other narrative meter was available to him. As a vehicle for Homeric dactylic hexameter, the Saturnian is grotesque, but Andronicus's achievement is none the less remarkable. The scanty fragments of his translation are not only surprisingly accurate; in addition, they show a penetration into the nature and meaning of the Latin language quite surprising in a man whose native language cannot have been Latin. Furthermore, Andronicus's *Odyssey* is the first known example in the Western world of a literary translation. Treaties, laws, business documents and the like no doubt had been translated from Greek to Latin and from Latin to Greek before this time; we know too that the Jews of Alexandria, at least a century before, had translated the Septuagint from Hebrew into Greek. None of these, however, can truly qualify as a literary translation, for they were all made with a purely practical aim. In translating the *Odyssey* for the children of Salinator, Andronicus was not only attempting to provide them with a pedagogical exercise—a school-book, so to speak—but also to show them, in rudimentary form, something of the literature of Greece. Livy (*History* 27.37.7,13) reports that Andronicus also composed, in the year 207 B.C., a lyric

9

hymn of expiation addressed to the goddess Minerva; unfortunately he goes on to say that the hymn was not worth reproducing. We should have been glad to have it, regardless of its quality, for it would have been our earliest example of the Latin lyric. This remarkable man is also credited with the establishment in Rome of a College of Actors and Poets, which had its headquarters in the temple of Minerva on the Aventine Hill. He must have been brilliant, versatile, sensitive, and industrious; it is entirely pardonable in us to think of him as the founder of Roman literature, and to allow his two plays to mark the date at which Roman literature began.

Andronicus died in 204 B. C., but before his death a second literary genius had appeared in Rome. This was the poet Naevius (277–199 B. C.). He was no Greek and no slave; tradition has it that he was born in Campania and that he served as a common soldier in the First Punic War. He seems to have imported something of the roughness, the earthiness, and above all the stubborn independence that characterized the people of this region of Italy. An outspoken and not particularly tactful man, at one point in his career he found himself in serious trouble with the powerful family of the Metelli, of whom he had the discourtesy to remark that it was probably only by a stroke of bad luck that they had become consuls in Rome. The Metelli replied by putting Naevius in jail, where he languished for some time. Later in life, Naevius fell into disgrace again and was compelled to leave Rome for North Africa where he lived in Utica until the time of his death. His epitaph was characteristic of the man:

> If it were lawful for immortals to mourn for mortal men,
>     the holy Muses would weep for Naevius the poet.
> Once he was handed over to the treasure house of hell, men
>     at Rome forgot how to speak honest Latin.*

Greek that he was, it is highly unlikely that Andronicus should have attempted to give any particular Italian or Roman character to the translations he made. It was his intent, so it seems, to intro-

---

*Immortales mortales si foret fas flere
flerent divae Camenae Naevium poetam
itaque postquam est Orchi traditus thesauro
obliti sunt Romae loquier lingua Latina
        (Warmington, *Remains of Old Latin* [see p. 7, note],
        Vol. II, 1961, p. 154)

duce to his uncouth captors and owners, in their own uncouth tongue, at least some shadowy likeness of the glories of Greek literature. Naevius, on the other hand, was less impressed with the glories that were Greece, and while he was perfectly willing to take the Greeks for his teachers and models, he was too much the native Italian to be content with the mere Latinization of a foreign literature. Like Andronicus, he began by making translations, or at any rate adaptations, of Greek tragedy and comedy, particularly the latter, since his native ebullience made him lean more naturally in the direction of comedy than of tragedy.

The scanty fragments of Andronicus's comedy did not reveal much about its provenance; the fragments of Naevius's, however, make it clear that he turned for his comic models not to the Old Comedy of Aristophanes (445–387 B. C.), but to the much simpler type known now as the New Comedy, whose chief representative was Menander (342–291 B. C.). The Old Comedy, with its dancing choruses, elaborate costuming and probably equally elaborate stage-settings, did not suit the Roman's purse nor appeal to his taste; furthermore, its heavy dependence on the personalities and problems of mid-fifth century Athens made it a form very nearly impossible of imitation, even if the Roman had been content, as was the Greek, to have his politics made into a dramatic caricature, and his public figures paraded like buffoons across the stage.

By contrast, the New Comedy presented virtually no problems at all. It was a simple form, employing only a few actors, without a chorus, with a setting so unvarying that it could be built permanently onto the stage, and with no costuming other than standard Greek dress. Its characters, plots, and general subject matter were so general and typical that they readily found analogues in Italy; that same general character was insurance against dangerous political sentiment and risky personal satire. Furthermore, the plays of the New Comedy were available in large numbers, for although Menander was its chief exponent there were a host of others, including Diphilus (c. 336 B. C.) and Apollodorus (c. 280 B. C.), both of whom are known to have furnished models for the Roman playwrights.

But to Naevius, the Greek New Comedy was only a model and a starting point. Not content merely to translate and adapt, he began the much bolder venture of writing original plays on Italian themes. The fragments that remain of them are not sufficient in extent to tell us in what degree they differed from his Greek derived plays or to make it clear why this particular form never flourished in Italy, but to all intents and purposes it died with its inventor.

The reasons advanced for its demise are two-fold; first, that it brought the toga, the Roman national garment, onto the stage, and this the Roman audience would not tolerate; second, because it had engaged in discussion of public issues and personalities, and this again was something that the Roman audience could not accept. It is also entirely possible that the plays were not very good, and that the Roman playwright, being less inventive than his Greek confrere, found himself floundering when he cut loose from his models.

The last years of Naevius's life, when he was in exile in North Africa, were spent on the composition of his masterpiece, his epic, the *Punic War (Bellum Punicum)*. For his meter, Naevius like Andronicus before him chose the bumpy old Saturnian; but for his materials he reached back into the legendry and mythology of the Italian peoples, for it was his plan to let his central theme, the First Punic War, stand as the climax of the history of the Roman people up to that time. The fragments of his epic show clearly enough that he began his poem with the destruction of Troy and the flight of Aeneas from the burning city; the poet also followed the travels of Aeneas from Troy to Italy and, although the fragments are not entirely clear on this point, may well have included the story of Aeneas and Dido. Naevius did bring Aeneas on into Italy and told of the founding of the cities of Lanuvium and Alba Longa; he then quickly sketched Roman prehistory and history up to the beginning of the first conflict with Carthage. The extant fragments do not allow us to reestablish the architecture or plan of the poem; there seems little question, however, that the largest part dealt with the First Punic War. As for its literary excellence, the few lines that remain suggest a writer of considerable imagination, skill, and vigor. In any event, Naevius's epic did not suffer the fate of his Italian-based comedies and tragedies, for Horace— not, to be sure, with any vast enthusiasm—speaks of having studied Naevius in his own school days (*Epistles* 2.1.53–54).

In the development of Roman literature, Naevius is a figure of prime importance. Not only is his the first native Italian name that we meet in Roman literary history; further, he was the first to set the Romans on the path that was to lead them to greatness in a literature that was incontrovertibly their own. Andronicus had pointed out to his friends and masters that, no matter what they might have produced in the way of a "pre-literary literature," they were bound to waste much time and effort if they did not turn for instruction in the literary arts to the Greeks, who with incomparable genius had laid down the basic guidelines and rules on which all Western European literature, not only the Roman, was ultimately to rest. Naevius's work confirmed all this; it also taught the Roman his first great lesson in national literature, that, no matter from what source it might derive its basic rules and forms, it must never be content merely to imitate and to re-present, but must search its own heritage, its own personalities, its own milieu; in short, it must learn to speak its own language. Naevius's epitaph shows that he himself thought he had failed to teach his lesson, but he was mistaken; with all that the phrase could mean, both literally and in its broadest implications, "men at Rome" had indeed learned to "speak the Latin language honestly." From the time of Naevius on until Latin literature disappeared in the Middle Ages, the literature of the Romans remained a felicitous combination of Greek form and native Roman content, a national literature as unique in its spirit, content, and meaning as any that has been produced in Western Europe.

However fundamental and indispensible may have been the work of Andronicus and Naevius, it was almost completely overshadowed by the work of the next figure to appear on the Roman literary scene. To Romans of every succeeding period, Quintus Ennius (239–169 B. C.) remained, as Cicero lovingly styled him, "Father Ennius," the true founder of Roman literature. He was born in Rudiae in Calabria, almost lost in the hinterlands of the heel of the Italian peninsula. That section of Italy is even today almost as much Greek as Italian; in antiquity, the influence of Greek cities like Tarentum must have been far greater than it is now. Ennius was probably bilingual from childhood, speaking both Latin and Greek; later on, from long residence near Naples, he also acquired fluency in Oscan, the native tongue of Campania. To Ennius, his familiarity with these three languages was rather more than a linguistic happenstance; it pleased him to feel that his linguistic accomplishments were the natural expression of the deep affection he felt for the three cultures, Greek, Roman, and Campanian, that had become such fundamental parts of his personal, as well as his literary life. He said, in fact, that he had "three hearts," one for each of these, and it is perhaps not too much to see in this combining of three cultures, three languages, and three peoples in the one man, a symbolic foreshadowing of the combination of peoples, tongues, and cultures that, as Vergil so accurately saw, was to be the essence of the Roman Empire.

Details of Ennius's life, as with most ancient authors, are hard to come by. He served in the Roman army in Sardinia, where he came to the attention of the quaestor, Cato; the two men became such close friends that Cato brought Ennius with him when he returned from Sardinia to Rome. It is also reported that Ennius taught Cato Greek, thus perhaps assisting in some degree to soften the old fighter's life-long enmity toward the Greeks and their culture.

It is interesting to note that Ennius's lifetime entirely spans the Second Punic War (218–202 B. C.), that worst of the three and the one that so nearly resulted in victory for Carthage. Apart from his service in Sardinia, Ennius's part in the war is not known; he did hold the rank of centurion and, to have attracted the attention of Cato, he must at least have been a disciplined and efficient soldier. It is interesting to speculate that his experiences in the Second Punic War, his friendship with Cato, and his subsequent move from Naples to Rome may signalize the rise of that "Latin" heart of his to a position of primary influence in his thought, and may ultimately have prompted him to the writing of his great epic, *The Annals*. He seems to have lived in very modest circumstances all his life, and apart from his military experience, to have been completely absorbed in writing. Cicero tells us that in his later years Ennius "bore the two burdens of poverty and old age in such a manner that he seemed almost to be enjoying them" (*De senectute* 5.14). The picture we get is of an enthusiastic and industrious playwright, poet, critic, and scholar, a gifted artist and thinker, a warm-hearted and unpretentious man with a vivid imagination and a rich sense of humor.

Ennius was a prolific writer. He composed at least twenty tragedies, all but one apparently translations or adaptations from Greek originals. The tragedies from the Greek are drawn chiefly from the cycle of stories surrounding the conflict between Greece and Troy, and the Greek tragedian to whom Ennius chiefly turned for his models was Euripides. His one "native" tragedy was the *Rape of the Sabines (Sabinae)*. Again the fragmentary state of these tragedies makes them hard to evaluate; the extant bits and scraps show a man who had studied Andronicus and Naevius and learned from them how to handle the problem of putting Greek into Latin. The quality of his work with tragedy is attested at least in some degree by the fact that his plays were read and revered as masterpieces for many centuries after his death. The fragments of his *Rape of the Sabines* tell us virtually nothing about it; we may conjecture that it suffered from the same deficiency that seems to have afflicted all Italian-based ancient drama; like the rest of them, it was an effort nobly conceived but pathetically unsuccessful. Ennius also wrote a few comedies, at least one of which again may have been on a native Italian theme.

Ennius was also the author of a series of *Satires*, really miscellanies, perhaps best described as critical essays on a great variety of subjects, ranging all the way from spelling-reform to gourmanderie. Some of these were in prose, some in verse, some in a combination of the two. One of them contained his version of the old Aesopic fable, *The Meadow-Lark and Her Nestlings* (Aulus Gellius, *Noctes Atticae* 2.29); another discussed the physical make-up of the world; still another seems to have been an attempt to rationalize the ancient pagan gods as deifications of great heroes. All in all, they suggest a man of lively intellect and wide-ranging interests.

But the masterpiece of Ennius's life, the work on which he spent the longest time, the greatest effort, and in the execution of which all his poetic arts reached their highest point, was his poem, *The Annals*, an epic in eighteen books. Like Naevius before him, Ennius chose a historical subject, but he seems to have contented himself with a quick sketch of early prehistory and to have passed very lightly over the First Punic War with the remark that this had already been treated "by backwoods poets of an earlier day."* By contrast, he writes in great detail on the early history of Rome in Italy, telling, for example, the stories of the birth of Romulus and Remus, the founding of the city of Rome, the events of the numerous wars waged by Rome with her Italian neighbors, and with King Pyrrhus of Epirus, and continuing in this vein up to the events of his own lifetime.

Like the rest of Ennius's work, the poem is extant only in fragments, but in this case there are enough of these to enable us to form some judgment about its literary qualities. Its salient characteristics are certainly vigor, directness, and color; there is little grace, but no lack of human feeling. The following passage depicts Romulus and Remus taking the auspices to determine which of the two should be the founder of the new city:

---

*"versibus quos olim Fauni vatesque canebant"
    (Warmington, *Remains of Old Latin* [see p. 7, note],
Vol. I, 1961, p. 82, no. 232-34)

Remus prayed for a sign; all by himself
he watched for a welcome bird. But Romulus the Fair
stood on the Aventine, watched for the winged breed.
They vied for the name of their city: "Remora" or "Rome?"
The people all worried which should be commander.
They waited, as, when the consul prepares to give
the signal, all men greedily watch the stall-gates:
How soon will he send the cars from their painted ways?
So the people waited and showed fear on their faces:
Who had won the victory; who, a mighty throne?
Meanwhile the white sun dropped into nether night.
Then white-rayed, gleaming, daylight came bursting forth.
Right then from heaven a splendid good-luck sign
Flew down: a bird on the left. Up rose the golden sun.
Down from the heavens came thrice four holy birds;
They moved toward quarters that meant good luck and joy.
By this, Romulus knew himself first choice:
The bird-sign awarded him dais, throne, and crown.*

The lines—perhaps because they were not quite accurately quoted —do not make it entirely clear that it was Romulus who saw the more propitious sign and was therefore elected to be the founder of Rome; they are jerky; they are also over-ponderous. But their dignity and forcefulness are not to be questioned, and these qualities are to be found in a great many of the extant fragments. *The Annals* doubtless deserved to remain, as in fact it did, the great national epic of Rome until the writing of Vergil's *Aeneid*. Cicero loved it, and knew large parts of it by heart; the second century A. D., a sentimental, archaizing age, saw it for a brief time elevated above the *Aeneid* in popular favor.

Whatever the literary qualities of *The Annals*, in the course of writing it Ennius took what is probably the most important single forward step ever taken in the history of Roman literature. His predecessors, Andronicus and Naevius, had stayed with the old native Saturnian, a clumsy, bumpy meter totally inadequate to the epic manner. Ennius was not content to follow them. Instead he determined to create a Latin dactylic hexameter, to domesticate the meter of the *Iliad* and *Odyssey*, and thereby to create a Latin meter equal to the demands of the epic style.

The sheer mechanical magnitude of the task that Ennius set for himself can hardly be overestimated. All Greek meters are

*Warmington, *Remains of Old Latin,* Vol. I, pp. 28-30, no. 80-100.

based on the quantitative principle; they depend for their rhythmic quality on a precisely regulated pattern of long and short syllables. In their composition, accent, whether of word or of sentence, plays relatively little part; because accent in Greek is of pitch rather than of stress, the Greek poet did not feel constrained to create accentual patterns in his verse, but could content himself with conforming to the canon of long and short syllables demanded by the verse form in which he chose to write.

The nature of accent in Latin has been much debated, but it seems agreed now that Latin, like English, had a stress accent, and in this respect was totally unlike Greek. When Andronicus and Naevius began to use Greek tragedy and comedy as models for their work in Latin, they found, very fortunately for the success of their venture, that the commonest dramatic meters in Greek, an eight foot trochaic line and a six foot iambic line, could be imitated in Latin with relatively little difficulty. The quantitative patterns of the trochee (long—short) and of the iamb (short—long) were found to be almost as readily available in the Latin language as they had been in the Greek. Furthermore, the relatively heavy stress accent of Latin tended to soften the quantity of any syllable that fell in the "short" position, and this permitted the Latin metrist to substitute the spondee (long—long) with far greater freedom than had been possible for his Greek predecessors. These early Latin meters emerge as a remarkably graceful compromise between the quantitative and the accentual principles; in theoretical structure, they remain true to their quantitative Greek models; their rhythmic patterns with amazing ease and grace follow the natural rhythms of the Latin language.

The problem that Ennius faced in creating the Latin dactylic hexameter was more complicated than this. In the dramatic meters, the softening or slurring-over of syllables in the "short" position made for quite casual substitution of a long for a short in that position; this meant, further, that the Latin metrist need be concerned about the true quantity of only every other syllable in his line. In other words, he need only watch carefully the quantity of the syllables in the "long" position; so long as these were correct, he need not worry too much about the others.

But with the dactylic hexameter, no such slurring is possible; the dactyl (long—short—short) is a foot mathematically precise and allowing no substitution whatever other than a long syllable for the two shorts. In order to write it acceptably, the poet must be absolutely certain of his quantities; he could not count, as could the writer of dramatic verse, on the heavy stress of his language to carry him along over "incorrect" quantities. But before Ennius's time, it is highly unlikely that anyone, poet or metrist, had bothered to determine with any precision the rules for length of syllables in the Latin language; writers had found the natural rhythms of the spoken language quite sufficient to carry them along through trochees and iambs and had therefore never felt the need for a strict and precise determination of quantity.

With the dactylic hexameter, this was no longer the case; Ennius's first task was to determine the rules for quantity in Latin. The rules that he (and perhaps a good many others, for we have no idea how many poets may have worked on the problem) eventually came up with were remarkably simple, and were in fact borrowed directly from the Greeks: a long syllable is any syllable that contains a long vowel or a diphthong, or one in which the vowel, whether long or short, is followed by two or more consonants. Syllables of the second category (we call them now "long 'by position' ") were easily identified; those of the first were not so easily disposed of. Although the speaker of Latin at all periods was conscious of the length of vowels in a way quite unfamiliar to speakers of English, still haste of utterance, sentence stress, sentence melody, and a host of other linguistic phenomena must have left the quantity of many a Latin vowel in considerable doubt. Before Ennius could write acceptable dactylic hexameters, he had almost literally to determine the true quantity of every vowel of every word that he wished to use. How he did this we shall never know; the fact remains that his determination of the quantity of vowels shows almost no deviation from the work of later, more sophisticated writers, and equally little deviation from what linguistic science has taught us in more recent times about the true quantities of vowels in Latin. Even if Ennius had not been a great poet in his own right, his work as a metrist in the creation of the Latin dactylic hexameter would be sufficient monument to his genius. His hexameters show some crudities, and take a number of metrical liberties that later poets eschewed; a few lines of Ennius, placed alongside any random group of lines from Vergil or Ovid, will inevitably sound rough and ungraceful. But with the writing of *The Annals*, the metrical foundations on which a great national poetry must rest had now definitely been laid. Rome was ready for the poets who were to come; the heritage that Ennius left them richly entitled him to the epithet of "Father" that Cicero later bestowed upon him.

# CHAPTER III

# Plautus

Fragmentary authors are never very satisfactory; the random bits and scraps that familiarity, affection, and interests sometimes far other than literary have preserved are often no more than tantalizing, leaving us with the insecure feeling that our appreciation of the author and our judgment of his qualities are at best imperfect and may be ludicrously in error. It is with a sense of genuine relief that we turn to the first Latin author from whose hand we have some complete works. Titus Maccius Plautus (c. 254–184 B. C.), a playwright, was a native of Sarsina, a small hill-town about forty miles southwest of the modern city of Rimini. Aulus Gellius, that prolix polymath and collector of random curiosa, gives an odd and probably garbled account of the life of Plautus. He says (*Noctes Atticae* 3.3.14) that Plautus was first engaged in "stage work," and that in this occupation he amassed a considerable fortune which he proceeded to invest in trading ventures of some kind. Apparently he had no more head for business than do most literary men, for he soon found himself bankrupt, and in order to keep alive was forced to take employment in a gristmill. In the time he could find free from this occupation, he wrote plays, which a century or so later were collected and edited by the scholar Varro.

This whimsical little sketch is full of difficulties; it is hard now to imagine what Gellius meant by "stage work" *(opera artificum scaenicorum)* and even harder to imagine how Plautus could have amassed any large sums of money in any job connected with the theater. Actors, more frequently than not slaves, were paid no vast sums for their services: the common suggestion that Plautus was a "stage carpenter" and that he made his money building the temporary wooden theaters which were the only kind known in

Italy in his day, seems again not to suggest a very lucrative occupation. But if we let it go and assume that whatever it was it gave Plautus enough money to enable him to buy shares in some kind of trading venture, then we are faced with the equally difficult problem of determining how the poet, spending endless dusty, hot days in a gristmill, had the energy and enthusiasm to write plays. Gellius's account shows every evidence of having passed through a number of romanticizing minds; hidden in it somewhere are doubtless several kernels of truth, among them the practical certainty that Plautus had been associated with the theater from his earliest youth, for his sure sense of stage and audience can only have been gained from long association. We know the place and approximately the date of his birth; we know the date of his death and have been able to determine the dates of first production of a number of his plays; since the discovery in the mid-nineteenth century of the great Ambrosian manuscript, we know the correct form of his name.*

Other than these few facts, and the indubitable love of the man for the theater, there is little that we can determine with certainty about Plautus. The plays themselves tell us that he was a man of wit, discernment, with a degree of human sympathy and a considerable measure of poetic ability. In the Western European literary tradition, he is also one of the acknowledged masters of the colloquial style; the easy, lively flow of his Latin, his skillful introduction of slang, trade argot, verbal coinage and witticism have produced as good a sample as we have of the way in which the Latin language was actually spoken. Varro is reported to have said that if the Muses had spoken Latin they would have spoken Plautine Latin; the compliment was far from undeserved.

We are not sure how many plays Plautus actually wrote. Gellius, at the end of his odd little biography, mentions three, two of which he gives by name, the third of which he had forgotten. The names of the first two, *Saturio* and *Addictus*, do not appear in our Plautus manuscripts, a curious phenomenon for which no satisfactory explanation has ever been offered. We are told that originally in antiquity one hundred thirty plays circulated under

*Previous to this time, he had been known as Marcus Accius Plautus. The great Ambrosian manuscript is of the third or fourth century A.D. It is a palimpsest; that is to say, the text of Plautus had been erased and the sheets of parchment used for the transcription of another entirely different text. However, since the ink of the original text could not be entirely obliterated, the shadowy outlines of the Plautine text can still be read.

the name of Plautus. The scholar Varro undertook to edit these; he divided them into three lists: one, the genuine; two, the probable and three, the spurious. The "genuine" list seems to have comprised the twenty-one plays we now have; it appears that this "Varronian Rescension" was as standard in antiquity as it is now; if consistency in style, composition, and theatricality are any criteria of single authorship, then Varro's twenty-one plays seem very well chosen. If we allow for certain small changes probably introduced into actors' copies by later stage directors or by the actors themselves, all of the plays give every evidence of being by the same hand, and there is surely no reason now to doubt that that hand was Plautus's. Enormously popular in his own day, during the succeeding centuries, Plautus's plays, along with those of his younger contemporary, Terence, emerged from the Middle Ages to set a standard for all subsequent continental European comedy.

The plays of Plautus, and it is to be presumed those of Andronicus and Naevius before him, were produced in an outdoor theater that was a variant on the Greek theater. The Greek orchestra, originally a circle, was reduced to a semicircle, across the flat side of which rose the long, narrow stage, elevated some five feet or more above the level of the orchestra floor. The stage might be as much as one hundred twenty feet long; it was ordinarily about fifteen feet wide. Backstage rose a perpendicular wall high enough to represent the fronts of houses, and pierced with two or three doors. (Since some of the plays require two houses, and some three, as their scenes, it may be that the number of doors could be varied.) These doors, of course, represented the entrances into houses; under ordinary circumstances this was all the "scenery" that the Roman stage afforded.

In some of the plays, there appears to have been a kind of alleyway between two of these housefronts; it is uncertain now whether this alleyway was an actual entrance to the stage, or was merely a niche or recess. In any event, we commonly hear of characters stepping into the recess as a vantage point from which to eavesdrop on the conversations of other characters on the stage. The stage itself represented a street, most commonly a street in Athens, although the scene is sometimes set in other cities. Access to the stage could be gained at either end; by convention the end to the spectator's right led downtown, that on the spectator's left to the harbor or to foreign parts.

Since all of Plautus's plays were derived from the Greek New Comedy his characters all wear the standard Greek dress (called *pallium* in Latin) and, at least in theory, all of the realia of the plays are Greek: place names, legal institutions, political institutions, coinage, all are at least nominally Greek. The world of the Plautine stage is presented to us as Greek; that Plautus is not entirely consistent in this, and sometimes allows Italian realia and Italian allusions to slip in, proves nothing but that he was a somewhat exuberant composer, primarily interested in theatrical effect and singularly unconcerned about scholarly accuracy.

Plautus's plays are for fun; if he occasionally slipped and said *consul* instead of *archon*; if his characters occasionally spend *denarii* instead of obols and drachmas; if they made reference to peculiarly Italian and Roman institutions of which the ordinary Greek would have been ignorant, this was, for Plautus, and probably also for his audiences, only part of the fun. One fixed principle Plautus does observe: no Roman ever appears on his stage. Greeks, a Carthaginian, slaves of many nationalities, take part but never any person who is demonstrably of Roman or even of Italian provenance.

In transferring the Greek plays that were his models to the Italian stage, Plautus did not slavishly translate or even painstakingly adapt his originals. He introduced much material that is his own. Individual lines certainly and whole scenes probably are of his own composition, and the many puns and other wordplays that are comprehensible only in Latin must be his own. Plot, characters, scene, and the general plan of action and development are largely Greek; much of the dialogue, too, is Greek derived. But for all their plausible Greek dress the plays have a distinctly Italian air; Plautus handled his Greek materials in such a way as to produce a Roman-Italian comedy in Greek dress.

In point of fact, since the Greek New Comedy, with the single exception of Menander's *Dyskolos*, is extant only in fragments, we gain our best impression of its nature from the Latin plays of Plautus and Terence. Their comedies show us a simple type of drama, in which the action revolves around certain more or less standardized plots and a set of very nearly stereotyped characters. In play after play, the plot is concerned with the love of a young man for a young woman, called *meretrix* in Latin, and *hetaira* in Greek. English lacks a proper name for this lady; the term "prostitute" smacks too much of the night police court; "whore" is an insult, for she is no common streetwalker. Classicists in general have contented themselves with the prissy term "courtesan"; and in default of anything better, it will probably have to do.

The women in question were really professional entertainers of men; schooled in poetry, philosophy, music, and dancing, they provided the educated Greek gentleman the kind of cultivated feminine companionship that is of enduring interest to any normal male. That these women also provided men with sexual delights is patent; they were schooled in these arts, too. But they were not available to all comers at a price; they appear to have reserved their pleasures and delights for one, or at most two or three men, who under an arrangement of semipermanent cohabitation, undertook to supply them with the necessities and, insofar as their means would permit, the luxuries of life. Commonly, these women were slaves owned by a pimp *(leno)* who housed them and saw to it that their lovers paid appropriate sums for them, and from whom lovers sometimes purchased them for their own exclusive use.

Sometimes, too, the lady was already a freedwoman or a foreigner, operating, as one might say, on her own. One fact about her must be kept clearly in mind: whether she were slave, freedwoman, or foreigner, her Athenian citizen lover was legally debarred from marrying her. The love affairs of the comedy revolve without exception around women of this sort—and for that matter, so does virtually all of the ancient literature of love. Ancient society expected its young men to contract liaisons of this sort, and demanded only that they be handled with a degree of discretion and without inordinate expense, and that when the time came for proper marriage with a citizen-girl, the young man gently but firmly dismiss his ladylove, and undertake not to consort again with her or her kind.

In the comedies, love affairs are always beset with difficulties, but these are most commonly of a financial sort, and only occasionally involve social or moral disapproval. In play after play, the plot takes its start from the young man's discovery that he does not have the funds to satisfy the demands either of the lady or of her owner; filled with passion and frustration, but not blessed with much intelligence or inventiveness, the young man turns for help in his predicament to his loyal and intelligent slave. Between the two, a scheme is laid whereby the necessary funds are obtained by trickery, either from the young man's father, or from a too-trusting banker, or sometimes from the pimp himself. Once the money has been obtained and "boy has got girl," the story is at an end.

Around this rather thin thread of plot, various distractive and elaborative elements can be arranged. A crusty old father, who has forgotten his own gay youth, may be introduced to put difficulties in the way of the young man's obtaining the money he needs; sometimes the young man has a rival, too, often in the person of a soldier, who boasts endlessly of his military exploits, but who has come back from his campaigns well supplied with money and ready for a month or two on the town. The clever, sophisticated slave may have as his foil a stupid, boorish slave with whom he may engage in exchanges devised more for the amusement of the audience than for the furthering of the plot. Sometimes a respectable lady, mother or aunt of the young man, will step in to defend the young fellow against the churlish attacks of his father; the basic plot situation too can be varied by the introduction of a second pair of lovers, with problems that parallel or cross those of the protagonists. The plot may be varied, too, by the introduction of a host of dramatic devices that are still sound theatre: the drunk scene, mistaken identity, the comedy of situation, and bald-faced clowning and slapstick.

One much-favored figure is the "parasite," a character become conventional on the stage, who probably owes his origin to a class of impecunious aristocrats, men who by some misfortune had lost their inherited wealth and, being far too proud to work, had been reduced to living off their more fortunate friends. On the comic stage, the parasite is almost invariably a clown, a caricature of the down-at-heels gentleman, whose sole interest in life is food and who contributes to the amusement of the audience by shamelessly toadying to, and passing wicked asides about, the character to whom he has attached himself.

But certainly the most interesting single variation to be introduced into this potpourri of fun, foolishness, and frustration, is the recognition-motif, by which the girl either already possessed by her lover but about to be torn from him by reason of his lack of funds, or still virgin, but on the brink of initiation into her profession, is discovered to be an Athenian citizen. Lost in childhood either by exposure or by kidnapping, she is now restored to honorable status by the discovery of some token, such as a pin, a ring, or a bracelet, still in her possession after having been originally left with her by her distraught mother or carried away by her when she was kidnapped. Once established as free-born, she is automatically and immediately released from slavery, and the young man, whose original intention had been to win her as his mistress, now very properly takes her as his wife.

To our way of thinking, this recognition device must seem baldly coincidental and obviously contrived. In antiquity, however, it probably was not so, since exposure of unwanted children, particularly girls, was a regular practice of ancient society, and the kidnapping of young girls by pirates or other marauders who helped to supply the slave traffic, was probably not an uncommon incident. It is certainly not hard to imagine the unhappy mother, ordered by her husband to dispose of a newly born girl-child, dropping the baby on some doorstep, and leaving with her some bit of jewelry, in the forlorn hope that the child might be allowed to keep it and by that means some day perhaps be recognized as free-born.

It is quite certain that all the stories presented upon the Roman comic stage were thoroughly familiar to the audience before the play began; if there were any doubt, this would be dispelled by the prologue, in which the audience was told what the story was to be. The only use of suspense in stories of this sort is to set the audience to wondering how the playwright will bring to their inevitable end the circumstances he has contrived, but since the devices for variation even here are limited by the demand that the playwright not stretch the credulity of his audience beyond all reason, he had to rely on other devices, notably on dramatic irony, to maintain interest. Time and again we are amused by noticing that facts known to one character on the stage are not known to another, or that we of the audience know things that the characters on the stage do not know.

In spite of their surface similarity, the comedies of Plautus show an amazing variety both in plots and in characters, so much so that it is rather difficult to select one play that might be called typical of his work. Most nearly conventional, perhaps, is the *Cistellaria (The Jewel-box)*. As in many of the comedies, the action of the play involves only the final incidents of a story that began long before, and that is revealed to us in the prologue. (In an otherwise unexampled fashion, Plautus has displaced the prologue to the *Cistellaria* from its usual place at the beginning of the play, and located it after the first two scenes.) As the prologue tells it, Demipho, some eighteen years before, on a trip from his home in Lemnos to Sicyon, in the course of a drunken festival had raped a free-born young woman of the place. Without then revealing his identity to the girl, he had returned to his home in Lemnos where he had later married and had had a daughter by his wife. The wife subsequently died; upon her death Demipho returned to Sicyon and there married the girl whom he had raped. As a result of that incident, she too had borne a daughter, but had handed her over to a slave, Lampadio, to be exposed. Lampadio had watched the baby and had seen her picked up by an old woman and delivered to the house of Melaenis, a courtesan, who had brought the girl up decently and honestly, and given her the name Selenium. As the play begins, we find Demipho's daughter by his Lemnian marriage engaged to a young man, Alcesimarchus, who is himself in love with Selenium. The play is concerned with the machinations by which Alcesimarchus, chiefly through the clever offices of Lampadio, is disentangled from his alliance with Demipho's Lemnian daughter and enabled to marry Selenium, who by means of a box of trinkets has been recognized as the the daughter of Demipho and Phanostrata, the Sicyonian girl whom he had raped years before and to whom he was now properly married.

The Greek original of the *Cistellaria* was by Menander, and Plautus's handling of it gives every evidence of his having followed his model quite closely. Yet a hint of the freedom with which he treated all his Greek originals is afforded by the prologue, at the end of which the speaker steps out of his role and addresses the audience:

"Goodbye all! Keep on winning victories by honest courage as you have done before! Stand by your allies, both the old and new; encourage them to help you by treating them justly under your laws! Destroy your enemies; win glory and the crown of victory! Defeat the Carthaginians and make them pay for the wrongs they have done you!" (197–202)

This obvious reference to the Second Punic War can hardly have appeared in Menander's original, and must be by Plautus himself.

This type of plot, in which the problems posed by a love affair are solved by the recognition of the girl as free-born, is used by Plautus in five others of his plays.* In two plays, the *Casina* and the *Stichus*, the plots are concerned with the adventures of couples already married; the *Poenulus*, or *The Carthaginian*, is of special

---

*Curculio, Epidicus, Poenulus, Rudens,* and *Truculentus.*
In one other play, the *Persa,* the recognition theme is used but in a rather different way: Saturio, the parasite, sells his daughter to the pimp as a slave. Once he has the money, Saturio reveals the free status of his daughter, and the pimp under the law is required immediately to give her up. Saturio, of course, keeps the money, which he has obtained to help a young friend in his purchase of the girl of his choice. Brief summaries of the plots of all of Plautus's plays may be conveniently found in H. J. Rose, *A Handbook of Latin Literature* (London, 1949) pp. 42–56.

interest because it includes a passage in the Punic language (930–49) followed by a scene in which the Latin is liberally sprinkled with Punic words and phrases. Since the Plautine audience was unlikely to have sat still for so long a passage in a language they did not understand, it follows that the Roman populace, in the course of their long and not very happy relations with Carthage, had picked up at least a smattering of the Punic language. One lone play, the *Captivi*, has no female characters at all; Plautus has his prologue in this play deliver himself of a distressingly self-righteous plea for special attention:

> "It will be really worth your while to give some time to this play. It has not been written according to the usual trite plan or just like all the others: it contains no dirty lines that will not bear repetition; it has no perjured pimp or sinful courtesan or boastful soldier. . . ." (54–58)

Unfortunately, the play, which deals with the efforts of a well-to-do father to ransom his son who has been taken prisoner of war, lacks Plautus's usual spriteliness, and would probably rarely have been read in modern times, if its sexless story did not make it admirable classroom material.

Another play, the *Aulularia*, has special interest for the modern reader, since it was destined to be the model for Molière's *L'Avare*; if it were not for the unfortunate fact that the last scene of Plautus's play has been lost, it could have provided us with some delightful arguments about the relative merits of the two playwrights. Even in its mutilated state, the play stands up well by comparison with Molière's; it is not mere professional loyalty that has led most classicists to prefer Plautus's version.

Another play that had the distinction of being used as a model by a later and far greater playwright is the *Menaechmi*, a farce with virtually no plot at all, and concerned from beginning to end with the efforts of one of a pair of twins, long separated, to find the other. This play was the original for Shakespeare's *Comedy of Errors*. The genius of Shakespeare perhaps suggests that comparison of his play with Plautus's is inadvisable; again, however, the classicists, and again not entirely out of professional loyalty, will point out that Shakespeare's addition of a second pair of twins seems rather to gild the lily of a story sufficiently amusing as it stands.

Plautus's *Amphitryo* has also had its modern imitators, the

latest being Anouilh, whose version, *Amphitryon 38,* was translated
into English and had a long run on Broadway. This play is based
on the story of the begetting of Hercules, when the god Jupiter,
having fallen in love with Alcmena, the sweet and virtuous wife of
Amphitryon, disguised himself as her husband in the certain knowledge that unless he could trick Alcmena into thinking he was
indeed Amphitryon, he would be unable to induce her to commit
adultery with him, king of the gods though he was. Alcmena has
often been described as the noblest of Plautus's female characters;
she certainly has dignity and loyalty; she has, moreover, a certain
motherly and wifely aura about her that renders the old god's
seduction of her distinctly obscene. Her bewilderment at being
confronted with two husbands, the one quite undistinguishable
from the other, and her puzzlement at Amphitryon's apparently
irresponsible changes of plan were no doubt meant by Plautus to
be very funny, but they have about them a pathos not entirely unrelated in type to the roles made famous by Charlie Chaplin. As if
the basic story were not rich enough of itself, Plautus has added to
its hilarity by the addition of a further instance of mistaken
identity: Mercury, Jupiter's divine attendant and messenger, dis-
guises himself as Amphitryon's slave, Sosia. They turn out to be a
finely matched pair of wits, with Mercury having the edge only by
virtue of his divine status; their scenes together are among the
best in the play.

Except for a minor deity or two who appear in one or another
prologue, this is the only play of Plautus's in which divine characters are used; his broad burlesque of divinity fails to startle the
modern reader only because we no longer think of Jupiter and
Mercury as gods but only as figures from an old and outdated
mythology. To Plautus himself, they were very much divine figures;
his lighthearted treatment of them merely proves once more that
the ancient pagan saw no reason whatever not to laugh at and
with his gods, particularly Hercules, that great, muscular, bum-
bling, kindly tramp perhaps best portrayed in Euripides' *Alcestis.*
Every story told about him, beginning with his miraculous begetting
by Jupiter on the body of the virtuous Alcmena, and continuing
through the tale of his wondrous labors and feats, seems tinged
with humor, and Plautus's account is no exception.

Worthy of some special note is the play called *Mostellaria,*
another nearly plotless play distinguished chiefly by its individually
hilarious scenes. In one of these we find a drunken young man
soliloquising at great length on his fall from grace. Comparing the

life of a man to that of a house, he shows how, as wind and rain destroy the house of a slovenly owner, so love and wine have ruined in him the life and character of a good young man:

> "I could break down and cry, when I think what I am and what I used to be. There wasn't a fellow worked harder than I did or was any better in athletics. Discus, javelin, ball, racing, manual of arms, horsebackriding: I took first prize any time I felt like it. I could live on next to nothing; there was nothing too hard for me; they used to point me out as an example to the others. All the really decent fellows used to try to get me to show them how to do it. And now that it is too late and I am no good for anything, I have sat down and figured this out all by myself." (149–56)

In another long scene, a retired courtesan, now grown too old for her profession and employed as a waiting maid, gives a younger woman sage and bitter advice on how best to feather her financial nest by the satisfaction of the affections and lusts of men. In still another scene, the clever slave of the play, Tranio, terrifies his old master with a wild tale of how his house has become haunted in his absence. In still another scene Plautus shamelessly exploits the timeworn but invariably effective scene of the drunken revel. It is easy to see that the play is a hodgepodge of amusing scenes strung together on a very thin thread of plot, yet it remains one of Plautus's most successful pieces of theater.

Of the remaining plays, the greater number—*Asinaria, Bacchides, Mercator, Pseudolus, Trinummus,* and the fragmentary *Vidularia*—are quite conventional and on the whole rather undistinguished performances. One play, the *Miles Gloriosus*, might earn our attention as an egregious example of wild slapstick developed around the theme of the braggart soldier; its clowning is still good for laughs, as anyone who has seen the play performed can attest, but it is otherwise rather thin and unsubstantial. Everyone who has read Plautus, of course, has his favorite play or plays, and the virtues of individual pieces are likely to be hotly contested by professional classicists—a fact which probably attests to little but that the plays are basically very good. But it would be hard to find among them one that surpasses the *Rudens* for interesting characters, logic and clarity of plot development, charm and originality of scene and setting, and judicious blending of hilarious clowning, gentle humor, and deft satire.

Among all the extant examples of the Roman comedy, the *Rudens* is unique, having its setting not on a city street but on the seashore, on the North African coast near the city of Cyrene. The stage itself represents a road which, to the audience's right, leads to the city of Cyrene itself, and to the audience's left, toward a wild stretch of coast. The usual housefronts have been replaced, on the audience's left, by a little temple to the goddess Venus, and on their right by the rustic cottage of Daemones, the old man of the play. The whole left end of the stage, from temple to exit, represents a rocky beach or promontory covered with large rocks, patches of swamp, and reeds. The front of the stage is to be imagined as the beach, and the orchestra as the ocean. We do not know how much of this scenery was actually represented by stage sets, and how much of it was left to the audience's imagination. It is interesting to speculate, too, whether a temporary extra set of steps may not have been placed against the front of the stage near the end to the audience's left (the "promontory"), since in Act 1, Scenes 2 and 3, the action of the play requires that the two girls enter the stage from the audience's left very nearly simultaneously, but hidden from each other by the rocks and reeds.

Daemones has been driven from his home in Athens by near bankruptcy caused by his overgenerous efforts to help his financially distressed friends; he and his wife (who never appears on the stage) and their slave, Sceparnio, are living a simple farmer's life in their cottage. They once had a daughter, but she had been kidnapped from them in early childhood, and their loneliness is now tempered only by the occasional visits of worshipers at the little temple next door—visits which, Daemones remarks, sometimes have become something of a nuisance.

As the play begins, Daemones and Sceparnio enter and begin to assess the damage that has been done to their place by a violent storm the night before. Soon a young man, Plesidippus, enters looking for a pimp, Labrax, who had agreed to meet him at the temple for a sacrificial meal, and to make formal delivery to him of the young woman, Palaestra, for the purchase of whom Plesidippus had negotiated a contract with Labrax. But Labrax has weaseled on his agreement and has in fact, the night before, at the instigation of Charmides, a rascally friend of his, packed up all his goods and his troop of girls and set sail for Sicily in the hope of finding there a more lucrative market for his wares. However, the gods and the sea had taken a hand in the deal and had caused Labrax's ship to be wrecked by the storm; all his goods had been sent to the bottom, and the two girls, Palaestra and Ampelisca, had taken to the ship's boat, which upset as they were washed near the shore. The two girls made their way through the surf to the beach and were taken in by an old priestess, Ptolemocratia, who led them into the temple to clean up and rest.

Subsequently, Ampelisca comes out to fetch a pitcher of water from Daemones' house next door; on the way she meets Trachalio, the slave of Plesidippus, who is out looking for Labrax and his girls. They recognize each other, and in their conversation it is revealed that among the effects that the pimp had lost in the ship-wreck had been a little chest containing the tokens by which Palaestra hoped someday to establish her free birth, and to locate her long-lost parents. A little later, the two old rascals, Charmides and Labrax, appear on the scene, cold, wet, and full of seawater; Labrax, learning that the two girls are in the temple of Venus, attempts to claim them as his property. It is clear, now, of course, how this play must be resolved: it must be shown that Palaestra is not only free-born, but actually the long-lost daughter of Daemones; this fact is established by the little chest of trinkets which mean-while has been dredged up from the bottom of the sea by another of Daemones' slaves, the fisherman Gripus. Daemones delightedly betroths his newly found daughter to Plesidippus. Labrax gets most of his money and valuables back: these had been dredged up by Gripus along with the little trinket-box.

In working out this story, Plautus has created some of his most interesting characters. First there is Daemones, amazingly patient and good-humored in spite of his misfortunes. He puts up with insolence from Sceparnio, challenging him only when he sees his behavior is distressing Plesidippus. He is endlessly long-suffering with Gripus' demand that he adjudicate the dispute between him-self and Labrax over ownership of the chest and its contents. When he hears that Labrax is attempting to force the two girls to leave the temple and come back to the city with him, Daemones is furious, both because he feels sympathy for the unhappy girls and also because of Labrax's intended sacrilege: the girls, being in the temple, had asylum, and by one of the ancient world's most ancient laws were entitled to immunity from seizure. Nor is he without humor, as when he complains that the frequency with which the worshipers at Venus's temple come to borrow implements, fire, and water from him, makes him wonder whether he is maintaining his place for himself or for Venus. Later on, with a wink at the audi-ence, he tells how delighted he is to have found as his clients two

such charming and pretty young women, and grumbles good-
naturedly that his wife is certainly keeping an eye on him so that
he won't be passing any signals to them. Perhaps it is his generosity
and ebullient good humor that at the end of the play prompts him
to invite everybody in to dinner, even telling the audience that
he would invite them, too, except that he has nothing in the house
to eat.

The three slaves, Sceparnio, Trachalio, and Gripus form a
splendid triangle of characters, Sceparnio vulgar, coarse, and
shrewd; Trachalio intelligent, sophisticated, and kind; Gripus,
loyal, hard-working, the perfect example of the "sea-lawyer," clever,
persistent, and argumentative, and just well enough versed in the
law to be able to hold off, although ultimately not to defeat, the
claims of both Trachalio and Labrax to the chest. Trachalio forms
the apex of this pyramid, and is played off against the coarse
Sceparnio, and later against the clever Gripus, in such a way as to
afford the audience a rich variety of comic scenes. Gripus, however,
has the distinction of having assigned to him the most socially
significant lines in the play; having dredged up the chest, he allows
himself to drift off into lovely dreams of the wealth and power that
he will acquire with the contents as a starter. His speech would
be nothing but an amusing fantasy except for the undercurrent of
bitterness that runs through it, for Gripus knows very well how
little chance he has of ever rising out of the status of fisherman-
slave. He is, in fact, the universal proletarian of the type made
famous by our own literature of the early part of the current
century; his dreams of wealth and power end with this not entirely
funny reflection:

> "Me and my big ideas! Right now I better hide this chest.
> Millionaire, are you? Well, 'millionaire,' time for dinner—red
> wine and salt mackerel—and no sauce." (937–37a)

As a foil to all these quick, strong, and very masculine characters, appear the two girls, Palaestra and Ampelisca. They are
both intensely feminine, with the soft and appealing exterior that
hides inner strength and courage. Of the two, Ampelisca seems
somewhat the older; she knows the world perhaps a little too well.
Yet the experience with men that enables her deftly to escape the
unwelcome attentions of Sceparnio, who has decided she is just
what he wants for a night's entertainment, has by no means soured
her toward all men: toward the clever Trachalio, who is her equal

in intelligence and experience but not quite her match in wit, she displays the easy warmth of a woman who is well aware of the difference between the commercial enterprise of Labrax's house and the selflessness of love.

Palaestra is the gentler of the two; even though she was kidnapped as a child, and has grown up in the house of a pimp, she has preserved, in remarkable degree, that air of innocence that was supposed, in ancient as well as in more recent times, to be the bred-in-the-bone heritage of the "gently born." As she climbs up out of the sea and onto the rocks, Ampelisca complains that her life, which has been chiefly one of troubles, appears now to have reached its hopeless end; but she will not give up her one remaining hope, that Palaestra is still alive, and will go on looking for her as long as she can. Palaestra, on the other hand, complains bitterly about the injustice of the gods, who have so mistreated her when she has done nothing to deserve it; cold, wet and hungry, she sits down on a rock and cries, grieving over her own hard lot and over the mother and father from whom she had been so cruelly separated years ago. Yet, curiously, it is on Palaestra's strength that Ampelisca relies for courage and the will to try to find their way of of their predicament. Here, too, we seem to be following the traditional character of the "lady"; when the chips are down, it is she, and not the low-born slave, who displays the required strength.

As for the pimp, Labrax, and his friend, Charmides, Plautus has quite frankly made slapstick clowns of them. Struggling up the beach, cold, wet, ragged, and sick, they accuse each other of being the Jonah that caused the shipwreck; later, when Labrax is mercilessly bullied by Plesidippus and Daemones, Charmides discreetly keeps out of the way, and when Labrax is finally dragged off to jail on a charge of breach of contract, Charmides refuses to go with him and help him. But after Labrax has been dragged away, Charmides leaves the stage with the comment that he will go after him after all—"to see that he gets put in jail the faster."

The least interesting character in the play, as usual, is the young man Plesidippus, and even he displays a measure of decency and resolution, which puts him a cut ahead of most of Plautus' heroes. Even old Ptolemocratia, the priestess of Venus, who appears only in one brief scene, comes in for her share of character depiction, for in her few lines she reveals herself as time-worn, industrious, conscientious in the performance of her duties as priestess, poor and shabby, but ready to share what little she has with the unfortunate girls—the perfect picture of a pagan abbess.

Even the prologue of the play is unusually interesting. It is spoken by the star Arcturus, who tells how during the daytime when he is not busy shining in the heavens, he comes down to earth, where he walks around observing the behavior of men, and like a very censor, compiling lists for Jupiter's benefit, of those whose good or bad conduct deserve his particular attention. He especially warns men that Jupiter's goodwill is not to be bought by gifts and sacrifices, but is to be earned by decency and honesty. Then, to illustrate his point, he tells how he came down and caused a storm that wrecked the ship and ruined the dishonest plans of Labrax and Charmides.

The action of the play, too, is rich and lively. In the opening scene, through the eyes of Sceparnio, we are given a vivid description of the attempts of the shipwrecked travelers to escape the wreck and swim to shore; we see the two girls come up wet, ragged, and frightened, climbing over the rocks and calling out as they try to locate each other. In the scene that gives the play its name, a physical tug of war between Gripus and Trachalio is accompanied by its verbal counterpart, a delightful parody of Roman lawcourt procedure in which the two engage in vigorous debate over that provision of the law which holds that all things in the sea are the "common property" of all men. In still another scene, after the girls have run out of the temple and taken refuge at the altar of Venus, Labrax is dragged bodily out of the temple, where he had been attempting to reclaim the girls by main force, by two huge slaves, who belonged to Daemones. They drag the sputtering pimp off to one side and stand guard over him with two enormous clubs upraised, and when he demands his "legal rights" they dare him to move over to the altar and even so much as touch one of the girls. Finally Plesidippus enters, throws a loop of rope around Labrax's neck, and drags him off to court to face the judge on charges of breach of contract and of holding a free woman as a slave.

Activity on the stage never flags; there are no long soliloquies nor any of those dead spots in which the characters simply stand and talk to each other. Rather, through a series of infinitely varied scenes and an endless flow of dialogue, in which bright and sparkling wit alternates with shameless belly laughs, the play is led neatly and deftly along to its inevitable solution. *The Rope* has been compared, perhaps somewhat rashly, to Shakespeare's *The Tempest*, with which it shares little more than its setting on an empty, wild beach. It has none of Shakespeare's lyric beauty, and one would search far in it for any symbolic meanings or philosophic values, but the warm sympathy with which it portrays the women, the old man, and the various types and levels of slaves, brings it perhaps closer to great drama than any other of Plautus's compositions.

It is unlikely that Plautus ever thought of himself as a great dramatist or as a man with a mission or message. He was content to divert and amuse his audience with the timeworn devices of the comic stage: fast-moving dialogue, liberally spiced with puns and other plays on words, hilarious slapstick and wild buffoonery, plays in which richness of action and character were unencumbered by any but the simplest of plots, and, conversely, richly intricate plots acted out by uncomplicated characters and with no distracting high jinks on the stage. In the fresh new stream of Roman literature in which he forms so important a part, Plautus stands midway between the Hellenism of Andronicus and the nationalism of Naevius. Following the lead of "Father" Ennius, he demonstrates, in the less pretentious field of comedy, the sound literary doctrine that Ennius had propounded in more spectacular form in the epic: that for the Roman, the best—in fact the only—road to literary greatness lay in the development of a literature that, proudly conscious of its native cultural heritage, insisted on clothing Greek form with material drawn from the native Italian milieu.

# CHAPTER IV

# Terence

A generation younger than Plautus is the second of the great Roman comic writers, Terence (Publius Terentius Afer), who was born about the year 190 and died in 159 B. C. An interesting and rather detailed account of his life, written originally by the biographer Suetonius, has been preserved by a fourth-century commentator, Donatus. From this biography, we learn that Terence was born at Carthage, that he came to Rome as the slave of a senator, Terentius Lucanus, was given the education of a gentleman and set free at an early age. Terence later became the intimate friend of two of the most prominent men of his times, Scipio Africanus the Younger, and Gaius Laelius. These two men, the one a soldier and statesman, the other a scholar and jurist, took close personal interest in the young playwright, and even advised and assisted him in the writing of his plays.

Suetonius tells an interesting story of Terence's first public appearance; he wished to present his first play, the *Andria*, to the aediles, the Roman officials who had charge of public spectacles, games, plays, and the like, but was directed by them to submit his play first to the playwright and critic, Caecilius, to obtain his opinion of its worth. Terence was ushered into the presence of Caecilius when the latter was at dinner; he was invited, in a somewhat patronizing way, to take his place on a little bench at the foot of Caecilius's couch, and from that position to read his play to the great man and his friends. Terence had read only a few verses of the play before he was invited by Caecilius to join the company at dinner, after which he read the rest of his play to the accompaniment of loud applause.

After this auspicious beginning (the *Andria* was produced in

166 B. C.), Terence wrote five additional plays, the *Heauton Ti-moroumenos (The Self-tormentor)* (163 B. C.), the *Eunuch* (161 B. C.), the *Phormio* (161 B. C.), the *Adelphi (The Brothers)* (160 B. C.), and the *Hecyra (The Mother-in-law)* (165 and 160 B. C.). After completing these six plays, Terence traveled to Athens, with the intent of making a thorough study of the plays of his chief model, Menander. While there, he is said to have written a large number of new plays, but on the way back from Greece to Italy, his ship was wrecked and his bundle of manuscripts was lost along with his baggage. So deeply grieved was he by the loss that a few days later he died, at the age of 35 or 36. There seems to be no doubt but that the six plays we now possess were the six that he wrote before his trip to Athens.

Some questions have been raised about Suetonius's account. For example, it is hard to explain how anyone born in Carthage around 190 B. C. could have become a slave in Rome, since at that time Rome and Carthage were at peace, and therefore the usual route to slavery, that of being captured as a prisoner of war, would have been closed. It is always possible that the young boy, Terence, had been kidnapped by pirates or other criminal marauders, and had come to Rome as a slave this way, but even if this was the case, his route to Rome must have been somewhat devious, since Rome and Carthage were not engaged in commercial relations during Terence's lifetime. How he got to Rome will probably remain an unsolved question, as will the question of his racial background. Suetonius describes him as *fusco colore* ("of dark complexion"); this might suggest that Terence was a Moor or even a Negro rather than a native-born Carthaginian. But the word used by Suetonius to describe his complexion *(fuscus)* is too imprecise to give us any very definite clues. It could be applied to any person whose complexion was somewhat darker than that of the usual Italian; all we can really say is that it was obviously dark enough to have attracted attention. Terence's racial origin is of far less interest than is the fact that he came to Rome a foreigner, whose native language was most certainly not Latin, and there mastered the Latin language so well as to earn a place among the greatest Latin stylists.

We gain other information about Terence, particularly about his activities as a playwright, from the prologues to his plays. These prologues have very little to do with the stories of the plays; instead, they are concerned with refuting various charges that were made against Terence by those who were envious of his success or of his intimacy with Scipio and Laelius. Chief among Terence's attackers was a somewhat older contemporary playwright, Luscius Lanuvinus. Some of the charges that Lanuvinus brings against Terence now seem very trivial; he accuses Terence, for example, of *contaminatio*, which is the use of materials drawn from more than one model in the construction of a play. Why Lanuvinus should have considered this improper is a mystery: as Terence himself remarks, he had good precedent for so doing in the plays of his predecessors Plautus and Naevius; furthermore it seems hard to imagine how anyone could be criticized for helping himself to materials that were in the public domain.

On another occasion, Lanuvinus attacked Terence for writing in too placid a style; Terence's indignant reply is to the effect that Lanuvinus had better check over his own writing before he begins criticizing that of others. The only one of Lanuvinus' charges that could strike us as serious is the accusation that Terence did not write his own plays but merely acted as a front for his two great friends Scipio and Laelius; these men, we must presume, enjoyed writing plays, but felt that their prominent position in the state made it inadvisable for them to lend their names to so trivial an occupation. Unfortunately, Terence is not nearly so forthright in his attempt to meet this charge as he was in the case of the others; perhaps it is a tactful regard for the feelings of his two great friends that prompts him to say nothing more than that "everyone in Rome had had occasion to accept help of one sort or another from Scipio and Laelius" (Terence, *Adelphi* 20–21).

No doubt this reply leaves the question still open, but at this late date any debate over the authorship of the plays seems singularly useless: for over 2,000 years they have been considered to be Terence's own; we may as well go on thinking them so. It will probably be wisest to accept Terence's defense at its face value and to assume that the interpretation placed upon it by Suetonius and other later writers is simply one more example of the scandal-mongery in which these ancient biographers and critics took such pleasure.

Terence, like Plautus, based all his plays on the Greek New Comedy; his favorite model was Menander, upon whose plays four of Terence's are based (*Andria, Heauton, Eunuch,* and *Adelphi*). The remaining two, *Phormio* and *Hecyra*, are based on originals by a later writer, Apollodorus (300–260 B.C.). Terence's generation in Rome had seen a reaction to the proud nationalism of Naevius and the exuberant Italianism of Plautus; Hellenism was the rage among the intellectuals; Scipio and Laelius themselves were the leaders in a cultural movement, the chief aim of which seems to have been to make Italian culture and society as Greek as possible. In view of this new intellectual current, it is not surprising to find that Terence's plays are much more faithful to their Greek originals than were Plautus's. This is not to say that Terence slavishly translated his Greek originals; but where Plautus cheerfully tossed in words, lines, even whole scenes, of his own devising, Terence is preoccupied with presenting a Greek picture on the Roman stage. The Roman audience probably felt quite at home with Plautus's characters; they may have worn Greek dress, but they talked and acted very much like people they themselves knew at first hand. By contrast, Terence's characters must have seemed distinctly foreign, the representatives of an imported culture rather more polished and sophisticated than their own. It is clear that Terence deliberately strove not to break the Greek illusion; sometimes it almost seems as if the only truly Latin element in his plays is the language.

In view of all this, it is not surprising that the plays of Terence turn out to be somewhat more staid and conservative than those of Plautus. The scene is always "a street in Athens"; the characters are the standard old man, young man, courtesan, and slave; the chief variation here is the more frequent introduction of the elderly married lady, and of the young couple already married when the play begins. The parasite, when he appears (in *Phormio* and *Eunuch*), has been elevated from the status of buffoon to that of intelligent man-about-town; similarly, the pimp, when he appears (in *Phormio* and *Adelphi*), is much more the businessman than the scoundrel. The plays show almost no clowning, and no slapstick whatever. Nearest to rowdyish foolishness are the scenes in the *Eunuch* in which a braggart soldier, in the company of his parasite and an "army" consisting of two or three ragged numbskulls, lays mock siege to the house of the courtesan. The plays are well-nigh perfect in form; every scene is functional and serves to forward either the plot or some character-trait that is in need of delineation; not only are there no wasted scenes, introduced merely for fun; there are not even any wasted lines and hardly a wasted word. There are no immoral scenes, no drunken revels, few remarks that smack even of impropriety, let alone of obscenity, and no violence at all. Action on the stage is quiet and rarely undignified. That the plays move smoothly, gracefully, and rapidly is a tribute to the skill with which they were put together; for all their quietness, they never lose the fast action which is the essence of all comedy. Plautus was a master of the theatre; he knew instinctively how to keep an audience amused and attentive, and as long as he reached these objectives he did not care much about the abstract principles of play-construction. Terence, by contrast, is the dramatic artist, consciously striving to make his plays conform to the rules of play-construction, deeply sensitive to the complementary demands of logic, harmony, and graceful movement.

Again, Terence's plays move on a higher moral level than do Plautus's. In every one of the six, there is a "recognition" of one sort or another; in every one, except for *Hecyra*, in which the characters are already married when the story begins, hero and heroine properly end by becoming husband and wife. In *Andria*, *Heauton*, and *Phormio*, a long-lost daughter is found and recognized; in the *Eunuch*, the girl turns out to be the sister of a proper Athenian citizen. In *Hecyra* and *Adelphi*, the girls had been foolish enough to go out on the streets at night in the course of a wildly sexual religious festival and had been raped by unknown young men. In *Hecyra*, the young man in question has subsequently married the girl he raped, without realizing who she was; his somewhat self-righteous perturbation upon discovering that she was already pregnant—presumably by some man other than himself —causes the complications which the dramatist sets out to solve. In *Adelphi*, the young man has acknowledged his act and has promised to marry the girl, even though she is penniless and of humble station; the suspicion on the part of the girl's mother that the young man is about to go back on his promise forms one of the problems that this somewhat intricate play sets out to solve.*

Yet these conventional and repetitive plot elements form no more than a base on which Terence erects a remarkably varied set of stories, in which our attention is held not only by the unfolding of a tale but even more by the sympathetic presentation of an interesting set of human problems and—what is probably most remarkable of all—by a gentle and unobtrusive, but none the less persistent note of social criticism. Nearest to the conventional play of the New Comedy, especially if we are to take Menander's *Dyskolos* as truly representative of that genre, is the *Eunuch*. The play presents two stories. In the primary plot, the young man Phaedria has been temporarily displaced from his position as the lover of Thais by Thraso, a braggart soldier from whom Thais

---

*As with Plautus, the most convenient summary of the plots of Terence's plays is to be found in Rose, *Handbook* (see p. 26, note), 73-78.

hopes to regain possession of a little Athenian girl who had been lost to her some years before but who had now, by coincidence, turned up in the soldier's possession. Once the problem of getting the little girl back has been solved, Thais is presumably ready to take Phaedria back as her lover, but here the playwright gives his story a twist that is as near to being tasteless as anything he ever wrote: Thraso's parasite, Gnatho, persuades Phaedria to share Thais with Thraso, remarking that the stupid and openhanded Thraso will gladly pay all the bills and can easily be disposed of whenever Phaedria may desire it.

In actual fact, the chief interest of the play centers on its subplot, in which the little Athenian girl herself is the central figure, even though she appears on the stage only briefly and has no lines at all to speak. Thraso has given the little girl, whose name is Pamphila, to Thais, but as she was being brought through the streets to Thais's house, she had been seen by Phaedria's younger brother Chaerea, who had immediately fallen madly in love with her, and after some difficulty had traced her to Thais's house. Meanwhile, Phaedria had prepared his own gift for Thais: a little Ethiopian girl and an old eunuch, and has instructed his slave Parmeno to take them over to Thais's house. Chaerea now persuades Parmeno to take him there in place of the eunuch; once arrived, he is put in charge of Pamphila and, in fact, stationed in her bedroom to fan her while she takes a nap. As Chaerea himself later remarks, if he had not taken advantage of this opportunity, he would have been what he pretended to be. When Pamphila's misadventure is discovered by the other slaves, they are not only indignant but wide-eyed with wonder: "How could a eunuch have done it?" Meanwhile Thraso, who feels that he has been undeservedly put off by Thais, comes with his ragtag "army" to take Pamphila back by force; in the ensuing "siege" Thraso, like the Duke of Plaza-Toro, "leads his regiment from behind" and is finally driven off by the combined efforts of Thais and Chremes, the just-discovered brother of Pamphila. Thais keeps Pamphila, and after Chaerea's identity has been safely disentangled from that of the eunuch, Chremes betroths Pamphila to him. The play comes very near to being foolish; it is certainly the least interesting of all of them, yet it is said to have been the most popular, for reasons that are perhaps not too far to seek. The reader of English Restoration literature will recognize the *Eunuch* as the original of Wycherley's *The Country Wife*.

The *Phormio* has a double plot perhaps somewhat better bal-

anced than that of the *Eunuch*. There are two love affairs, one
concerned with the love of the young man Antipho for an orphan
girl, Phanium (who never appears on the stage), the other with
the passion of Phaedria for the usual courtesan. By a series of
clever tricks, the parasite Phormio, for whom the play is named,
succeeds in getting Antipho married to Phanium and obtaining the
money that Phaedria needs to purchase his ladylove. At the end of
the play, Phanium, as we have guessed all along, turns out to be
an Athenian citizen, in fact, the daughter of Phaedria's father,
Chremes, who is also bamboozled into letting Phaedria keep his
girl. The play is livelier and much better constructed than the
*Eunuch*; in it, Terence also dispenses with some of the fairly
coarse humor that had characterized the other play, and which he
never learned to handle with the lighthearted gaiety of Plautus.
This play was destined later to be the model for Molière's *Les
Fourberies de Scapin*.

Closest of all Terence's plays to a tender love story is the
*Andria (The Woman of Andros)*, probably best known to modern
audiences through Thornton Wilder's adaptation of the play to
novel form. The play centers on the usual love-of-young-man-for-
long-lost-daughter theme; the conflict is occasioned by the young
man Pamphilus's determination to keep the girl whom he has
married without his father's consent, and without really adequate
proof of her citizenship, and the equally strong determination of
his father, Simo, to separate the couple, not so much because he
disapproves of the girl, Glycerium, as because of his hurt that a
son of his should have flouted both Athenian law and custom by—
apparently—marrying a non-citizen woman.

In the end, the girl turns out to be a citizen, in fact, the
daughter of Simo's old friend, Chremes. The story might be quite
commonplace except for the curious way in which the character of
a dead woman, Chrysis, pervades it. She is the true "woman of
Andros." She came to Athens a penniless orphan, tried with
courage and persistence to earn an honest living, but, finding this
too difficult, dropped into the less happy but more prosperous trade
of the courtesan, and died just before the story of the play opens.
It is her courage, kindness, generosity, and deep devotion to the
young girl Glycerium that irradiate the whole play and give it a
human warmth and sympathy that it could not otherwise have
possessed. We never see Chrysis or hear her speak, yet a single
speech of hers, reported by Pamphilus just at the end of Act 1,
makes her central to the whole story:

"Even now those words are written on my heart—what Chrysis said about Glycerium. She was at the point of death when she called me to her; I came in; you all went out. There we were, all alone. She began, 'Dear Pamphilus, you see how young and pretty she is, and you know very well just how useful those qualities will be to her for protecting her honor and her property. Therefore, by your right hand and the god that guards you, by your honor, and by her unprotected state, I beseech you not to put her away from you nor desert her. If it is true that I have always loved you like a brother, and that she has always tried to please you in everything, I make you her husband, her friend, her guardian—yes, her father. I leave all this property of mine to you and give it into your trust.' She made her my lawful wife. Then, at that moment, death seized her; I took her and I'll keep her." (286–98)

Nowhere in the course of the play can Pamphilus be said to display real courage or resourcefulness except when he is sure that he is on perfectly safe grounds. Still he is no worse bargain than are most of the other young men of the Roman Comedy, and his association with Chrysis has at least given him a measure of goodwill and sympathy, and to some modest degree has helped to bolster his none too robust ego.

Our interest inevitably centers on the slave, Davus, who considerably outdoes his master in matters of intelligence and sheer manliness. Davus is clever, quick, and resourceful. He has a buoyancy of spirit that even the pillory and the lash cannot quench. More than that, he never loses his human dignity; he may be a slave, but he is nonetheless a man. On one occasion, when one of his schemes has gone awry, he is petulantly scolded by Pamphilus for his failure. Davus patiently hears him out and then replies:

"Pamphilus, I'm your slave, and as such it's my duty to work with might and main, night and day, to risk my life, so long as I may help you. It's your duty, if things don't turn out quite as expected, to forgive me. My scheme isn't going very well, but I'm still at it. Or why don't you find a better scheme yourself, and let me out?" (675–80)

As we might expect, this brief speech leaves Pamphilus spluttering and embarrassed; it is obvious which of the two is the better man.

The most interesting, and at the same time the most exasperat-

ing of the six plays, is the one called *The Brothers (Adelphi)*.
Formally, the plot is stereotyped, revolving around one version of
the boy-girl problem, but in fact, it is no more than a framework
on which to hang a story of fathers and sons. The play presents
two elderly brothers, Demea and Micio. Demea has two sons,
Ctesipho and Aeschinus, but he had given the one son, Aeschinus,
in adoption to the boy's uncle, Micio. The two elderly brothers
represent completely opposite types and philosophies of child-
rearing. Demea believes in hard work and stern discipline; he has
kept Ctesipho out on the farm, and the boy has apparently had
very little in the way of recreation except when he could sneak off
for a day or so to his brother in the city. Micio, on the other hand,
has spent all his life in town, and there has brought Aeschinus up
in a way that would now be called "permissive"; Micio thinks of it
rather as the way of patience, understanding, and love.

In the beginning, the two boys seemed to have responded to
these two kinds of upbringing much in the way that we might have
expected; Ctesipho is mean, sneaky, and selfish; Aeschinus, on the
other hand, even if somewhat of a gay roisterer, has a broad streak
of honesty and decency, and it is clear that he is fond of his uncle-
father, Mico. True enough, he had raped an unknown girl during
a religious festival, but, as a character in the play later remarks,
with the tolerance typical of ancient society, "night-time, passion,
wine, youth—all that is pretty persuasive, and boys will be boys"
(470–71). Such incidents, we gather, were not at all uncommon;
what is uncommon is Aeschinus's recognition of his act, his appeal
to the girl's mother for forgiveness, and his promise to marry the
girl. Aeschinus has a conscience, too; he is bothered because he
failed to tell his uncle-father Micio about the rape incident at the
time when it occurred, and bothered too, because he has rashly
gone ahead and promised to marry Pamphila, a penniless, unknown
girl, without his father's consent.

It looks for all the world as if Terence were going to show us
how right was Micio, and how wrong, Demea. Strangely, however,
this is not the way the play turns out. Demea, observing how
Micio has won the affection of both of his sons and has succeeded,
so he thinks, in enticing them into a dissolute and lazy life, decides
to play the part of generous father himself. The part that he
actually plays is an ugly caricature of Micio; in actions that can
only be termed shameless and vulgar, Demea mocks and ridicules
Micio's way of life, and seems thereby to be winning the contest,
for he enlists one party after another on his side, and in the end
badgers poor Micio into tearing down the wall between his house

and Pamphila's, promising to marry her decrepit old mother, giving away a valuable piece of land to a friend of Pamphila's family, setting free the rascally slave, Syrus, and even giving him a sum of money to set him up in business. As if this were not enough, at the very end of the play, Aeschinus, in a speech that seems to belie all the goodness that we had thought resided in him, deserts his kindly and patient adoptive father and turns himself and his interests over to the conscienceless Demea.

As might be expected, scholars have wrangled for years over the lesson that Terence intended to teach by this play; some have argued that Demea has been proven right and Micio wrong, some have taken the opposite position. If the play proves anything at all, it is that the bringing up of boys is an exasperating, worrisome, expensive, and uncertain business, no matter on what principles or by what philosophy it is attacked. Demea's nasty criticism and vulgar gloating hardly seem to prove him the ideal father; on the other hand, Micio's weak-kneed acquiescence to Demea's badgering and to the misbehavior and final desertion of his son Aeschinus seem somehow to stamp him too as lacking in the kind of character one would like to see in a father.

Perhaps all that Terence meant to say is that there is no one "right way," and that even if there were, most of us are too clumsy and eternally left-handed to be able to follow it with any success. The bewildered and self-pitying father of *Heauton Timoroumenos* (*The Self-tormentor*) with his foolish attempts to punish himself for what he fancies to be a mistake he made in bringing up his son, seems to confirm this view of Terence's opinion of fathers. Unfortunately, this play, which has a most interesting opening scene, quickly degenerates into one more boy-gets-girl story, and is saved from being commonplace only by the very clever way in which Terence manipulates its double plot.

The remaining play, the *Hecyra* (*The Mother-in-law*), had a curious history. On the first two occasions on which it was presented, the audience walked out before the play was over to go and see, on the one occasion, a tightrope walker, and on the other, a gladiatorial exhibition. Only on the third attempt did the play succeed in holding the audience until the final curtain. It is fair to suspect that this original bad luck has been at least in part responsible for the generally low rating the play still enjoys. Actually, it tells a charming story and tells it remarkably well, and as far as action is concerned, is at least as lively as the *Adelphi*. The plot—to repeat—concerns a young man who has raped a girl during a religious festival, and then later has married her without realizing who she was, only to be greatly distressed upon discovering that she was pregnant, apparently by some other man. The resolution of this tangle comes about through a variation of the "recognition" device: a ring, pulled from the girl's finger by the young man in the act of raping her and later presented by him to his mistress, a courtesan, is produced by the courtesan at the critical moment and establishes the identity of the young man's wife.

The curious role of the courtesan in this play immediately attracts our attention; generous and sympathetic courtesans are not unknown in the comedy, and particularly not in that of Terence, but this woman is the only one who deliberately, and out of sheer kindliness and generosity, engages in an act which must inevitably and permanently sever her from her former lover. Besides this, the play has two delightful pairs of old people who bicker and pick at each other as only those who have been comfortably married for many, many years can do. The young man, too, presents an interesting variant, for unlike the other young men in the comedy, who seem to have had mothers only through biological necessity, this one is devoted to his mother, so much so in fact that he considers her happiness more important than his wife's. Toward his father, he is loftily independent, and brushes the old man's suggestions aside as foolish or inconsequential. The play ends happily with the baby recognized and accepted by his father, the wife returned once more to her husband's arms, the two sets of in-laws joined in what appears destined to be a lasting friendship, and the courtesan, warm and glowing with a sense of her own goodness, and comfortably ensconced in the favor and protection of the young man's father.

About the only complaint that can be legitimately made of this play is that the situation Terence has described is probably richer in implications than he realized: we feel, as in the case of *The Self-tormentor,* that he might have done a great deal more with his story. This is, however, a criticism that could well be leveled at any of the plays of either Plautus or Terence, and probably indicates nothing more than that this was all of which this particular dramatic form was capable in their lifetime. Even so, Terence does not lack in boldness. A thoroughly gentle and tactful man, he is never pushing or blatant; still, through all his plays, there runs a persistent note of social criticism, directed particularly at the position of slaves and of women in Greek and Roman society. There is not a single slave or female character who is not decent, honorable, resourceful, and intelligent. This is certainly not due to inadvertence, nor can it be brushed aside as simple sentimentality. Rather, it is Terence's way of arraigning ancient society for the heartless indifference which it commonly demonstrated toward its slave population, and for the hypocritical casuistry with which it handled the class of women whom we have called "courtesans." Aristotle may have dismissed such individuals as inferior and deserving of no better fate than slavery; Terence, perhaps because he himself had been a slave, shows a sympathy toward them that must earn our respect both for his human understanding and for his courage. To us, the protest seems so mild as hardly to be noticeable; to the ancient audience, it may well have been disquieting. Like Plautus, Terence is no great dramatist; his plays, as documents of human nature, are not much better than Plautus's, but where Plautus saw in his fellowman chiefly an opportunity for creating an amusing situation, Terence viewed him with something very akin to love.

In a curious way never quite adequately explained, the Roman Comedy, at least in the form developed by Plautus and Terence, virtually came to an end with the death of Terence himself. No doubt other writers attempted it, but none with sufficient success to have attracted other than the most cursory attention. It is almost as if Plautus and Terence between them had made the comedy say all that it could say in Latin; later attempts would have been repetitive and banal. In effect, Plautus and Terence so overshadow even their predecessors and contemporaries in the field as virtually to preempt it for themselves; we almost forget that before them Naevius, Ennius, and Andronicus had also written comedies.

We tend to forget, too, a distinguished older contemporary of Terence's, Caecilius (Statius Caecilius, 219–166 B. C.). In fact, Sedigitus, a playwright and critic of the early first century B. C., gives first place among all the Roman comic playwrights to Caecilius (Plautus rates second and Terence a poor sixth), and from the frequency with which Cicero quotes him, his plays must have been nearly as popular as were those of Plautus and Terence. Unfortunately, only fragments of his work are extant; the most interesting thing that we know about him now is that he acted as official censor of new plays; it was in this capacity that he listened to Terence's reading of his *Andria* and by his approbation encouraged him to continue to write. Rather than write new plays, the Roman resorted to revivals of the works of Plautus and Terence, revivals that continued on down through the imperial period until the Middle Ages.

As for the native Roman comedy, the type called by the Romans themselves *fabula togata* (because the characters wore the Roman *toga* instead of the Greek *pallium*), plays that had native Italian stories, settings, and characters, although it had an early beginning in the works of Ennius and Naevius, it never achieved any great measure of success. The Roman seemed unable to tolerate the presence of his national garment, the toga, on the stage, and could never quite accept humor too nicely directed at himself and his institutions. It is entirely possible too that no writer of the *togata* was sufficiently original to take the Greek New Comedy, and instead of simply modifying it, build an entirely new comedy with it as model. It is altogether likely that the *fabula togata* was not only offensive to Roman feelings, but simply not very good drama.

Plautus and Terence apparently never attempted this form; the attempts of Naevius and Ennius are lost except for a few fragments. One other name has come down to us, that of Lucius Afranius (born about 150 B. C.) ; we are told that his plays enjoyed considerable popularity and that they were revived like those of Plautus and Terence during the Empire. Unfortunately again the scanty fragments of his work do not enable us to pass judgment on its quality. The inevitable conclusion is that the *fabula togata*, as a literary form, never quite attained true distinction.

At this point we must say a word about Roman tragedy. It will be recalled that Andronicus, in 240 B. C., produced both a comedy and a tragedy in Rome, and that this first attempt was followed by tragedies written by Ennius and possibly also by Naevius. A few other names of tragedians from this early period have come to us, but only two of these produced works of any lasting significance, Marcus Pacuvius (220 B. C.) and Lucius Accius (170–86 B. C.). For the most part, these men followed the lead of Ennius in using Greek models; it is safe to assume that their practice resembled that of Plautus and Terence; that is to say, they did not merely translate Greek tragedies but freely adapted them, changing them when necessary to make them comprehensible to the Roman audience, and in all likelihood adding lines and perhaps whole incidents or scenes of their own devising. Both Pacuvius and Accius also produced original tragedies based on Roman stories, but like the *fabula togata*, they seem not to have earned any degree of success. Even the dignity of the tragic stage, apparently, could not make an actor in the toga palatable to the Roman audience; in all probability too, the Roman tragedians were no more successful than their comic confreres in creating a worthwhile native drama. As for Accius and Pacuvius, men of taste and discernment, like Cicero, admired their plays; the extant fragments are too scanty to afford us any real grounds for judgment.

If comedy was destined not to outlive Plautus and Terence, a similar observation may be made about the tragedy, for nothing of any real note appears after Accius and Pacuvius. Tragedy, in fact, suffered the unhappy fate of becoming a plaything of the dilettante; a generation after the death of Accius, we find Roman gentlemen like Quintus Cicero, Marcus's brother, composing tragedies as a diversion, as if at the same time to amuse themselves and to give evidence of their cultivated tastes. Marcus Cicero also amused himself in this way. We have fragments of this work; they show grace, skill and understanding, but it seems reasonably certain that neither of the Ciceros expected their plays to appear on the stage.

To put it briefly, Roman comedy and tragedy had their flowering at a very early stage in the development of Roman literature; almost before any other form reached the point of literary respectability, the tragedy and the comedy were born, developed, and faded into insignificance. It is a little hard to account for this phenomenon; certainly the easy accessibility of the Greek New Comedy, which provided the Roman writers with an inexhaustible source of plays readily adaptable to the Roman stage and audience, was an important element in this early flowering, and may well account for the entire phenomenon. No other Greek literary form—certainly not the epic, the lyric, or the elegy, to say nothing of prose forms—could have slipped so easily from the Greek to the Latin; all the others had to wait upon the development in Italy of a richer and more flexible literary language.

As for the tragedy, apart from its two early practitioners, it never commanded the attention of a single major literary figure. Models were as richly available as for the comedy, but for some reason the Roman mind did not readily take to them. It may well be that the Roman never quite overcame his feeling that the stage was essentially undignified, and that the very act of producing kings, gods, and heroes upon it somehow demeaned them in a way uncongenial to him. For whatever reason, the tragedy in Roman hands became a literary tour de force; it leaves the stage and passes to the easy chair and the library, there to become scarcely more than a cultural ornament. When, two centuries or more later, the philosopher Seneca composed nine tragedies on Greek models, he produced a strange melange of melodrama, ghost story, and rhetorical bombast; they are not without their virtues, and at one time or another have had great influence on Western European drama; nonetheless, if Seneca's plays are characteristic of the Roman tragedy, it is no great wonder that it was a failure.

# CHAPTER V

# Lucilius

Near the beginning of the second century A. D., the pedagogue-rhetorician Quintilian, in making up a reading list of books that should be included in the education of the would-be orator, admits to the Greek provenance of most of Roman literature, and then remarks, "As for the satire, that is entirely our own" (*Institutes* 10.1.93). Quintilian's statement always comes as something of a shock, for the Greeks were certainly not lacking in the "satiric" spirit; how could they have failed to write satire? Quintilian meant, not that the Greeks did not write satire, but that they did not write *the* satire, the former being a method or manner of writing, the latter a literary form. Satiric writing exists in abundance in Greek literature; one need think only of the lyrics of Archilochus and the comedies of Aristophanes, to say nothing of the occasional barbed passages to be found in the orators and in the philosophers.

But the satire, in the form in which Quintilian found it in the writings of Lucilius, Horace, and Persius, and as it was presently to appear in the works of Juvenal, had in fact no analogue among the Greeks. It was written in verse; originally, various meters were used, but in the fully developed form, only the dactylic hexameter appears. It was rarely less than twenty, rarely more than four hundred lines long; it was written in the colloquial style, and dealt always critically, and sometimes abrasively, with one or more of the problems and issues of the day. Except for its being written in verse, it resembles nothing so much as the critical essay of today, with a range of quality, interest, and subject matter as broad as that which extends from the *Spectator Papers* of Addison and Steele to the effusions of the newspaper columnist. The

form—again in prose, not in verse—has become so familiar to us
that we find it hard to imagine any age that was not deluged, as
ours has been, with an avalanche of punditry. How the Greeks
should have missed it is hard to understand; nonetheless, they did,
and Quintilian was correct in assigning to his compatriots the invention of the satire as a literary form.

We do not know exactly how or when the satire came into
being. Livy in his *History* (7.4) speaks of an early literary or
quasi-literary form called the *satura* which he says was well developed as early as the fourth century B. C. However, the form he
describes bears little resemblance to the satire as it appears in the
works of later Roman writers; Livy's *satura* seems to have been a
dramatic production, a playlet or skit, presumably comic in content, in which the characters sang and danced as well as engaged
in dialogue. Tradition has it that Ennius also wrote works which
he called *saturae*; from what we read of them and from the fragments that remain, we gather that they dealt with many different
subjects, and were at least partly written in verse. Although the
evidence is far from clear, and the remains of Ennius's work
scanty, it seems as if this were the place where we should look for
the prototype of the later satire. Certainly it is likelier than the
*satura* described by Livy; it is probable that the two shared nothing but a common name, and the name itself was derived from
their *content* rather than from their *form*: *satura* means miscellany,
"potpourri," and may have been transferred to both from the
*satura lanx*, a platter containing a sample of each of the crops
and the fruits gathered at the harvest time and presented as a
thank-offering to the gods.

Whatever the original reason for the name, it was fastened
on the form from the time of Lucilius on. Later writers, for example Horace, seemed to have clung to the name partly because
it was traditional, partly because of a relationship they fancied
they saw between their satire and the Greek Old Comedy. It is
true that the Old Comedy presented many subjects and many persons in a satirical way; it also addresses itself to issues of the day;
at one point or another, for example, Aristophanes attacks the
tragedy of Euripides, Athenian policy toward Sparta, the philosophy of Socrates, and sundry political figures of his times. Treatment of these subjects on the comic stage comes closest to the form
and manner of the Roman satire when it is embodied in the
*parabasis*, a curious feature of this dramatic type in which the
whole action of the play is stopped while the chorus-leader steps

to the front to deliver himself of a long discourse on some topic of immediate interest. Superficially, the *parabasis* does bear a certain resemblance to the satire, but apart from other considerations it always remained part of a play, and never acquired an independent existence of its own.

It is clear that the Romans themselves were a little puzzled about the nature of the satire; in hindsight it may be viewed as the critical essay, which developed as a verse-form rather than prose for no other reason than that the Romans preferred verse-presentation for this type of subject.*

Whether or not we are correct in thinking that Ennius wrote satires, it is clear that to the Romans themselves the founder of this genre was Gaius Lucilius (180–102 B. C.). He was born at Suessa Aurunca near the border between Latium and Campania, and came of a family of wealth and distinction. But since he was technically not a full citizen of Rome, he held no public office and took no part in public life; however, he did become the intimate friend of Scipio the Younger and Laelius, the same two who were the patrons of the playwright Terence.

He is credited with thirty books of satires, of which enough fragments now remain to make a fair-sized volume. The earliest of these were written in meters borrowed from the comedy, the iambic senarius and trochaic septenarius. Lucilius also experimented with the elegiac distich, a couplet of which the first verse is dactylic hexameter and the second dactylic pentameter; a second group of his satires is written in this meter. In the end, however, he settled on the dactylic hexameter in a somewhat easier and more relaxed form than had been employed in the epic by Ennius; Lucilius's best, most mature, and latest satires were all written in this meter, which became from then on standard for the genre.

Horace, a century or so later, readily acknowledges his debt to Lucilius; he claims, in fact, that apart from a certain Varro of Atax (known now only as the author of an *Argonautica*) and certain others whom he does not think it worthwhile even to name, he was the first man to take the form developed by Lucilius

---

*There was concomitantly a second type called "satire" but bearing the special name of *Menippean*. This was written either entirely in prose or in a prose-verse combination; it too bears no generic relation to the type of satire we have been discussing. The Menippean satire was not a Roman invention but was, according to tradition, invented by a Greek, Menippus of Gadara.

and to give it final literary polish. Horace speaks with admiration of the vigor of Lucilius and praises him for having "rubbed the city of Rome down with many a handful of coarse salt" but criticizes him for his carelessness in matters of style and composition: he flowed "with a muddy stream"; "if he had lived on into our age," says Horace, "he would have done much pruning and polishing, and would have been more careful to confine himself within the accepted canons of writing" (*Satires* 1.10.67–70).

Horace's judgment on Lucilius is eminently fair. The remaining bits of his satires reveal a man who was an exuberant, enthusiastic, and prolific writer, with a sharp, incisive mind, and an irreverent sense of humor. Although he had great respect for the Greeks and for Greek thought, it is clear that he was out of patience with the Hellenomania that was sweeping over the cultured circles of his day. In one fragment (Warmington, *Remains of Old Latin* vol. III, 1961, p. 3, no. 15–16) he seems to be twitting his fellow Romans for thinking it was more dignified to use Greek rather than Latin words for common objects like beds and lamps; in another (87), he lashes out at someone by the name of Albucius, a name straight from an Italian barnyard, scornfully castigating him because he would rather be thought a Greek than the compatriot of husky centurions, great soldiers, and distinguished men. Albucius apparently insisted upon being greeted with the Greek *Chaire* instead of the Roman *salve*; "Very well," says Lucilius, "whenever I meet you, I will say '*Chaire*, Titus!' My attendants, the whole kit and kaboodle of them, will say '*Chaire*, Titus!' But from that point on, Albucius, you shall be to me an enemy, both public and private" (*ibid.*).

This must not be taken to mean that Lucilius was opposed to all Greek expressions. Apparently the Latin of the second century B. C. was liberally peppered with domesticated Greek loanwords, and Lucilius can see no reason for not using these, especially when they handily express ideas for which Latin words are lacking. But he argues for the additional inclusion in the literary language of words of Italian origin, many of them from barnyard and workshop, but all expressive and colorful. At another point he protests a suggested spelling reform that would have required Romans to write long vowels as double vowels (long *a* would be *aa*); he views this as pedantic, and cites Greek precedent in defense of the existing Roman custom (*id.* p. 114, no. 368–72).

But linguistic matters were far from being Lucilius's only or even his chief concern; he was far more interested in the observation and criticism of men and policies of his times. Book IV seems to have been a discourse on the gladiatorial games; at any rate we find reference in it to two famous gladiators of the time, Pacidianus and Aeserninus. In vigorous, homely language Lucilius describes the insults the two tossed at each other before they actually began their battle. In Book V he appears to be taunting his friends for their lack of concern at an illness of his own; Book VI contains the figure of a miser, and may well have been an attack on greed. In Book XI, he attacks petty men who dare to set themselves up against men of greater stature like Scipio the Younger; Book XVI contains a discussion of philosophy, with particular emphasis on its value as an antidote to superstition. Book XVII may have been a satire on marriage or perhaps on women in general. An extant fragment (*id.* p. 178, no. 567–73) suggests that there is no woman— not even the great Helen of Troy—not possessed of some disfigurement. A fragment of uncertain location takes someone—presumably the Roman people—to task for a type of moral degeneracy more commonly associated with the later days of Rome:

> But nowadays from early morning until nightfall, on feast days and ordinary days, our whole population, commons and patricians together, go rushing down to the market-place, and there they stay. To one interest and one art they have devoted themselves, the art of deceiving without being caught, of fighting with no holds barred, or competing in dishonesty while they wear the face of the simple, honest man. They try to entrap each other as if they were so many hostile armies. (*id.* p. 372, no. 1145–51)

Another passage which, because of its ragged composition, looks, as one of the editors of Lucilius has remarked, as if it were one of those that Horace says the old satirist wrote "standing on one foot" (Horace *Satires* 1.4.10), sings the praises of Virtue:

> Virtue, Albinus, consists in being able to set a true value upon those things that concern us and make up our lives; virtue consists in knowing what any given thing may mean for us; virtue consists in knowing what is right, what is advantageous, what is honorable for us, what is good, what is bad, too, what is disadvantageous, unseemly, dishonorable; virtue consists in knowing what end and limit to place upon the acquisition of things; virtue consists in being able truly to evaluate wealth;

virtue consists in granting to public office that which it is in fact entitled to; virtue consists in being the enemy of evil ways and evil men, and on the contrary, the defender of good ways and good men, honoring these latter, loving them, being their friend; it consists, too, in putting in first place the welfare of our fatherland, in second place, that of our parents, in third and last place, our own. (*id.* pp. 390–92, no. 1196–1208)

Lucilius may have been prolix, and a sloppy composer; he may have had more enthusiasm than literary ability; but his apparently careless manner of composition may have been with him a matter of literary doctrine; he may well have thought that looseness and informality, being a reflection of popular, spoken Latin, was the proper vehicle for his quick, incisive sketches of Roman life and character. There is also a possibility that Lucilius's rough style was part of his protest against the over-Hellenization of Italian society, the excessive devotion to all things Greek, that characterized the circle of the younger Scipio and Laelius, and was responsible for that degree of overrefinement which we find in the comedies of Terence. Lucilius felt that if Rome was to make her mark in the world of culture, she must speak with the voice of Rome, if need be even roughly and harshly, and must never allow herself, in the name of any degree of refinement and cultivation, to become the mere ape of Greece.

# CHAPTER VI

# Early Prose, Cato

The figure of Cato the Elder (Marcus Porcius Cato, 234–149 B. C.) opens up the field of Roman prose. Experience with the histories of national literatures has generally shown prose to be a late development preceded by centuries of poetic expression. In Greek literature, for example, the epic, the lyric, the elegy, and the drama have reached a high peak of development before prose literature begins to make its appearance. At Rome, the development of prose began at an unusually early period; for some reason, the Romans seem not to have required the usual long period of poetic development before they could set their hand to the writing of artistic prose. The reason usually assigned for this—in all likelihood a valid one—is that the Roman from the beginning had an intense interest in all aspects of law and government, and that since communication in these fields inevitably takes the form of prose, he turned earlier than do most people to the development of this type of literary expression.

In the traditions, if not in the actual remains, of early Latin we find indications of the existence, perhaps from the very earliest times, of two distinct forms of prose, the oratorical and the descriptive. The oratorical grew up in connection with the activities of lawcourt and assembly; one of the characteristics of this style, maintained throughout its history, was the preservation of an attitude and manner clearly suggestive of living speech; the composer of oratorical prose always writes as if he were addressing an audience and were responding to the reactions of the audience to his words. Oratory, to the Roman, never consisted of a written form intended for oral delivery; on the contrary, it was always composed as if it were a spoken form subsequently written down for purposes of the record. Even when the Roman wrote out and memorized the speech that he intended to give, he always wrote it with the living speech and living audience in mind; he interpolated audience interruptions, heckling, and applause, even before these actually occurred. If in fact overt audience reaction did occur, he was always prepared to change his memorized oration to meet the occasion.

Unfortunately, no actual speech has survived from these early years, but from historical studies like Cicero's *Brutus* and from accounts like those of Livy, it is clear that from the earliest times the Romans consciously made use of such rhetorical devices as the alliterative phrase, the rhetorical question, and above all, of the illustrative anecdote. Livy for example reports (2.32) a speech made by a certain Menenius Agrippa early in the fifth century B. C. at a time when the plebeians had left Rome in a body, refusing to serve in the army against the advancing Aequi until their demands for greater participation in the government were granted. Menenius was appointed to ask them to return. In the course of his plea he told them the story of *The Body and the Members.* There had been a time, said he, when the various parts and organs of a man had not reached the consensus that they now enjoyed, but tended rather to reach decisions and to act individually and singly. The other parts of the body became indignant at the stomach; they worked, they worried, they served, but everything went to the stomach; there it sat in the middle, at its ease, with nothing to do except to enjoy the pleasures handed to it. The other members thereupon formed a conspiracy; they agreed that the hand would no longer carry food to the mouth nor the mouth receive it if it were placed there nor the teeth chew it if it should come their way. The result of this quarrel and of their attempt to starve the stomach into submission was that all the members found themselves nearly in a state of collapse. At that point it became clear that the services performed by the stomach were far from negligible, that it did not just absorb nourishment but also passed it along, since it distributed to all parts of the body the stuff by which men live and maintain activity. For the stomach digested the food, enriched the blood with it and thus divided and parceled it out impartially through the veins. By pointing out that the angry withdrawal of the plebeians was like the quarrel of the other members with the stomach, Agrippa persuaded them to return to the city.

Other stories of the sort exist; they all give the same impression of a simple, mordant, yet far from naive style of speech, and this at a time when Rome was as yet untouched by Greek rhetoric. It is probably fair to say that the early Romans, through love of law-court and assembly, had taken instinctively to the art of persuasion, and very early had developed the art of speaking to such degree that only the addition of a more polished and sophisticated rhetoric was needed to bring Roman oratory to the perfection that it ultimately achieved.

As for purely descriptive prose, it is immediately set apart from the rhetorical type by the fact that it was always written. Its earliest forms scarcely deserve the name of literature; they are embodied in such prosaic documents as laws, treaties, and contracts, and show little if any elegance. Their aim is strictly practical; their chief virtue lies in their relentless clarity. The Twelve Tables can scarcely lay claim to elegance, but there is little doubt about their meaning. It is a fair supposition that the clarity of the Twelve Tables is to be found reflected in the writings of the Roman annalists and historians.

The first historian of whom we hear anything was Quintus Fabius Pictor (fl. c. 216 B. C.). Fabius wrote an annalistic history of Rome, that is to say, a history written in year-by-year fashion, in the manner of official records. Fabius's history may have been Roman, but it was not Latin: it was written in Greek. Nonetheless, it rapidly became the chief source book among the Romans for their early history, and we are told that not long after Fabius completed it, it was translated into Latin, although not by its author.

Fabius was followed by a series of other historians who also wrote in Greek: Lucius Cincius Alimentus (fl. c. 210 B. C.), Aulus Postumius Albinus (fl. 155–146 B. C.), Gaius Acilius (fl. c. 155), and —although we are not certain in this case whether his work was done in Greek or in Latin,—Publius Cornelius Scipio (fl. c. 180 B. C.), the father of Scipio Africanus the Younger. The works of all of these men, like that of Fabius, may be presumed to have been annalistic in character; why all of them chose to write in Greek remains a mystery. It has been alleged that they used this language because Latin lacked the necessary vocabulary; in the face of the works of Ennius, Plautus, and Terence, to say nothing of Lucilius, this seems rather an odd theory, especially as it is hard to imagine that a group of men with sufficient initiative to engage in the writing of history should have lacked the imagination and originality to think up Latin words if appropriate ones were not at hand.

But these were all practical men; perhaps they did lack literary imagination. The fact that Greek was at this time the lingua franca of the whole Mediterranean, while Latin was still the language of a small group of people in Italy, may also have had its influence on them. Certainly they were impelled to the writing of history of Rome in some measure by national pride; they may have felt that histories written in Greek would be more likely to convey the message of Roman greatness to the world than would similar works in Latin. Perhaps the chief importance of these early writers of history is the fact that they demonstrate the early interest taken by the Roman people in themselves: the writing of history shows that there was arising among the Romans a consciousness that Rome and her people had a story worth the telling. They echo the same consciousness of national pride, the same sense of national identity and purpose that are clear to see in the works of Naevius, Plautus, Ennius, and Lucilius, the embryo of the idea of empire that was later to inspire Vergil, Livy, and Tacitus.

It is probably only coincidence that Cato's book *On Agriculture* is the first piece of Latin prose extant in complete form. No doubt other men wrote prose before him, perhaps on more titillating subjects, and Cato himself was the author of a large number of other prose treatises: he wrote, besides an encyclopedia, books on medicine, on the civil law, and on military science; he published over one hundred orations and carried on a voluminous correspondence. Chief of his works was probably the book that he called *The Origins*, the first certain example of a history written in Latin.

The sheer bulk of Cato's works is amazing in view of his indefatigable labors as statesman and soldier. He held successively the offices of quaestor, aedile, praetor, and consul, the last-named in 195 B. C.; in 184, he was censor, and carried out the duties of that office so thoroughly and conscientiously that he came to be known forever after as "Cato the Censor." He was actively engaged in a number of wars, serving sometimes as supreme commander, sometimes in a more subordinate position, but always with vigor and distinction. When he was in his eighties, he took part in an embassy to Carthage, which at the time was at peace with Rome, and was there so impressed with the growing power of Rome's traditional enemy, and so convinced that no sharing of empire or interests between them would be possible, that he ever thereafter pursued an anti-Carthaginian policy, trying again and again to impress the Romans with the importance of attacking Carthage before she attacked Rome.

In addition to all this, he was a vigorous farmer, who scorned absentee ownership and took immediate and active part in the

working of his farm. A man of enormous energy, prodigious courage, and granitic conviction, he was a Roman of the old mold, with
no patience for softness in any form and with a deep and abiding
mistrust of the Greeks and everything that they represented. In his
old age, we are told, he softened to the extent of learning Greek,
but whether from some access of enthusiasm for Greek literature
and culture, as Cicero not too seriously suggests, or from the more
practical desire of beating the Greeks at their own game by master-
ing the language of their trickery, cannot now be determined.

In any event, Cato's convictions must represent, at least in
part, his reaction to the Hellenophilia which predominated in the
intellectual circles of the day. Rome had been in contact with
Greek culture and various Greek peoples from the earliest times,
for all of southern Italy and Sicily had been colonized by the Greeks
before Rome made her first tentative gesture outside of Latium.
But never before the middle of the second century B. C. had so
concerted an impact been made by Greece upon Rome. By the
terms of the treaty concluded after the battle of Pydna (168 B. C.)
the Greek states were required to send 1000 hostages to Rome as
guarantee that the new treaty would be observed. The hostages
stayed in Rome for seventeen years. Somewhat later came Panaetius the Stoic; he and a number of other philosophers occupied
their time by giving public lectures on philosophy. In a world just
awakening to philosophic speculation and exploration, the ideas of
Panaetius and his fellows acted as a catalyst; Stoicism in particular
caught the Romans' fancy, partly because of its emphasis on the
duty of man to serve the State, partly, too, no doubt, because of its
doctrine of the brotherhood of man which seemed to provide some
philosophic basis for the Roman's incipient dream of world empire. Among the hostages was also the historian Polybius, who
found himself fascinated by Rome and the Roman people, and
inordinately impressed by their intelligence, their legal, political,
and military genius, and their unimpeachable honesty. Polybius's
admiration for the Romans could scarcely have diminished their
admiration for him and for the other Greeks of his company.

In the year 155 B. C., even before the Thousand Hostages were
sent home, the Athenians also sent to Rome an embassy composed
of three philosophers, Critolaus, Carneades, and Diogenes the
Stoic. These three men, too, lectured widely in Rome and added
their teachings and influence to that of Panaetius. As a result of all
these activities, Greek culture fairly flooded into Italy, and even a
decree of the Senate, passed in 161 B. C., by which the Greek

philosophers and rhetoricians were ordered to leave Rome, could not check the tide of interest in Greek ideas or dampen the enthusiasm of young Roman intellectuals for Greek literature and Greek culture.

Greek culture came to Rome and the Romans at a most appropriate time; young, strong, vigorous, and now the unquestioned masters of the largest share of the Mediterranean, they were blessed, for the first time in their national history, with sufficient wealth and leisure to begin to do more than amuse themselves with the drama, and to tolerate, if not actually to encourage the epic. To borrow a phrase used whimsically by Cicero of Cato, "They took to Greek literature and culture as if seeking to slake a thirst of long standing" (*De senectute* 8.26).

That they went to excesses in some instances is clear. We have already observed the near-sterilization of Roman comedy caused by Terence's over-devotion to Hellenic perfection, and we have seen evidence, in the *Satires* of Lucilius, of the foolish affectation by some Romans of Greek speech and manners. If Greek influence had gone unchecked and unimpeded there would have been very real danger that Rome would have become, as Horace later was to phrase it, "the captive of captive Greece" (*Epistles* 2.1.156).

Fortunately, however, corrective forces were not lacking. Lucilius's strictures against excess of zeal for Greek culture were mild compared to the violence of Cato. He was certain that Greek philosophy would corrupt Roman thought, that Greek morality would destroy Roman morals, that Greek rhetoric would debase and distort the Roman's native genius for speaking, and, in short, that nothing Greek could possibly be good for Rome. Cato was convinced that the invasion of Italy by Greek culture was a deliberate and fiendishly calculated plan to soften and effeminize Rome, and thus to make her fall an easy victim to her enemies. He was even convinced that Greek physicians intended to poison their Roman patients.

In some ways it seems strange that a man of Cato's intelligence and experience should have reacted so irrationally to the advent of a great culture, which if properly assimilated could not do other than assist in the intellectual development of Rome. Perhaps Cato, like many brilliant men, had his blind side; perhaps he was perturbed by the sudden and spectacular way in which Greek culture had taken over the country, and felt it necessary to provide some counterbalance to these new ideas. The later history of Latin literature tends to prove him right, at least in some degree; Rome needed the culture of Greece in order to build and perfect her own; she needed a Panaetius, a Diogenes and a Polybius, to apply the spur of speculative thought to her already lively practical imagination. But she also needed to be warned not to be carried away and not to turn her back on her native heritage.

This was the warning that Cato provided. His works were voluminous and covered a wide variety of subjects; his style is that of a genuine primitive in rhetoric: rough, direct, salty, and entirely honest. That he wrote in prose, and never laid hand to verse, is no more than we should expect of the man who spoke with pride and approval of the early days in Rome when "Nobody paid any attention to poetry; anybody who did take an interest in it was called a loafer." For an art of rhetoric, he invented his own: "The orator," said he, "is a decent person who knows how to talk." Integrity of character came first; after that, nothing more than a natural way with words. Perhaps with the feeling that his definition was a little vague and imprecise, he added the further principle, "Know your subject and the words will take care of themselves."

Nothing could afford more positive proof that he himself followed his own principles than his one remaining extant work, the book entitled *How to Run a Farm (De re rustica)*. Characteristically and without any attempt to win over his reader, he plunges immediately into his subject:

> Sometimes trade isn't a bad way to earn a living, except that it tends to be risky. The same may be said of banking, if only it were honorable. It was our ancestors' opinion, and they put it into law this way, that a thief should be condemned in double damages, a usurer in quadruple. From this we can figure out how much less desirable a citizen they thought the usurer than the thief. When they wanted to praise someone as a worthy citizen, they called him a good farmer and a good tenant. Praise like this, they thought, was the highest anybody could get. I'm sure that your business man is a hard worker and genuinely interested in the acquisition of wealth, but as I said before, he takes great chances and runs great risks. No, it's our farmers who produce our finest citizens and bravest soldiers; their profession is a decent and respectable one; it is thoroughly solid and substantial and excites no one's ill-will: men whose time and energy are absorbed in this pursuit are highly unlikely to fall prey to immoral or subversive thoughts.
> (*De re rustica,* preface)

With this as a beginning, Cato takes his reader through all the operations of running a farm, from the choice of site to the proper way to crush olives. For Cato's farmer was no cash-crop expert, growing something for sale and depending for the necessities of life on the nearby market town. He grew crops for sale, to be sure, but his farm was also expected to provide all the basic necessities—food, shelter, and clothing—for the farmer himself, his family, and his household of slaves.

Nothing usable was to be wasted; willow trees lined the irrigation ditches and provided shade; their withes were collected for the manufacture of baskets. Olives provided relishes when green, and food when ripe; they also provided oil.* Cato has a use even for the watery residue that remains after the oil has been drawn off; sprinkled on a threshing-floor, it discourages ants and prevents the growth of grass; mixed discreetly with the food and water of the cattle, it is a prophylactic against disease; it acts as a protective finish on wood, and when applied to the inside surfaces of a storage chest, it is a moth preventative.

Cato's book is full of information of this sort: how to cure the illnesses and injuries of animal and man, how and when best to gather and press olives, how to prepare salad, how to make honey-cake, where best to locate the vineyard, the apple orchard, the pasture, and the grain field, how to plant asparagus (and his directions in this instance are almost identical with those printed on a modern seed packet), how to say prayers for the well-being and fertility of the farm, and for the health and strength of the draft animals (he declares that no woman may take part in or even observe this latter ceremony). It is hard to imagine any aspect of farm life which Cato might have left untouched. "What," says he, "is the good farmer's first law? Plow carefully. What, the second? Plow again. What, the third? Spread manure" (*De re rustica* 61.1). "On rainy days look for work that can be done indoors. There must be no loafing! Clean house! Remember that even if no work

---

*This product may well have enjoyed wider use in the ancient world than any other single thing: it was used in countless ways for food, both raw and cooked; burned in lamps, it provided light; rubbed on the body, it eased sore muscles and was the ancient substitute for soap; used by itself or in combination with other ingredients it was a healing unguent to be applied to every imaginable break in the skin, whether of man or of animal; combined with various perfuming agents, such as rose petals and spikenard, it became that perfume that every Greek and Roman expected to be poured liberally on his head at any convivial gathering.

is done, expenses go right on" *(ibid.* 39.2). But perhaps Cato's whole attitude toward the farmer's profession is best summed up in his chapter of directions to the owner, the "head of the household" *(paterfamilias):*

> As soon as the owner enters the house, he should pay his respects to the gods of the household. Immediately thereafter, if possible, he should make a tour of inspection of the farm. If he cannot do this on that same day, then he should do it no later than the following day. He should inform himself about the way in which the farm has been run: what tasks have been done and what not done. On the next day he should call in his overseer and ask him what parts of the work have been completed, what remains still to be done, whether the jobs that were done were completed in good time, and whether he can also complete the tasks that remain to be done. He should ask for a report on the wine, the grain, and all other things. When he has obtained this information, he should ask for a detailed report of the work that was done and of the times at which it was done. If a task turns out not to have been completed, the overseer will say that he himself had worked hard, but that the slaves had been unwell, the weather had been bad, there had been a number of runaway slaves, he had had to work the public roads. After he has offered these and the rest of his long list of excuses, call the overseer's attention once again to the list of jobs, both major and minor, that must be done. When the weather is wet, there are jobs that can be done on rainy days: scrubbing and caulking storage jars, cleaning house, shifting grain, shoveling out manure, building a manure-heap, sorting seed, splicing ropes, making new rope; the whole household could be employed in mending coats and headgear. On feast-days, old drainage-ditches could be dredged, public roads could be worked, brush could be cleared, the vegetable garden could be hoed, pasture-land could be cleared, faggots could be bound, brambles could be grubbed out, coarse meal could be ground, and things in general cleaned up. If slaves should happen to be sick, they should not be given as much food. After owner and overseer have studied this list over quietly and sensibly, the overseer must be told to see to it that any tasks still remaining are carried to completion. The owner should go over the cash account and the grain records, and determine what has been got in for fodder. He should examine the figures on wine and

oil: what supplies have been sold, what supplies exhausted, what supplies still remain, what might still be left that could be sold. Where there is need for a full supply, let him make sure that it is full; where there are any shortages, let them be filled up. Plans should be made a year ahead: whatever may be needed should be purchased; whatever may be superfluous should be sold. Where work must be contracted for, the contracts should be let. The owner should give his orders, and leave them in writing, as to the work that he wishes done and the tasks that he wishes to be let out on contract. He should inspect the farm animals. He should hold an auction and, if the price is right, should sell all surplus oil, wine, and grain; if there are over-age oxen, diseased cows, diseased sheep, surplus wool, hides, worn-out plows, worn tools, over-age slaves, sick slaves, and anything else superfluous, he should see that it is sold. The owner should be more interested in selling than in buying. (*ibid.* 2)

This tough, hard-bitten old farmer, statesman, and soldier would probably not have relished being considered a literary figure; nonetheless his contribution to Roman literature must not be underrated. His harsh prose calls the Roman back to the actualities of his life, to the value of the simple expression of reality. To Cato, honesty, sincerity, solidity of intention and validity of content were more important than formal perfection or literary beauty. His point of view is limited and all too susceptible of being turned into the ludicrous distortions of the supernationalist. Nevertheless at that time his views were much needed as a counterbalance to an excessive zeal for all things Hellenic that was in danger of overshadowing the Roman's native heritage. And if Cato's code of personal conduct sometimes seems excessively stern and even cold-hearted, it stands in healthy and decided contrast to the glossy ethics and shallow immorality of Hellenistic philosophy and life. Cato afforded, in fact, an astringent antidote to Hellenomania. Because of his work, his writings, and his life, the Roman learned never to forget that his land and his nation, his customs, traditions, history, heroes, myths and stories, were worth preserving in his literature.

# CHAPTER VII

# The "New Poets" and Catullus

The period that stretches from the deaths of Cato and Lucilius to the time of Cicero, was a time of revolt and turmoil, as the Roman economy, society, and governmental system attempted to adjust themselves to the new conditions of life that resulted from the subjugation of the Eastern Mediterranean and the defeat of Carthage. Rome found herself in possession of wealth that came flooding in on her from the newly conquered provinces; she also found herself faced with internal dissension, stress, and strain, as her citizen-body strove, sometimes legally and reasonably, sometimes violently and with much bloodshed and suffering, to effect a more equitable sharing of new-found wealth and power.

The reforms instituted by the Gracchi (133–123 B. C.) were directed at improving the lot of the plebeians and assuring their greater participation in the nearly worldwide power they had assisted to create. The patricians resisted these reforms, partly out of honest conviction that such great wealth and power were not wisely to be entrusted to the inexperienced and unreliable populace, partly out of sheer selfishness and determination to hang onto the wealth and power that they had themselves acquired. Revolt and counterrevolt, riot and repression, continued on down into the age of Marius and Sulla (107–78 B. C.), where they ended in a temporary truce and stalemate with the relatively new party of the prosperous middle class (the "knights," *equites*) providing a precarious balance between the patricians on the one hand and the plebeians on the other.

In such a restless time it is not surprising that few literary figures of any importance emerged. We have the names of a few historians, of whose works only meager fragments now remain, and who are important chiefly as the sources to which Livy was later to turn for information about the earlier history of the Roman people. We hear of the *Annals* of Gaius Sempronius Tuditanus (fl. 129 B. C.), and of a history of the Second Punic War, in seven books, written by Lucius Coelius Antipater (c. 121 B. C.), a writer later to be praised by Cicero for his style and perhaps of some interest as the first known writer of a Latin historical monograph. A certain Lucius Calpurnius Piso Frugi (fl. 149–108 B. C.) also wrote an *Annals* in Latin, in which he is reported to have attempted to give a rational account of a number of early Italian myths, among them the story of Tarpeia. Somewhat later than these came the *Annals* of Quintus Claudius Quadrigarius (fl. c. 80 B. C.) and of Valerius Antias (c. 80 B. C.). Oratory continued to flourish; we hear of Marcus Antonius, Licinius Crassus, and Quintus Hortensius, all of whom were later to find mention in Cicero's history of oratory (the *Brutus*). In the later years of this period belongs a work of unknown authorship addressed to a certain Herennius, the *Auctor ad Herennium*, the earliest and, except for Cicero's later work, the most exhaustive treatise on oratory extant in Latin. As a work of literature, it has little merit, but it is of interest as showing the degree to which the Romans, in this fairly early period, had systematized their understanding of the art of speaking. In the realm of poetry we hear of Laevius (fl. c. 100 B. C.), who composed among other things a collection called *Erotopaegnia (Occasional Love Lyrics)*, a work which appears to have begun the liberation of Latin poetry from an almost exclusive devotion to the epic, the drama, and the satire, and to have given a first clear indication of the adaptability of the Latin language and the Roman poetic genius to the brief occasional poem, especially to the poem of love. A particular service of Laevius was the introduction and domestication in Latin of a number of Greek lyric meters; he also broadened and enriched the Latin poetic vocabulary by the infusion of colorful colloquialisms, and encouraged the use of the brief, uncomplicated sentence, and the relaxed, informal syntax of ordinary speech.

Amid all this welter of minor names, only one of any real importance emerges. This is Valerius Cato (fl. c. 80 B. C.), a native of the northern part of Italy, perhaps the foothills of the Alps, who appears to have set up in Rome as a teacher and mentor to the aspiring poets of the day. Certainly a man of some learning and scholarship, he is credited by Horace with an edition of the *Satires* of Lucilius; he also wrote poems of his own. Because so little is known of Valerius Cato's work, we are unable to form any judgment of its poetic worth; if, as some think, the poem called the *Dirae* is properly ascribed to him, we cannot feel that he had any vast poetic genius. The probability is that he was more teacher and critic than poet—as his young friend Bibaculus remarked, "Professor Cato . . . [is] the only man alive who can teach a man to be a poet, and can tell a poet when he sees one." (*Cato grammaticus . . . qui solus legit et facit poetas.* (Bibaculus, frg. 1 [Baehrens, *Fragmenta poetarum Romanorum*].) Except for a small coterie of friends and pupils, which included the poet Catullus, he seems to have gone almost unnoticed in his own lifetime, but his influence upon the young men around him was deep and abiding; through their mediation it passed on to help shape the work of the poets of the Augustan Age. Valerius Cato may well have occupied a position in the history of Latin poetry analogous to that occupied by Gerard Manley Hopkins and Gertrude Stein in the development of twentieth-century English and American writing: his personal influence far outweighed his contribution in original poetry.

It is impossible to tell now to what degree the poets who surrounded Valerius Cato formed a coherent group with a consistent set of literary principles and ideals, or whether they were a more or less random group with no common interest other than a desire to free Latin poetry from exclusive devotion to history, geography, social comment, and the movement of the heavenly bodies. In several widely separated passages which appear to have no generic relation to each other (*Ad atticum* 7.2.1; *Orator* 161; *Tusculan Disputations* 3.19.45), Cicero speaks of young poets whom he calls "these young whippersnappers," *(hoi neoteroi)* poets who in his opinion are guilty of violating some of the laws of Latin metrics, of young men who show an inordinate fondness for a heavy variety of the hexameter considered by Cicero himself to be archaic and inelegant, and of writers who fail to show due respect for Cicero's beloved "Father" Ennius.

It is hard indeed to find any common element in the groups that Cicero mentions; scholars have tried valiantly to lump them all together as a school, calling them, after Cicero, the "New Poets," but the results have been something less than convincing. Poets have never been noted for their willingness to organize; there seems little reason to think that the young men writing in the middle of the first century B. C. should have been more likely to join in some sort of common poetic cause than are the highly individualistic and staunchly independent young men who are writing poetry today.

Being in rebellion against something is a feeble bond of union that collapses as soon as the more positive aims of the protesters gain even a modicum of public recognition.

Rebels these young people were; many of them were probably also personal friends. They may well all have been associated in one capacity or another with Valerius Cato or with other men like him, but there is no reason to think that their poetic aims and ideals showed any great degree of unanimity. Some of them devoted themselves to the epic, trying to write now on contemporary rather than on historical themes: we hear, for example, of an epic on Caesar's exploits in Gaul. Some turned to religious poetry; Helvius Cinna spent nine years on a *Zmyrna*, which appears to have been no more than an exhaustively learned theological treatise in verse. Some devoted themselves to the light occasional lyric, some to obscenity and scatology. Some wrote love poems, some, satire.

With but one exception, the poems of Catullus, nothing except a few fragments remains of the work of any of this group; they all seem to have been washed away by the tide of revolution that followed the assassination of Julius Caesar in 44 B. C.

As for Catullus himself (Gaius Valerius Catullus, c. 87–54 B. C.), the known facts of his life are very few. He was born at Verona in northern Italy, apparently to a family of some wealth and standing: Suetonius, in his biography of Julius Caesar, tells us that Catullus's father used to entertain Caesar on his passages between Rome and Gaul, and from this we may conclude that the family were people of consequence. He is supposed, though on what evidence is not entirely clear, to have come to Rome as a very young man and there to have completed his education—whatever that may mean. Suetonius tells us further that Catullus composed a large number of bitterly critical lampoons against Julius Caesar; when Caesar found these lampoons being circulated in Rome, instead of ridding himself of the young man, as he could easily have done, he invited him to dinner and so charmed Catullus that the two parted fast friends.

There is reasonably sound indication that Catullus spent the year 57 B. C. in Bithynia on the south shore of the Black Sea, as a member of the staff of Memmius, the governor of the province. There is evidence, largely to be sure derived from the poems themselves, that he owned a villa on the promontory of Sirmio in Lake Garda, and at one time owned or rented a villa near the hill-town of Tibur. In Rome, again to judge from the poems themselves, he moved in social circles that included some of the most brilliant men of the day; besides Caesar, he knew Cicero and Cicero's young friend, Marcus Caelius Rufus; he seems to have known members of the two illustrious families, the Calpurnius Pisos and the Manlius Torquatus's—these of course in addition to his acquaintance among the circle of young poets that surrounded Valerius Cato. If a somewhat shaky literary tradition is correct, he also met at Rome the infamous Clodia, sister of Cicero's arch enemy Clodius, and fell madly in love with her. This at any rate is the story we hear from Apuleius, who nearly 200 years later reports that the real name of the woman whom Catullus in his poems called Lesbia was Clodia. That he died young, presumably in his 30's, is also well established, although the precise date of his death must remain a matter of dispute. For some curious reason, Catullus never mentions any member of his own family except a brother, and he appears in the poems only after his death, an event which appears to have caused the poet great and lasting sorrow.

This is about all we know of Catullus's life; of his day-to-day activities, of the time of his first arrival in Rome, of the length of his sojourn there, of the travels that he must have made between Rome and Verona, of the times he presumably spent in his villas on Sirmio and at Tibur—of all this we know nothing whatever. We can scarcely so much as set a date upon the composition of his poems; even those that refer to specific historical events do so in oblique and imprecise ways or refer to events the dating of which is still far from certain. A few of the extant poems, like those that specifically mention Caesar and the one that mentions Cicero, gain some meaning for us because we know the persons to whom they refer, but in all honesty it must be admitted that the rest do not suffer because the persons named in them are either relatively or totally unknown. Even the poems addressed to Lesbia are in no way illuminated by the supposed identification of this woman with Clodia; even if we were certain of the identification—and we are not—the poems would gain nothing from it.

In the case of the poems of Catullus, the circumstances virtually force us to do what we really should have done anyway, that is, to interpret the poems as they stand, as products of poetic imagination and genius, with no attempt to link them with specific persons, events, or happenings, other than to recognize them as the products of a poet who lived in the middle of the first century B. C. We know from history the kind of world in which he lived; we know that it was exciting, interesting, dangerous, and immoral; we know that there were great men on the scene and that cataclysmic changes in the life of Rome were impending. This was Catullus's world, and to a degree he reflects it; far more, however, he reflects the mind of a sensitive and imaginative man, to whom personal relationships and their meaning and impact upon himself were the most important things in the world. It is this personal world that Catullus explores and explains in his poems; in virtually every instance, the poem itself tells us all that we need to know in order to create the world in which it moves, to observe its artistry, and to comprehend its meaning and message.

In the intensely personal character which Catullus set upon his lyrics he at once cast himself free of the impersonal objectivity of much of Greek poetry and set forever upon all Western European lyric and upon much other Western poetry as well, the stamp of the personality of the writer. Paradoxically, this does not mean that the writer is self-absorbed or egotistic; rather, it means that, first, he has a depth of mind and breadth of heart that enables him to trace in himself the feelings of all men, and second, that by walking out, so to speak, into the world of the poem that he creates, and by setting himself there clearly and unequivocally, he invites his reader to join with him in the experience depicted and in the ideas described.

Like most practicing poets, Catullus eschewed the role of the critic and only rarely and summarily took time to explain his theory of the art of poetry or to defend the way in which he wrote his poems. One principle, however, seems to govern all his work; this is *venustas*, a term commonly translated as "charm" or "grace" but in fact implying a great deal more than that. The poems of Catullus are remarkably various, and in their short compass display an amazing range of interest and a kaleidoscopic variety in style and manner of presentation. But through them all, the poet's conviction of one principle of poetic composition remains unequivocal and clear: no matter what the subject of the poem, it must display an inner consistency and harmony. Subject matter, vocabulary, sentence structure, relative length of the parts and total length of the whole, meter, rhythm, sound patterns, rhetorical devices—all of these elements must be worked out so that they agree and harmonize one with the other, and so that the end result is a poem, which, within the limits set by its subject and the poet's intent, shows no lapse from good taste.

It should be immediately noted that this is not a theory of "respectability" in poetry; "good taste" *(venustas)* is literally to be described as the inner harmony of all elements of which we have been speaking; if only this harmony is present, the poem may range in subject matter from the scatological to the sublime. Even in the small corpus of his poems that has come down to us, Catullus manages to range over this whole spectrum. He can be as vulgar as the brothel and as ethereal as the angels; he can be as starkly simple as a Doric column or as full of dados, curlicues, and gingerbread as a lumber baron's mansion. It all depends on the nature of the total complex which is the poem of the moment.

Although Catullus, as a frankly experimental poet, wrote on a wide variety of subjects and in a wide variety of styles, he was best known in antiquity and is still best known for his short occasional lyrics, those poems in which he gives expression to events of the day and his feelings about them. A friend returns from a trip to Spain:

> Veranius, of all the friends I have
> You who are worth 300,000 of them,
> Have you come home to your own household gods,
> to your brothers who share one heart, and to your gray-
>      haired mother?
> You have come! Oh what happy news for me!
> I'll see you safe and sound, and hear you tell
> tales of the Spaniards: cities, exploits, peoples,
> as is your way. I'll draw you close to me
> and give your lips and eyes the kiss of joy.
> Oh, all you men of happiness everywhere,
> What greater joy or happiness than mine? (9)

Passing through the forum, Catullus overhears a chance remark:

> I laughed a moment ago at some chap in the crowd
> who when my friend Calvus had marvelously
> unfolded the charges against Vatinius
> was thunderstruck, threw his hands in the air and shouted
> "Great gods! What an eloquent little runt!" (53)

His poem on the death of Lesbia's pet bird is probably his best known:

> Weep, Venus, Cupid, weep;
> weep every man of true good taste!
> The little bird is dead,

her bird, her darling.
She loved it more than her eyes,
for it was honey-sweet, and knew its beloved
as well as the girl knew her own mother.
And it never went away from her lap,
but hopping about now here, now there,
it piped and sang to its lady alone.
Now it's going down the road of shadows
to the place whence, they say, no one returns.
Well, damn you anyway, damned night of Hell;
you gulp down everything that's lovely!
Such a pretty little bird you stole from me!
It's too damned bad!
                    Oh, you wretched bird;
you did it! My poor girl's eyes
are all red and swollen with weeping! (3)

Scarcely less famous—because Tennyson once referred to it in a poem of his own—and perhaps one of the really great poems of sorrow from antiquity, is Catullus's poem on the death of his brother:

Through many nations and over many seas I traveled,
and have come, my brother, to say my poor prayers for the
    dead
to give you the last gifts of death
and to speak, though in vain, to your voiceless ashes.
For Fate has taken you yourself from me—
Oh, my poor brother! It was not right that you be
    taken from me!
Still now, for the moment, take from me—
as the ways of our fathers would have it—
these gifts, set forth in sad office of the dead;
they are wet, wet with a brother's tears.
And forever and ever, my brother,
Goodbye. (101)

Catullus could also express scorn, as in his famous epigram against Caesar:

I don't much care to win your favor, Caesar,
or even to know if you are dark or fair. (93)

He could be venomous:

> Cominius, if the people took a vote
> and sent your hoary halo of white hair
> with every spot of moral muck still on it
> down to the grave, I'll tell you what I think:
> First off, the tongue that hated all good men
> would be cut out to stuff a buzzard's craw;
> they'd dig out your eyes and throw them to the crows,
> your guts to the dogs and to the wolves the rest. (108)

These poems might be said to mark the various boundaries of Catullus's lyric effort; within the field they circumscribe lie short lyrics expressive of almost every degree of feeling, from the deepest hatred to the gentlest concern, from the lively and playful to the profoundly passionate. Within their limits too lie most of Catullus's love poems; these, however, present a very special problem and will be dealt with separately.

Even these few examples will show clearly enough that Catullus had that spontaneity and natural ease of expression that belong to a man who does not have to search his own mind, let alone the minds of other men, for ideas for his poems. Paradoxically, this most spontaneous of all the Roman poets had attached to his name from very early times—perhaps in his own lifetime—the epithet *doctus* ("learned") as if he were some kind of scholar-poet devoted more to books and libraries than to the life around him. In actuality we are not at all sure what the epithet meant; Catullus himself uses it of a young woman to whom he attributes an unusual degree of poetic taste, and it may have been meant to convey nothing more than the idea that Catullus was a great artist in words, as indeed he was. The spontaneous and easy flow of his lyrics should not for a moment lead us to think that they are the artless outpourings of a full poetic heart, unchastened and unstrained by the conventional and artificial limitations of formal literature. Even the most cursory examination of the poems will show that they are beautifully and delicately constructed according to clearly conceived and executed plans; every line, every word has been placed with consummate care to create not only a carefully devised pattern of meaning, but an equally carefully devised and balanced pattern of words. Catullus is a poetic artist, and a great one; his art is perhaps the subtlest of them all: the art that conceals art.

However that may be, and whatever the word *doctus* meant

when applied to Catullus, it has certainly been a contributing element to the theory that Catullus was an Alexandrian, that is to say, a follower of the school of poetry that flourished around the great library of Ptolemies in Alexandria in Egypt from the fourth to second centuries B. C. The poets of this school found themselves no longer able to cope with the heroics of great epic and great drama: these fields of literature, they felt, had been preempted by Homer and the great tragedians of Athens. The Alexandrian poets turned instead to the writing of light verse, short poems, the poetry of fantasy and humor, and even the poetry of learning per se, conducting elaborate research into variant forms of the great myths of antiquity and embodying the results in poems so obscure and loaded with learning as to have been well-nigh incomprehensible, even in their own day, without an elaborate commentary. In default of greatness, they sought for novelty; in default of wisdom, they sought for cleverness. They delighted in taking some small subject and working it out in beautifully polished and proportioned verse, seeking perfection of form rather than depth of meaning.

No doubt Catullus, and the rest of the New Poets, knew the work of these Alexandrians; among the extant poems of Catullus, in fact, we find a translation of a poem by the chief exponent of the Alexandrian school, Callimachus (c. 305–c. 240), the *Lock of Berenice (Coma Berenices,* 66). Like any educated Roman of his day, he had certainly read every scrap of Greek poetry, ancient or contemporary, that he could get his hands on, and no doubt the delicate artistry of the Alexandrian poets made great appeal to his mind. The aesthetic perfection of his shorter poems, their neatly turned balance and deftly executed patterns, probably owe much to the Alexandrians, and it is certainly from them that Catullus learned the elaborate nonfunctional verbal tracery of poems like his *Peleus and Thetis* (64) and the strange and murky mode and mood of his *Attis* (63). But his interest in literature was catholic; his reading had certainly included Homer and the great dramatists as well as early Greek lyric; from them he learned as much or perhaps even more than he did from the Alexandrians about the qualities and modes of expression that are appropriate to personal poetry. Careful study of his poems shows that the great poets of every age of Greek culture, up to and including his own day, had been his masters. To speak of him as an "Alexandrian" is to give a false impression of shallowness and devotion to sheer wordplay which, far from playing any part in his work, are utterly foreign to it.

As for "learning" in his poetry, we see that it takes two quite different forms, both of them original adaptations of the Alexandrian concept of learned reference. In Catullus's elaborate quasi-elegy (68), he weaves the story of Protesilaos and Laodamia, and of Helen and the seige of Troy, into a poem of disappointment with his love for Lesbia and sorrow for the death of his brother at Troy. The poem might have crossed the border into mawkish self-pity if Catullus had not slashed away sentiment by two rather startling devices. The first is sheer grotesquerie: the depth of Laodamia's love for Protesilaos is compared to the depth of the ditch that Hercules dug to drain the Stymphalian swamp (with a side glance at his "slavery" to "a lesser master," Eurystheus, and a strange "clause of perverse purpose," by which the purpose of Hercules's labors becomes the entry of one more deity into Olympus, and the termination of Hebe's virginity). The second and even more original device is the introduction into the poem of a bit of learning drawn from the Roman law: the depth of Laodamia's love, again, is compared to the deep glow of affection that comes over an aged grandfather who has no sons to whom to leave his property, but whose daughter after years of childlessness finally produces a grandson for him and gives him the double satisfaction that his family property will not be dissipated and that his collateral relatives, that "'horde of vultures" who have been waiting for him to die, have been beaten off and compelled to leave him in peace.

The second type of learned reference is more deft and in the end more productive. This type makes use of a suggestive epithet, either geographical or mythological in character, which, far from being merely decorative or conventional, tempts the reader to a flight of the imagination. In a light and amusing little poem (7), Catullus tells Lesbia that he wants as many kisses from her as there are grains of sand in "laserpiciferous" Cyrene, from the temple of Zeus Ammon (an oasis in the middle of the Sahara Desert) to the Shrine of Battus the Ancient, a monument that stood in the center of the city of Cyrene itself. The word "laserpiciferous" may well be a coinage of Catullus's own, and the mouth-filling word certainly had its humorous connotation; in addition to that, with its reference to *laserpicium*, a strong smelling condiment widely used in ancient cookery, it suggested images similar to those that would be suggested in English by such a phrase as the Spice Islands, but with a certain wry twist arising from the fact that the condiment in question (now called asafoetida), however exciting to the taste, had a most rank odor. In addition, the mention of Cyrene probably suggested to the Roman much what Babylon suggests to us: flesh-pots and high living. And Catullus tops it all off with a reference to Battus, the tough old Greek adventurer who had founded the city of Cyrene on the coast of North Africa. This type of "learned" reference is one with which we are now quite familiar (one need only think of Milton's magnificent use of it in *Paradise Lost*), but Catullus seems to have been one of the first poets to use it in this way.

This is about as far as Catullus's learning extends; in general the simple, unaffected language of his poems, the indirect and uncomplicated mode of expression, and their almost total lack of obscurity in any form seem a far cry from the tortuous and deliberately obscurantist erudition of Callimachus and Lycophron. That Catullus studied the Alexandrian poets is beyond question; that he learned much from them about the art of verbal arrangement and the balanced architecture of poetry is equally beyond doubt, but whether or not this qualifies him to be called an Alexandrian remains a serious question.

Far more characteristic of Catullus is his insistence on a return to living people and living speech. Poetry resided for him in all the actions of people, including some of the more intimate matters which we normally feel are not fit subject for poetry. What people did and what people said were to Catullus endlessly fascinating; he saw his task as a poet to be the embodiment of these acts and this language in poems each of which would be a perfect expression of an incident, and of the level of society, activity, and language, in which it lay. We are familiar enough with poetry that is expressive of men's higher thoughts and more delicate feelings, and by far the greater bulk of Catullus's poetry is of this kind. But he never shrank from the coarse, the vulgar, and from what we choose to call the obscene: in these realms too, he thought, lay materials susceptible of poetic expression. It is in this spirit that he writes a mocking little poem teasing an old man for letting his playful, lusty young bride cuckold him (17), and in the same mocking tone addresses a common whore as "my darling little missy" (*Ipsithilla*), begs her to receive him at the siesta and prepare to make love with him nine times, one right after the other (32). He can write of a man whose body odor is so strong that it drives all decent girls away (69) and of another man whose breath is so foul that he's not quite sure whether he prefers him right-side-up or up-side-down (97).

Yet none the less realistic and intensely alive are his religious poems; his *Hymn to Diana* (34) preserves all the legalism of pagan Roman prayer (identification of deity and worshiper, pedigree of deity, chief aspects and functions of deity, particular function in virtue of which the present prayer is offered, and finally the prayer itself) yet the quiet dignity of its movement and its totally functional language express a degree of religious feeling that we may justly suspect was only rarely evoked by the actual cult practice of the day. The wedding song of Vinia and Manlius (61) gives us a step by step poetic version of a Roman wedding ceremony and procession: we invoke the god of marriage, Hymen, call the bride out of her house, escort her through streets to the bridegroom's home, on the way teasing her and embarrassing her by singing ribald songs, escort her into the bridegroom's house where her young husband-to-be is hanging over the edge of his dining couch in eagerness to see her, put her to bed, call the bridegroom to her, and close with the wish that the young couple "may enjoy each other more times than there are sands in the desert or stars in the sky" and soon produce children. The poem contains, incidentally, one of the few realistic portraits of babyhood that have come down to us from antiquity:

> a tiny Torquatus I'd like to see
> safe in his mother's circling arms
> hold out his darling baby hands
> and give to his father that first fleet smile
> with little lips half parted. (61.216–20)

Equally realistic is his picture of the orgiastic worship of the Great Mother of the Gods, Cybele (63), with its bloody scene of self-castration, its wild dances and music, its grim picture of the eunuch priest, neither man nor woman, condemned to eternal slavery to the goddess, and closing with the poet's fearful, awe-struck prayer that such madness may never visit his house.

It almost stretches credulity to turn from such realism to the self-consciousness, verging on sheer prettiness, of Catullus's "little epic," the *Peleus and Thetis* (64). This poem of a little over 400 lines contains two stories, one inside the other. The outer story is a much romanticized version of the tale of the love affair and marriage of Peleus and Thetis, a highly proper tale of love at first sight and subsequent marriage, blessed—and in fact actually attended—by all the gods except Apollo and Diana. (Why Catullus says they did not attend is one of the few unexplained bits of erudition in his poetry.) As the wedding guests enter the hall, they see the wedding couch, symbol of marriage, spread with an embroidered coverlet on which is worked the story of an illicit love affair, that of Theseus and Ariadne. The bulk of the poem is actually concerned with this latter story, again given in much romanticized form, but beginning in deceit and elopement, proceeding through extravagant passion and almost unaccountable absentmindedness, as Theseus "forgets" his stolen lady on the morning after, and sails away leaving her deserted and alone on the beach of the island, Dia, from which she is ultimately rescued by the god Dionysus.

The poet now returns to his first story and concludes it with an account of the prophecy by the three Fates about the birth of the hero Achilles. The language of the poem and its movement match its self-conscious prettiness and nearly stuffy morality. The action of the two stories is related in jerky, staccato style, with here and there an awkward flashback to pick up the antecedent incidents; the much more extended sections, in which the poet depicts the emotional reaction of the various characters involved, seem unnecessarily drawn out and adorned with nonfunctional verbal ornamentation—at one point, for example, the poet seems to be trying to find out how many different ways he can say "water," and his attempts to describe the first ship that ever sailed the seas, the Argo, without using the word "ship," border on the ludicrous. Probably the poem is best regarded as an experiment in the Alexandrian manner with some attempt on the part of the poet to give his composition a Roman tone, as he pleads the case for righteous love as against unrighteous, and concludes his lengthy narrative with an almost too solemn coda, in which he laments the passing of the good old days when men, by their piety and decency, could still earn the love and respect of the gods. Granted its own set of standards and ideas, the poem is expertly executed; it may not be much to our taste, but again within the limits the poet has set for it, it preserves the inner harmony and consistency which to Catullus was the essence of poetic art.

In spite of Catullus's wide and remarkably varied interests as a poet he has doubtless always been best known as a poet of love. The identity of the woman he calls Lesbia, the various incidents and titillating character of the affair he carried on with her, even the sheer chronology of their relationship, have all been subjected to intense and well-nigh endless scholarly scrutiny. As for Lesbia, as we remarked earlier, the writer Apuleius in the second century A. D. tells us that her real name was Clodia, and it has been widely assumed that the Clodia meant was the famous, not to say infamous, sister of Clodius Pulcher, that wild and undisciplined leader of popular gangs who was Cicero's deadly enemy. About this particular Clodia we know a good deal; she was beautiful, fascinating, and dangerous, a seductive creature who loved to gather around her brilliant men of all sorts and interests, and through her manipulation of them to enter into the intellectual and political activities of the day.

Cicero's references to Clodia suggest that she had far more beauty than morals; if she was indeed Catullus's Lesbia, then her relationship with him was frankly adulterous, for she was married to a certain Metellus Celer (consul 60 B. C.). Some support for the identification is to be derived from one of Catullus's own poems (79) in which he sneeringly remarks that "Lesbius" is "Pulcher" ("handsome") and remarks that Lesbia seems to prefer him to the poet himself. Clearly, if "Lesbia" is "Clodia," then "Lesbius" might well be "Clodius" and the adjective "pulcher" could well be a pun on Clodius's cognomen. This would make the two brother and sister, if we have correctly understood the poem, and we might even go on, as many editors have done, and assume that the "preference" which Lesbia was showing for Lesbius was incest. There was, to be sure, another Clodia, the younger sister of the infamous lady of that name; about her, nothing is known save her existence.

In point of fact, nothing could be less important for an understanding of Catullus's love poetry than the physical, personal identity of the woman he calls Lesbia. What he wants us to know about her he tells us in the poems themselves and, in all conscience, this is precious little. He says that she was "beautiful all over" (*pulcherrima tota*, 86.5), whatever that may mean. He says that she "had all the charms any woman ever had" (*omnibus una omnis surripuit veneres, id.* 6), a charming thing to say but again not precisely revelatory. He once calls her his "blond goddess" (*candida diva*, 68.70) but something seems to be wrong here. Cicero says of Clodia that she was "ox-eyed," a physical characteristic that does not go with being "blond." Perhaps Catullus only meant to say that Lesbia was as beautiful as a blond goddess, or perhaps she was one of those fortunate women who have fair complexion but dark eyes and hair. Catullus wrote no poems in which he described her physical charms, he wrote no poems in which her identity as this or that woman is in any way crucial to an understanding of the poem. As far as the poems themselves are concerned, whether as works of art or as expressions of love, Lesbia could have been any woman; Apuleius has done nothing but confuse the issue.

Only one thing about Lesbia is of any importance at all; this is the fact, related with agonizing clarity by the poet himself, that she did not care for or even understand the unique quality of the love he offered her. For Catullus's love poems are not about Lesbia; they are about Catullus. Intensely personal, they tell us how *he* has reacted to the vicissitudes of passion, how love has affected *him*. However large a part she may have played in their actual personal relationship, in the poems that resulted from it she is only the embodiment of female force and feminine personality, who might perhaps better have been left under the anonymity of the name he gave her.

Far more important than the identity and the personality of Lesbia, in fact, even more important than the identity and personality of Catullus himself—for his poems would be no less impressive even if we did not know who he was—is the special and unique quality and nature of the love about which he wrote so many poems. The love literature of antiquity, both Greek and Roman, deals almost exclusively with the ephemeral relationship of a man with his mistress. It has nothing whatever to do with marriage, either existing or contemplated, and is best illustrated for us, if in rather flat and bourgeois style, in the comedies of Plautus and Terence. Writers more interested in women and love than these two were have given the affair rather more exalted and sensitive expression; even so, the ancient literature of love begins with the thesis that only beautiful women can expect to be loved, and that they will be loved only so long as their beauty lasts. "Gather ye rosebuds while ye may" is the essence of the ancient love affair, at least so far as the women were concerned. This does not mean that ancient love poets were not interested in anything but sex, or that they were so absorbed in physical beauty that they were unaware of intellectual and emotional charms; on the contrary, we find more than one poet protesting that his lady, besides being lovely to look at, danced, sang, and conversed brilliantly, and that all this was part of her attraction for him. Even so, her physical beauty was paramount, and it is quite clear that once that beauty were gone, his interest in her would quickly fade away.

It is in this respect that the love poems of Catullus are so startlingly different. He is not unaware of Lesbia's beauty: far from it; for although he never describes it, he tells how overpowering it

was (51) and how later, in all the bitterness of his disappointment
with her, her physical beauty still exercised upon him not so much
an attraction as a demand, that was almost literally maddening.
But to Catullus, this combination of physical attractiveness and its
corresponding response in himself, the sheer sexuality of love, was
only one element, albeit an important one, in the total complex
of ideas, feelings, sensations, and responses which in his poems he
described as his feeling for Lesbia. Nowhere else in ancient literature do we find a poet so absorbed in the nature of love itself;
nowhere else do we find a poet to whom love is such an agonizing
enigma.

Catullus clearly did not know why he felt as he did about
Lesbia; he was not entirely certain how he felt, but whatever his
feelings, he found himself engaged in an endless struggle to understand and express them. He was aware that the love of a man for
a woman involves physical attraction, sexual delight, and satisfaction; he was also aware that, at least for him, love was something
less than right if it did not also include emotional and intellectual
sympathy, loyalty, honesty, and a sense of belonging, that were
totally nonphysical in character. Unlike the other love poets, he
had come to see that love was not sexuality with intellectual
trimmings, but a complex in which sexual and nonsexual elements
were rather delicately counterpoised. Looking back at his poems
from our own vantage point at the end of a long romantic tradition, we can see clearly enough what it was he experienced and
attempted to express; it was, of course, the modern romantic concept of love, and the writings of many generations of romantic love
poets have given to the English word "love" the intricate bundle
of meanings which we have come to accept as normal and regular.

To Catullus, not only was this bundle of meanings not normal
or regular; it was something that he had never heard of, and something for the expression of which he found the Latin language
totally inadequate. His love poems reflect his endless struggle to
understand and to express his feelings. He cannot say simply that
he "loved" Lesbia, as a modern poet might, for the Latin verb
*amare* does not involve the complex of ideas for which he demanded expression, nor is there any other verb in Latin that could
say what he needed and wanted to say. Words were not lacking for
the primarily sexual concept of love that had long been standard
in ancient erotic literature; it was for those other aspects of love,
the nonphysical side of it, that he found himself lost for words.

In a curiously paradoxical way, it is only in the poems written

about the bitterness and disillusionment that follow the loss of love
that this struggle with definition begins to emerge. In one poem he
attempts to state his feelings positively:

> No woman can ever say
> that she was loved so much
>  (that is if she tells the truth)
> as you were loved by me
>      My darling.
> No loyalty was ever
> in any bond so great
> as in my love for you
> on my side was discovered. (87)

Here it is the intensity of his feeling and the bond of loyalty that
are uppermost in his mind.

An epigram of two lines shows in simplest form the inner conflict that was beginning to torment him:

> I hate and I love. Well, why do I, you probably ask.
> I don't know, but it's happening, and it hurts. (85)

The poet is dismayed, as no other ancient poet ever was, by the
realization that the sexual, physical side of his passion was as strong
as ever, but that the complex of loyalty, goodwill, and sympathy
that had made up the nonphysical side of love had turned to hate.
He finds the paradox not only puzzling but painful.

As if a clear definition of his love for Lesbia would help him
to understand and perhaps to be rid of the sense of guilt that has
been fastened upon him by the persistence of sexual desire in the
absence of the nameless complex of feelings that had escaped his
powers of expression, he attempts a definition so intensely and
typically Roman that it must sound strange to us:

> You used to say
>  (that was, oh, long ago)
> that Catullus was the only man
> you wanted to know,
> Lesbia, and that before me
> you would not wish Jove's own embrace.
> My feelings for you then were not just those

that anybody has for a girl he'd make love to
but like those of a father for his sons
or for the young men that have married his daughters.
Now I know what you are,
yet though my desire for you flames
more wildly than ever, still
you seem to me more and more
like some poor worthless, thoughtless thing.
How can that be, you say?
Because when a man's in love
and you hurt him the way you hurt me
it stokes his lust
but chills his heart. (72)

We must inevitably find it strange that he would compare the love of a man for a woman to the love of a father for his sons, let alone for his sons-in-law. The idea reflects that family solidarity that was so characteristic of Roman society, and the affection of a father for his sons-in-law gains new force when we remember that only in marriage did the Roman girl find a career and a life worth living. That a Roman father should feel deep affection for the young men who had given his daughters their lives, so to speak, is really not surprising.

In any event the important part of this concept, the idea that was certainly uppermost in the poet's mind, was the totally non-physical character of such a love. He does not mean that he felt like a father or like a father-in-law toward Lesbia; such an idea would have been as grotesque to him as it is to us; what he is trying to say is that his love for Lesbia had the same nonphysical, nonsexual quality that must characterize the love of a father for his sons and sons-in-law. To us, the expression seems fumbling, and fumbling it was. This bewilderment, in fact, is a large part of the tragedy of a man whose love had come many centuries too soon, before the Romantic movement had placed women and men's love for them on that very exalted level which Catullus had so painfully antici-pated.

Catullus's struggle for definition and understanding of love continued on through a number of other poems, but in the end logic failed, and the poet felt himself engulfed in a tide of con-flicting feelings, torn between surging sexual desire and sickening scorn for the woman to whom he had offered a love unparalleled and unprecedented, only to have her openly flout it by her endless coupling with other men.

In a poem which many editors, perhaps with more sentimentality than sound critical judgment, have designated as the last of the Lesbia poems, Catullus does what, as a good poet, he should have known enough to do in the beginning: instead of attempting to analyze and define the love that he felt but could not understand or express in logical language, he resorts to a picture. Addressing two friends whose protestations of eternal friendship and willingness to travel with Catullus "to the ends of the world" have decided overtones of irony, he asks them to take this message to a Lesbia who had apparently been trying to win him back:

> "To her and her kept lovers, a fond farewell,
> those hundreds whom she holds in one embrace;
> she loves not one, but bursts—again, again!—
>     their swollen passion.
> She'll find no more a haven in my love,
> for by her fault it fell, as on the lea's
> last edge and end a flower, when the plow
>     passed by and touched it." (11.17–24)

The figure of that last flower at the farthest edge of the field, a flower so delicate that only the touch of the plow was needed to destroy it, expresses far more clearly than any logic the quality of the love that Catullus had offered to Lesbia.

As we look back at Catullus's work, especially from the vantage point of the mid-twentieth century, when literary experimentation has virtually run riot over the whole field of experience and even of imagination, the contribution made by Catullus to the art of Western European poetry seems modest, and his work seems scarcely radical or experimental at all. Where he succeeded in expressing himself clearly and satisfactorily, as in the short occasional lyrics, he is only doing with the lyric poem what we ourselves have done long since. When he writes in the torment of bitterness and frustration, as in so many of the Lesbia poems, while we may deeply appreciate the expression he gives to a kind of heartache that is by no means peculiar to his own age, we are bound to find his expression a little uncertain. It emerges into clarity only when he forcibly prunes his thought back to its simplest terms or when, with sure genius, he turns to a figure like that of the flower on the edge of the meadow. When he speaks simply or in symbols, he has the touch of greatness, and we can see that the lyric is what it is today at least partly because of the work that he did with it.

When he becomes more elaborate and fanciful, as in the *Peleus and Thetis* and his more frankly experimental and Alexandrian poems, he produces work that, though excellent of its kind, has little appeal to contemporary taste. Yet even here we must credit him with showing the poet what words can be made to do under given circumstances and in certain environments. Coming to a Latin poetic vocabulary that was stiff and formal, not to say stuffy and stodgy on the one hand, and crude, shapeless, and unpolished on the other, he enriched the one by the infusion of popular speech and popular syntax, and brought the other to more civilized form by pruning out its awkwardness and crudity and by meticulous insistence on the principle of internal harmony, balance, and good taste. Although, along with his contemporary, Cicero, he was destined almost to fade from the public scene in the early years of the Empire, he was known and loved and studied by every Roman poet after him, for it was he who laid the foundation for the great classical poetic Latin style of the age of Augustus. Perhaps if there was ever a "poet's poet" at Rome, it was Catullus, for there is not a single later verse-maker in Rome who was not in his debt in some degree. He continued to be read and studied until well into the fifth century A. D. Then, except for a brief emergence in the ninth century, his text seems to have been completely lost. Only in the fourteenth century, at his home town of Verona, was a single manuscript of his poems discovered. Although the manuscript that was found at that time has since again been lost, copies were made of it, and through their mediation the poems of Catullus have continued to be known and read down to our own day.

# CHAPTER VIII

## Lucretius

It is a curious fact that the most original, venturesome, imaginative, and thoughtful mind of the middle years of the first century B. C. should have occupied a somewhat anomalous position among the poets of the day. Lucretius (Titus Lucretius Carus, c. 96–c. 53 B. C.) is unique not only in his own period, but in the whole history of Latin literature. Although he knew his predecessors and presumably also his contemporaries, and sometimes seems to borrow from them, he is totally unlike any of them; and in the succeeding years, no other poet, as far as we know, ever attempted to follow in his footsteps. The subject of his poem, *On Nature (De rerum natura)* is the philosophic system of the Greek philosopher, Epicurus (342–270 B. C.), a philosophy neatly logical in conception and execution but not, on the face of it, likely to excite the imagination of a poetic mind. Yet Lucretius found it personally satisfying and poetically inspiring; out of this combination of personal satisfaction and poetic inspiration, he produced the only philosophic poem that has come down to us in complete form from antiquity.

Of his life, the chronicler Jerome tells a strange story, remarking that Lucretius was driven to insanity by a love-philter and that in the intervals of his insanity he wrote "books" which Cicero later "edited"; he then committed suicide in his forty-fourth year. The account is suspect for more than one reason. Love-philters were common enough in antiquity; along with other magical trash and mumbo-jumbo, they were used to stir lagging passion, to attract the interest of someone hitherto indifferent, to transfer affection from one person to another, and for a variety of other purposes associated with the passion of love. Made up of a variety of ingredients, largely foolish nonsense, such as furry leaves gathered by moonlight and cut with a bronze knife, they seem commonly to have included bits of liver, since the ancients were convinced that the seat of sexual passion was in the liver. They may well have been rather vile-tasting and vile-smelling concoctions, but the chances that they would drive anyone into psychosis seem remote. It has been suggested that Jerome got the idea of the love-philter from the long passage in Book IV of Lucretius's poem, in which he attacks sexual passion as a maddening and distracting force in human life. The point seems hardly important. That the poet should ultimately have gone mad, and that he should have committed suicide, may well be true. Lucretius's poem is the work of a highly imaginative, intensely sensitive intellect, only too alive to all aspects of human life, a man, moreover, whose deep seriousness of purpose and dedication to his "mission" might well in the end have brought him to the bitterness and disillusionment that can lead to suicide.

This is all that Jerome has to say, and all that we can deduce from the poem itself. Beyond this, we know nothing about Lucretius's life, other than that he was a friend of the same Gaius Memmius whom Catullus accompanied to Bithynia and whom he so cordially detested. In Lucretius's poem, Memmius appears as patron, friend, and deeply respected pupil, for the poem is written as if to instruct Memmius in the doctrines of Epicureanism. It is useless to speculate as to why Lucretius should so have revered the man whom Catullus so hated; personal feelings of this sort are beyond fathoming at any time, nor have they any bearing whatever on the understanding and appreciation of the works of either poet.

No other contemporary is mentioned by Lucretius in his poem; we knew nothing of the poet's family, where he was born, where he lived, or anything else about him. The name, Lucretius, is an illustrious one in Roman history; one need only think of the lady of that family whose rape by the infamous Tarquin occasioned the revolution that set Rome free of the kings. But the name was not uncommon, and the merest freed-man could have borne it. The chances are that Lucretius was a Roman gentleman, well educated and of some position, who moved on familiar terms with Memmius and other members of the Roman aristocracy of the time.

Of more interest is Jerome's cryptic remark about the "books" that Lucretius wrote which were subsequently "edited" by Cicero. By "books" Jerome presumably meant the poem *On Nature*; at any rate we know of no other work by Lucretius. What he meant by "editing" is more puzzling; the Latin verb *emendavit* could cover anything from a casual examination of the poet's manuscript to the

most thorough critical rescension. From a letter that Cicero wrote
to his brother Quintus (2.9.3) we gather that both of them had
read Lucretius's poem and found it of more than passing interest:
"Lucretius's poetry is exactly as you describe it: it is filled with
flashes of genius, but at the same time shows great technical skill."
The remark, however, does not tell us whether Cicero or his brother
Quintus has done more than just read the poem; that one or the
other of them might have undertaken, after the poet's death, to
prepare his manuscript for publication remains at least a possibility.

On the face of it, the Epicurean philosophy would seem an
unlikely subject for poetry. With all the pedestrian dullness of a
system based on the exclusive validity of sense-perception, it lacked
the excitement and sense of adventure that might have been given
to such a system by the addition of mathematics and the experimental method. Nor was its founder the kind of man about whom
poems are written; a modest, gentle, and retiring soul, he was
better known and more honored for the integrity of his life and
the warmth of his affection than for the brillance of his intellect or
the artistic excellence of his writings. His followers, too, were on the
whole an unexciting lot, given to simple, not to say austere living,
retiring from politics and other sorts of public activity, and occupying themselves chiefly with memorizing, repeating, and expounding
the "Golden Sayings" of their master. Because their doctrine that
pleasure is the criterion of good was widely and perhaps even
deliberately distorted, they gained the undeserved reputation of
being selfish pleasure-seekers and sensual debauchees—a cruel canard
that led their philosophy to discredit in ancient times and has
pursued them to the present day. Their real fault, if any, lay in the
opposite direction; they were too austere, too unpretentious and
unambitious for the violent and flamboyant world in which they
lived.

In practical effect, the Epicurean philosophy which Lucretius
attempted to express in verse was not far in its basic doctrines and
attitudes from the position taken by modern science. Starting with
the question, "How do we get our knowledge?" Epicurus concludes
that we get it through sense perception. The fundamental starting
point of his philosophy is the doctrine that sensation is true. If we
would determine the nature of any thing, we must examine it
through the power of the senses and must accept what they tell us,
and only what they tell us, as true. Nor was Epicurus unaware of the
fact that many phenomena lie beyond the limits of sense perception;
in such instances we must theorize concerning the nature of these

phenomena on the basis of what the senses do tell us, and accept only those theories which, when appropriately analyzed, do not contradict the evidence given us by the senses. In this limited way, Epicurus allowed for the extension of the powers of the senses through logic and reason, very much as the modern scientist extends those powers through instruments of various kinds and through the mathematical process.

Starting with this basic premise, the philosophy proceeds with as nearly relentless logic as was ever to be found in the ancient world. If sensation is truth, then it follows that all Being is material, for our senses show us no other sort of existence. But the senses show us also that matter moves; if it moves, it must have space in which to move, therefore there must be empty space, or void. If we examine the behavior of matter, we find that we can explain it in only one way that is compatible with the evidence of the senses; this is that matter is composed of atoms, particles so small as to be far below the range of human sensation and possessing only the properties of indivisibility, size, and shape. From their indivisibility, it follows that they can neither be created nor destroyed; since they could not have been created, they must always have been. It follows that time is infinite, and the continuing presence of atoms in infinite time demands that the atoms themselves be infinite in number. The atoms possess size and shape, but since no atom is large enough to be seen by the human eye, there must be a limited number of such sizes and shapes, but of any given size and shape there is an infinite number.

All "things"—and by this we mean all objects perceptible by human sensation—are aggregates of atoms and void; the varying proportions of atoms and void account for such phenomena as relative weight; the varying sizes and shapes of atoms, and the ever-varying patterns into which their combinations are formed, account for color, taste, smell, texture, and even for life itself, since living objects are no more than particularly subtle and highly specialized combinations of specific types of atoms commingled with void. In contrast to the atoms, all "things" are mortal; they begin when the appropriate atoms, moving freely in the void, come together in such ways as to form the requisite pattern. They remain in this pattern so long as the combination of interior stress and blows inflicted by atoms from outside remains too weak to break the bonds that held the atoms together. Ultimately these bonds weaken, and when that happens, internal and external stress and strain combine to break the atomic bonds. Thereupon the "thing" in question is broken up into its atoms, which fly off into the void to resume their normal movement. In this way, from infinite time in the past on into infinite time in the future, infinite atoms move through equally infinite void, now colliding and joining together, for a greater or shorter time, now colliding only to fly apart again, now breaking from their temporary combinations with other atoms and resuming their endless movement through the void.

What caused the atoms to move in the first place? Nothing "caused" them to move; they were always in motion, for the atom by definition can never be at rest. As for the direction of atomic motion, earlier atomic philosophers, e.g. Democritus, had taught that they move ever downward—in whatever direction "downward" may be in an infinite universe—following parallel paths. Epicurus saw the basic flaw in this doctrine, for if the atoms always move in parallel paths, there will be no way in which one atom could touch another, and therefore no "things" could be formed. In order to remedy this basic defect in the system, he conceived the idea of atomic swerve, teaching that although the natural movement of the atom was indeed downward in parallel paths, as Democritus had taught, nonetheless at some unpredictable time and place and for no assignable reason it could and inevitably would swerve from this path. As soon as it did so, it would strike the adjacent atom and drive it from its path, and thus a chain reaction would be set up, the end result of which would be the random swirl of the atoms in the void, by virtue of which, combinations of atoms could and did take place. This "declension of the atoms," as it is sometimes called, was undoubtedly Epicurus's greatest stroke of genius; its validity is substantiated in a curious way by the Heisenberg indeterminacy principle of modern physics.

These fundamental postulates about the atoms and their nature, and about the void in which they move, was concluded by Epicurus to be capable of explaining all phenomena of every sort. Even psychological phenomena and others of the type that we would class as nonphysical were taken by Epicurus to be nothing more than the interaction of certain classes and types of atoms in the make-up of a man. Even man's soul was described as atomic, for since it existed, it must be material like all other existing things. The soul, like the body, was simply an aggregate of atoms, atoms so fine and so delicate that their presence could be detected only by their effects, but atoms nonetheless. The soul was conceived and grew along with the body, it maintained its identity only so long as it was contained within the body, and upon the dissolution of the body at death the soul also was dissolved: its atoms, like those of the body were set free to join the eternal swirl of the atoms in the infinite void.

Obviously, by this doctrine, there could be no afterlife, for the soul like the body was mortal, and its life ended with the life of the body. Death then was the total extinction of the person and the personality; as Epicurus put it, after death it would be no different for a man than if he had never been born. Since death is total extinction, the fear of death becomes nonsense; there will be no afterlife in which we must expect to pay penalty for the misdeeds of this life. Therefore we need have no fear of death, no fear of punishment, no fear of the gods. The gods exist, to be sure, but they have no influence whatever upon our life, now or at any other time; they influence no phenomena of any sort; in fact, they do nothing but exist in the spaces between the worlds, where they live a kind of perfect life of Epicurean peace, models of the life that man might have for himself if only he would accept the truth about nature and nature's laws.

It is in similar fashion that Epicurus arrived at his ethical doctrines. Relying once more on observation, he claimed that all living creatures instinctively seek pleasure and avoid pain; it follows that pleasure is the sole good and pain the sole evil. Pleasure is the normal and natural state of existence, when the atoms that make up a given thing are moving comfortably in their normal patterns and not being disturbed by any force, internal or external. Pain, by contrast, is the dislocation and disarrangement of the atoms when they clash and conflict in abnormal and unnatural ways. Pleasure is in fact a completely negative state; it is that condition that exists in the absence of pain, and the presence of the smallest degree of pain will destroy it. The task of the true philosopher becomes to keep free of pain, to avoid all things that not only do cause pain but may potentially cause it at some future time. All pleasure is good; in this respect Epicurus was entirely consistent: the physical pleasures—eating, drinking, and sex—were all good. They did however suffer from this deficiency, that if engaged in to excess they could easily eventuate in pain; they must therefore be pursued with great restraint and caution for fear of crossing over the line between pleasure and pain and turning what was meant to be a virtue into a vice.

The safest thing of course was to avoid physical pleasure as much as possible, and this was indeed what Epicurus recommended; he himself and the most devout and faithful among his followers lived a simple, almost ascetic life, devoting themselves to those pleasures—the pleasures of the mind—which of all the pleasures available to man are least likely to cross the threshold from pleasure into pain. To Epicurus, the truest form of pleasure was the acquisition of knowledge, the study of the laws of nature, the laws that create and govern the things man sees, and control and explain his reaction to them.

Nor is man a mere mechanistic creature, behaving as he does because of the patterns of atoms existing within him; he has free will, and can choose the good life if he will. But quite consistently man's free will is explained by Epicurus on grounds of the behavior of the atom itself; as we have seen, the atom has the power to swerve, the ability to move from its predetermined path for no assignable cause, the freedom, one might say, to initiate movement on its own. From this independence of movement, inherent in the atom itself, came the power of free will in man. The world man lives in is a purely mechanistic creation; no intelligence built or guided it; no supernatural being has power to influence it in any way. It is what it is, acting only in obedience to its own laws and to the laws of chance. Within this world exists man, a creature with a material body, a material soul, mortal like all other things, possessed of an intellect that is a product of the atoms that go to make him up, in all his actions and all his being, a purely material thing. But again because his atoms are what they are, he is possessed of the all-important power of free choice and free will.

It is this philosophy which Lucretius set himself to expound, describe, and explain in verse. His poem, *On Nature,* in six books, was, as far as we know, his only literary production; how long he was occupied upon the writing of it we have no way of knowing, but it is patent that the work was never finished. The poem as it exists contains unfinished bits, repeated passages, illogical progressions of thought, sections here and there that look as if they were in trial position waiting for the final hand of the author for their disposition. Each of the six books of the poem deals with a different aspect of the Epicurean philosophy. In Book I, Lucretius lays down the fundamental postulates of the system. He gives in summary form an exposition of the theory of the atoms, describing them as solid, indivisible, eternal particles moving in limitless void; he proclaims the twin principles of the indestructibility and the increatibility of matter. He continues with a brilliant exposé of rival theories of the nature of matter, taking them up one by one and showing that while some of them may have been moving in the right direction, they did not go far enough, but were too quick to content themselves with theories of primal matter which left it complex, divisible, and basically weak, in every instance not primal but secondary and derivative.

The book is framed, so to speak, in two intensely vivid and poetic passages, It begins with an invocation to the goddess Venus, in which the poet asks for help in creating the peace which is essential to him in the writing of his poem. This proemium has been much criticized, chiefly on the grounds that it is inconsistent with Lucretius's doctrine of the nature of the gods, who, according to Epicurean theory, have no influence whatever of human life, and therefore cannot logically be appealed to for help. But Lucretius is not only a philosopher; he is also—in fact, primarily—a poet, and as such it is only natural that he should speak in the language of symbols. Venus is such a symbol; she represents peace and harmony; she also represents dynamic, creative being. She is at once life itself and the forces and powers that give rise to life. In a very real sense, she *is* the "Nature" which is the subject of Lucretius's poem. In the latter part of the proemium appears her counterpart and opposite, Mars, symbol of dissension, disharmony, strife, and death. The beautifully plastic figure of Mars succumbing to the blandishments of Venus is Lucretius's anthropomorphic symbol of the totality of existence, which is the result of the triumph of creativity over destruction. More than this, the figure of Venus was never intended to be; to attempt further to rationalize it is to destroy its poetic and philosophic validity and to make a grotesque caricature of the poet's intent.

Complementing this picture of creative and harmonious nature, the book ends with an almost Miltonic picture of the chaos and destruction that must inevitably result if the supply of atoms were not infinite. Unfortunately, the first lines of the postlude, if we may so call it, are lost. It began, no doubt, with an assertion that the atoms must be infinite in number, and then continued:

> lest, like flames, the walls of the world take wing
> and suddenly scatter in fragments through the void,
> and all the rest follow after in like fashion;
> lest, too, the heavens, high home of thunder, rumble,
> and earth be ripped from under our feet, to fall
> amid the crumbling wreckage of a world
> and heaven confounded, down through the empty deeps,
> to leave, in a second, no remnant of themselves

except blind atoms and abandoned space.
For wheresoever you first allow a shortage
of atoms, there you open a door to death,
and through it all matter will madly whirl away. (1.1102–13)

Book II is the most highly technical of the six. It is concerned
with the theory of the atoms, which is now discussed in great
detail. Beginning with the thesis that peace of mind is the truest
form of pleasure, and that it is there for the taking if man had
only the wit to see it, Lucretius excoriates men for their willful
blindness, for selling themselves out to ambition and lust, and for
refusing to see that it is knowledge of the truth that sets men free
—knowledge that is to be obtained by the study and contemplation
of the "outer view and inner law" of nature.

It is to this outer view and inner law of nature that Book II
is devoted. Lucretius explains that the atoms are always in motion,
never at rest; he shows why this must be so, even though this motion
is below the level of human sensation. As for atomic speed, he
maintains that it is greater even than the speed of light, a quite
logical error since he saw that light (which he also viewed as
atomic) had to move through air, which, being material, would
impede its progress, whereas the atoms moved in a vacuum, the
void, where there was nothing to slow them down. For their motion, said he, there were two causes; the first was their natural
weight, or gravity, the second was their striking against other atoms
or being struck by them; the rebound in the one case and the
impulse in the other caused them to move in ever-varying paths.
As the atoms themselves were indestructible, so their motion was
endless; things might be, and commonly were, in a state of repose;
the atoms that made them up never were. Lucretius also touches on
the infinite number of the atoms, and on the large but indefinite
and finite number of each of the *kinds* of atoms; he explains how
these varying kinds can join in varying patterns to create all the
forms that existence can take.

At the end of the book he reminds us that the universe is
infinite and that our world is only one of countless worlds that
exist somewhere in the infinite reaches of the void. Our world, like
all other worlds, is only a "thing," a completely fortuitous combination of atoms and void, subject to constant stress from atomic
motion within itself, and also to the endless blows of moving atoms
that rain upon it from outside itself. Although some of these
external atoms may stick to the earth and thus tend to increase its

bulk, the net result is a loss, for more atoms fly away from earth than are received onto it. Ultimately, as in the case of all other things, the combination of internal and external stresses and blows will become too much for the structure of earth; it will disintegrate, and the atoms that go to make it up will fly off and be received once more into the endless swirl of the universe. This process of deterioration is going on right now, and we can observe it:

> The aged plowman sighs and shakes his head
> again and again—all that work gone for naught!—
> compares the present times with times gone by
> and often remarks how lucky his father was.
> Discouraged, the vintner tends his tattered vines,
> curses the weather and prays till heaven is tired;
> he growls of an age long gone, when men were good,
> and found life easy though their world was small,
> and the land that each man held was then far less.
> He does not see that all things slowly weaken,
> and fall to ruin, worn out by ages past. (2.1164–74)

Of all the books of the poem, Book III is probably the best known and best loved, for here Lucretius embarks on a subject very close to the thoughts of all men, the question of the mortality or immortality of the soul. In general, the ancients believed in an afterlife, and held the not very inspiring view that that life consisted simply of a shadowy, unsubstantial, intrinsically unreal extension of our life here on earth. It is not at all surprising that in the *Odyssey* the ghost of Achilles should say to Odysseus, "that he would rather be slave to the poorest man on earth than king of all those that dwell in the underworld" (11.488–91). The underworld was not, as our Hell has always been, a place of punishment, nor like our Heaven, a place of reward. Only the spectacularly evil or the spectacularly good could expect any sort of special treatment in the life after death. The abominably, heroically sinful—chiefly those who had sinned against the gods themselves—were often thought of as subjected to hideous punishments of one sort and another, and the particularly noble might hope to be allowed some day to enter into the Elysian Fields where, if they did not dwell in eternal bliss, they at least enjoyed a limited form of happiness in the pursuit of those interests that in this life had rendered them great. Some of the great philosophers, e.g. Plato, had more cheerful visions of the life to come; there was in fact a persistent feeling among cultivated and educated men that life after death simply by definition had to be good.

In view of these persistent ideas, it is strange that Lucretius should so vehemently have attacked the idea of punishment after death, almost as if he had had a distorted prevision of Judaeo-Christian Hell. Nothing, to him, is as evil as the fear of death which these false ideas about the afterlife occasion in men; it is the root of all evil, and the religion that fosters and supports it is itself an evil thing. In Book III, Lucretius devotes himself to dispelling the fear of death by showing men that the soul is not immortal but, like the body, is a mere mortal thing that dies along with the body; death is then "more secure than any sleep." It is nothing, nothingness, total annihilation, the absence of being. If the soul, as he says, does not exist after death, then clearly it cannot possibly suffer in any way, for only that which exists can suffer.

Approximately the first half of Book III is devoted to a discussion of the nature of the soul. Like all other forms of existence, it is atomic, and consists of a conglomeration of the very finest of all the atoms, atoms so light and fine that their presence or absence cannot be detected by any of the instrumentalities of sense. The atoms that go to make up the soul are four in number. First is "wind," perhaps best thought of as moving air; this is the cool or chilling element, the one that accounts for the calm and deliberate aspect of character. The second is "heat," the warm and energizing factor, which gives us our liveliness and sensitivity, and in excess accounts for fury and anger. The third is "air"; this is a kind of neutral element that mingles with the other two and serves to keep them in proper proportion and balance.

These were the only elements in the soul Lucretius felt himself able to identify. Clearly, however, he was well aware that the combination of these three kinds of atoms, no matter how intricately built up, could not account for life, for in spite of everything they remained simply inert matter. For this reason, he now adds the fourth element, the *quarta natura*. To this he says he can give no name, and can only describe it by saying that it is far lighter, finer, smoother, more movable than any of the other three. Possibly, if either he or Epicurus had been more sophisticated, they might have posited this fourth nature as life itself and have spoken of atoms of "life." Neither of them ever did this; the imagination of the ancients never reached this far; for them, the "fourth nature" remained only that element without which the soul was not complete, without which here could be no life.

Lucretius saw the soul, then, as a conglomerate of four elements. With good practical imagination but faulty physiology, he locates the soul in the "breast," vaguely the mid-section of the human body, and explains that while the subtlest, finest and most sensitive parts of the soul are all located there, it in fact extends out into all parts of the body and is scattered through it all, although not evenly; there are more atoms of soul present in some parts than in others. These scattered parts of the soul are the ones upon which exterior forces impinge; struck by atoms coming onto the body from outside it, the scattered soul-atoms transmit these impulses to the concentration of soul-atoms in the breast, where they are sorted and interpreted, and from which, if this be appropriate, a demand for reaction is transmitted to the appropriate part of the body.

It is all too easy to see in Lucretius's description of the soul an analogy to our brain and nervous system. Lucretius never drew such an analogy, for in common with most of the ancient world, although he knew of the existence of the brain and of nerve-fibers, he had no clear idea of their function. It certainly never occurred to him or to any other Epicurean thinker to equate the soul with any part of the body tissue, for he held the soul to be so fine as to be invisible, entirely below the powers of human sensation. Lucretius's soul combines in itself the functions of the brain and the nervous system as we now know them, and also includes all those powers and faculties which we would now describe as psychological or spiritual. It must be remembered, of course, that to Lucretius there was no such thing as "spiritual" existence, and that as the soul itself was a material thing, so all its functions and activities must be described in terms of atomic motion of one kind and another. Lucretius never doubted the existence of the soul; he saw it, as the ancients in general did, as that part of a man that makes him alive and that combines within it all his intellectual and emotional life. But whereas the ancients, very much like ourselves, tended to identify the soul with the self, and again like ourselves, to give that self a permanence which the body could not possess, Lucretius thinks of the soul rather as merely a part of the total "thing" that is a man, something that functions within him very much like another organ, and possesses only the one distinctive quality of being life-giving; as part of a man, it has no identity apart from the man himself, and in fact owes its identity to the body in which it is located. Once that body is gone in death, the "container" of the soul is also gone and the soul will be dissipated, as will the body itself, into its component atoms.

Having thus described the nature of the soul, Lucretius launches into a series of seventeen separate proofs that the soul is mortal, not immortal. Although these proofs are presented in vivid and imaginative ways, they can be reduced to three basic propositions: first, that the soul is too tenuous and delicate a thing to be capable of maintaining its identity outside its container, the body. Not only are its particles smaller even than those of fog or smoke, they are so delicate as to be moved by the mere *image* of smoke and fog; second, it is clear from all its behavior that it has a specific location in the body and is closely physically entwined with the body itself; it is in fact like any other part or organ of the body, and just like them cannot exist as an entity apart from the body; third, we see proof after proof that the soul can suffer damage, for example in illness or drunkenness, and that it can be cut into parts: we see the limb cut off in battle still twitching and jerking as it lies on the ground. It could do so only if atoms of soul were present in it, atoms that have now been cut off, divided, separated from the soul to which they belonged. But things that can be damaged and divided can be destroyed, in fact they inevitably are destroyed as soon as they meet with a force stronger than the forces that bind them together. Since the soul is clearly an entity of this kind, it inevitably must suffer death.

One of the most interesting aspects of Lucretius's proof of the mortality of the soul is the ingenious way in which he uses what one might call the standard or orthodox proofs of the immortality of the soul to prove its mortality. According to the orthodox point of view, the lightness, speed, and nimbleness of the soul were proof that its nature was opposite to that of the body; and since the body was demonstrably mortal, the conclusion was that the soul was immortal. Lucretius uses this same lightness, nimbleness, and speed to prove that the soul is far too unsubstantial and tenuous to exist as an entity outside the body. Orthodoxy held that the illness, dullness, and frustration of the soul were caused by its imprisonment within the obstructive and antipathetic flesh, from which it longed to escape into the purer, rarer atmosphere of the absolute and eternal. Lucretius uses these same defects and limitations of the soul to prove its intimate and intensely sympathetic connection with the body, to show, in other words, that it was just like the body and therefore must die as the body does. One of the most persistent, and to modern thought the strangest doctrines of antiquity was that of "memory" (anamnesis), whereby it was held that the soul remembered in this life things that it had learned in an earlier existence. Since logically no limit could be placed upon the number of such previous existences, the conclusion was they were infinite in number. That which was infinite in the past, so to speak, must logically also be infinite in the future. Thus the soul's power of memory proves its infinity, i.e. its immortality. This doctrine Lucretius mentions only to dismiss it with contempt, asking us only to consider whether in reality we do remember, even to the slightest degree, the great and cataclysmic events of earlier years, for example, the Trojan War. The soul, he concludes, does not have memory of any previous existence, for the very simple reason that it never had one, but was born along with the body and in consequence must die along with it.

> Death, then, is nothing to us, nor matters a bit,
> since the soul has proven to be a mortal thing.
> (3.830–31)

With these two lines Lucretius sums up his proofs of the mortality of the soul and continues with a series of nine exhortations to men to cast aside all fear of death. The future, says he, will be exactly like the past, a total blank, and will concern us no more than the past does. Destruction of the body, loss of love and the physical bonds between ourselves and our family and friends, will be nothing to us, since death is like sleep:

> "Asleep in death": so shall you be for all
> that's left of time, cut off from grief and pain.
> . . . . . . . . . . . . . . .
> And so we may ask this man what is so harsh
> and cruel (if everything ends in sleep and peace),
> as to make man waste his life away in tears.
> (3.904–11)

Life's pleasures are endlessly repetitive and hopelessly tedious; should we wish them to go on for eternity, or rather be glad to escape from them into the nothingness of nonexistence? Once again, Lucretius picks up one of the standard commonplaces of ancient consolation for death and uses it for his own purposes. For those who were concerned about their own death or were grieving for the death of someone else, the ancient commonly commanded him to reflect on the fact that greater men than he or his loved one had died; death was the common lot of all men, and if he does not even spare the great, why should we common men object to our translation into another world? With withering scorn rather than gentle persuasiveness, Lucretius turns this argument to his own purposes:

> Even the eye of Ancus the Good grew dark,
> and he was your better—for shame!—a thousand ways!
> And other thousand kings and potentates
> have died, the governors of mighty nations.
> He, too, who once paved highways over the sea,
> and built his legions a road across the deep
> (taught them to walk atop the pools of brine,
> and prancing horse to spurn the ocean's roar)
> fell ill, saw daylight fade, and breathed his last.
> Scipio, thunderbolt-warrior, scourge of Carthage,
> gave bones to earth just like the meanest slave.
> Add the discoverers of truth and beauty;
> add Helicon's host, of whom great Homer sole
> earned kingship: like them all, he rests in peace.
> Then, too, Democritus, when ripe old age
> warned him that mind and memory were fading,
> went freely to place his person in death's path.
> Epicurus himself died when life's light ran out,
> he who in mind surpassed all men—eclipsed them
> all, as the sun hung high in heaven the stars.
> Will you hang back, indignant that you must die?
> Alive and conscious, you live next door to death;
> you waste in sleep the greater part of life,
> and even waking, you snore, and dream, dream on;
> you wear a heart confounded by hollow fears
> yet rarely can tell what caused them, when oppressed
> and drunk and wretched with unremitting cares,
> you wander, waver, and wonder where to turn.
> (3.1025–52)

All these brilliant exhortations may be summed up in the single proposition that this life, for all its potential pleasures and joys, is not so full of unremitting happiness as to make any sensible man wish to prolong it forever; he should far more turn with relief to the thought:

> Think back to ancient times, the endless past;
> how little that means to us—before our birth.
> Here nature holds her mirror to the future;
> so will it be for us when we are dead.
> Where here is the grim and ugly face of terror?
> Is this not a state more peaceful than all sleep?
> (3.972–77)

Book IV deals with the all-important problem of sensation; how do we see, hear, taste, smell, and touch? Since to the Epicurean sensation is the only source of knowledge, it is important that it be explained in a manner both consistent and persuasive. The book begins with a somewhat over-decorative prologue in which Lucretius compares his poetic activity to gathering fresh new flowers, and "seeking the laureate's crown whence Muses never ere now had veiled the brow of any man" (4–5). Students of Latin literature will recognize here a Lucretian version of the claim to originality made by so many Roman poets. Nothing, apparently, so tickled their egos as the thought that they had been the first, each in his own field, to have adapted to Latin speech and Roman forms one or another achievement of Greek culture. Sometimes the claim is patently questionable; sometimes it seems rather fatuous—this, perhaps, because no man in his right mind could now make any similar claim. That Lucretius should have so long postponed his particular claim to originality, and then have nearly buried it under pretty images of flowers, fountains, and the Muses, seems to betoken it as scarcely more than a bow to convention, even though in Lucretius's case it may well be justified.

The prologue continues with a sentimental picture, that of the sick little boy tricked into taking his bitter medicine by the doctor, who paints the lip of the medicine-cup with honey and thus inveigles the little fellow into taking the healthful draft before he becomes aware of its vile flavor. Lucretius—seemingly not without a touch of humor—compares his own poetic activity to that of the doctor. "His philosophy," says he, "often seems a little grim to the beginner," hence:

> . . . . . . . . . . . . I wish to tell
> my tale in sweet Pierian song for you—

to "paint" it with the "honey" of the Muses—
hoping that thus I might fix your attention
upon my verse until you clearly saw
the nature of things, and understood its value.
(4.20–25)

With that, the poet launches into his explanation of sense-perception. His theories will strike us now in many instances as naive, yet they are amazingly ingenious, relentlessly logical—almost to the point of being mathematical—and in many instances not so far removed from actual scientific truth as might at first appear.

In formulating his explanations of the operations of various senses, Lucretius theorizes that all sensation is essentially one, namely, the sense of touch. Earlier, in Book II (434–36), he had proclaimed touch the queen of the senses:

For touch, yes, touch, by all the powers of heaven,
is what we sense, either when things outside
penetrate the flesh, or something within offends us.

Lucretius's reasoning in this matter is quite clear and logical. Sensation is a physical phenomenon; it must therefore be caused by the impact of one physical thing upon another physical thing, for there is no other way in which one thing can be affected by another. The senses of seeing, hearing, tasting, and smelling are therefore merely variations of the sense of touch; in each instance they are caused by a physical contact between the sense-producing agent and the appropriate specialized atoms of soul and body. Only certain kinds of atoms can be affected by certain other kinds of atoms, for their configuration must mesh and their general characteristics must be in harmony one with the other. The atoms that produce the sense of smell, for example, are specialized and of course are of various kinds, ranging from those which produce pleasant odors to those that produce the nauseous and fetid. In every instance, the sense of smell is produced when a stream of the appropriate kind of atoms, driven forth by sheer atomic force from the odoriferous substance, comes into forceful contact with those specialized soul-atoms that are located in the nose. These atoms in turn transmit the impact, in chain-reaction fashion, to the soul-proper, which thereupon interprets the nature of the impact and dictates appropriate action to the body. Hearing is caused in exactly the same way, except that the particular atoms involved on the active and the passive side are different from those that cause and react to smell. They too have a specialized location, the ear. An identical process again with the involvement of particular and specialized atoms on both sides produces the sense of taste.

Most ingenious, perhaps, is Lucretius's explanation of the phenomenon of sight. Here, the problem of impact could not be so easily solved, since the relation between the eye and the object it sees is not as obvious as that between the organs of taste, smell, and hearing and the objects that produce these sensations. Nonetheless, Lucretius saw the process as essentially the same. Sight, too, must be caused by physical impact; something must actually touch the specialized atoms of the soul in the eye that are capable of receiving the sensation of sight. All things, said Lucretius, constantly emit from their surfaces extremely delicate films of atoms. These atoms, impelled again by sheer atomic force, fly in all directions at very nearly absolute speed. When they strike the soul-atoms located in the eye, they, like all other such atoms, transmit the impulse to the soul-proper in the breast, which interprets these impulses, identifies the sense-producing agent, and dictates to the body an appropriate reaction. Sight, of course, has one further requirement not shared with the other senses: it can operate only in the presence of light, which Lucretius clearly views as a kind of catalytic and adjutory agent which prepares and assists the soul-atoms in the eye for the reception of the appropriate atomic impulses.

Touch of course remains the most widely diffused and most essential of all the senses: atoms sensitive to touch are located all over and through the body, although, as Lucretius was careful to observe, they are more heavily concentrated in some parts than in others.

Although at first blush these theories may appear crude and naive, a little thought and examination will show that they are basically sound. We cannot, for example, quarrel with his theories of the nature of taste and smell; except for his explanation of the actual mechanical operation of the soul in the process, his analysis of the two chemical senses is essentially correct. As for both hearing and sight, he is only one step away from the vibration and wave theory which we now accept as correct. Of all the senses, it is clear that sight most fascinated Lucretius; he explores its operation in great detail, showing not only how the eye operates to see, but also how it determines relative distance, size, shape, texture, and color. He explains why the image in a flat mirror is reversed, while that in a concave mirror is not, how we can see out of a dark place into one that is lighted, but not the reverse.

It is when Lucretius turns from sensation to the problem of thought that he is put most upon his mettle, for the whole process of thought lies outside and beyond the realm of the immediately perceptible. The soul that produces sensation is of course identical with the mind that engages in thought; they are one and the same thing, a conglomeration of atoms centered on those that are located in the breast. Since mind is material, thought must be a material process; ideas, too, must somehow be material, atomic things.

What, then, is an idea, and how does it affect the mind? Lucretius's theory of the nature of ideas is an extension of his theory of sight. In addition to those films cast off by all things, that can affect the atoms of soul in the eye and thus cause sight, there are other films, also cast off in an endless stream, that are of too delicate and tenuous a character to be perceived by the eye, but can pass through and make impact directly upon the soul itself. The world is literally full of films of this kind; they float everywhere and are always available, so to speak, to the soul for the processes of thought. They may even make impact upon the soul-mind during sleep—in fact, it is at this time, when the soul is completely relaxed that it is most susceptible to such impulses. By Lucretius's theory, thought becomes a process of impulse, reaction, and interpretation, all taking place within the mind itself and at a level far below that of ordinary sensation. No eye has ever seen an idea; only the "mind's eye" can see them. By receiving, perusing, contemplating, combining and recombining the impulses made by these floating images, we think.

The explanation is again not too far from modern theories, especially if we think of the thought-process as physiological, consisting of the neural patterns that cross and recross the brain. To a people whose air is literally alive with wave-patterns of radio and television, Lucretius's floating films, too tenuous to be grasped by the eye but capable of making impression on the more delicate atoms of the soul, should not seem as strange as it probably does. The system's greatest weakness is its inability to cope with mathematical concepts and to make adequate allowance for the process of invention, imagination, and discovery. Mathematical abstractions have little or no connection with material things in any form; it is well-nigh impossible to imagine how they could have taken the shape of thin films of anything. This inability to cope with mathematics and mathematical abstractions is the greatest weakness of the Epicurean system, and is responsible for many of its more palpable errors.

As for discovery, invention, and imagination, there would appear to be no place for them in the Epicurean system, for if thought is the result of the impact upon the mind of films of atoms cast off by things, then no mind could conceive of a thing until the thing itself had already been in existence. In effect, this would mean, for example, that the wheel could not have been invented until it was already in existence and hence able to cast off a film of itself. This seeming paradox can be partly resolved by theorizing that the wheel, shall we say, would have existed far in outer space, perhaps far back in the years of infinite time, and from that vantage point have cast off an image of itself that, at long last, came into contact with the mind of some particularly sensitive and perceptive individual here on our earth.

But this is merely to prorogue the question, not to solve it. Epicurus's solution here was to allow for a process which he calls "anticipation" *(prolepsis),* perhaps something like the process of putting a known "two" together with another known "two" and coming up with a hitherto unknown "four." Logically, the process of anticipation begs the question, for it posits a form of thought not previously allowed, but it seems to have been the best that Epicurus or Lucretius could do with a very thorny problem.

As for the "stuff of dreams," the fact that in sleep we see visions of strange creatures the like of which never existed on earth, see men taller and stronger, and women more beautiful than in nature, see impossible creatures like centaurs, and the faces of those long dead, this is more readily explicable as in part the persistence, by chance, of images from some long dead and forgotten age, and in part by the purely fortuitous entanglement and combination of images that did not in nature belong together: the image of a man combined with that of a horse, for example, would explain our visions of centaurs.

Lucretius's discussion of dreams leads him by way of the phenomenon we now call a "sexual dream" to the problem of sex itself, and to this he devotes the last 250 lines of Book IV. The passage has often been misunderstood as a tirade against love; critics have wondered how a man of such evident kindliness and compassion, so keenly aware of the values of family life, could have been so bitter when it came to the subject of women. What experience the poet himself may have had with women, we shall never know; we should certainly not take Jerome's story about the love-philter as serious indication that Lucretius was sexually unresponsive and therefore unsympathetic to women. A careful reading of this famous tirade will show that it is indeed sex, and not love, against which the poet is here inveighing. He is thinking of the relation between the sexes that is the substance of the love affairs of the Comedy, and in fact of virtually all ancient love literature. These, he feels, are misleading, debasing, frivolous, and all too likely to lead to folly and misery. To Lucretius, sex, viewed sensibly, is a simple physical necessity, which should be taken care of in the quickest, easiest, least expensive and least complicating way, that is, through the services of the prostitute. Lucretius warns us several times in the course of his diatribe that he is not talking about marriage or married love; it is clear that to him sex formed only a subordinate part of the marriage relationship, where it served the purely practical end of procreation. Like a good Epicurean, Lucretius regards sex as indubitably pleasant and therefore essentially good, but all too susceptible of being ill-managed, and of passing thereby from the good of pleasure into the evil of pain.

Book v begins with another fulsome encomium on Epicurus; Lucretius ventures to style him a god, and declares that his exploit of clearing the human mind of error far outweighed Demeter's gift of grain, or Bacchus's gift of wine, and asserts that beside it the famed labors of Hercules pale into insignificance:

> But if the heart's not whole, what struggles then,
> what dangers must engulf us 'gainst all will?
> How then will the stinging sabre-slash of lust
> and guilt trouble a man—what fears besides?
> And pride, bad temper, baseness—what disasters
> can they inflict? What, sloth and self-indulgence?
> He who drove all these evils from our hearts—
> purged them with words, not weapons—should not he
> be deemed one man meet to be counted god?
> (5.43–51)

After a brief recapitulation of material contained in the first four books, Lucretius announces as his subject for Book v the constitution and institutions of the world in which we live, beginning with the fact that, like all other things, it is a conglomeration of atoms and void that had a day of beginning and will have a day of destruction. This world includes not only our earth but also the heavens and the visible heavenly bodies, the sun, the moon, and the stars, all of which Lucretius views as parts of a single unit which he styles "the world." He will account for all these parts and their behavior; specifically, he will discuss the nature and origin of life on this earth, the development of the various kinds and species of living creatures, and the beginning of growth of such human institutions as language, government, religion, and the arts of civilization.

As if the application of the term "god" to Epicurus had suggested it, Lucretius now turns to the subject of the gods themselves, their nature and their relation to this world of ours. We have already seen them described (at the beginning of Book III) as living a life of eternal, perfect peace in the spaces between the worlds; now we are told that their nature is of the most tenuous sort, far too fine to be apprehended by our coarse sense-processes; their delicately poised and eternally blissful equilibrium is, and forever has been, utterly beyond any concern for us, and perfectly oblivious to any troubles of ours or to any petitions we might address to them. Divine creatures of this sort certainly never would have troubled themselves to build a world, let alone concern themselves with the crude, imperfect creatures that might inhabit it.

In any event, says Lucretius, when we look at this world how could we imagine that it was the work of the gods? It is an ugly, clumsy, ill-conceived, exasperating place, at times seemingly devoted to nothing so much as to its own destruction—as for example in the hurricane and earthquake—and certainly a most uncongenial and unfriendly place for man, who finds himself thwarted and frustrated at every turn by its intransigency.* It is a hard and endless struggle for man just to keep alive, surrounded as he is by wild beasts, disease, and natural disaster of all sorts. He comes into the world naked and helpless, his advent accompanied by the screams of his agonized mother; small wonder that

> he fills the world with wails—and well he might,
> such woes await his passage through this life!
> (5.226–27)

This world of ours is of course atomic in nature, but Lucretius, perhaps conceding a point to contemporary orthodox physics, allows his atoms at this point to take the form of molecules, for he

---

*It may be worth noting here that Lucretius, in his discussion of the world's flaws, falls into the anthropocentric fallacy. For if the world is, as he claims, the result of the interplay of purely mechanistic and impersonal forces, and is totally without purpose, why should mere man's discomfiture be a sign of weakness or imperfection in it?

thinks of the world as formed of the familiar four elements, earth, air, fire, and water. In an Epicurean version of the settling of the heavy elements, earth and water, and the rising of the lighter ones, air and fire, Lucretius describes the formation of the earth, seas, air, and heavenly bodies; these processes took place simply because the atoms and the void are what they are and because by the sheerest chance they were formed into the four compounds, which then proceeded to behave in accord with the properties of the structure that chance had given them.

Lucretius's theories of the nature, movement, and size of the heavenly bodies are distorted by his lack of mathematics. He thinks he has observed, for example, that men do not misjudge the size of a fire as long as they can feel its heat; since we can feel the heat of the sun, all we need do is look at it and form an estimate of its size and we shall not be far wrong. Furthermore, as long as we can clearly discern the configuration of a source of light, we are similarly capable of judging its size; since we can quite clearly discern the shape and configuration of the moon, we must also be able accurately to judge its size. The movements of the sun and the moon and the other heavenly bodies, Lucretius naively ascribes to winds or currents of air, the regularity of which should not surprise us, since nature seems to be full of things that occur at regular intervals, e.g. the succession of the seasons, the growth, maturation, and dying away of plant life, etc. (That the argument here is circular, he obviously did not see.)

As for the succession of night and day, the rising and setting of the sun, and the phases of the moon, in the midst of child-like maunderings he stumbles onto the right explanation in each case: he suggests that the sun might move under the earth at night (an at least passable version of the modern theory) and that the disparity of the lengths of the day and the night at various times of the year is due to the fact that the passage of the sun "under" the earth takes longer at some seasons than at others. The phases of the moon, he says, might be accounted for by the relative position of the moon with respect to the sun and the earth, such that at some times all, and at other times only a part of the surface caught and reflected the sun's light to earth. In each of these instances, Lucretius is at least on the right track.

But once Lucretius turns from the heavens to the earth and begins to discuss the nature and origin of life, he is on much firmer ground. He asserts that plant life preceded animal life; he also sees correctly that all forms of life came out of the earth—although his paleontology slips a little when he claims that no earth-creature could possibly have originated in the sea. As for the beginning of life itself, his theory represents a refinement of the doctrine of spontaneous generation; he holds—perhaps not entirely incorrectly, as modern theory may appear to indicate—that life was caused by a spontaneous combination of appropriate kinds of atoms under appropriate circumstances. But from there on his theory goes awry. Believing as he did that in his own day the earth, now grown old and tired, still could produce small animals, he theorizes that in her younger days, a vigorous and fecund earth easily produced much larger creatures. He draws a Dali-esque picture of every imaginable form of animate life being born out of "wombs" in the earth, and then finding their first nourishment at "mammary glands" filled with sweet milk like a woman's breasts, these again being the spontaneous product of a youthful and burgeoning earth.

As for the development of the various kinds and species of living things, Lucretius presents us with a curious variant on Darwinian theory. Totally unacquainted as he was with the study of comparative anatomy, it never occurred to him to connect one species of animal with another; rather, he has them all start from scratch, from those fabulous wombs in the earth, with appearance and habits very much like those they have now, but with the important exception that many of the kinds of creatures produced by earth were not able to survive and therefore died out. He sees that only the fittest could survive, only those who were able to find sustenance and to engage in the appropriate procreative activities could continue to live and reproduce their kind. The rest died out.

Although he is unable to envisage the development of one species out of another, Lucretius does allow for the evolutionary process in the development of the individual species themselves, once they have been created. By the law of survival of the fittest, by natural selection, and by sheer chance, the individual kinds of living creatures of the world have experienced a gradual process of refinement, though not of violent or fundamental change. Man, for example, was a great, shaggy, muscular animal, who roamed the forest in search of food, slept on beds of wet leaves, and coupled rudely with any member of the opposite sex whose path he happened to cross. Apart from the fact that Lucretius's primitive man is solitary rather than gregarious, his picture is remarkably accurate. Accurate, too, is his picture of primitive society: nomadic, consisting of groups of hunters and gatherers living off the natural products of earth, having no permanent homes of any kind and employing only such primitive weapons as sticks and stones.

The process of civilization, Lucretius says, began through the influence of love; men and women who had hitherto coupled promiscuously, began to feel tenderness and a kind of lasting attachment to each other, an attachment which the birth of children cemented into permanent affection. From this association grew the family, and from the association of many families, the tribe. Association of man with man in this fashion brought forth language, which was not the special creation of one man but was the inevitable result of two things: first, the possession by man of the appropriate sound-producing organs, and second, his possession of an intelligence that was capable of organizing random sounds into a logical and reproducible pattern.

From this point, Lucretius's history of the development of man proceeds. First comes the discovery of fire with its civilizing effects, then the organization of tribes into cities, at first ruled by monarchs, later by the spontaneous formation of a social contract which resulted in the institution of magistracies and laws. Here for a moment Lucretius digresses onto his old whipping-boy, religion: with law, says he, came punishment; from punishment came the fear of punishment, from the fear of punishment came the fear of punishment after death, and from this arose the theory of godhead and its punitive activities.

Returning to the main thread of his narrative, Lucretius explains how men discovered the art of smelting and working metals, the domestication of various animals, particularly the horse and the cow, the development of the arts of warfare, the coming of weaving, agriculture, the song, and the dance. Finally in quick summation come the chief of the civilized or learned arts, astronomy, international law, poetry, reading and writing, navigation, architecture, roads, painting, sculpture, etc. One man has learned from another, one age from another, until, Lucretius says, we have finally reached our present peak of civilization.

If any specific proof were needed for the unfinished character of Lucretius's poem, it could readily be found in the sixth book. It is not without the flashes of genius that Cicero noted, nor is it entirely lacking in the skillful technique which he conceded the poem also possessed; nevertheless with its very opening passage, one gets the feeling of a piece of work that could have stood some polishing and refinement. It appears to have been the poet's in-

tention to frame the book within references to Athens; it begins
with extravagant praise of the city, not, as we might expect, for its
familiar glories, but because it brought Epicurus to the attention
of the world. This we might accept; it is really no worse and no
more overdone than some of the other passages that refer to the
philosopher, but the repetition of the attack on men's blindness—
men who simply will not see that pleasure is so very easy to get—
seems a little forced and threadbare at this point; and when
Lucretius goes on to compare non-Epicurean man to a piece of
dirty and leaky pottery, which, if men would only listen, they
could find scrubbed clean and repaired by Epicurus's "true-speak-
ing words," the whole thing threatens to pass from Lucretius's
usual good taste to vulgarity and grotesquerie.

Balancing this introductory tribute to Athens is the very end
of the book, in which Lucretius gives us a versified version of
Thucydides's description of the plague at Athens in 430 B. C.
(Thucydides 2.47–52), a grisly description of the disease that swept
the city in that year. The attempt to frame Book VI in references
to Athens is clear enough; just what the frame was supposed to
prove is another matter. Is it "Athens, once great, now fallen on
evil days?" Is "Athens, mother of Epicurus" and "Athens, wallow-
ing in filth and horror" symbolic of what happens to mankind
when Epicurus's great message is scorned? Parts of the frame do
have certain analogies with, for example, the frame of Book II,
which begins with the picture of carefree men, happy in the
bosom of a benign nature, and ends with the tired, discouraged
plowman bewailing the decline of the powers of earth and lament-
ing the passing of the fecundity he had known in her as a young
man. The somewhat tentative nature of the frame of Book VI is
perhaps most clearly indicated by the fact that the prologue ends
with the repetition of two passages, now grown just a bit tired, in
which the fears of mankind are compared to the terrors of little
boys in the dark.

The largest part of Book VI is given over to atomic explanations of various celestial and terrestrial phenomena. Lucretius is
at great pains to attempt an explanation of lightning and thunder;
although, with his total ignorance of electricity, he is wide of the
mark, he does at one point envisage the building up of enormous
pressures caused by "wind" and "fire" within a cloud mass which
finally burst forth in the form of the thunder and lightning. He
is observant enough of natural phenomena to notice that sound
travels more slowly than light and to use this as an explanation of

why we see the lightning before we hear the thunder, although they are produced simultaneously.

In his explanations of clouds and rain, Lucretius again approaches correct understanding. He sees clouds as a gathering of water in the air, and attributes rain to the building up of the weight of water and the consequent downward pressure, but is not aware of the effect upon clouds of changes of temperature in the upper atmosphere.

Turning to the earth, he first takes up earthquakes and, once again with a remarkable intuition, suggests they might be caused by the collapsing of internal caverns in the earth—a theory not too far removed from more recent discoveries of the effect upon the earth of the slipping of one stratum of rock upon another. As in all these instances, Lucretius offers a number of explanations, many of them quite fantastic; his defense of these would be the one he has always offered, namely, that although in all likelihood only one of his theories is correct for this earth of ours—and he does not know in any instance which one this might be—there are innumerable worlds scattered throughout the infinite cosmos, and his various explanations are bound to fit either in one place or another, since, at least as he sees it, none of them violates the atomic principle.

He passes on from the earthquake to volcanic eruptions, the reasons for the constant size of the ocean, and for the flooding of the Nile, an anomalous phenomenon that constantly worried the ancients. Along with Herodotus (2.19–27), Lucretius offers a variety of explanations for the floods, including the correct one, that it is caused by the melting of the snows in Ethiopia in the summertime. Herodotus had scouted this explanation as fantastic; Lucretius adds it to his list without comment.

From here he moves on to a series of miscellaneous phenomena, including among them an ingenious explanation of the nature of magnetism, as being caused by "effluences" which stream out from the magnet, part the air, and create a vacuum, into which the linked atoms of iron proceed to fall, one drawing another after it, and ultimately causing the whole piece to move into contact with the magnet. If a nonferrous metal, such as brass, is interposed between the iron and the magnet, the effluences of the brass interrupt those of the magnet and the iron and thus negate the magnet's power. Lucretius's "effluences," although again distorted by his lack of knowledge of electricity, do bear a strange resemblance to the "lines of force" of modern science.

As we have noted earlier, the book ends with a disquisition on disease, which Lucretius attributes to the gathering of noxious seed in the atmosphere—an atomic refinement, no doubt, of the theory of miasmas or "bad airs" which in the ancient world were generally held responsible for the occurrence of disease, whether in the regular cycle of the seasons, as in the "fever season" at Rome, or in sudden accesses of pestilential seeds, as occurred at Athens during the plague. The description of the plague, gruesome though it is, is brilliantly executed and has excited the admiration not only of literary men, but of the medical profession. It brings Book VI to an abrupt end, leaving us in little doubt that the poet, if he had finished his poem, would have added some more graceful conclusion to it.

There has been considerable discussion of the appropriate place of Lucretius in the history of Latin literature. It seems fairly clear that his ideas of poetry are not quite the same as those of Catullus and other members of the school of "New Poets," although in all honesty one cannot see how he would have quarreled with the principle of *venustas*; nor is there anything in his poem to suggest that he might have found Catullus and his fellows uncongenial. Although Catullus himself never wrote any epic-length poems, other members of the school, e.g. Furius Bibaculus, did, and there is little reason to doubt that the *Zmyrna* of Helvius Cinna fell not much short of epic length. Lucretius's style has sometimes been characterized as conservative or even archaic; it is said that he harked back to the older poets, e.g. Ennius, and that in particular he handled the verse-form that he used, the dactylic hexameter, in a manner more reminiscent of the old epic poet than of later writers like Catullus.

But the precise nature of the "school" of New Poets is much in doubt; if they were indeed a group of young rebels who chose each in his individual way to revolt against established standards in poetry and to develop distinctive ideas and styles of their own, there is certainly no reason to imagine that Lucretius would have found himself in strange territory among them. He himself boasts of his innovating; he certainly tackled a subject that until then had not been widely treated by Italian poets, and his style is "Ennian" only in some of its metrical aspects, for in his imagery and in the brilliance and broad scope of his poetic imagination, he is a far cry from the older poet.

Probably no poet of the Latin language, not even Vergil himself, exhibits so vast a range of imagery, so catholic a vision of the world and its poetic possibilities, as does Lucretius. The feel of a pebble in the shoe, the touch of the feet of an insect, a strand of cobweb brushing across the face, the acrid smell of a just-extinguished wick, the taste of bitter medicine, the various parts of the human body: eyes, nose, hands, ears, internal organs, nerve-fibres, bones, and even teeth and their agonizing ache; the dead body, tumescent and full of worms, a pig's-bladder balloon exploding, the hiss of hot iron dashed into water, sparks flying from stone struck against stone, or stone against steel, the crash of a falling tree, clothes that grow damp when laid out near a body of water and then grow dry again when hung in the sun, the rumbling of carts over the paving stones of a Roman street, the wobbling of a vase when the water within it is disturbed, sheep on a mountain-side, armies clashing on a plain, the foot of a bronze statue worn smooth and shiny where passersby have touched it, the light of the sun shining through varicolored awnings stretched over a theater, the springtime gaiety of birds and animals and even of fish, the curious snakelike majesty of the elephant and his trunk, and the sloppy contentment of pigs in the mud: these are only some of the many aspects of life that Lucretius uses for poetic and argumentative purposes. Although he is not often thought of in this manner, he is in fact one of the most brilliant word-painters of life in the ancient world; his poem affords us a wide panorama of the Mediterranean world in the first century B. C.

For in spite of his putative fascination with philosophy, Lucretius is a poet rather than a philosopher. His logic is often faulty, but his poetic images never fail to make their point. Like the poet William Carlos Williams, Lucretius saw that ideas are to be found only in things, and that nothing proves a point quite so neatly as an appropriate series of pictures from life. Lucretius was a poet with an eye for everything and a sure hand in the description of what his eye had seen. Like the philosophy he attempted to teach, Lucretius was a good many centuries ahead of his times; Cicero's perceptive but not very sympathetic estimate of his work is probably characteristic of the way in which it was greeted by most Romans; if they had any sensitivity to poetic values at all, they could not help admiring the poet's skill and inspiration, but his brilliance probably embarrassed them just as his philosophy, with its incessant attacks on the sacred cows of ancient orthodoxy, frightened and repelled them.

Whatever small reputation he may have earned was eclipsed by Vergil; in the second century A. D. Lucretius enjoyed a brief period of popularity, a popularity probably not based on genuine appreciation but rather on sentimental archaizing. In the Middle Ages, he was unpopular; the church considered him, if not an atheist, at least anti-religious. As late as the seventeenth century, a devout French bishop, de Polignac, took the trouble to write an epic called the "Anti-Lucretius" in which he attempted to refute, point by point, the principles of Epicureanism. The good bishop showed a remarkable understanding of Lucretius, and an amazing skill at imitating his style; one cannot help wondering if he perhaps wrote his poem as much to convince himself as for any other reason. Lucretius never was and probably never will be a truly popular poet; even our own age, which finds in its scientific discoveries many a correction, extension, and confirmation of some of his tentative, hesitant, and imperfect theories, seldom takes the trouble to read him.

By the end of the fifties, B. C., with the death of Lucretius and Catullus, Roman poetry clearly came to the end of an era that had been characterized by stubborn individualism, vast inventiveness, revolt against traditionalism, and exuberant experimentation. The poets of the Roman republic were fairly bursting with ideas about every aspect of poetry, its form, its techniques, its content, and its purpose. Their works ranged from the boisterous laughter of Plautus to the almost tragic seriousness of Lucretius, from the proud nationalism of Ennius and Naevius to the sensitive cosmopolitanism of Catullus, from the gentle social prodding of Terence to the corrosive "salt," as Horace was later to phrase it, of Lucilius. The result is a body of poetry of vast variety, rich imaginativeness, and refreshing liveliness. There is also a strangely personal quality about all Republican Latin poetry which sets it off both from its Greek predecessors and from its Roman successors. The Roman poet makes no pretense of being objective; on the contrary, he obtrudes himself and his own personality and ideas into everything that he writes. He is not a mere describer of life, but a participant in it; to read his poems is not to stand and watch something happen, but to walk with the poet through the middle of the event. This is a quality most signally to be observed in the works of Catullus, who was perhaps its most brilliant exponent. But it can also be seen in the epic of Ennius and Naevius, both of whom insert their own personal feelings and place the stamp of their own personalities upon their accounts of Roman history and myth. With every line of his fragmentary works, the personality of Lucilius strikes us with force; for all that only rags and tatters of his work exist, we feel as if we had met the man. The laughter of Plautus and his veiled jibes at Roman society, contrasted with the gentleness of Terence, as he urges attention to some of the social problems of his day, show clearly to what extent the personalities of these two playwrights entered into their plays. And Lucretius is profoundly involved in the lessons that he is attempting to teach. He preaches, he urges, he exhorts, he argues, he even jokes with his reader; his poem is one long plea to man to walk with him through the world and see how everything proves the truth of his convictions.

If the Roman revolution had not intervened, Roman poetry might have become as rich and varied as English poetry. But in the course of those terrible years of stress and strain, of economic disaster, political bewilderment, and cruel and bloody civil war that followed the death of Julius Caesar in 44 B. C., nearly every important intellectual figure of the Republic disappeared from the scene. One or two, like the scholar Varro or the historian Sallust, survived for at least a part of these years, but the intellectual climate of Rome suffered as complete a revolution as did her political institutions. In the succeeding Augustan Age, poetry reached greater heights of technique and perhaps, too, of inspiration, but although its roots were deep in the poetry of the Republic, it was an achievement of a radically different character.

Most of the other poets of the final years of the Republic are hardly more than names to us now. Laevius and Valerius Cato have already come to our attention as important if shadowy figures in and around the coterie whose chief figure was Catullus; we have made a brief note of Gaius Helvius Cinna whose tortuous *Zmyrna*, nine years in the writing, Catullus so greatly admired. Catullus's close friend Gaius Licinius Calvus, although primarily famous as an orator, was a poet of some distinction. Calvus wrote mostly brief lyrics; Marcus Furius Bibaculus seems to have done the same, but is also credited with an epic on Caesar's Gallic Wars. Because Horace later thought him sufficiently important to name, mention should be made of Varro of Atax (not to be confused with the scholar of the same name), a writer of satires which Horace, at any rate, considered failures. Because they are the authors of the earliest known Latin epigrams, the names of Lutatius Catulus and Valerius Aedituus (c. 100 B. C.) should be included in any list of the poets of this period, although nothing else is known about them. The names of two writers of mimes, Decimus Laberius and Publilius Syrus, along with some fragments of their work, have come down to us; the fragments show a bent for epigrammatic statement and a pleasant Latin style, but nothing that would lead us to rank them with Plautus or Terence. One poet of the period, almost certain to be forgotten, is Cicero, whose verse has been buried under his prose. Fairly extensive fragments of Cicero's poetic works are extant; they range from a poem on his own consulship to a number of translations from the Greek, including the *Phaenomena* of Aratus, and various Greek tragedies; they show great technical skill and are invariably neat and graceful.

# CHAPTER IX

# Cicero

The work of Cicero (Marcus Tullius Cicero, 106–43 B. C.) is so extensive, and so distinguished, both for technical excellence and for intellectual breadth that he would easily have overshadowed his predecessors even if their work were extant. As it is, he fairly explodes onto the scene of Latin prose without our having available materials that would enable us to trace the long development of the prose arts that must have preceded his work. The only complete prose work extant to us from the period before his time is Cato's book on farming, a work not without its own peculiar excellence, but hardly to be placed in the mainstream of the development of formal Latin prose. Cato himself was, to be sure, an orator of no mean ability, but since only fragments of his orations are extant, we can scarcely do more than include his name in the long list that Cicero himself gives in his *Brutus*, his book on great orators, in which he sketches the development of Latin oratory up to his own day. Apart from Cato, most of the men whom Cicero mentions are no more than names now, although some, like Appius Claudius Caecus, the Gracchi, Scipio, and Laelius, are known to us as statesmen and men of public affairs. Cicero says that they were important in the development of Latin oratory, but the steps of its development from such speeches as that of Menenius Agrippa on *The Body and the Members* to the polished perfection of an oration like Cicero's *On the Manilian Law* are forever lost.

We know that the Greek rhetoricians from Sicily and southern Italy had considerable influence on the development of Latin oratory; we know that the great Latin orators studied Greek oratory and its methods. Cicero himself, for example, studied with

Molo of Rhodes; and works like the anonymous *Auctor ad He-rennium*, and Cicero's own *De oratore*, are clear evidence of the painstaking study the Romans gave to the art.

There are probably few prominent figures of the ancient or even of the modern world who are as well known to us as Cicero. His own voluminous works, particularly his letters, of which some 800 are extant, reveal almost every facet of his character and every phase of his career. He was born on January 3, 106 B. C. at Arpinum, in the southeastern corner of Latium; his family was well-to-do, but not of the aristocracy; they were members of the class called the "knights" (*equites*). Like most young Romans of his class, he was educated at Rome, where he studied law, rhetoric, and philosophy under a series of distinguished teachers. He began delivering his speeches in the Roman law courts when he was scarcely twenty years old, and in the year 80 B. C. spoke in defense of a certain Roscius Amerinus, who was being prosecuted by a freedman of the dictator Sulla. It is a tribute not so much to the arbitrary powers of Sulla as to the brilliance of the young Cicero that he found it healthful to leave Rome shortly after this case was concluded; this moment, he thought, was just the one for a trip to Rhodes and Athens, there to perfect his style by study under some of the great masters of Greek rhetoric, including the already mentioned Molo.

After the death of Sulla in 78 B. C., Cicero returned to Rome and continued the oratorical and political career for which he had been laying the foundations. In the year 70, he was approached by the people of Sicily to assist them in the prosecution of their former governor, Verres, who during his term as governor had appropriated for his own personal property all of the movable wealth of Sicily on which he could lay hands. Cicero prepared a series of orations for the prosecution of Verres; but after he had delivered the first of these, Verres saw that his conviction was inevitable, and removed himself to exile in Marseilles (Massilia) where he remained for the rest of his life. His departure from Rome deprived Cicero of the opportunity to deliver the rest of his orations, but he published them nonetheless, and their brilliance, as well as the thoughtfulness and thoroughness that they displayed, were of material help to him politically.

From then on his rise in power and prominence was uninterrupted, until finally, in the year 63, he became consul. No doubt it was comforting to Cicero, but it must remain a matter of regret to us, that Cicero's friend Atticus, to whom he addresses his most revelatory letters, was himself in Rome during the year of Cicero's consulship. The result is a lack of light on Cicero's activities as consul which makes this most critical and important part of his career difficult to assess.

The outstanding event of that year was the conspiracy of Catiline, a disaffected member of the patrician class who, having failed to be elected consul himself, attempted to seize the government by a coup d'etat. Cicero uncovered the plot and suppressed the intended insurrection; the four orations, *Against Catiline,* that he delivered on this occasion are familiar—perhaps all too familiar —to most who have studied Latin past the first or second year. Stylistically, the orations are superb, although they cannot contend for depth and thoughtfulness with those against Verres or the one *On the Manilian Law.* But there has always been a lingering suspicion that Cicero, who was extremely vain, exaggerated both the extent of the conspiracy, its potential danger to the state, and the wickedness of its participants. The historian Sallust has also written an account of the conspiracy, but beyond showing that Catiline himself was a man of resolution and courage, does little to clarify the picture.

Rather more important than the conspiracy itself was its effect upon Cicero's career. The point of law involved is still under debate, but it is clear that he committed an egregious political blunder by putting some of the conspirators to death without allowing them the right of appeal to the Assembly of the People, a right very ancient in Rome and understandably cherished by the citizens. Cicero claimed that under the "Emergency Decree" (*Senatus Consultum Ultimum*), he had the right to do this, since the decree instructed the consuls to see to it "that the state received no harm," certainly a very loosely phrased directive.

In the end, it did not matter then, and it does not matter now, whether Cicero's legal point was well taken or not; the populace resented his apparent violation of their constitutional rights, and as a result his career came under a shadow from which it never emerged. The depth of his obloquy is clearly illustrated by the story that is told about the conclusion of his consulship: when, as was customary, he arose in the Senate to take the oath "that he had not violated the constitution," a tribune interposed his veto, and Cicero was then thrown back upon the weak expedient of affirming "that he had saved the state."

Less than five years later, this alleged constitutional violation was used as an expedient for forcing Cicero into exile, where he

remained in utter misery, from April of 58 to August of 57 B. C
Finally with the help of his friends and of his ever-loyal wife—to
whom, incidentally, the great man showed a measure of petulant
ingratitude strange in one ordinarily so humane—he was enabled
to return to Italy, where he continued his political activities until
the year 51 when, much against his will, he was made proconsul
of Cilicia, a post that to him was only just this side of exile. Nevertheless, he carried out his duties conscientiously and honorably,
his only blunder being a pitiful attempt to win a military triumph
by provoking and winning a minuscule war against some mountaineers. He was deeply hurt when his friends refused to support
his request for a triumph on this occasion, but the probabilities
are that they did Cicero a better turn than he knew. For the statesman and orator to have claimed the virtues of a commanding
general, and to have marched through the streets of Rome trailed
by a ragtag and bobtail outfit of captured Cilician mountaineers
would almost certainly have brought him ridicule rather than
glory.

Returning from Cilicia in 50, he found himself in the middle
of the growing quarrel between Caesar and Pompey, a dispute
which faced him with the bitterest choice of his lifetime. He did
not like Caesar, but he admired him and recognized his genius;
he saw, however, that Caesar was determined to overthrow the old
Roman constitution, and since Cicero's whole life had been devoted
to its support, he could not accept Caesar. As for Pompey, he
recognized his ability as a military commander, but was intensely
aware of his inadequacies in the political field; out of uniform, so
to speak, Pompey was conceited, overbearing, pompous, and—at
least so Cicero thought—unintelligent. Still, he was at least nominally on the side of the "republicans" and so, after much vacillation, Cicero decided to support him. When the quarrel between
Pompey and Caesar reached the point of open warfare, Cicero,
very nervously and after much hesitation, followed Pompey into
Greece, but soon left him and returned to Italy, where he went
into virtual seclusion during the remaining years of the dictator-
ship of Caesar.

Upon the assassination of Caesar, Cicero was once more thrust
into prominence and found himself again faced with a choice only
less bitter and less difficult to make than had been his choice
between Caesar and Pompey, for now he must choose between the
mature and brilliant statesman and general, Mark Antony, and

the callow, fumbling, unattractive Octavian, the adopted son of Julius Caesar. Again after much vacillation, he threw his lot in with the young Octavian as a *pis aller*: for all his apparent deficiencies, the young man at least had not been carrying on with Cleopatra or giving himself the airs of an Oriental despot.

The end of Cicero's story is all too well known. He not only stood with Octavian, but delivered the fourteen *Philippic Orations*, in which he scathingly attacked Antony. This crime against his dignity Antony never forgot. When he and Octavian, in the company of Lepidus, formed the Second Triumvirate, one of their first acts was to draw up a proscription list, that is to say, a list of the names of individuals whose lives and fortunes were declared forfeit to the state, presumably on grounds of subversive or treasonable activity. Octavian, mindful of his debt to Cicero, did his best to keep his name off the list, but in the end agreed to trade him for a relative of his own whom Antony wished dispatched, a disgraceful betrayal of the old statesman which is all too often glossed over in accounts of the glories of Octavian, later called Augustus, and his reign. Cicero made a halfhearted attempt to escape from Italy, but was betrayed by a young man whom he had befriended and educated; when he saw his assassins approaching, he told his servants to set down the litter in which he was riding, and then, as Plutarch has phrased it, "He stretched out his neck and was slain, being then in his sixty-fourth year." Antony, in an act of barbarity that even the Roman populace could not quite condone, nailed the head and hands of Cicero to the rostra in the Forum, a hideous act only in part atoned for by his own ignominious death not too many years later.

It is hard to imagine Augustus having a conscience (in his position he could scarcely afford one) yet the total eclipse of Cicero in the Augustan Age when, apparently, no one dared mention his name, suggests not so much that the emperor feared the dead Cicero as a martyr around whom disaffection might gather force, as that he was too ashamed of the deal he had concluded with Antony ever to wish to hear Cicero's name again. His real feelings about Cicero are perhaps best illustrated by Plutarch's concluding story. He tells how, on one occasion, Augustus was walking through the halls of the palace and came across a young nephew of his who, since he was reading a book of Cicero's, was frightened and tried to hide the book in his gown, but the emperor saw him, took the book from him, and stood a while reading it, then handed it back with the words, "This was a learned and eloquent man, my boy, and a true patriot" (Plutarch, *Cicero* 49.3).

Cicero's literary activities span the whole of his adult life, and for all we know may have begun much earlier than that, for when we first meet him as a writer, in the early orations, he is already showing a skill that could have been developed only by long practice. Oratory came from him in a steady stream, beginning in the late eighties B. C. and terminating only with his death in 43; there were, to be sure, two relatively brief periods during which he delivered virtually no orations; these were the years 55 to 51 B. C., when Caesar was consolidating his power and, in order to prevent his opponents from rallying around the still imposing figure of Cicero, deftly but firmly removed him from the political scene. Again in the last few years of his life, the political turmoil that marked the end of Caesar's life, the assassination of Caesar himself, and the subsequent period of terror drove him once more into semiretirement. But these two blanks in his oratorical activity were filled with other kinds of writing, the first chiefly by his rhetorical works, the second by his philosophical treatises. And along with all this formal writing, the sheer bulk of which is astounding in view of Cicero's many other activities, responsibilities, and distractions, run the almost unbroken series of letters beginning in 60 B. C. and ending with his death in 43.

It is hard in this modern age to be patient with Cicero's oratory, for with our almost unlimited facilities for the preservation of words, the concept of a literary work of art that would last only as long as its speaker was delivering it has lost all meaning for us. To be sure, most if not all of Cicero's speeches were taken down in shorthand by his secretaries, then polished and perfected by the orator himself and published in written form. But for Cicero it was the spoken version itself that was of primary importance; it was on this that he expended all his oratorical arts, not only those of purely literary and rhetorical character, but also such matters as gesture, facial expression, variations in pitch and stress and, in short, all the arts of the actor: it was not for nothing that he had studied with Roscius, the greatest actor of his day.

At best, the published orations of Cicero are only pale reflections of the actual delivered speeches. Furthermore, the orations are heavily contemporaneous, and depend for comprehension and appreciation on a knowledge of the history and personalities of the period. The orations *Against Verres* are models of the lawyer's prosecution; they also have general meaning as attacks on political corruption and private greed; the oration *In Defense of Archias* is a graceful defense of the liberal arts, and of literature in particular. But orations like the *Manilian Law*, and the *Philippics*, are of interest now chiefly to the historian, and the many speeches delivered in defense of individuals, for example, the defense of Caelius, can have little meaning to anyone who does not know the personalities involved. Ages other than our own have counted the orations among the great achievements of the Western literary mind.

Somewhat similarly, Cicero's rhetorical writings, except where they digress onto the problem of the education of the orator or onto matters of literary style in general, deal with ideas that would be of interest chiefly to an age in which oratory itself was highly regarded. Perhaps the greatest of these works is the essay *On the Orator (De oratore)*, a study of the philosophy of oratory and a discussion of the proper education of the orator (Cicero believed that his technical training should rest on a firm basis of the liberal arts). To lovers of the Latin language, particularly to those who can enjoy the grace and dignity of great prose, the essay *On the Orator* remains one of Cicero's masterpieces; written about a subject with which he was thoroughly conversant both in theory and in practice, it is composed with the hand of a master of language and style and with the mind of one who, probably more than any other Roman of the age, understood the resources and capabilities of Latin as a prose vehicle.

Most of Cicero's other rhetorical works are so highly technical as to command little general interest. The *Brutus* gives a brief, anecdotal history of Roman oratory; its companion piece, the *Orator ad Marcum Brutum,* presents Cicero's picture of the perfect orator. In essence, these two works are really a defense of Cicero's own rhetorical principles. During his lifetime controversy raged between two schools of oratory, the one known as the "Asian," the other as the "Attic." The differences between the two are not entirely clear now; it does appear, however, that the Asian school tended toward the florid and flamboyant style, the Attic toward the puristic and severely disciplined. Cicero rather characteristically adopted a middle course both in theory and in practice. While he granted that the Asian style was inclined to become overblown and bombastic, he felt that the Atticists were likely to be flat and jejune. In his own work, he strove to preserve what seemed best to him in both styles.

It is when we turn to Cicero's philosophical works that we

find ideas that speak more directly to us. Although they are really expressions of one basic point of view, Cicero's work may be conveniently divided into two categories, his political and his ethical philosophy. These are the two branches of ancient philosophical thought that interested him; in its purely speculative aspects he had little interest. His *Timaeus* is part of a translation of Plato's dialogue of the same name; Cicero may have intended to use it in a discussion of physics or of the problem of Being, but it is clear that he never finished the project. To this might be added three theological works, *On the Nature of the Gods (De natura deorum), On Divination (De divinatione),* and *On Fate (De fato).* The last-named work is incomplete. In these three works Cicero presents varying points of view concerning the nature of the gods and their relations to men, and the degree to which we are able to foretell the future and to govern our own lives. Like all of Cicero's works, they have been admired for their stylistic grace and the clarity of their argument, but they are hardly to be placed in the forefront of his philosophic efforts.

Throughout his life Cicero was plagued by indecisiveness; to make up his mind as to which of two courses was the right one or which of two ideas was the more accurate, was for him exquisite torture. It is not surprising, then, that in philosophic matters we should find him an eclectic; of all the philosophies current in Rome during his lifetime, the one that appealed most to him was the Stoic, both for its insistence on the primacy of reason as a guide to thought, and for its placing of involvement in public affairs among those activities that were preferable for man. But Stoicism demanded from its devotees a kind of total commitment of which Cicero was incapable; while he could accept virtually all of the main tenets of Stoicism, he could not at the same time reject out of hand all of the teachings of other philosophic systems. In particular, he found himself attracted to the Academics, the intellectual heirs of Plato and Socrates, whose cardinal doctrine of the need for careful weighing of evidence and suspension of judgment appealed strongly to Cicero's sense of man's imperfect nature and to his own eternal bent for compromise.

The doctrines of both of these two schools appear in Cicero's philosophical writings, sometimes separately, sometimes in combination; the only major school of philosophy which he rigidly excluded was the Epicurean. This he rejected as ridiculous, and there is some indication that his prejudice against it led him to refuse to understand it. He is as obtuse as most of his Roman contemporaries in his failure to grasp the true implications of Epicurus's doctrine of the nature of Being, and in his steadfast refusal to grant even the slightest validity to Epicurus's doctrine of pleasure, no matter how carefully "pleasure" were defined. For all that he had read Lucretius, and undoubtedly was acquainted with the major works of the Epicurean philosophers, and in spite of the fact that his most intimate friend, Atticus, was a practicing and devout Epicurean, Cicero's attitude toward this philosophy never wavered; the old Roman prejudice against any philosophy that denied divine intervention in this world and based its ethical doctrines on pleasure, was too strong in Cicero ever to be overcome.

Although as a doctrine of pure philosophy, Cicero's essay *On the Republic* (*De re publica*) is hardly in a class with Plato's dialogue of the same name, and although it contains little that is truly original, it has had an abiding influence on Western political theory and is a repository of much sound political sense. Unlike Plato's *Republic*, which was a purely theoretical model built not to teach the form of a proper government, but to analyze and demonstrate the nature of justice, Cicero's essay is a genuine study in statecraft; it not only describes the state from a historical point of view but recommends that form of government and that set of political institutions which its author deems would be best calculated to give man a just and effective government.

The Stoics held that the Good was the ultimate end of all existence, and that all parts of the universe, therefore, should so order their substance and behavior as to be in harmony with this transcendent aim. The state, says Cicero, best finds its way to harmony with ultimate purpose if it is just; the problem of the statesman, then, comes to be so to order and organize the state that it will come closest, in this imperfect human world, to serving the ends of justice. This is to be done, says Cicero, by following the rule of law and by preserving a decent order in social and civil institutions, so that all men may expect and receive the same fair treatment, and each man may fit into the niche in which he will be most effective, both as an individual and as a citizen.

In considering the proper form for the state, Cicero examines the three forms of government that were traditional in his day: monarchy, aristocracy, and democracy. He observed that each of these had its inherent weaknesses; monarchy involved too great

a concentration of power in the hands of one man, and was therefore entirely too subject to the personal attributes of the monarch
himself: an evil monarch would turn the whole state evil. Aristocracy, the rule of the "best" elements in society, had much to
recommend it, but fell short of justice in that it excluded too large
a share of the citizen-body from the privileges and responsibilities
of rule. Also, like the monarchy, it was uncommonly subject to the
personal qualities of the aristocrats themselves, for if they were to
become degenerate there could be no effective check on their evil
influence. As for democracy, Cicero saw it as a "culpable leveling,"
in which no provision was made for gradations in rank, where the
wellborn had no more to say in the guiding of the state than those
of humble birth, and might indeed be outvoted and overpowered
by them. Looking back to the history of Athens and of Rome itself, Cicero could adduce entirely too many examples of political
folly that was the result of unchecked popular rule.

The facts of history seem to show us, says Cicero, that human
governments tend to pass through a regular cycle of forms; first
comes monarchy, the rule of the richest and the strongest man;
political, social and economic jealousy result in the deposition of
the monarch and his replacement by a council of the aristocrats
who, at least at first, attempt to run the state for the good of all
the citizens, but inevitably become selfish, ambitious, and dishonest,
with the result that their rule turns unjust and oppressive. Hereupon, the people rise en masse and replace aristocratic rule by the
rule of the people, i.e. democracy, with every man participating to
the best of his ability in the government of the state, all sharing
the responsibilities and assisting in the making of decisions. Unfortunately, the greatest portion of mankind is not either intelligent or responsible; democracy works well so long as the weaker
elements in the population allow themselves to be taught and led
by the abler and more intelligent, but sooner or later the lower
classes become jealous and restive; they rise against the democratic
government, overthrow it, and replace it by irresponsible mob-
rule. But mob-rule cannot long last, for the folly and greed of an
undisciplined and largely unintelligent melee of people soon ex-
haust both the coffers and the powers of the state, and chaos
results.

Into this mass of turbulence now steps the tyrant, an astute,
unprincipled, sometimes greedy and violent man, but persuasive
and powerful. Surrounding himself with armed bodyguards, he

forcibly seizes the government, reorganizes it with himself in a position of sole political power, forces the citizen-body into subjection and order, pacifies the people by well-timed donatives from the public treasury, and distracts their attention and dazzles their gaze with magnificent public spectacles and works. If the tyrant is successful, as the years go by he consolidates his position, and by appropriate legal moves changes it from usurpation to legally constituted rule; at this point, the tyrant becomes a king, and the cycle begins again.

The history of the ancient world tends to substantiate this cycle of governments; they do in fact seem to have proceeded very much according to a pattern of this sort. But to Cicero such political instability was intolerable; he was looking for a form of government that would make such periodic upheavals unnecessary if not impossible. The disorder and injustice inherent in the succession of governments was to him deeply offensive, since it seemed most signally not to be in accord with the Law of Nature. Since he saw that each of these forms of government, with the possible exception of tyranny, had in it an essential element of good, he attempted to combine them into a composite form of state which would keep the good aspects of monarchy, aristocracy, and democracy, and would allot power to each in such way that they would keep each other in balance, allowing each to perform that good of which it was capable, but preventing any one from lapsing into evil:

> I feel that in our government there should be one element that is commanding and royal; another should be granted to the aristocracy as their share, and certain matters should be reserved to the judgement and will of the many. A constitution like this has, first of all, a kind of all-inclusive fairness, without which men can scarcely remain free for any length of time; secondly, it has stability. Those we discussed first (*sc.* the royal, aristocratic, and democratic constitutions) easily change over to their negative and destructive variants: a king becomes a tyrant, an aristocracy a cabal, and a democracy lawlessness and anarchy, and each of these types is subject to frequent change into one of the others. But in our conjoint, judiciously compounded form of government, this can scarcely occur unless our leaders turn spectacularly vicious; for there is no occasion for revolution when each component part is

soundly and suitably located in its proper slot, and there are no hidden pitfalls into which it might tumble. (*De re publica* 1.45.69)

We see in this, of course, a somewhat idealized picture of the actual Roman constitution, the "king" being represented by the consuls, the "aristocracy" by the Senate, and the "many" by the various popular assemblies. It is likely that Cicero, in constructing his ideal constitution, was thinking not so much of his own day as of the Rome of the mid-second century B. C. when, under the able and benevolent leadership of men like Scipio and Laelius, the Roman government, at least as viewed from the vantage point of a century later, seemed to be in a well-nigh perfect state of balance and harmony. Cicero intended that the orderliness of the balanced constitution should be expressed by the orderliness of the government based on it, with the people pursuing a policy of harmony, mutual understanding, goodwill, and patriotism. Externally, too, the state in its policies was to reflect the orderliness of the constitution; it was to work toward a harmony of the whole world in a spirit of universal brotherhood, with Rome playing the part of the wise and benevolent king. In Cicero's balanced constitution, we are entitled to see the theoretical ancestor of our own system of checks and balances; in his policy of world brotherhood under the benevolent rule of Rome, we may observe the genesis of the Roman Empire, and of the philosophy that motivated and justified it.

Of somewhat less interest to the modern reader is Cicero's companion work, *On the Laws* (*De legibus*). This work, patently unfinished, attempts to interpret the ideal constitution in terms of specific laws. The argument is again Stoic in nature, based on the universal Law of Nature, which is that all things should be ordered toward the Good.

It is when we turn to Cicero's work on ethical philosophy that we find both the greatest interest to ourselves and the best indication of Cicero's clarity of thought, and the proofs of his deeply humane nature. Cicero's philosophic works comprise three major studies and two short essays, all of these written in little more than a year, 45 to 44 B. C., when Cicero, deeply disturbed at the turn events had taken in Rome and seeing himself utterly powerless to check the downfall of the constitution for which he had labored all of his life, retired into obscurity, took no part in public affairs, and devoted himself to his writing. Two of these works are monumental in scope; the first, *On the Definition of Good and Evil* (*De finibus bonorum et malorum*), the second, the *Tusculan Disputations* (*Tusculanae disputationes*). The first attacks the problem that is fundamental to the study of ethics, the nature of good and evil, for until these have been defined, we can make no progress toward recommending the kinds of conduct to be pursued or avoided by men. The essay is divided into five books, and proceeds according to a rather unusual plan. In Book I, the chief speaker, Torquatus, discourses on the Epicurean definition of good and evil; in Book II, Cicero refutes his arguments. In Book III, Cato explains the Stoic point of view on these two questions; in Book IV, Cicero refutes Cato's arguments. Book V is entirely occupied by a discourse, put into the mouth of Piso, in which the point of view of the New Academy is set forth; since Cicero was in accord with this last definition, the volume contains no refutation of it.

The entire work, which is in dialogue form, is of course Cicero's own; the individual speakers were merely introduced for variety's sake and in an elaborate attempt at accuracy and fairness, since each of the persons of the dialogue was a recognized authority in his particular school of philosophy. While Cicero is charitable to all three points of view, it is clear that he favored the last two over the first; as we have seen before, Cicero was never quite able to stomach Epicurean philosophical theories. The work is enormously valuable as a source book on these three philosophies; except in the case of the Epicurean, Cicero's accuracy has rarely been called into serious question.

Rather more readable than *De finibus* is the *Tusculan Disputations*, since it deals with problems that are closer to our interests, less theoretical and more practical—problems, moreover, to which final answers have yet to be given. The general subject of the work is human happiness, or what one might more accurately call the good and effective life. Each of the five books of this long and meticulous study deals with a different aspect of the problem; Book I, for example, deals with the problem of death and the proper attitude of man toward this inevitable event. Cicero holds, as we might expect, that only by learning to scorn death as nothing more than an incident, can we hope to achieve a worthwhile life on earth, for the man who is preoccupied with or fearful of death can never render himself truly effective. Man must learn that death is only one of two things: either it is total annihilation, in which case any concern for it is sheer folly, or it is eternal happiness, in which case it is something to be welcomed as bringing man into closer contact with God.

Book II deals with pain and the proper way of bearing it. Cicero views pain as an inevitable part of human life, and again asserts that unless man learns how properly to face and bear pain, he cannot live a truly happy life. Scouting the Epicurean theory that pain may be borne because a long-standing pain is always moderate and therefore bearable, and a severe pain cannot last for long, Cicero turns rather toward the Stoic doctrine that pain is something that must be borne, that we must learn to suppress its effects by courage and patience, by self-discipline and by the development of a habit of indifference, all of which qualities are the result of the study of philosophy. Book III, on the mitigation of grief, argues that grief, simply because of its nature, a kind of delirium or madness, cannot possibly befall the true philosopher, who has trained himself to reject all such wayward forms of thought. In sum, those who wish to live the effective, good life must acquire the philosopher's control over their feelings. Book IV is in a similar vein, dealing with various perturbations of the mind which are shown to be neither in accord with nature or necessary; it is therefore within the power of the true philosopher to remain unaffected by them all.

The crown of the *Tusculans* is undoubtedly Book V. Here Cicero shows that the argument of the preceding four books has attacked the problem of human happiness piecemeal, that although the arguments advanced are all entirely valid, there is one underlying argument that supports them all: this is that the key to all human happiness, the sole protection against unhappiness and ineffectiveness, is virtue; the virtuous man is always happy no matter in what circumstances he may chance to find himself.

In order properly to evaluate this work of Cicero's, we must understand what he meant by "virtue," especially since this term has now come to have primarily sexual connotations. "Virtue," to Cicero, and to the ancients in general, has a meaning fairly close to what we call "excellence," and encompasses the effective sphere as well as the moral. It involves intellectual excellence above all, for the key virtue is "wisdom," and this is to be possessed only by those who have the intellectual capacity for it. Without wisdom, it is impossible to understand the nature of any other virtue, since virtue is a quality of the mind, and is acquired by the performance of good acts for the right reason. But right reason implies intelligence, the capacity to understand; the unintelligent man is excluded from virtue, for although he may perform right acts and do good things, he is incapable of performing or doing them for the right reason, since he is not intelligent enough to know what the right reason is.

Besides wisdom, the ancients recognized three other cardinal virtues: courage, temperance (or better, "self-control"), and justice. To these four a host of variations and elaborations were appended; the Stoics in particular defined virtue as acting "in accord with nature." By this they did not mean following one's natural inclinations, but rather putting one's self in harmony with the law that governs the universe and orders all things for the good. To be a virtuous man, to Cicero, meant to study himself and the world about him, and to learn their nature; to determine by the study of philosophy what principles will so govern his actions that they will always be aimed toward the greatest excellence of which he is capable. The man whose life is so absorbed may be called truly happy, for if his actions and thoughts are firmly based in philosophic principle, there will be nothing that can upset his equilibrium. It is in this sense that Cicero asserts that virtue, in itself and alone, is sufficient for human happiness.

Cicero's third major treatise on moral philosphy is the book called *On Duty* (*De officiis*). Cicero's concept of duty is once again founded on Stoic principle. Dividing all possible human activities into three categories, the virtuous, the vicious, and the indifferent, the Stoics further divided the third category into those which were preferable and those which were nonpreferable. The former were acts which either led in the direction of virtue or at least did not lead away from it; the latter were actions harmless enough in themselves but of such nature that they might tend toward vice if not carefully regulated.

From the practical—that is to say, the Roman—point of view this "indifferent" class was by far the most important, for it comprised most of the acts that human beings were likely to wish to perform. It is here that men must learn to distinguish the preferable from the nonpreferable, and must concentrate all their effort on pursuit of the former. Cicero's book, *On Duty*, is a study of those actions and ideas that he considered preferable for a good Roman citizen, the things that the good Roman ought to think and do. He begins by observing that every moral action requires choice; we are constantly being faced with situations in which two alternatives are presented to us, either of which may be accounted morally good but which cannot be pursued simultaneously. Our choice must be dictated not only by a study of the two alternatives themselves but of the immediate circumstances in which they occur, for all such considerations are pertinent to our choice; and our choice must always be that one of the alternatives which appears the better from all points of view.

Cicero next discourses on the problem of advantage, for it is clear that we often must consider not only whether a given act is morally good but also whether it will be advantageous to us to perform it. Here again, Cicero observes that the advantageous also involves choice, for we may be presented with two possible actions, both of which may contribute to our advantage. Clearly, our duty is to choose that which will be more advantageous. Finally Cicero, observing that the good and the advantageous sometimes coincide and sometimes do not, demonstrates to his own satisfaction that the conflict between them is only apparent, for in the last analysis only the morally good will be found also to be truly advantageous.

The work *On Duty* was enormously popular in the eighteenth and nineteenth centuries, particularly in England, where it was considered a good moral guide for the English gentleman; its fairly rigid code of morality coincided, at least superficially, with those rules of conduct that were approved in an England heavily influenced by Puritanism. In point of fact, Cicero is more practical than the Puritans, and his morality rather more hardheaded than theirs. The modern reader who has the patience to follow Cicero's slow and deliberate way of making a point will find much in the work *On Duty* that reflects the practical moral principles of our own day.

Paradoxically, the two brief essays which Cicero considered scarcely more than pleasant intellectual diversion make the greatest appeal to us today, perhaps only because they are brief and simple and do not try our patience with long chains of argument or niceties of definition. The essays *On Old Age* and *On Friendship* consume scarcely more than an hour apiece in the reading. Each is cast in the form of a dialogue; in *On Old Age*, the chief speaker is Cato the Elder, who is depicted conversing with two young friends, Scipio and Laelius, who have come to ask the old man for the secret of happiness in old age. In his discourse, Cato outlines four charges, as he calls them, that are commonly leveled against old age: first, that it takes us away from the active life, second, that it deprives us of physical vigor, third, that it deprives us of virtually all pleasures, and fourth, that it is close to death.

With the interposition of a strategic remark here and there by the two young men, Cato proceeds to show that each of these charges, although not entirely false, is in fact either meaningless or unimportant. Old age may, to be sure, deprive men of certain primarily physical activities, but in compensation it gives them personal prestige and influence. As for the charge of physical weakness, Cato observes that this is in no sense peculiar to old age, that many young men also suffer from physical weaknesses, and, in the last analysis, physical strength is not important to the old, since it is never demanded of them. Rather, they are levied on for their wisdom and experience, qualities for which physical vigor is not needed.

In the section dealing with pleasure, Cicero seems to be deliberately teasing his old friend Atticus, to whom the dialogue is dedicated, by making mock-virulent attack on Atticus's philosophy, Epicureanism. Cato declares that if old age does indeed deprive us of pleasures, we should be grateful to it, for pleasure is the enemy of moral excellence and intellectual accomplishment. It is, in fact, the source of all evil in the world; man is far better off without it than with it. And anyway, Cato remarks, the old do not lose all pleasures, only the more extreme and violent ones; for the moderate pleasures of healthful eating, drinking, and good conversation, and for such useful activities as farming, the aged have ample opportunity.

As for the charge that old age is too close to death, Cicero remarks, with all the wisdom of the Book of Common Prayer, that "in the midst of life we are in death"; in this hazardous life of ours the young are as much exposed to death as the old. Furthermore, death for the old is natural, and therefore good: when a man has had his fill of life, then death is no more than appropriate, and may even be viewed as desirable. As for the fear of what may eventuate after death, Cicero once again picks up the argument that he had used in earlier works: either death is total annihilation, in which case it is foolish to fear it, or else it is an eternity of happiness, in which case it is something to be desired. In quick outline, Cicero has Cato retail his arguments for belief in the afterlife and the immortality of the soul; he has him conclude, with Socrates, that this event which many regard as such an evil may in fact be the greatest good. Cato is looking forward to reunion with the great men whom he has known and with those of whom he has only read, and above all with his son, who died as a young man; the belief that he will indeed have such a meeting in eternity is one which he will not allow anyone to wrest from him. "And if," says he, "I find that I am wrong, at least I need not worry for fear dead philosophers may make fun of me" (*De senectute* 23.85).

This delightful little essay has all the beauty and dignity of Cicero's high, formal prose, but its style and manner are tempered by a geniality he does not often otherwise display, a geniality one would like to think sprang from real affection and concern for his old friend Atticus, for whom he wrote, as he puts it, "for our mutual benefit."

The second of the two little essays, *On Friendship*, is somehow less successful, although it has been much admired by scholars. Here and there, it shows signs of incompletion; there is repetition; there are arguments not led to logical conclusion. Cicero is wrestling with a problem that greatly mystified antiquity: why is it that men so value friendship? What is the nature of this relationship? Cicero attempts to show, through the mouth of his main speaker, Laelius, that friendship is closely related to virtue and that only the virtuous can form true friendships. Within this general proposition, he analyzes in considerable detail the kinds of acts that friends may properly perform for each other, the point to which they may stretch principle in the name of friendship, and the varying degrees of friendship which may properly exist between different classes of men. The essay, *On Friendship*, remains a charming literary effort; in it we see revealed the ideas on friendship of a man who was himself throughout his life a warm and loyal friend.

To turn from Cicero's formal writings to his letters is not to turn to a different person; rather, it is to have a more nearly complete view of the writer himself. As far as can now be determined, Cicero's letters were not intended for publication, but were meant only for the addressees themselves; thus we may expect to find in them as unvarnished a picture of the man himself as any man can paint for anyone but himself. In the *Orations*, and in works like the *Republic*, we see Cicero the statesman; in the letters we see him as the consummate politician with a hardheaded practical view of political power and the ways in which it is to be gained and kept. We see Cicero not in the least averse to accepting the help of influential friends, and in fact openly soliciting it; he was not even above accepting the help of men whose opinions he despised and whom he found personally obnoxious. Besides this revelation of Cicero the politician, we also see, in the political letters, a brilliantly delineated and often very detailed picture of the operation of the Roman government in Cicero's lifetime: the venality of the courts, the greed of provincial governors, the pride and ambition of brilliant men, among them Cicero himself.

The letters also show Cicero in his moments of relaxation with his friends—with Atticus, with Sulpicius, and perhaps most charmingly of all with his young friend Trebatius Testa, a brilliant lawyer in whose company Cicero spent many a convivial evening from which he returned, as he himself remarks, "fairly tight" (*bene potus: Ad familiares* 7.22). All the great men of the day are to be found in the letters, either as addressees or as writers, for the collection contains nearly one hundred letters written to Cicero by others: Caesar, Pompey, Brutus, Cato the Younger, Cicero's brother Quintus, Catiline—it would be hard to mention a man of any distinction whose name does not appear somewhere in some guise, for he knew them all. The picture that emerges is of a man of superb intelligence, in general honest, but canny enough for the political life, vain and ambitious, but more ambitious for his beloved Constitution than for himself, a warm friend, a gentle father (particularly toward his daughter, Tullia), a patient husband—but one whose patience could be exhausted, as his ill-tempered letters to poor Terentia, written on his return from exile, show. The letters are divided into four collections: first, *To His Brother Quintus* (*Ad Q. fratrem,* two books); second, *To Atticus* (*Ad Atticum,* sixteen books); *To Marcus Brutus* (*Ad M. Brutum,* two books); fourth, *To His Friends* (*Ad familiares,* sixteen books). The style of the letters is a far cry from his formal style; it is relaxed and easy, peppered with colloquial words and informal syntax, with many Greek loan-words—in short, just the sort of language we would expect from a learned and eloquent man when he was not on public display.

It would be difficult to overestimate the importance of Cicero as a literary man. Not only do his formal prose works give us an overarching view of the intellectual life of the age; in addition, the letters give us many a glimpse of its literary figures, including Cicero himself. In the opinion of most critics and scholars, both ancient and modern, Cicero's greatness as a writer of formal Latin prose was never surpassed or even equalled. No man understood as well as he the possibilities of the Latin language as a prose vehicle, or saw as clearly as he how the language could be so handled as to combine, with the most demanding artistry, a feeling of ease and naturalness: for all their complex structure, Cicero's sentences leave one with the feeling that he has heard someone talking in an easy and unaffected way. In his prose, balance, grace, and neatness are coupled with a dignity such as no other Latin writer ever achieved. Subsequent writers begin with him and work cautiously away from the standard he set. In the informal prose of the letters, Cicero also set a standard in colloquial Latin, for although he probably would have been shocked to know that his letters were regarded as literature, they are nonetheless models of the simple, unaffected, unpurged and unchastened speech that was the reservoir from which the great formal styles, including of course Cicero's own, were developed.

# CHAPTER X

# Caesar: from Republic to Empire

For most literary purposes, the age of the Republic may be said to end with Cicero. He is perhaps the last man of that age to whom the composition of literary works was not only a serious but also a major interest—for his assertion, often repeated, that he took to writing only to fill up his time during periods when he was perforce inactive politically, must be taken as scarcely more than a bow to Roman convention: it was not au fait for a Roman gentleman to confess openly to so absorbing an interest in literary composition.

There were, of course, other writers. Four important names occur to us at once: Julius Caesar, the first sentence of whose *Gallic Wars* is probably the single most often repeated Latin tag in existence; Cornelius Nepos, that busy professor of history, some of whose not very inspired biographies of famous Greeks and Romans are still extant; Sallust *(Sallustius Crispus)*, whose monograph on the Catilinarian conspiracy has already been referred to, and who also wrote a monograph of similar scope on the *War with Jugurtha (Bellum Jugurthinum)* and a work known simply as the *Histories*, in five books, covering the period 78 to 67 B. C. (extant only in fragments); and finally, the encyclopedic scholar and polymath, Marcus Terentius Varro, to whom can be assigned very nearly fifty known titles, only one of which is extant in its entirety: the book *On Farming (Res rusticae)*, a distinctly bookish production hardly to be placed in the same class with Cato's. Probably Varro's most important work was his study, in twenty-five books, of *The Latin Language (De lingua Latina),* of which even the extant portion (Books 5–10) is of great value in showing us what a learned Roman knew (or thought he knew) about his own language. Most tantalizing of all of Varro's works are his *Menip-*

*pean Satires,* of which only fragments are extant; these are full of wit, boisterous humor, atrocious puns, and gay obscenity.

Except for Caesar, all three of these men survived the revolution and lived on into the thirties, B. C., but Caesar is certainly the only familiar name among them. His *Gallic Wars* (*Commentarii de bello Gallico*) were, for many centuries, the *corpus vile* on which incipient Latinists and unhappy schoolboys made their primary gross dissections of the Latin language. The awful fate of having become a schoolbook has tended to obscure the literary merits of the *Gallic Wars* and its companion piece, the *Civil War*; the lucidity of their exposition, the sure sense of drama they exhibit, and their intensely disciplined style have earned them a place among the masterworks of the Latin language; anyone who can read them without unhappy visions of schoolrooms in the month of May will find them fascinating.

Caesar's political and military genius has unfortunately overshadowed his rôle as a writer. He produced, for example, two books *On Analogy* (*De analogia*) embodying his own interpretation of the nature of the Latin language, an interpretation at odds with that of Varro. He composed many orations, carried on a voluminous correspondence, and when he was attacked by Cato the Younger for his political views and ambitions, published a series of brilliant documents, the *Anti-Catos* (*Anticatones*), in refutation of Cato's attack.

The *Gallic Wars* is Caesar's account of his campaigns during the years 58 to 52 B. C. to reduce Gaul to Roman domination. In addition to narrating important events, Caesar also tells much about the terrain, the important personalities, and the various peoples of the country. The book was written in the form of a series of reports to the Senate in Rome of his own activities on behalf of the state; its main purpose was to create, in the eyes of the Senate and the Roman people, the image of a brilliant and resourceful commander. In this, Caesar succeeded.

The *Civil War* is Caesar's account of the conflict between himself and Pompey during the years 49 to 48 B. C. This also takes the form of a report, but in fact seeks to justify Caesar's part in the defeat and ultimate death of his great rival for power. Caesar even found time to write poetry; his epigram on the playwright Terence, in which he praises Terence for his art, but says that he lacks *vis comica* ("genuine humor") and calls him a "half-Menander" (*Menander dimidiatus*), has long been famous; he is said to have composed a large number of such literary apothegms. In addition, he is known to have written an epic poem called simply

*The Journey* (*Iter*) telling of the events of one of his numerous trips between Gaul and Rome.

Caesar was certainly Rome's greatest military genius, one of her greatest statesmen, and in all probability one of her most charming writers. Cicero, in his letters, tells how on one occasion he perforce entertained Caesar at one of his villas; the impending visit nearly left him in a state of nervous prostration, but although he never felt easy with his guest, he is compelled to admit that they had spent a most delightful evening together discussing literary questions. Those who knew Caesar—even his assassins—confessed to their affection for him and their fascination with his brilliance; it is unfortunate that we have only the two *Wars* by which to judge the qualities of his mind.

A comparative table of the dates of the most important authors of the Republic and of the Augustan Age will show at once the decisive break between the two, and at the same time some curious and strategic instances of overlapping.

| | |
|---|---|
| Cicero 106–43 B. C. | Vergil 70–19 B. C. |
| Catullus 87–55 B. C. | Horace 65–8 B. C. |
| Lucretius 96–53 B. C. | Livy 59 B. C. – 17 A. D. |
| Caesar 100–44 B. C. | Ovid 43 B. C. – 18 A. D. |
| Sallust 86–35 B. C. | Propertius fl. 29–15 B. C. |
| Varro 116–27 B. C. | Tibullus d. 19 B. C. |
| Varro of Atax 82–27 B. C. | |

From this table we observe that at the time of the death of Catullus and Lucretius, Vergil was about fifteen, Horace about ten, while Ovid, Propertius, and Tibullus were probably not yet born. At the death of Cicero, Vergil was twenty-seven, Horace was twenty-two; Ovid had just been born, and Propertius and Tibullus were still unborn or were small boys. Livy was a boy of sixteen. The three greatest of these names, Vergil, Horace, and Livy, would have had all or the greater share of their education before the death of Caesar and Cicero; Horace says that his father took him to Rome for his schooling when he was still a boy; if this is the case, he must have been physically present in the city for at least the last years of the Republic; the assassination of Caesar, the dramatic appeal of Mark Antony for popular support of the Caesarian party, and the subsequent flight of Brutus, Cassius, and the other assassins from Rome, the nailing of the head and hands of the dead Cicero to the rostra, must have been events of which he was intensely aware, even if he did not actually witness them. It is a good guess that Horace had already done a good deal of writing by the time of these events, although anything he may have written then is not only lost but is not even mentioned by the poet himself. As for Vergil, so far as we know, he was never in Rome during these years, but presumably was at his home near Mantua, in the Po Valley. Similarly, we learn nothing of any early visits by Livy to Rome; he presumably spent these same years in his home at Padua (Patavium).

In any event, none of these writers confesses to any knowledge or experience of events prior to the battle of Philippi in 42 B. C., although it is to be presumed that these events formed part of the—now lost—later books of Livy's *History*. If this was a general conspiracy of silence, it was remarkably successful; it may also represent compliance with the known wish of Augustus, that neither he nor the Roman populace in general be too often or too vividly reminded of the events that preceded his elevation to the principate; it may be too that, to the literary men of the Augustan Age, the acts and policies of Augustus had brought a blessed relief from the confusion of Republican-democratic rule, and from the bloodletting of civil war, and they preferred to forget.

But although physical contact between the great personalities of Augustan literature and those of the last years of the Republic is difficult if not impossible to establish, intellectual contact between them is obvious on virtually every page of the works of the later writers. In a day when books descend on the world in a flood that no one can compass, it is difficult to imagine a time when men of education, taste, and discrimination could well have read every scrap of literature that was in existence. Even if the proof were not there to find in the pages of the Augustan writers, it would be a certain, even a necessary supposition that they had read all the Greek and Latin works of the pre-Augustan period that we now possess, and doubtless many more that have since been lost. Horace's lyrics are full of echoes of Catullus. He knew Cicero too, and Lucretius, Plautus, Terence, Naevius, Ennius, and Andronicus. Vergil, too, knew, loved, and echoed Catullus. Even a cursory reading will disclose in his works the influence of Lucretius, Cicero, and Ennius, and a bit of digging will turn up echoes of virtually every other known earlier poet. The other important Augustan poets, Tibullus, Propertius, and Ovid, are no less dependent on the work of their predecessors. As for the great Augustan prose writer, Livy, he was, of course, totally dependent on Republican histories for his sources; his prose style, although very much his own, is nonetheless heavily dependent on Cicero.

# CHAPTER XI

# Horace

Of all the writers of the Augustan Age, the one whose lifetime most clearly spans the period of the revolution and whose work most clearly demonstrates and delineates the lines of literary influence that link Republic and Augustan Age together, is Horace. Quintus Horatius Flaccus was born in 65 B. C. in Venusia in southern Italy. The accounts we have of his family are strangely one-sided; he has much to say about his father, but of his mother not a word. Whatever may have become of her, it is reasonably clear that Horace never knew her. His father was a freedman, thus occupying the lowest rung of the Roman social ladder (for a slave could not be said to be on the ladder at all); he was either himself an auctioneer or an auctioneer's assistant—the Latin term is *coactor*—a man certainly of very modest station, concerned not at all for his own standing in Roman society but selflessly ambitious for his talented son.

For his boy, the local schools at Venusia were not nearly good enough; in some fashion not now clear, the elder Horace got together enough money to move to Rome, where he put his son in the school of a certain Orbilius, a stern but apparently effective taskmaster, whom Horace himself later styled as "old Swat-'em Orbilius" (*plagosus Orbilius*). Here Horace studied the Greek and Latin classics; he apparently enjoyed the former more than the latter, for he has few kind words to say of any of his Latin literary predecessors, and he recalls with particular distaste his studies of Andronicus, Naevius, and Plautus. In Roman times, education of the sort described by Horace was generally available only to the aristocratic and well-to-do; boys who attended school were regularly accompanied by a slave, called a *paedagogus*, who both carried the boy's books and other effects, and saw to it that he was not molested as he passed through the streets. Such an attendant was clearly beyond the means of the elder Horace; with truly remarkable self-abasement, he assumed this role himself—and Horace never says whether his father preserved the anonymity of a slave or let his identity be known.

Horace was eternally grateful to his father, and throughout his life accorded him all the respect and honor, as well as affection, that were the due of so selfless a man. Rising as he did to the top of the Roman social scale, becoming the intimate of the great and the friend of the emperor himself, Horace not only never apologizes for his humble origin, but is warmly proud of the father to whom he owed so much. Not many literary men have been so fortunate in a father; even fewer, perhaps, have so sincerely acknowledged their obligation and expressed their gratitude.

Horace does not tell us when his father died or under what circumstances, but he must have left his son with some small means, for we learn that Horace moved on from Rome to Athens, there to continue his studies of literature and philosophy. He was in fact in Athens in the year 44; when, after the death of Caesar, Brutus appeared there on the search for young Romans to enlist in his army, Horace was among those who volunteered to serve; how this totally unknown and thoroughly plebeian son of a freedman came to be enrolled as a *tribunus militum*—a fairly exalted military rank comparable perhaps to a colonelcy in a modern army—must remain a mystery. Either the young man was remarkably personable and persuasive, and had made some unusually influential friends during his student days, or else Brutus was indeed frantic for genuine Roman citizens to place in positions of responsibility in his hastily collected forces.

Aside from his lack of social standing, Horace was certainly a most unmilitary young man. In an ode (2.7) written some years later, he says that at the battle of Philippi he hardly distinguished himself, for he threw away his shield and ran from the field with the rest of the defeated army. The story is not to be taken too literally, for as we have remarked, poems are not biographies; in this particular instance, too, we have good reason to suspect that Horace was following a poetic tradition, for Archilochus (frg. 6), Anacreon (frg. 51 D), and Alcaeus (Herodotus 5.95) all incorporated nearly identical incidents in poems they wrote, and all of them, apparently, in the same half-whimsical tone of resignation.

With the defeat at Philippi, Horace was left virtually penni-less, for his property at Venusia, apparently his only source of in-come, was confiscated, and there is no telling what he might have done to survive, if Augustus had not magnanimously offered am-nesty to the defeated troops of the tyrannicides. Horace returned to Rome and invested what little money he still had in the purchase of a post in the imperial revenue service and a membership in the guild of scribes. He was unable to escape the drive to write poetry; during his leisure hours he began the composition of his *Satires*. Some of the early *Epodes* probably also belong to this period; he himself says that he made the mistake of trying to write Greek poetry, until he realized how foolish it was for him, an Italian, to attempt to compete with the Greeks in their own field (*Satires* 1.10.31–49). It is a practical certainty that in these early days he also began the work in Latin lyric that was to culminate in his *Odes*, for even the earliest of these is patently the result of much labor and practice. In one of the *Epodes* (11) he claims to have led a fairly wicked life and says that his name "became a by-word all over the city"; again we do not know how seriously or literally to take this; he undoubtedly found other young poets with whom he enjoyed working and associating; they must have read their poems to each other, drunk their wine together, en-joyed the company of the same interesting and willing women, and generally behaved in the way that has always been characteristic of the young and creative mind.

Among the acquaintances of these early days must have been the poet Vergil, for in the year 38 B. C. Vergil and his friend Varius introduced Horace to the great patron of the arts, Maece-nas. In what is probably an accurate account, Horace says (*Satires* 1.6.56–62) that he was dreadfully embarrassed, gulped out a few words, and went away thinking that the interview had been a colossal failure. But nine months later Maecenas gave him a formal invitation to join his circle of authors; about five years after that, he presented Horace with his Sabine farm, a spot for which Horace developed a deep affection, and which provided him with a modest but adequate income for the rest of his life.

One of the puzzles of Horace's life is his relation to the emperor Augustus. To judge again from the *Odes*—and again we must be cautioned that they are not necessarily or even probably reliable evidence of historical fact—the two men held each other in mutual respect. Horace, originally a supporter of the old Re-public, had come to see the inevitability of change, and to realize that Augustus's plans for the now established Empire offered far greater hope for peace and prosperity than the cumbersome old Republic could ever have done; Horace had come to respect the personal qualities of the emperor, his administrative ability, his sagacity in the choice of subordinates, and his remarkable patience with those who refused to grant him the deference that might seem naturally to belong to his powerful office. It appears—again to judge from the poems—that Augustus on a number of occasions put considerable pressure on Horace to write poetry in praise of his, the emperor's, accomplishments, both military and civil; to the end of his life, Horace resisted this pressure, giving in to it no further than his convictions would allow. For what he liked in the emperor and the new order, he had carefully measured praise; further than this, he refused to go. The independence that Horace maintained, not only against the emperor but against his patron Maecenas, whom he never regarded in any other light than as friend and equal, is the more remarkable in view of Horace's unique rise in the Roman social scale: he is the only literary man of whom we have knowledge in classical times who was able to make his way from the lowest to the highest levels, and that without losing his pride, honesty, and independence. He died at the age of 56, in 8 B. C., just a few months after the death of his friend and patron Maecenas.*

*This matter of the recusatio, which Horace shares with Vergil, Propertius, and perhaps other poets of the Augustan Age, has greatly troubled scholars; they dread to find in the lucubrations of these writers some indication of hypocrisy or sycophancy. A recent writer on Vergil, Kenneth Quinn (Virgil's Aeneid, a Critical Description (Ann Arbor, 1968), pp. 29–40) has I believe at last found the solution to this vexing problem. It is not that any of them was insincere, hypocritical, or sycophantic; nor was any of them finally bludgeoned into proclaiming a position he did not honestly accept. Pressure there undoubtedly was, on all of them; nothing could have been more natural than that the emperor and his chief friend and advisor should suggest to their friends and protégés that poetry in support of imperial policy would be welcome both in government circles and out. As Quinn has very neatly shown, the resistance of the poets to these suggestions sprang primarily and very largely from their artistic interests and predilections. The poetry of patriotism and national glorification is, viewed as an artistic problem, distinctly limited in scope. Patriotism is a noble sentiment and one never to be despised, but its colors and its expression tend to be either flat and obvious, or pale and washed with sentimentality. Neither stance appeals to the sensitive poet who knows all too well that if he adopts either extreme he will be dull and unworthy of his

The publication of the various parts of Horace's poetic work can be dated with considerable accuracy. His first collection, Book I of the *Satires*, was published in 35 B. C. Five years later, in 30 B. C., came the publication of the *Epodes* and of the second book of *Satires*. For the next seven years, he seems to have been engaged on the first three books of the *Odes*; these were published in 23 B. C. In 20 B. C. came the first book of *Epistles*, about 18 B. C. the second book of *Epistles*, and in 17 B. C. the *Carmen saeculare*. Alone among Horace's works, this was a command performance, written at the emperor's request to be sung during the celebration of the Secular Games—for with a bit of mathematical lergerdemain, it had been figured that this year marked the seven-hundredth anniversary of the founding of the city of Rome. Among the spectacles offered by the emperor to the public on this occasion was a grand processional, in which Horace's *Secular Hymn* was sung by a chorus of twenty-seven boys and twenty-seven girls.* Horace's last publication was the fourth book of the *Odes*, published in 13 B. C.

Since none of Horace's juvenilia have survived, it is difficult to determine where and how his work had its first beginnings, what influences first shaped it, and the stages of development through which it passed. In the semi-biographical *Satires* 1.10, Horace sets himself up against a group of poets who, he says, indulged in literary ancestor-worship and resented what they imagined to be Horace's attempt to supplant their great idol and model, Lucilius. Further, he claims, they vulgarized and weakened the Latin language by insisting on including Greek loan words in their vocabulary, and courted a cheap popularity by affecting a bombastic, sensationalistic style; at best, says he, they were the mere apes of Calvus and Catullus. Most of the names Horace mentions in this ill-tempered tirade mean little or nothing to us; a disputed text suggests that one of them was Valerius Cato, the

---

art, but if he attempts to operate somewhere between the two extremes, he is all too likely to be either clumsy or misunderstood. Only a man of the stature of a Vergil had the genius to see what could be done with the patriotic theme, and he reached the solution only after many years of agonizing.

*There still stands, in the National Museum in Rome, the marble slab on which the emperor had had inscribed a detailed account of this great celebration. Few archaeological finds have brought any personality of the ancient world so vividly alive to the classicist as the words still to be read on this slab: *carmen composuit Quintus Horatius Flaccus*

teacher whom Calvus and Catullus and the other New Poets so greatly respected; another conjecture identifies the *Alpinus* of verse 36 with the poet Furius Bibaculus, who is generally considered to have been a member of the circle of New Poets in the time of Catullus.

Critics cannot even agree on whether or not Horace, in speaking contemptuously of men who merely aped Calvus and Catullus, meant the slur to be directed at the imitators or also at the two poets themselves. If he did, then he stands convicted either of lamentable ignorance or of flagrant ingratitude, for Horace's debt to Catullus is everywhere apparent. He may not have known Catullus himself, but he certainly knew his work and studied it carefully, and there is at least some evidence that his early efforts in poetry, like his politics and his social behavior, were as rebellious and indecorous as were those of any of the New Poets. Some of the *Epodes* and early *Satires* (e.g. *Epodes* 5, 8, 11; *Satires* 1.2–3) show an interest in horror and scatology that seems quite startling in a poet who later so carefuly pruned all such undignified and improper materials from his works, and perhaps even from his thoughts. One point at least seems to be clear: the two poets came into contact with the same poetic influences, were thrown into the same poetic environment, and for a time at least worked in the same or very similar genres. Scatology was not a major interest with either of them; with Catullus it was an aspect of his creative personality which he was able to work out with some skill. With Horace, it was a side of his genius at which he labored briefly and failed to express adequately. As the vast bulk of his poetic work shows, he had the good sense to turn his efforts in a different direction, to the more congenial fields of popular philosophy and personal relations.

In so doing, he affected to turn his back on the New Poets; where their interest ranged all over the field of human conduct, and they took an eclectic's delight in searching out odd corners for poetic ideas, Horace resolutely confines himself to the respected and respectable. The direction he thus gave to Latin poetry was very nearly as radical in its implications and effects as was the earlier revolution of the New Poets themselves, for at least partly from Horace's work is derived the doctrine, persistent until very recent times, that the proper realm of the lyric is the good, the true, and the beautiful, and the feeling that that which is merely true, particularly if it is not especially attractive or restful to the mind, should be left to the writers of prose or to the composers of satire and epigram. Horace caused the refreshing *Ungebundenheit* of the Republican poets to be replaced by a more restrictive ideal, one that was at once easier to live with, and at the same time, perhaps paradoxically, nearly as richly productive of great poems.

A passage in one of the *Satires* (2.6.70–76) comes very close to summing up the subject matter of Horace's poetry once he had turned away from the experimental early *Satires* and *Epodes*:

> Well, we start talking, but not about other people's country or city places, not about Lepos—whether he's a good or a poor dancer; no, we discuss matters of more immediate concern to us, matters of which it is downright wrong to be ignorant: Is it wealth or virtue that produces the happy life for humankind? What motivates us to make friends: mutual advantage, or the search for excellence? What is the nature of the good, and what its highest form?

From this time on, there is hardly a line Horace wrote that is not in one way or another connected with these questions.

Horace was not writing philosophy, but making poems; for this purpose, he used whatever philosophical precepts or ideas were ready at hand and adaptable to the particular poetic problem he had in mind. Although his poems often mention the pleasures of life, he is far from being an Epicurean. He was most certainly not a Stoic; as a practical Roman and a sensitive man, he had neither time nor patience for doctrines of absolute virtue, even as these were modified and softened by later Stoic philosophers. The doctrines of both schools not only failed to appeal to Horace's temperament; in addition, they were poor material for poetry, particularly for the poetry of thesis and antithesis, of balance and grace, that Horace wished to write.

By contrast, the doctrine of the Golden Mean, with its concomitant injunction to accept "the day" as the valid measure of life, were made to order for a type of writing which constantly sought to oppose one element to its opposite, and to resolve the stress thus created by finding that mean-point between them on which the mind could rest with comfort. For to Horace, the mean is not merely a philosophic ideal and idea; it is also a principle of poetic composition; again and again, his poems, in good Aristotelian fashion, "aim at the mean."* Again and again, Horace's

---

*"Virtue is indeed a sort of mean, since, you see, it makes the midpoint its aim" (*Nichomachean Ethics* 2.5.1106b).

poems begin on one side of a poetic proposition, proceed to a general statement, then continue with an opposite or complementary statement of the same proposition; when the whole poem has been read, it will be seen that its two "extremes," like Aristotle's virtue, "aim" at its mean-point, which when properly interpreted, both sheds light on the two sides of the proposition and neatly binds them together into a unity.

Aristotelian, too, is the way in which Horace locates his mean, for like Aristotle's, it rarely if ever falls at the arithmetical midpoint between the two extremes; the merest line-counting, to say nothing of the balancing of sets of ideas, images, or word-groups, will show that the point at which the tension of the poem is resolved by an appropriate "mean" lies not halfway through the poem but to one or the other side of the midpoint. It would almost appear that for Horace the principle of poetic imbalance, by which the machine-like dullness of precise balance is avoided, was generically related to the doctrine of the Mean; Horace saw there a vehicle that provided him at once with a subject matter and a structure that harmonized with his concept of the art of poetry.

In the writing of his *Satires*, the first book of which was published in 35 B. C., Horace is following the tradition already set by Lucilius a hundred years earlier. Like the old master, whose works he deeply respected, although he felt that they lacked finished style and structure, Horace views the satire as a verse-essay, composed in dactylic hexameters, relatively brief, and in general vocabulary and style, couched in colloquial rather than in formal language.

In subject matter, the *Satires* deal with practical philosophy and moral conduct, human relations, particularly friendship, and in somewhat less degree, literature itself. Two satires of somewhat different character lighten an otherwise over-serious content: *Satire* 5, with its amusing account of Horace's journey, with Maecenas and his staff, from Rome to Brundisium. The trip was made partly by barge down the canal through the Pomptine Marshes, where, Horace said, the company was kept awake by frogs, mosquitoes, and the bargeman singing about his absent sweetheart, and partly by mule-team. On one occasion the group was entertained by a pair of clowns. In *Satire* 9, Horace tells how he was stopped one day in Rome by a tiresome and insistent acquaintance, who wanted him to introduce him to Maecenas. With infinite patience and tact Horace tries to put the man off, but to no effect; when Horace's friend Aristius Fuscus appears, Horace thinks he can pawn his tiresome interlocutor off on him, but Fuscus—as Horace might well have known—was much too clever for him, and the satire ends, as Horace says, with the poet "under the knife."

More nearly in accord with our general impression of Horace as a satirist, and probably intended by the poet himself to set the tone for his first book of satires, is *Satires* I.1. The poet begins with a question:

> Why is it, Maecenas, that nobody, no matter what his lot in life, whether the result of deliberate choice or mere chance, lives content with it, but rather praises people who follow other paths? (*Satires* 1.1.1–3)

There follow a series of examples: the soldier praises the seafarer, the seafarer the soldier; the jurist praises the farmer, the farmer the city-man, etc. And yet if some god were to offer them the opportunity actually to make the exchange, they would refuse.

At first blush, it appears that Horace is about to castigate men for their eternal discontent, but almost immediately it turns out that this is not the case: it is not man's discontent with his lot, but rather the reason that prevents him from changing it that occupies the poet's interest. Men persist in uncongenial occupations because in them they have found a way to acquire wealth: like the ant, they are storing up provisions against the day when they may retire in security. "What!" says the poet, "The ant? The ant is a hard worker, but he has the good sense to stop when he has enough. You go on piling up more and more, forever discontented if there is one man in the world richer than you are" (*id.* 31–40).

Thus neatly and deftly Horace introduces his favorite topic, the Golden Mean, for the real point of his essay is that man creates misery for himself by failing to observe due limit in his efforts, whether to obtain wealth or anything else:

> Proper limits do exist in this world of ours, and there are fixed boundary-lines, beyond which and short of which we cannot stop and still be right. (*id.* 106–7)

This, the poet concludes, is why men are eternally dissatisfied with their lot: they never know when to stop, when to place a limit upon their activities, of whatever kind they may be:

> And so it comes about that we can rarely find a man who will admit that he has had a happy life, and who, when his time

runs out, is content to depart like a banqueter who has had his fill. (*id.* 117–19)

The thought was hardly a new one, even in Horace's day. The examples were familiar to every Roman; apart from the ant, whose industry, as proverbial in antiquity as it is now, is here given an ironic new turn, there is not a trace of novelty or invention in the images and ideas that occupy the poet.

The excellence of the satire consists in the clarity, skill, and cogency with which the poet presents these familiar pictures and ideas. We are not likely soon to forget Horace's picture of the sailor, the soldier, and above all of the miser, who gladly suffers the hisses of the crowd for the sake of his moneybags, the sight of which makes him glow with self-satisfaction. The essay is brief, too, and makes its point quickly, by means of a vivid picture or a neat turn of phrase; at a steady unhurried pace the writer leads his reader from one idea to another with a minimum of waste motion.

In manner of organization, too, the satire is interesting both in its own right and as foreshadowing the type of composition the poet was later to employ in his *Odes*. For it will be noticed that Horace does not attack his topic directly, but begins, so to speak, at an oblique angle: he tempts our fancy by leading us to suppose that he is going to talk about one topic, then shows us that the topic had quite a different dimension from the one we had expected, and that it is on this latter that he intends to discourse. Through a series of examples, he seeks to prove his point, at last bringing us to the real topic of his essay, the need to observe proper limits in all human activities. He then ends the essay by deftly tying together his original and his later illustrations, and showing how they are indeed all germane to his central point. The architecture of the satire is like the Mean itself, for the truth it announces lies somewhere between its beginning and its end. And in this instance, at least, the Mean is at a considerable distance from the arithmetical midpoint; thus the structure of the satire itself reflects in graphic fashion the ideal of the Mean.

Book II of the *Satires*, published in 30 B.C., lacks the vigor and spontaneity of Book I. In a fashion that seems now a little tired as well as tiresome, Horace discourses on the evils of luxurious living (*Satires* 2 and 4), on the Stoic paradox "that all fools are mad" (i.e. that all those who lack the philosopher's true wisdom are in effect brainless; *Satires* 2.3), on a second Stoic paradox,

"that only the wise man is free" (*Satire* 7), and on the evil prac-
tices of those who are socially and economically overambitious
(*Satire* 5). *Satire* 8, on the banquet of Nasidienus, is a flat and
tasteless bow in the direction of Lucilius; one suspects that it was
composed solely because, by tradition, a book of satires ought to
include at least one on this subject.

The remaining two satires are, however, among Horace's best.
*Satires* 2.1, which in order to be best appreciated should be read
in conjunction with *Satires* 1.10, shows Horace, now assured of his
acceptance as a writer and poet, justifying his pursuit of this metier
to Gaius Trebatius Testa, now grown from the witty and learned
young friend of Cicero to a veritable Oliver Wendell Holmes of
his day. In no more than half-serious fashion, Horace insists that
he writes satire because he can't help it—and anyway, if he doesn't
write verse he can't sleep. When Trebatius suggests that he might
at least change his topics and write about the great achievements
of Caesar, he replies that he will, when the occasion arises—a remark that should have silenced for all time the canard that makes
Horace the emperor's toady, and his *recusatio* a mere pose. *Satires*
2.6 is on the perennially pleasant topic of the joys of the simple
life—and Horace is careful to make the point that only the simplicity that is a matter of choice is truly pleasant; no one in his
right mind would want the simplicity that abject poverty enforces.
The satire no doubt is best remembered for Horace's version of
the old Aesopic fable of the city and the country mouse:

> Once upon a time, so the story goes, a country mouse re-
> ceived a city mouse in his modest hole (a pair of old friends,
> the two of them). The country mouse was rough and ready,
> strictly business, but when it came to hospitality, he was quite
> capable of letting his limited soul expand a bit. Why make a
> long story of it? He quite ungrudgingly drew on his store of
> chick-pea and oat; he brought in his mouth a shrivelled raisin
> and what was left of a piece of bacon, and served them: his
> guest, you see, had shown a very fastidious tooth and had
> scarcely touched the food, and the country mouse was eager to
> win him over by serving some fancy dishes. The master of the
> house himself stretched out on some new straw and ate weed-
> seeds, passing up the tastier parts of the feast.
>
> Finally the city mouse said to him, "My friend, why do
> you find it amusing to live here in hardship on a hogback hill
> in the woods? This is positively uncivilized! Don't you think

that people and cities would be more interesting than the wildwood? Take to the road, my friend! Believe me, it's the lot of all of us who live on earth to have mortal souls; great or small, not one of us can escape death. So, my boy, while you can, be happy; live where it's nice; live with this thought in mind: Life is short!"

His suggestions really hit the country mouse hard, and he jumped up, eager to leave. Off the two of them went on the trip they'd planned, anxious as they were to creep into the city as soon as it got dark.

Night had about reached the middle of its course in heaven when the two of them found themselves scurrying through a rich man's house. Everywhere was purple upholstery and furniture gleaming white with ivory overlay; there had been a big dinner the evening before, and dish after dish was left over, all of them piled in baskets stacked on one side of the room. The city mouse made a couch out of some purple cloth for his country friend, and then, like a good host, tucked up his gown and rushed back and forth with a continuous stream of edibles; he even performed his duties like an honest-to-goodness slave, for he took a preliminary lick at every dish he brought! The country mouse lay there having the time of his life: "What a change! This was the life!" And he was playing the part of the happy dinner-guest when a sudden crash of opening doors knocked the two of them off their couches. They were scared to death, and ran all over the dining-room, and they very nearly died of fright when the house began to echo to the barking of dogs. Whereupon the country mouse said, "I can get along without this kind of life. Goodbye and good luck! I like the security of my hole in the woods, where nobody is ambushing me. That and a bit of grass-seed will comfort me." (*Satires* 2.6.79–117).

At about the same time as the publication of the second book of satires, Horace's book of *Epodes* also appeared. This little collection of seventeen poems no doubt includes some of Horace's juvenilia; it contains in addition at least four that are quite frankly political (4, 7, 9, 16), the longest of which, 16, is a bitter protest against the civil war, and might well stand as Horace's treatment in extenso of a theme that recurs in his poetry again and again, and never without some bitter reflection on the folly, cruelty, and impiety of the war of brother against brother. Others (1, 11, 13), are poems of friendship, dealing with one or another aspect of Horace's relation to Maecenas and to others of his friends. *Epode* 15 is a kind of love song; *Epode* 14 combines the love theme with Horace's *recusatio*—that refusal, which Horace stood by throughout his literary career, to commit himself to the writing of heroic verse. But undoubtedly the queen of the collection is *Epode* 2:

"Happy is he who far from trade and toil,
    like mortal man in days gone by,
with his own oxen works his fathers' land,
    free of all bonds and debts;
whom brassy bugles never call to arms,
    who fears no angry seas;
he shuns the law-court and the haughty halls
    of greater power and wealth.
Yes, when his grapevine sprouts and grows full-length
    he weds it to tall poplar trees,
or in secluded valley hears his cows
    lowing, and watches where they stray.
With pruning-hook he snips the sterile branch,
    slipping in more fertile ones;
he strains the honey and stores it in clean jars;
    he shears the feeble sheep.
When autumn, on his farm, lifts up her head
    crowned with the beauty of ripe fruit,
how happy is he! He picks the grafted pear
    and grapes of royal purple—
a gift for you, Priapus, and for you,
    Silvanus, guard of boundaries.
At will he rests beneath an ancient oak
    or where the grass grows thick and fast;
waters meanwhile glide past their steep cutbanks,
    birds whistle in the woods,
springs trickling softly make a pleasant noise,
    a summons to easy slumber.
But when it's winter, and thunder fills the sky,
    foretelling the fall of snow and rain,
he and his hounds surround the battling boar
    and drive him into waiting nets.
Or else on polished rod he hangs a mesh,
    a trap for the greedy thrush;

for timorous hare and migrant stork he sets
    his snare and bags them with a smile.
Who doesn't forget the wails and woes of love
    amid such scenes as these?
But if a loyal wife should do her share
    with home and child and happiness
—a Sabine girl, say, or the sunburned wife
    of a son of nimble Apulia—
should pile the holy hearth with seasoned wood
    at the time when a tired man comes home,
and driving her cheerful flock within the fold
    should drain their swollen dugs,
and from its sweet jar pouring this year's wine
    set table with never a penny spent—
Lucrine oysters would not please me more,
    not sole or sturgeon more,
(if winter thundering over the Eastern wave
    has driven them to our sea);
bird of Africa and Ionic grouse
    would not descend into my gut
more gaily than olives gathered from the branch
    where they hang thickest on the tree,
or sorrel, lover of meadows; mallows, too,
    (so good for ailing flesh)
or lamb killed on the Feast of Boundary Gods,
    or a goat grabbed from the wolf.
At such a board, what joy to watch the sheep
    come hurrying home from pasture,
to see the tired oxen, heads hung low,
    come dragging the upturned plow,
and a ring of slave-boys, brood of a wealthy house,
    sitting around my smiling Lares!"
These were the words of banker Alfius,
    a farmer tomorrow, for sure!
He called in all his loans two weeks ago,
    and now he's looking for borrowers.

This poem has been justly famous for its bucolic charm and grace and for the quite convincing way in which it sings the praises of the simple country life. And yet for all that the poem is satirical; with his sudden introduction, at the very midpoint of the

poem, of the woes and miseries of love—a topic for which no prepa-
ration has been made by the poet—Horace warns the reader to
expect something other than the usual ending of a poem in praise
of the farmer's life; from here on, the reader reads Horace's lines
with something of a puzzle in his mind. The puzzle is of course
resolved, but only with the very last word of the poem, for until
that word, we really do not know quite what to expect of Horace's
"banker Alfius." With something of a start, we learn that the
thing Alfius is looking for, once he has called in all his loans, is
not, as we might have expected, a farm suitable to his purposes,
but rather—a borrower! Now we know what Alfius's trouble was:
some girl had jilted him, and in his heartbreak and misery, he has
threatened to sell out his business and retire to the peace of the
countryside, with a peasant-woman to keep his house for him. But
in the end he can't make it; girl or no girl, misery or no misery,
he is back at his counting house again. The unique feature of this
epode is its successful combination of the contemplative and the
satirical; Horace's lines on country life are quite enough to make
us love the idea of life on a farm, and we are not disillusioned
when Alfius in the end says that he didn't mean it; our reaction is
instead to think what a fool Alfius is.

Horace's *Satires* have their charm and grace and, in ages when
restraint and decorum had more open claim on men's thoughts,
held an important place, both as literary and as moral documents.
The *Epodes*, for all their liveliness and picturesquesness, have never
held a position of prominence in the Horatian tradition; they were
minor works to begin with, minor works they have remained. Even
the English schoolboy, who for centuries was brought up on a diet
of Horace, was unlikely to have much acquaintance with the
*Epodes* beyond *Epode* 2. Any realistic appraisal of Horace's position in Western European literature must show his claim to distinction firmly based on the *Odes*; these were and always have been
his masterwork.

But while verse-essays, like the *Satires,* lend themselves readily
enough to translation into English, and while the *Epodes* are too
unsubstantial to suffer greatly in the process, the *Odes* remain
totally untranslatable: to those who cannot read them in Latin
they must be a book forever closed. What Cicero is to prose, Horace
is to poetry, both of them so intensely Latin that no modern idiom
can even with mere adequacy capture what they have to say. The
reason in both cases is that the "what" is so intimate a function

of the "how": with Cicero, it is intricate balance and counter-
point, the precise and weighty flow of the periodic sentence; the
greatest master of the periodic style in English, John Milton (e.g.
in the *Areopagitica*), could at best approximate the Ciceronian
manner, and it has been many a year since anybody cared or dared
try to imitate him.

As for the Horatian ode, its excellence is so immediate and
intimate a function of its structure, and that structure in turn is so
intimately and immediately dependent upon the nature of the
Latin language that, short of the appearance of a poetic genius so
great that he had better be employed on something more reward-
ing than translation, we will never see an English Horace that is
anything more than remotely Horatian. Because the *Odes* are
eternally fascinating to poets (for if there was ever a poet's poet,
Horace is he) many English versions have been produced, but
even the most charitable judgment will give them nothing more
than the barest passing mark. Critics of Horace generally are
agreed that the two best translations of the *Odes* are Milton's *Odes*
1.5, and A. E. Housman's *Odes* 4.7:

> What slender youth, bedewed with liquid odours,
> Courts thee on roses in some pleasant cave,
>     Pyrrha? For whom bind'st thou
>     In wreaths thy golden hair,
> Plain in thy neatness? Oh, how oft shall he
> On faith and changed gods complain, and seas
>     Rough with black winds and storms
>     Unwonted shall admire,
> Who now enjoys thee credulous, all gold;
> Who always vacant, always amiable,
>     Hopes thee, of flattering gales
>     Unmindful! Hapless they
> To whom thou untried seem'st fair! Me, in my vowed
> Picture, the sacred wall declares to have hung
>     My dank and dripping weeds
>     To the stern God of Sea.
>
>                                         John Milton

> The snows are fled away, leaves on the shaws
>     And grasses in the mead renew their birth,
> The river to the river-bed withdraws,
>     And altered is the fashion of the earth.

The Nymphs and Graces three put off their fear
    And unapparelled in the woodland play.
The swift hour and the brief prime of the year
    Say to the soul, *Thou wast not born for aye.*

Thaw follows frost; hard on the heel of spring
    Treads summer sure to die, for hard on hers
Comes autumn, with his apples scattering;
    Then back to wintertide, when nothing stirs.

But oh, whate'er the sky-led seasons mar,
    Moon upon moon rebuilds it with her beams:
Come *we* where Tullus and where Ancus are,
    And good Aeneas, we are dust and dreams.

Torquatus, if the gods in heaven shall add
    The morrow to the day, what tongue has told?
Feast then thy heart, for what thy heart has had
    The fingers of no heir will ever hold.

When thou descendest once the shades among,
    The stern assize and equal judgement o'er,
Not thy long lineage nor thy golden tongue,
    No, nor thy righteousness, shall friend thee more.

Night holds Hippolytus the pure of stain,
    Diana steads him nothing; he must stay,
And Theseus leaves Pirithöus in the chain
    The love of comrades cannot take away.
        A. E. Housman, *Diffugere Nives*
        (*Collected Poems,* pp. 163–64)

The former is a triumph of precision, but its excellence is apparent only to those who know the Latin original, as of course Milton assumed his readers would; the latter, although about as good a job as has ever been done in the modern idiom, betrays a Shropshire melancholy and a British mistiness that in the end are foreign to Horace's Roman forthrightness and Italian clarity.

What then is this "how" that is so essential to the understanding of the Horatian ode and so much bound up with the language in which he writes? As everyone who has had even the slightest acquaintance with Latin knows, it is an inflected language; its syntactical patterns, its grammatical structure, are signalled and revealed by the endings of the words: we know which words belong together, which words pattern with which others, what is the subject, the object, what is the predicate in a given sentence, because of the endings the words display. For the speaker of Latin as well as for the poet, this means that he is free of limitations imposed by laws of word order; syntactical patterns—his "grammar"—do not depend on his uttering or writing his words in a particular order; within certain limits, he may put his words in any order he likes, and still come out with a comprehensible utterance.

In English this is difficult if not impossible, for in English, syntax, grammar, "sense" of utterance are determined by word order; in the sentence, "John hit William" it is the order in which the words appear that tells us who hit whom, and if we vary that order we are in danger of reducing our utterance to nonsense, or of making it say the opposite of what we intended (except in the presence of a carefully constructed context, "William hit John" cannot mean the same as "John hit William"). It would be hard to name a single poet other than E. E. Cummings who has ever succeeded in using extensive word order variations as a poetic device in English, and he has succeeded only because he was willing, with enormous patience, to build up the needed contexts, and with equal patience to devise visual patterns (i.e. the arrangements of words on a page) and a system of punctuation that reveal syntax and sense in spite of unorthodox word order.

It is on this innate ability of the Latin language to vary its word order without losing syntax or sense that Horace's excellence as a lyric poet in large measure depends. He was not the first poet to take advantage of this characteristic phenomenon; the varying of word order patterns is so natural to the speaker and writer of Latin that its use as a stylistic and artistic device was apparent from the beginning, and there is no author now extant, not even the earliest, most primitive, and most naive, who does not display a conscious manipulation and variation in word order patterns to this end. In Catullus in particular it is everywhere obvious, and in his more elaborate poems, e.g. the *Peleus and Thetis* (64), the device is employed in ways that directly foreshadow Horace's work.

With the prefatory warning that English is not Latin and in its connotations reflects a culture very different from that of the Augustan Age in Rome, a passage or two from some of Cummings's lyrics may serve at least to show the shape and perhaps in some degree the artistic and poetic effect of word order patterns de-

liberately devised for special stylistic effects. To take a very simple
example, Cummings opens one of his spring poems with the line:

"Spring is like a perhaps hand"

On first reading, this line sounds like a strange perversion of English; the adverb "perhaps" would, as we say, "normally" appear
either before "spring" or between "is" and "like," or after "hand";
Cummings, by putting the word in an unorthodox position, has
created a number of interesting thought and word patterns. The
fact that the word "perhaps" could appear in any one of three
orthodox positions in this simple statement illustrates that it is at
once an important and versatile word. It suggests immediately that
the poet does not know for sure to what he should compare spring;
it is as if he had thought over a number of possibilities, none of
which quite satisfied him, and finally had come up with the figure
of a hand as at least worth considering. By placing the word "perhaps" where he does, Cummings compels the reader to stop short
and to experience with the poet his own feelings of wonderment
and indecision about the likeness of spring.

Thus by the use of a displaced word, Cummings brings the
reader immediately into the poem with him, makes him, as it
were, stand alongside the poet and think with him. From the
point of view of structure, the word "perhaps" divides the first
part of the sentence "Spring is like a" from its last part "hand"
and thus creates a three-part or quasi-triangular arrangement: the
first part of the line forms, so to speak, the rising side of the triangle, of which the word "perhaps" is the apex, and the last part
of the sentence forming its descending side. It should be noted
furthermore that in the last analysis Cummings's line is not at all
distorted English; the line accurately represents the way people
speak, starting a definition, stopping to wonder in just what
terms to phrase it, and then using the word "perhaps" to suggest
a possible definitive term. The poem continues by telling us in
what respect spring is like a "hand," drawing for us a picture of
spring's eternal creativity, its gentleness and orderliness, and of its
nondestructive character. The word order manipulation which we
see here presents, in concise and simple form, the principles that
are basic to Horace's poetry: the deliberate retardation of movement in order to compel the reader to think with the poet, and
the creation of antithesis and balance.

One final point should be added: in Cummings's poem, the

juxtaposition of "perhaps" and "hand" suggests that, in spite of the supposed English rule that adverbs cannot modify nouns, the two words do belong together; the word "perhaps," with its suggestion of tentativeness and experimentation, does suggest the character of the "hand" to which spring is being compared. Ambiguity of this kind is very nearly a constant in Latin, which commonly uses syntax to create a fundamental pattern of meaning, and superimposes on this a set of variations, or suggested meanings, that arise from the juxtaposition of words not syntactically bound together.

Devices of this sort are part of the internal structure of a poem and serve to place its individual bits in an interesting and aesthetically pleasing relation one to another; no less important for the understanding of the Horatian ode is its overall structure, its architecture. In this respect, Horace was richly imaginative; his odes display many different architectural patterns, and one ode may involve two or more of them, one superimposed upon another. One of the commonest of these takes the form of a triangle or pyramid, centered on a single mordant idea, or a particularly clearcut and suggestive image. One side of the ode leads up to this central thought and the other side, away from it; in a further refinement, beginning and end of the poem are tied together by a series of verbal correspondences, thus creating, one might say, the base of the pyramid.

As it happens, a poem by Emily Dickinson very neatly illustrates this architectural type:

> Of all the Souls that stand create—
> I have elected—One—
> When Sense from Spirit—files away—
> And Subterfuge—is done—
>
> When that which is—and that which was—
> Apart—intrinsic—stand—
> And this brief Drama in the flesh—
> Is shifted—like a Sand—
>
> When Figures show their royal Front—
> And Mists—are carved away,
> Behold the Atom—I preferred—
> To all the lists of Clay!

Emily's poem is centered on the beautifully graphic line "Is shifted like a sand"—and it was sheer genius that suggested "*a* sand," with its simultaneous suggestion of a wind-blown ridge of dry sand, and the equally wind-blown movement of a single grain of sand over such a ridge. Associated with the picture and immediately suggested by it, are the brevity and helplessness of human life, "this brief drama in the flesh," and the fact that life consists of two opposites, the real and the apparent, which for a time seem to be combined and to operate to their mutual concealment, but in the end are separated one from the other as a single ridge of sand might be blown into two ridges by the wind ("when that which is," etc.).

With passing note of the fact that the central point (the line "is shifted like a sand") stands at the mean rather than the midpoint of the pyramid, we may now go on to examine the outer structure of the poem. Balancing correspondences immediately appear: line 1, "Of all"; line 12, "To all"; line 2, "elected one"; line 11, "atom I preferred"; line 3, "files away"; line 10, "carved away." In each of these instances it will be noted that the pairs of expressions are balanced neatly and precisely, but not to the point of literalness; the second member of each pair shows a slight variation on the idea or image presented by the first.

When we come to the final pair, we see that balance is still preserved but in a way different from that of the other pairs: line 4, "subterfuge is done" balances with line 9, "figures show their . . . front"; both members of the pair express a truth, but while the first member expresses the idea negatively, the second member expresses it positively.

These four pairs of expressions thus form the two sides of the pyramid, the one ascending, the other descending. Of particular importance is that fact that of the four pairs the final one is not in the same form as the other three; by varying the last pair, Emily has prevented her poem from becoming mechanically balanced; she creates, as it were, a slight imbalance or inconcinnity in the structure of her poem, an element that clearly points up the difference between art and mechanics: the latter demands perfect balance; the former compromises with balance in order to create movement. The mind is not permitted to rest in smug assurance that it has seen all that the poet had to say; instead the reader is nudged into rereading the words and rethinking their relationships and meanings, again and again.

Perhaps a so-called literal translation of an ode of Horace will adumbrate the ways in which Horace uses structural devices of these kinds. *Odes* 3.23 is a Roman version of the Widow's Mite (*Mark* 12:42):

> Caelo supinas si tuleris manus,
> nascente luna, rustica Phidyle,
>     si ture placaris et horna
>       fruge Lares avidaque porca,
>
> nec pestilentem sentiet Africum
> fecunda vitis nec sterilem seges
>     robiginem aut dulces alumni
>       pomifero grave tempus anno.
>
> nam quae nivali pascitur Algido
> devota quercus inter et ilices
>     aut crescit Albanis in herbis
>       victima pontificum securis
>
> cervice tinget: te nihil attinet
> temptare multa caede bidentium
>     parvos coronantem marino
>       rore deos fragilique myrto.
>
> immunis aram si tetigit manus
> non sumptuosa blandior hostia
>     mollivit aversos Penates
>       farre pio et saliente mica.

\*   \*   \*   \*   \*   \*   \*   \*   \*

> To heaven extended if you raise your hands
> at borning moon, farm-girl Phidyle,
>     if incense is your propitiation and the new
>       grain, for the Lars, and a greedy pig,
>
> no pest will harm, from Africa,
> your fertile vine, nor will a sterile crop
>     go rusty, or your darling lambs
>       in apple-time fall sick—*that* time of year.

For up on the snow-cap feeding—Mt. Algidus—
doomed, amid white oak and ilex,
   or fattening at Alba on the grass
     is a victim: the high-priests' axes

his throat will stain. You? It's no concern of yours
to vex with a flood of blood from sheep
   the little flower-crowned-with-rose-
     mary gods, and with crumbling myrtle.

Pure to the altar if you set your hand,
no wealth will add sweet influence to your gift:
   kindness comes to unhearing house-gods
     from a crust, with prayer, and leaping salt.

The first two and the last two strophes of this poem are concerned with the simple life and piety of the peasant-girl: her prayer, her flocks of sheep, her little household gods. Standing in strong contrast to this is the third strophe with its picture of fat, sleek animals grazing in mountain pastures. These are the perfect creatures, the "unblemished hecatombs," which alone are suitable for public sacrifice to the great gods. Standing as it does in strong contrast to strophes 1 and 2 on the one side and 4 and 5 on the other, the third strophe nonetheless links the others into a unified poem, the subject of which is piety. Moreover its position in the center of the poem indicates that the structure of the poem is pyramidal: a set of pictures rise toward the central image on the one side and another set decline from it on the other side. Of special interest is the way in which the poet avoids allowing his central figure to occupy the mathematical midpoint of the poem; in a poem of five strophes, clearly strophe 3 is the arithmetical middle. But the image of the midpoint is not confined to the third strophe, but runs over into the fourth, occupying one half of the first line of the fourth strophe, and showing once again the slightly skewed structure which obviates mechanical balance.

In overall structure, Horace's ode is precisely parallel to Emily Dickinson's poem; both center on a strong and striking central image, both show a clear but slightly skewed pyramidal shape. However, the resemblance goes much farther, for in Horace's poem as in Emily's, there are a series of matched pairs on the two sides of the pyramid. In Emily's poem, these pairs were most easily seen by beginning with the outermost pair first; in Horace's ode, we had best begin with the innermost pair; the difference does not affect basic structure, but is far from being accidental. Emily's poem shows its strong points concentrated at beginning, center, and end; Horace's ode shows its strongest images clustered around the center and begins and ends with less colorful, or one might better say, "gentler," figures. The difference in the end is one of emphasis, not of fundamental architecture.

The pairs in Horace's ode are as follows: line 7, "darling lambs" (*dulces alumni*), line 14 "sheep" (*bidentes*); line 6, "crop" (*seges*), lines 15–16 "rosemary" (*marino rore*); line 6, "fertile vine" (*fecunda vitis*), line 16, "crumbling myrtle" (*fragilique myrto*); line 4, "greedy pig" (*avidaque porca*), line 18, "gift" (*hostia*); line 4, "the Lars" (*Lares*), line 19, "house-gods" (*Penates*); lines 3–4, "new grain" (*horna fruge*), line 20, "a crust, with prayer" (*farre pio*); line 2, "borning moon" (*nascente luna*), line 20, "leaping salt" (*saliente mica*).

All these pairs are concentric; that is to say, if circles were drawn through them with the third strophe as the center, none of the circles would intersect. However, the pairs are not perfectly matched; that is to say, element A is not balanced by a second element A but by something like it or closely related to it; one might say that *A* is not balanced by another *A*, but by *a* or by Greek *alpha*. "Darling lambs" pairs neatly with "sheep," although in Latin the pair is a little less precise; "crop" pairs with "rosemary" chiefly in that they are both plants and in each instance are single words (strictly speaking, *ros marinus* is two Latin words, but they are to be taken together as the name of a plant; in the English version the adjective, "sterile," is forced into association with the noun "crop" by metrical necessity; in the Latin, the adjective modifies another word). "Fertile vine" pairs with "crumbling myrtle": both are plants; each member of the pair is expressed by two words; "greedy pig" is balanced with "gift"; the balance is more precise if we recall that the Latin word for "gift" in this instance is *hostia*, which means specifically a gift, sacrifice, or "victim" offered to a god. "New grain" pairs with "a crust with prayer"; again the pairing is a little more obvious in the Latin, in which each member consists of a noun plus an adjective; the final pair, "borning moon" and "leaping salt" are paired only in that the modifier of the noun in each instance is a present active participle; the pairing is thus formal, or, one might say, phonetico-grammatical in nature.

Even within these carefully balanced pairs, then, there is a degree of variation, of an inconcinnity that prevents the pairs from being too precisely balanced. But this is not the end of the story; there remain two pairs, each of which cuts across the concentric pairs already described. Least precise of the two is the pair, "pro-pitiation" (*placaris*, line 3), and "kindness comes" (*mollivit*, line 19); both verbs express the placating of the gods which is the main aim of the ancient pagan worshiper, but different verbs are used in each instance, and the verbs appear each in a different personal form (the exigencies of translation make this less than apparent in the English version; more literally, *placaris* means "you propitiate," and *mollivit*, "has made gentle," or "has softened up").

More striking and more clearly illustrative of the principle involved is the second pair, "hands," line 1, and "hand," line 17. Once again, the demands of translation tend to obscure the neat and delicate way in which Horace has skewed this pair: *manus*, line 1, has a long *u* and is the accusative case, object of *tuleris*; *manus*, line 17, is the nominative case, subject of *tetigit*. The words appear each in the same position in their lines and are visually identical; pronunciation and syntactical patterns differentiate the two, one from the other. And finally, if we were to adopt the ex-pedient of drawing circles through the pairs, we would see that these two pairs each intersect one or more of the others, and, in-cidentally, each other.

Thus Horace's ode displays a pattern, both external and in-ternal, rather more complex than the one shown in Emily Dick-inson's poem, but of precisely the same type. It displays the same sorts of balanced but not quite identical pairs, each member ar-ranged on its respective side of a pyramidal structure. Both this structure and the sets of pairs are so constituted as to avoid mere mechanical, precise balance; the effect is of firmness and grace, rhythm and movement. It is this artistic aim rather than any lack of imagination on the part of the poet that accounts for the rela-tively limited subject matter of Horace's odes—or perhaps one had better say, accounts for the repeated appearance in them of the old and hackneyed theme of the Golden Mean and its various corol-laries and derivatives. Like the mathematicians' constant, it pro-vides a firm ideological base upon which a very nearly infinite number of structures can be erected.

Much the same may be said for other salient aspects of Hor-ace's *Odes*. Seafaring, army life, the farmer, the athlete: these are levied upon again and again for illustrative images. Nearly as frequent are wine, the banquet, and love—if one may so characterize the rather unexciting amorousness that is the chief content of Horace's erotic poetry. In nature, it is her cultivated forms that most appeal to him: oak, olive, pine, poplar, and ivy, all of them placed in relatively tame and domesticated settings, afford the forms of natural growth he likes best; aside from the ocean, which he generally views as a fierce and unfriendly element, the cool, sparkling hillside brook and the bright clear mountain water of the irrigation ditch, provide him richly with images; except for the generic term "flowers" the bright and many-colored blossoms with which Italy is blessed make almost no appearance in Horace's lines. In mythology, it is the standard Olympian deities in their Greco-Roman forms, plus an occasional local Italianate deity like Faunus, or the Lares and Penates, who provide him with the necessary illustrative materials; in history, apart from the Civil War, which hangs over so much of Horace's poetry like an oppressive cloud, the Trojan War is very nearly the only event to make much appearance; the Punic Wars, apart from one dramatic incident related in *Odes* 3.5, afford Horace chiefly the figure of "perfidious Hannibal"; here and there an old hero like Fabricius, Scipio, or Cato puts in brief and sometimes very effective appearance. Geographical locations, apart from those of the immediate Mediterranean Basin, are most commonly designated by the names of the peoples who inhabit them; here Horace ranges all around the outer edges of the world as he knew it, but although his list of names sometimes seems long and bewildering to the modern reader, it was almost certainly not so to Horace's contemporaries; he was not one to try to startle them by importing strange and bizarre names into his lines.

In fact one may take it as a fixed principle of Horace's lyric that the bizarre, the outlandish, the extreme, even the unconventional, are to be resolutely avoided. Horace's odes nowhere contain forced notes of any kind, whether of vocabulary, syntax, or structure; they are perfectly adapted and totally in harmony with the language in which they are written and the age and the culture from which they sprang. It remains a matter for amazement that out of all these elements, on the face of it so conventional and decorous, not to say downright commonplace and dull, Horace has managed to construct such eternally fascinating poems.

To attempt any further description here of the individual odes would be wide of the mark. All afficionados of Horace have their favorite poems; on nearly every list appear *Odes* 1.1, the dedication to Maecenas, 1.3, the propempticon to Vergil, 1.5, the Pyrrha ode, 1.9, the Soracte ode, 1.22, the *integer vitae*, 1.35, the hymn to Fortuna, 1.37, the Cleopatra ode, 2.10, the expression par excellence of the Golden Mean, 2.14, the Postumus ode, 3.5, the Regulus ode, 3.13, the Fount of Bandusia, and 3.30, the *exegi monumentum* ode, which balances 1.1, the dedication to Maecenas. Book IV, perhaps unjustly, has been less read and less loved than the other three; certainly 4.7, the spring ode, is among Horace's best, and it would be hard to find a more touching tribute to friendship than 4.12. By any standard, these are all great poems, and their gracious and graceful movement, their infinite decorum, and above all their structure, both in gross and in fine, executed with such meticulous care and such unerring genius, have rightfully earned for Horace a preeminent place among the lyric poets of the Western world.

The twenty epistles of Book I, published in 20 B. C., are pretty much of a piece with the *Satires*. For all their epistolary form, they too are really essays in verse; the introduction of a specific addressee in each case serves primarily to give them direct impact on the reader, who is brought more immediately into the discussion than in the less personal *Satires*. The themes of the *Epistles* differ hardly at all from those of the *Satires*: the ever-present Golden Mean, here garbed in various new guises, but still basically the same, the advocacy of simplicity, goodwill, and decorum, the importance of friendship, the desirability of finding one's metier and staying with it: these are the not very original subjects of most of the *Epistles*. The writer of these verse-essays is wise and well seasoned, possessed of the calm and dignity that so naturally accompany success both as a person and as a writer; they are the work of a man who could say without affectation and without fear of contradiction:

> As men pass by they point me out:
> "Our poet, the lyric voice of Rome!"
> (*Odes* 4.3.22–23)

Again, as always with Horace, readers have their favorites among the *Epistles*. *Epistles* 1.6 perhaps sums up as well as does any single work of Horace's the principle of moderation that underlies so much of his thought. *Epistles* 1.7 is a warm document on friendship, in which Horace successfully and convincingly advocates that combination of affectionate unselfishness and independence of spirit which alone can bind men together for any length of time. *Epistles* 1.16 begins with a brief but charming description of

Horace's famous Sabine Farm, and goes on to advocate integrity and sincerity as among the most important guiding principles in life.

The second book of the *Epistles* makes hard reading. Each of its three verse-essays is over two hundred lines long—the third, in fact, runs to nearly five hundred lines—and the manner and subject matter suggest the retrospection of a man who has passed his prime and is content to look back on what he has already accomplished. Best known is the third, commonly called *The Art of Poetry* (*Ars poetica*). It is addressed to two young men, the brothers Piso, who apparently have come to Horace for advice in the writing of tragedy. Why Horace should be an authority in this particular literary genre does not immediately appear, and while the advice given to the two young men is sound enough, the essay seems a bit tired and shopworn. It also tends to be restrictive of originality in a way that Horace himself would never have tolerated in his youth; the insistence on the traditional "unities" of the drama, the laying down of canons to govern the manner of depiction of various traditional characters, the warning against flights of the imagination, whether in plot or diction—all of these are the symptoms of an art grown overripe and self-satisfied. There is a certain air of smugness about the whole essay, which, since Horace was above all else not smug, suggests at least to some critics that he never meant it to be taken too literally or seriously.

The quality of the fourth book of Horace's *Odes*, published in 13 B. C., varies greatly; some sound like the faded efforts of a poet grown too old for inspiration; others are among Horace's masterpieces. They are at best a somewhat miscellaneous collection, made chiefly at the insistence of Maecenas and Augustus, published perhaps quite unwillingly by the poet, and whatever their excellence, probably not to be classed with the first three books.

The one remaining work of Horace's, the *Carmen saeculare*, or *Secular Hymn*, published in 17 B. C., is more valuable as a historical and biographical monument than as poetry; Horace was doubtless honored by Augustus's request that he write the ode for this occasion; he struggled manfully with the historical, legal, political, and military data which perforce had to be included in it, and produced a passable lyric; it is no worse, certainly, than other such "command performances"; it requires no more than that its existence be recognized.

Horace, both in his life and in his poetry, may be said to link

Republic and Empire. In his youth a supporter of the assassins of Julius Caesar, in his mature years he became a warmly acquiescent, if not solidly enthusiastic supporter of Augustus and his new order. In his youth, a writer, if not a spectacularly successful one, of the stamp of Catullus and the other New Poets, in his maturity he developed a style of poetic artistry quite unlike that of his earlier efforts, and turned from *Ungebundenheit* and experimentation to the poetry of grace, dignity, and decorum. The change in both instances was quite consonant with the changes that were worked in Roman society and politics by the fall of the Republic and its replacement by Augustus's imperial system. By the time of Horace's death in 8 B. C., the undisciplined freedom of the Roman Republic had been replaced by the stability, dignity, and decorum, of a government and culture that were to bring several centuries of peace to the Western world.

# CHAPTER XII

# Vergil, *Eclogues* and *Georgics*

But for all Horace's brilliance, the distinction of being the one supremely great poet of Rome must be reserved for Vergil. The emperor Justinian, writing in the sixth century A. D., declares that when Romans speak of "the poet" and do not add a name, they always mean Vergil (*Institutes* 1.2), and if Vergil never quite attained the unique condition of universality that the Greeks attached to Homer, he remains nonetheless Rome's greatest poet and, in poetry at any rate, her most influential mind.

Publius Vergilius Maro was born in 70 B. C. in Andes, near Mantua in the Po Valley. His family were people of property and substance, although not of wealth or distinction; the young Vergil was sent to study at Verona, Milan, and, ultimately, at Rome. We do not know when he first began to write, but the technical skill of his first book, the *Eclogues*, published between the years 42 and 37 B. C., demonstrates clearly enough that they are the result of many many years of practice.* If Vergil was a poet like most of his kind—and there is no reason whatever for thinking that he was not—he undoubtedly began writing poems in childhood; the absence of any early works that can be with certainty attributed to him tells us only that he was a perfectionist, and for consciousness of their imperfections never permitted to be published the thousands of lines that he must have written before the year 42.

It was while Vergil was engaged on the writing of the *Eclogues* that his family property near Mantua was confiscated by Octavian,

---

*The few minor poems that appear in the Vergilian Appendix, and are, albeit with some hesitation, attributed to Vergil, tell us little but that their putative author was acquainted with the works of Catullus.

who after the battle of Philippi in 41 B. C. was obliged to find
farm land with which to pay the rewards that had been promised
to his veterans. Fortunately for Vergil, one of the officials charged
with the confiscations was Asinius Pollio, a close friend of Octavian's and a man of taste and discrimination in matters of literature. Through his intervention, Vergil's lands were returned to
him, but the poet seems not to have spent much time thereafter
in the north of Italy. He chose rather to live at Rome and at
Naples, where he had a villa.

At about the time of the negotiations for the return of his
property, he also made the acquaintance of Maecenas, the friend
and close confidant of Octavian, and an earnest patron of literature. He made Vergil his friend and protégé, and saw to it that
from that time on the poet was left undisturbed and in reasonable
comfort to continue the writing and endless polishing and per-
fecting of his poems. The ten *Eclogues* appear to have occupied
his attention for at least five years, the four *Georgics,* for seven
(37–30 B. C.). His masterwork, the *Aeneid,* had occupied him for
eleven years at the time of his death in 19 B. C.; he is said to have
judged the poem far from finished and to have preferred that it
not be published; in his will, in fact, he directed that the manuscript be destroyed. Fortunately, the emperor intervened to count-
ermand this provision of Vergil's will; the manuscript was saved
and turned over for editing to two of Vergil's friends, Varius and
Tucca, with the understanding that they were not to add anything
to the text, but only to remove repetitions, obvious errors, and
other unmistakable blemishes, before the manuscript was published. So far as we know, they carried out their work conscientiously.

Throughout his life, Vergil was a poet. So far as we can tell,
he had no other interest. He had friends, to be sure, among them
Octavian himself (later called Augustus), and Maecenas, and Horace, to say nothing of Varius and Tucca, Asinius Pollio, and doubtless many others. Vergil was not an unfriendly man, he was only,
like many poets, intelligent, sensitive, imaginative, and endlessly
industrious, qualities that often give the false impression of self-
absorption and shyness. He was warm enough to elicit from his
friend Horace a poem of farewell (propempticon) in which Horace
wishes him a safe trip to Greece and prays God to keep him safe,
since he is "the half of my own soul" (*animae dimidium meae,*
*Odes* 1.3.8).

With Vergil as with Horace, question has been raised concerning the nature of his relation to the emperor. It has been asserted that both poets were under considerable pressure from the emperor and his associates to write poetry in praise of the emperor's accomplishments and in support of his new order; both poets have been accused of putting up a show of resistance to this, but of succumbing in the end in spite of their anti-imperial leanings, and of becoming, in fact, scarcely more than propagandists for the new regime. We know that Horace in his youth was an enthusiastic supporter of the Republic, but that his admiration for the emperor and his policies grew steadily as he witnessed the pacification and stabilization of Italy after the civil wars, and saw a world brought from endless bloody quarreling and wrangling to order, law, justice, and peace under a government that, as far as the times allowed, must be judged humane and tolerant.

That Vergil's feelings might have developed much as did Horace's seems on the face of it reasonable and probable. He too had seen what Horace saw, had lived through the terror of the civil wars, had seen Italy brought to internal peace, and a bloody and eternally quarreling world brought under the firm but benevolent rule of Rome. He knew there was a price to pay; he had seen the price paid around his homeland in the Po Valley; he had no illusions about the degree of perfection, whether of intelligence, perspicacity, or morality, that he could expect in Augustus or Romans in general; he was acutely aware, as only a sensitive man could be, of the cruelty and suffering, both psychological and physical, that a growing empire perforce inflicts upon those who stand in its way, but his only requirement here is that Rome never forget her weaknesses and shortcomings, never succumb to the sin that the ancients called "hybris" and that we sometimes call self-righteousness.

With Vergil, in fact, we may see a certain tempering of his feelings about Augustus and the Empire; our first impression, in the *Eclogues* and the *Georgics,* is of an almost servile gratitude and fulsome adulation. (We are of course to understand that Vergil is using the formal laudatory style of his day, a style which we no longer accept or tolerate, but which in reality means nothing more than our simpler language would mean.) Adulation of this sort is totally absent from the *Aeneid*; here, the figure of Augustus is deeply shadowed by the figure of Aeneas himself, who represents not Augustus but Rome, and who, far from being shown as the perfect hero, commits moral lapses and errors of judgment that the emperor, if he were indeed to see himself figured in

Aeneas, would have found less than complimentary. Where the emperor does appear, as, for example, on Aeneas's shield in Book VIII, he is only one of a long company of illustrious Roman heroes, and is granted only the praise that goes with the language of apotheosis. Vergil loved and admired the Empire, he loved and admired Augustus, but he accepts both Empire and man as human creatures and therefore of necessity imperfect.*

Vergil's earliest works, the *Eclogues* or *Bucolics* (42–37 B. C.) can have little appeal to the modern reader. They are couched in the idiom of the pastoral, set in a kind of half-real, half-make-believe world, inhabited by poetic shepherds, playful and complaisant shepherdesses and soft, fleecy sheep, all of them placed in a landscape dominated by groves, grottoes, tinkling streams, blue skies, and benevolent sunshine. The prevailing motif of the pastoral is the contest in song, in which one shepherd pits his singing ability against another's, while a third individual sits in judgment, and determines which of the two has sung the better song.

The pastoral goes back at least to Theocritus (c. 310–250 B. C.); Vergil's dependence on Theocritus includes names of characters, general style and manner, and in some instances (e.g. *Eclogue* 8), adaptations so literal as to be close to translation. The *First Eclogue* is often viewed as a thank-offering to Augustus for his restoration of Vergil's lands; if it is indeed such, it is couched in such highly symbolic and abstract language that the compliment must have gone nearly unnoticed. The *Sixth Eclogue* contains a beautiful tribute to the poet Lucretius in the form of a quick summary of Epicurean physical theory placed in the mouth of the country god Silenus; *Eclogue* 10 is a tribute to Vergil's old friend and patron, the poet Cornelius Gallus. The *Second Eclogue* is frankly homosexual, and is probably the source of a good deal of foolishness that has been spoken about Vergil's sexual habits. Byron, in *Don Juan*, tells how English schoolboys were required to read Vergil's *Eclogues*:

> But Virgil's songs are pure except that horrid one
> Beginning with *Formosum pastor Corydon* (*Don Juan*, 1.45)

To any dispassionate reader, the homosexuality of the poem makes it neither more nor less interesting than the others; it is just another pastoral.

*See footnote, p. 146.

Unique in the group is certainly *Eclogue* 4. Here, for once, are no shepherds and shepherdesses, no contest in song, not even the usual soft, pretty-pretty scenery, but instead a strange and highly dramatic poem, couched in language and filled with symbols, the like of which are not to be found in any other piece of literature from Greco-Roman antiquity. The poem can be dated by its reference to the consulship of Asinius Pollio in 40 B. C.; this was also the year in which Mark Antony and Octavian temporarily settled their disputes by the Treaty of Brundisium. This treaty, which doubtless many Romans hoped would mean the end of civil strife, may perhaps account for the solemnly optimistic tone of the *Eclogue*.

In this poem, writing in astrological terms, Vergil speaks of the return of the Great Year, the year, that is, in which the constellations would have the same positions and dispositions they had at the time of Creation; this astronomical event was to indicate the end of the Age of Iron and the beginning of a new cycle of ages, starting with a new Golden Age. The advent of the new age, says Vergil, is to be signalized by the reestablishment of Saturn as King of the Gods, by the "return of the Virgin," and by the descent of a "new race of men from heaven." A boy, too, is to be born, and his birth will mark the end of the Age of Iron and the beginning of the new Age of Gold. The first step in this event would be taken during the consulship of Pollio, under whose leadership fear, terror, and sin will be banished from the earth. The boy himself will be granted the life of a god; in the company of the other deities he will pacify the world and govern it "with the goodness of his fathers." Nature will rejoice at his birth; strife will disappear; Nature will spontaneously produce milk, flowers, and perfumes for the delectation of man; the lamb will lie down with the lion, the serpent and the poison herb will die. As soon as the boy shall have reached adolescence (Vergil seems in a curious way here to refer to his schooling, his learning of the glorious deeds of heroes and the accomplishments of his father), the fields will spontaneously grow golden with grain, the bramble will bear the grape, and the oak will sweat honey-dew.

Even after this, "some traces of man's earlier wickedness will still survive," there will be other Argos, another Troy, another Achilles. But when the boy has reached full maturity, all such infamous and artificial activity will come to an end; the perfect state of perfect nature will return; every vestige of artificiality and deceit will be gone. It will not even be necessary to make wool "lie," for the sheep in the pasture will show fleece now of purple, now of yellow, now of vermilion:

> O enter upon your great office (the hour will soon be at hand), dear child of gods, great blessing of Jupiter! See how the weight of a universe trembles and bows, the earth, the stretches of the sea, and the depth of heaven! See how all things rejoice in the age that is to come! O let my life be long and let my last years see that day, and grant me a heart great enough to tell of the things you shall do: then not even Orpheus of Thrace will surpass me in song, nor Linus, though the one have his mother, the other, his father at his side—for Orpheus, Calliopea, for Linus, the handsome Apollo. Even if Pan should vie with me, and Arcadia be our judge, yes, even Pan—and Arcadia be our judge!—would confess himself defeated. Smile, tiny boy, and show that you know your mother (your mother has borne the misery of ten long months). Smile, tiny boy: they who do not smile at a mother, will never be deemed worthy by a god of his table, nor by a goddess, of her bed. (*Eclogue* 4.48–63)

It is patent that this poem contains many puzzles, virtually all of them still unsolved. Who was the boy? Who was the Virgin? Where did Vergil get the idea that the birth of a child would mark the coming of a new era? Many have assumed that by the "boy" Vergil meant a specific person; it has even been suggested that the poem was written in honor of the impending birth of the child of Scribonia and Octavian. (Unfortunately for this theory, the child in question turned out to be a girl.) Asinius Gallus, the son of Asinius Pollio, later claimed that he was the "boy," since he was born in the year 40; if this was the case, Vergil's predictions for the child seem sadly misplaced, since Asinius Gallus never distinguished himself in any way.

The temptation is great, and the early Church succumbed to it, to see in this *Eclogue* a prediction of the birth of Christ—garbled, to be sure, as it was bound to be by a pagan, but nonetheless a prophecy, and worthy to be classed with those of the Hebrew prophets. This idea found some bolstering in the fact that the language of the *Eclogue* does seem on occasion to reflect the language of the *Book of Isaiah*, and it is tempting to think that Vergil might have read this portion of the Scriptures. He may have, but if he did, he is nearly unique among the Romans in having found Jewish thought of any other than very perfunctory interest. The early Church, charmed by the thought that even a pagan might have heard God's message, ventured to place Vergil among the saints, and his supposed tomb at Naples was venerated as a holy place. This tradition, too, is no doubt part of the reason that prompted Dante to take Vergil as his guide through Hell and Purgatory, even though he refuses him the place in Paradise that he grants to some of the great figures of the Old Testament.

In the end, the poem tells us only, in highly symbolic and allegorical language, that Vergil saw in the events of the year 40 real hope for the world, in particular hope for unity, peace, and goodwill among men; the poem also reflects his realization that no such hope was to be realized overnight, but that long years of inspired leadership and divine benevolence would be necessary before a cruel and bloody world could even begin to hope for a new order of things. In fact, the *Eclogue* says, in short and symbolic form, much what the *Aeneid* was later to say in more elaborate fashion. It is a poem of hope tempered by good sense, and by the realization of men's weaknesses; it is a prayer for peace. All attempts to make it any more than that, and particularly all attempts to tie it to particular events and individuals, have ended in nothing but distortion and special pleading. For the curious and perhaps misguided adulation of the early Church, we need only be thankful, for this may well have accounted for the care and devotion with which the texts of Vergil's poems were preserved.

About the *Eclogues* there hangs a certain air of confusion and indecisiveness; for all their artistry, they seem like the work of a man who has not yet made up his mind as to what he wants to do, what kind of poems he wants to write and what sorts of ideas he hopes to embody in them. The poems are lovely, but tentative, and they could never have been the final efforts of a fully developed poet.

This becomes immediately clear when we move on to the *Georgics*. With the ancients, the tradition of a literature of farming, including poetry on this subject, was an old one; the second oldest poet in the Greek tradition is Hesiod, the crusty old Boeotian who in the eighth century B. C. produced a poem called the *Works and Days*, which is in fact a poetic farmer's almanac. Rather less inspired than his predecessor Homer, Hesiod nonetheless wrote a poem that was justly famed for its accurate and often touching pictures of Boeotian peasant life; his poem became the model for all subsequent poetic efforts in this direction.

Before the time of Vergil, we hear little of poems on farming in Rome; two prose works exist, one Cato the Elder's practical guide to ancient farm management, the other a skillful but rather bookish study of the subject by Varro. Cicero, too, in part of his little essay on old age (15.51–59) writes of the joys of farming, with all the charm, grace, and sensitivity that only a literary man can command; to him and to his readers, agriculture remained a spectator sport, appreciated from the viewing stand but hardly to be engaged in hand to hand.

It is the triumph of Vergil not only to produce the first great literary treatment of agriculture in Rome, but even—at least in the opinion of some critics—to surpass his model, Hesiod himself. The *Georgics* are a remarkable combination of superb technical skill, deep and sensitive appreciation of the art of farming, and honest pictures of the farmer's work More than that, the tentativeness, the hesitation of the *Eclogues* is gone; in the *Georgics* we have the work of a poet who knew exactly what he wanted to do, and exactly how to go about it.

The first book of the *Georgics* deals with the raising of grain, the second, with the raising of vines and trees, the third with cattle and sheep, and the fourth with bees. The very order of the subjects themselves is interesting, proceeding as it does from those two staples of ancient life, bread and wine, on into the raising of cattle, sheep and goats, creatures which for the ancients—at least those of the ancients who did not come into too close contact with them— were lightly brushed with romantic feeling. Bees—the last in Vergil's series—have always fascinated man. Alone in the insect world, they are incontestably useful to him; they produce a substance of unusual gustatory delight, and incidentally the only form of sweetener that the ancient world knew; they are pretty little things; they do no one any harm unless they are disturbed, and then, with a thrust of their sting, they die romantically in defense of their integrity and their kind; they are patterns of industry, providence, thrift, political efficiency, and patriotism; they are even competent engineers, with an understanding of structural stress and of the strength of materials. No other living creatures, not even the birds, have so captured the imagination of men and so titillated their minds with dreams of the perfect society. Maurice Maeterlinck's *The Life of the Bee* is only a recent example of that same romantic delight to which Vergil himself succumbed.

In his *Georgics*, he leads us step by step from the sternly practical to the sweetly—and he would not have minded the pun—delightful, from dusty grainfields, beautiful enough in their way, to be sure, but primarily of interest for their usefulness, to the soft, gray willows, to river banks, and to the rose gardens of Paestum, from the grim reality of Caesar Augustus, a name to be spoken only in a circumambience of the highflown language of formal respect, to the perfect society of the bees, where there is only honesty, industry, and love, and where even the "king" (so Vergil styles the queen bee) is the creature—the very manufacture—of his subjects, who serves rather than rules, and that for only so long as the powers required of him exist in full vigor.

The *First Georgic* begins with an appeal to various deities, all of them in one way or another connected with farming, for help in the writing of this book of four poems; the list ends with Caesar, and there follow those lines so hard for the modern reader to stomach, in which the emperor is imagined as having his choice of the godhead he would assume and of the spot in the heavens that he would occupy:

> Or will you, a new constellation, join in the slow
> procession of the months, there where a gap stands
> wide between Virgo and Scorpio, who trails behind
> her? Yes, the fiery Scorpion himself is already
> drawing in his claws and leaving you more of heaven
> than you really need.
>        \*  \*  \*  \*  \*  \*  \*  \*  \*  \*
> Grant me a smooth course, and bless my bold emprise!
> Have pity with me on the farmers who know not how
> to tread the path! Grow used even now to being
> summoned in prayer!
> (*Georgics* 1.32–35, 40–42)

The eighteenth century in England understood this kind language and used it freely in dedications to sundry members of the British aristocracy, some of whom deserved such praise far less than did the emperor at Rome; we need understand nothing other than that the language represents a deference for which societies like our own have little use.

The poet then launches into his specific task, which is to explain to the farmer the "works and days" of his calling, so far as these have to do with the cultivation of grain. The poet continues with warnings of the pests that trouble the farmer: "that nuisance, the goose, the cranes of Strymon, chicory with its tough and bitter

leaves: these are all harmful. Shade, too, can cause damage"
(*Georgics* 1.119–21).

This leads the poet to a digression on the origin of labor, which
he ascribes to Jupiter, who, he says, "never wanted the road of
tillage to be an easy one, invented the artful turning of the soil,
sharpened the mind of man on the hone of care, and would not
let his kingdom grow lazy, sluggish, and fat" (*ibid.* 121–24). "In the
sweat of thy face shalt thou eat bread" (*Gen.* 3:19) seems to be
Vergil's theme, yet he goes on to show that this is not his picture
of the ideal life, but rather that state of idyllic natural peace and
abundance that preceded the reign of Jupiter, to whose singularly
unlovable and unloving heart Vergil ascribes all the thousand labors
of that most fundamental of crafts, the production of food. Man
faced these difficulties and overcame them by his resourcefulness
and hard work; *"labor omnia vincit"* ("Toil conquers all things")
the poet seems almost to crow, as if in pride at the triumph of
man's industry and ingenuity. But—and this is frequently forgotten
by those who proudly quote Vergil's words in support of the nobility of labor—the poet goes on to add his less than adulatory opinion
of hard work by attaching to the word *labor* the adjective *improbus,*
saying in effect, "Toil conquers all things, but it's degrading."

The *Second Georgic* deals in a rather discursive and casual way
with the cultivation of the vine, and of various types of trees, particularly the olive. Vergil speaks of different methods of propagating
these forms of plant life; the one that interests him most is grafting,
which the ancients found endlessly fascinating, perhaps because of
its apparent violation of the laws of plant growth. The poet also
considers the types of soil that are best suited to different grapevines
and trees; this part of the poem contains his only exhaustive discussion of the subject of soils (*Georgics* 2.177–258). Nearly lost in
the discussion are a number of interesting digressions in which the
poet reveals a romantic love for the land of Italy, for the scenes it
presents, and the life that it permits and encourages for its people.
To Vergil it is above all a kindly and productive land; it may lack
the wealth of the Orient, but it has never been burdened with the
monsters that, by tradition, infested the East:

> But its fields are heavy with grain, and Bacchus's "Dew of Mt.
> Massicus" keeps it filled; its lords are the olive and sleek herds.
> . . . Here spring lasts on and on, and summer in months not
> her own; twice a year flocks bear young; the tree twice offers its

fruits for our use. But here are no rabid tigers or the savage
seed of the lion, no aconite to trick the fools who pick it, no
scaly serpent to haste his huge loops across earth and gather
his great dragging length into a coil. Think, too, of all those
wonderful cities and the works of men's hands that have
clustered our towns atop steep cliffs; think of rivers that slip
by under walls many centuries old. . . . Hail, great mother of
man's bread, land of Saturn, great mother of men! For you I
enter on an art long practiced and praised, and dare to tap a
sacred spring: I sing my "Song of Ascra" through Roman
towns. (*ibid.* 143–76)

With this should doubtless be coupled the other major digression—digression only in the sense that it is tangentially germane to
the subject of vineyarding, but in reality containing within itself
the whole life and art of the farmer of Italy, the real object of the
poet's interest and affection:

O blessed beyond measure, farmers, if only they knew what
happiness is theirs! For them the earth itself, far from discord and war, in perfect kindness offers an effortless living
from her soil! Even if no lofty palazzo, with its arrogant doors,
vomits from every corner of the house an abortive mass of
morning visitors, and they do not stand stupidly gaping at
columns inlaid with pretty tortoise-shell, or at coverlets tricked
with gold, or at bronze of Ephyrë; even if clean wool is not
distempered with poisons of Assyria, and the honest, clear olive
is not corrupted by perfume, yet here men sleep secure; here is
a life that never heard of lies, a life rich in goodness of every
kind; here are broad fields and an hour of rest, here caverns
and living lakes, here cool valleys and the lowing of cattle, and
sweet sleep under a tree. Here are open fields and wild animal
trails; here, young men who are glad to work and live on a
little; here men pray to the gods, here men bow to the old;
when Justice went out of this world, it was here that she left
the last print of her foot (*ibid.* 458–74). . . . The farmer moves
earth this side and that with his curved plow; here is his
season's work; by this he upholds homeland, house, and home,
by this his herds of cows and his loyal oxen. The season knows
no rest: now it is abundant with fruit or with the young of the
flock or with sheaves of grain; produce flattens the furrows and
bursts the storehouse. Winter comes; olives of Sicyon are ground

in the mill, pigs come home fat with acorns, the forest gives
wild fruits. Autumn too bears all kinds of produce, and up on
the hill the fragrant vineyard ripens where the sun is warm on
the rocks; meanwhile, sweet children circle his neck for kisses,
a chaste home keeps guard on purity, cows drag milk-filled
udders, and on the lush grass, kids butt and lock horns in
battle. As master of the house, he celebrates holiday, and lying
on the grass in front of the altar-fire, while his friends fill the
wine-bowl to the brim, he gives you libation, Lernaeus, and
says his prayer; he sets up a target on an elm-tree for a javelin
contest between his shepherds; and farm-boys bare their iron-
hard muscles for the wrestling-match. This was the life the
Sabines led in days gone by, this, the life of Remus and his
brother; it was thus Etruria grew strong—yes, and Rome, that
greatest of all wonders, was built, and alone in the world,
surrounded herself with seven walled hills. Before the day, too,
when that king of Dicte earned his throne, and sacrilegious
man killed his oxen and made feast of them, Saturn the
Golden made a life like this in the world, in a day when men
had yet to hear the blast of the trumpet and the clang of the
sword laid on the heartless anvil. *(ibid.* 513–40)

It seems hard to believe that these wistful pictures of an Italy
rich and beautiful, yet still so far removed from the perfect peace
and fecundity of the Age of Saturn, should ever have been regarded
as propaganda to get the Roman proletariat "back to the land." Any
Italian who had ever attempted to till the none too fertile soil of
Italy—if indeed any such Italian would ever have been likely to lay
hand on a copy of Vergil's poems—might have been charmed, but
certainly would have been amused, by Vergil's picture of idyllic
farm-life; both he and the poet would have known better than to
take such writing literally and seriously. And if any proletarian,
innocent of the facts of agricultural life—again, if any such had
happened to lay hand on Vergil's poems—had been led by the loveliness of the *Georgics* to hurry out, hoe in hand, to the Sabine hills,
a season or two of backbreaking labor with grapes withering on the
vine, wheat ruined by rust, and oxen dead of the colic, would have
sent him back with even greater speed to the comfortable and
familiar byways of the Subura.

Vergil was not attempting, as Cato did, to write a practical
book on farming; rather, out of carefully selected materials, all true
in themselves and all germane to the art of agriculture, he was

attempting to create a beautiful work of art. Like a painter, Vergil opens a window on agriculture, and again like a painter, puts within that frame the truth that he sees there, arranging it with care so as to preserve harmony, balance, and unity. His theme is the beauty of the land, and it has its truth to tell; its aim is to show what is beautiful, graceful, gracious, and harmonious about the life of the land, even in his own less than perfect day; his picture was for instruction and delight, not for deception.

The first two books of the *Georgics* deal with the practical arts of grain-raising, vineyarding, and orcharding; at the same time they preserve an almost even devotion to the grace and beauty of the life of the land. With the third *Georgic*, method and tone change almost dramatically. The poet begins by promising, in terms that were surely intentionally imprecise, to write some day of the glories of Roman imperialism. Thereafter he launches immediately into the subject of the breeding of horses and cattle, including even a brief digression on the gadfly and his unfortunate effect upon animals, particularly when they were pregnant. On the whole, Vergil's treatment of the care and raising of animals seems rather general, almost as if he were not particularly attracted by this aspect of the farmer's life. In grainfield, vineyard, and orchard he had seemed to be at home; in pasture and stable he appears to be less so. In a way that is very nearly paradoxical, he turns almost with relief to an aspect of animal breeding that gives more scope to his talents: the description of an epizoötic plague which, he says, at one time caused great havoc in the Po Valley. He includes, in fact, the description of two separate diseases in his account; the first (440–77) is the scab, a form of mange that attacks sheep. The shepherd tried washing the animals, anointing them with *amurca*, that watery lees of olive oil which served the ancients for so many antiseptic and protective purposes. They tried a mixture of silver oxide and sulfur; they tried painting the lesions with pitch and wax, and with a mixture of squill and hellebore, but all these measures proved ineffective. The only cure was lancing of the lesions, and even this was none too salutary. In the end, says the poet, the shepherd folded his hands, "sat back, and prayed God for better luck next time" (455–56). The severity of the disease is well attested, says he, by fields and folds still deserted and empty.

The other disease was far more violent and attacked animals of every kind, both wild and domesticated. It was characterized by sudden onset of violent fever followed by insatiable thirst; the blood flowed thin and sluggish, and in the end the animals were afflicted by a deep cough, and by a sort of madness that drove them to run aimlessly about, tearing at their own flesh with their teeth, and vomiting bloody foam. So complete was the destruction wrought by the disease that even the hides and fleeces of the animals could not be salvaged; human beings who touched them were themselves afflicted with painful skin eruptions.

It is a relief to turn from the end of the *Third Georgic* to the beginning of the *Fourth,* from plague and disease to "honey, gift of heaven and air" and to "watching and wondering at that small society, with its brave leaders, its kinds and classes, its occupations, battles, peoples." We know at once that the society of the bees is going to be laid before us as an ideal that we might do well to contemplate, if not actually to emulate. To begin with, the work of the bees is with that loveliest of the creations of nature, flowers; their sweetness and perfume are transmuted by the bees into a product almost as sweet, and certainly more useful to man than the flowers themselves. It is no more than fitting that this most perfect of natural products should be the work of a perfect society. Jupiter himself made the bees as they are in return for their having fed him when he was an infant on Mt. Dicte:

> Alone of living creatures they have their children in common, share their homes; their whole lives are governed by law. Alone of living creatures they know but one homeland and one home. Mindful of winter that is to come, they carry out their labors in summer, and store away their gains for all to use. Some have sleepless concern for food, and by bond and pact work in the fields; others within the walls of the house take Tear of Narcissus and sticky drops from bark to lay a base for the comb; from this they suspend the tight-clinging wax. Still others instruct the Hope of the Hive, now they have reached adulthood; others pack in the clear-pure honey and fill the cells to bursting with bright nectar. There are those chosen by lot to guard the doors; they take turns watching for clouds and signs of rain; sometimes, too, they take over the burdens of those who are returning, or form ranks and drive the drones, that lazy breed, from the feeding chambers. It is a seethe of labor, and the honey is fragrant and sweet with thyme. . . . All rest together, all work together. In the morning they rush from the gates; there is never a moment's rest; and when evening warns them that it is time to leave their gathering in the fields, then only do they come home and care for their

creature needs. There is a buzzing and humming about the bounds and doorways. Later, when they have laid themselves in their chambers, there is silence on into the night; every tired body knows the sleep it has earned. . . . You will wonder, too, that bees are happy not to engage in sex; no lethargy of love exhausts their strength nor do they labor to bear their young; no, with their mouths they gather their babies from leaves and sweet herbs. They make their own king, and of themselves supply their baby citizens, and repair their waxen palaces and kingdoms. . . . Furthermore, not even Egypt and mighty Libya, not even the peoples of Parthia, or the Mede by Hydaspes, so revere their king. While the king lives, all are loyal to him; when he has died, they break their pledge, and tear apart the honeycomb they have made, and break up the fabric of the hive. He is custodian of their toil; him it is they revere. They pack themselves thick around him and surround him with loud buzzing. Often they raise him on their shoulders and offer their lives for him in war, seeking the wound that will mean a glorious death. (*Georgics* 4.153–218)

After various instructions on the handling and managing of the bees, the prevention and cure of their diseases, and so on, Vergil attacks the problem of creating a swarm where none existed, or when a swarm has been lost. He reverts here to a bit of mythology widely current in antiquity, to the effect that bees may be generated by the decaying body of a calf, provided that the proper preparations had been made. A chamber must be constructed with openings facing each of the four winds; a bullock is then to be killed, not by the usual process, but by smothering; the body is to be crushed without breaking the hide, then placed in the chamber and covered with fresh herbs. Ultimately, as the body decays, little legless creatures will appear in it, and these will presently be transformed into bees.

The source of this superstition is not far to seek. There is a certain resemblance between the larvae of bees and maggots; bees, moreover, for all their love of flowers, are also attracted by carrion, and nothing could have been more natural than that the ancient should have thought that the bees that gathered on the rotting corpse should be the adults of the worms found in its flesh.

As if Vergil were conscious that he had drawn no very lovely picture, he appends an account of how this practice was first discovered. A certain Aristaeus had lost his hives of bees; his mother, the water nymph Cyrene, instructed him to go and find the god, Proteus, who after attempting to escape him by changing from one form into another, would eventually revert to his original shape and could then be compelled to answer Aristaeus's questions.

Aristaeus does as he is instructed and is informed by Proteus that the reason for the loss of his bees is the anger of Orpheus, whose beloved Eurydice Aristaeus had attempted to seduce; in running away from him she had carelessly rushed through a field, where she had been bitten by a snake and had died. Aristaeus's mother puts the capstone on the tale by informing him that the nymphs with whom Eurydice had loved to dance had killed off Aristaeus's bees in sympathy for the girl and for her heartbroken lover. She then tells Aristaeus how to atone for his wrongdoing, and at the same time restore his swarm of bees; he is to select four splendid bulls and four heifers, to build four altars to the nymphs, and to slaughter his animals before these altars. Then he must throw their carcasses into a leafy grove. Nine days later he is to offer "poppy of Lethe" to the ghost of Orpheus, slaughter a black sheep, and return to the grove; there he will find that the sacrifice of his cattle has placated Eurydice and the nymphs. Everything of course happened exactly as Cyrene had predicted; on the ninth day the bees were there; they burst out from the decayed bodies of the cattle and obligingly swarmed on a neighboring tree, where we are to presume Aristaeus gathered them in.

There is a persistent tradition to the effect that the Aristaeus-Orpheus combination did not form the original ending to the *Fourth Georgic,* but that Vergil had written instead a long panegyric in honor of his friend, the poet Cornelius Gallus. After Gallus was disgraced and committed suicide, so the story goes, Vergil removed his panegyric and replaced it with the combination of stories we now find there. Whether or not this tradition reflects truth cannot now be told; on the face of it, it would seem rather difficult to have brought Gallus into a discourse on the raising of bees. Some have thought it might have come in by way of Vergil's bee-generating story, the locale of which was Egypt, where Gallus held the post of procurator. In any event, the neatly interwoven tales of Aristaeus and Orpheus do provide a graceful ending to Vergil's four poems on the art of the farmer.

# CHAPTER XIII

# Vergil, the *Aeneid*

The last eleven years of Vergil's life were spent on the composition of the *Aeneid*, and it is on this poem that his stature and fame as a poet rest. It is useless now to speculate on the meaning of the opening passage of the *Third Georgic*, in which Vergil seems to be expressing the hope that he may some day write an epic in praise of the accomplishments of Augustus: if we take Vergil's words literally, it would appear that he abandoned the plan, and turned instead to a mythological theme. There is in fact a persistent tradition to this effect, and a number of reasons have been suggested for his change of heart, among them, that the historical theme proved recalcitrant from a poetic point of view, and that the poet hesitated to write on contemporary events for fear of offending important and powerful men, perhaps even the emperor himself. On the other hand, if we view Vergil's words only as the expression of a hope that he might some day, in some way, prove equal to the task of putting the fact and ideal of empire into an epic poem of some sort, then we may say that the *Aeneid* represents no fundamental change of heart or of design, but only the final fruition of a poetic design.

For the *Aeneid* is a poem about empire. It tells us where, when, and how an empire came into being, what forces, cosmic, human, and purely personal went into the making of it, what helped and what hindered it, and finally, why it ever existed at all. The poem is not an apologia; it is an exposition. Vergil thought it hardly necessary to defend either Rome's position or his own. This does not mean that he thought of Rome as a perfect instrument; on the contrary, much in the *Aeneid* is best understood as showing how men falter when they try to carry out the divine will. Often they

188

fail even to understand it, and when they do understand, they blunder, sometimes nearly to the extent of defeating the very purpose to which they had devoted themselves. There is grandeur in Vergil's concept of empire, but there is no claim of perfection; there is greatness in Aeneas, but no suggestion that he is the perfect hero. If we find him hard to love and even to respect, sometimes pompous, sometimes stiff and bloodless, it is because he must be at once a fallible man and an infallible symbol, he must simultaneously be both himself, a man like other men, and Rome, an imperial ideal.

Inappropriate though they may be, comparisons between Vergil and Homer on the score of epic are virtually inevitable. One thing must be kept clearly in mind: Vergil did not want to be a latter-day Homer, the writer of a remodeled and redecorated *Iliad*—a sort of *Iliade à l'Italien*. If Homer looms large in the *Aeneid* it is chiefly because Vergil took the name of his hero, as well as sundry other Trojan and Greek names, from the *Iliad* and *Odyssey*, and a number of stories, similes, and stylistic devices from the older poet and put them in strategic places, where he knew his readers would enjoy finding them. These things catch our attention, and lead us to forget that the structure of the *Aeneid* is totally unhomeric, its purpose is unhomeric, and its poetry is of a different character from Homer's.

The difference between them lies in the nature of the basic plan and in the consequent differences in technique and manner of execution; the basic plan itself is different because the poet's task in each instance was different. Homer was composing a tale of adventure; his art rests on the demand to tell, in satisfying form, *what* happened at Troy. Vergil was writing a philosophic-religious poem about an idea and an ideal: his art depends on the need to tell, in satisfying form, *why* and *how* something happened in Italy. There may be hidden meanings in Homer's stories, and nobody minds if we take pleasure in looking for them; the point is that the instruction and delight that reside in the *Iliad* and *Odyssey* do not depend in any degree on our finding lessons in them. The *Iliad* and *Odyssey* are as good poems without lessons as they are with—perhaps even a little better. But the *Aeneid* without its lessons is only half a poem; if we do not with every episode see both a story and a symbol we shall gain little instruction or delight.

Viewed simply as a story, the *Aeneid* is relatively dull, not only because we know in advance how the major incidents will end, but also because the incidents themselves are largely conventional and contrived. If for example we compare the spying episode of Odys-

seus and Diomedes (*Iliad* 10) with the story of Nisus and Euryalus
(*Aeneid* 9), it is apparent which is more effective *as a story*. Homer's
tale is clear-cut, simple, and realistic; it contains surprise, suspense,
and even humor; we can read it again and again just for the story
it tells, and gain fresh instruction and delight with every reading.
Vergil's story, by contrast, seems over-lush with detail; it has enough
sheer stuff in it for a dozen stories.

The point is not that the *Aeneid* is inferior to the *Iliad* or
Vergil to Homer; it is that they, both poems and poets, are different. Vergil did not botch the story of Nisus and Euryalus; he wrote
it the way it had to be if it was to tell its *double* tale, of Aeneas
*and* of Rome. We are to think not of two friends, but of *what kind*
of friends, and particularly of the differences between them, not of
the volume of blood, and spilled wine—the sheer muck of slaughter
—but of what this might mean as a symbol of a people struggling for
world dominion. We are to read the death-episode with an eye to
the *kinds* of action and thought it involves, both on the Trojan and
on the Rutulan side. All these supra-literal considerations are
essential to the *Aeneid*; they are indispensable to the kind of poem
Vergil was writing.

The fact is that Vergil consciously and deliberately wrote on
two levels simultaneously and we are required to read his poem in
double-staff, like a piano score, from beginning to end. On the
literal, or narrative, level, we have the story of the fall of Troy and
the escape from its blazing ruins of a small company of men,
women, and children—today we would call them refugees. They are
led by Aeneas, son of the goddess Venus and member of a princely
Trojan house; under his direction and that of his old father,
Anchises, they build a fleet and set sail for "the West" in answer to
some imperative, again not too precisely defined, but clearly of
superhuman origin. Like any band of dispossessed and uprooted
people, they hurry pathetically first to one spot, then to another,
each time hoping to find the promised new home and each time
disappointed. After seven years of this, a freak storm blows them
to North Africa, to Carthage, where they are kindly received by the
local queen, Dido, herself a homeless refugee from the city of Tyre.
Some months pass; it begins to look as if Aeneas' people and
Dido's—Trojans and Tyrians—can work out a joint citizenship, a
sort of separate-but-equal arrangement in which both would co-
operate and neither dominate. This dream is blasted by new orders
from the gods: Aeneas must not rest until he has brought his people
to Italy, for only here will he find Hesperia, the "Westland" for

which he was ordered to search. Somewhat hastily and uncere-
moniously, the people and their chief slip away, and sail off to the
northwest. They stop at Sicily; here their old friend and ally,
Acestes, takes into his kingdom those of the Trojan company who
have had all they can stand of camp-life and shipboard. With the
rest, Aeneas sails on.

Once in Italy, he consults the Sibyl, the priestess of Apollo at
Cumae, and is told to go down to the underworld to get final orders
and directions from the ghost of his father, Anchises, who had died
before the company had arrived at Carthage. After appropriate
ceremonies, and under the leadership of the Sibyl herself, Aeneas
makes the terrifying journey to the realm of the dead; there, at
long and weary last, the whole story of his enforced pilgrimage is
revealed and explained to him; he is reassured of Heaven's love and
favor. The company set sail once more, to land at Tiber-mouth, and
there to find signs that they have at last reached the end of their
journey: this is The Place.

At first Aeneas is received with joy by Latinus, King of Latium:
he sees in Aeneas the "foreign husband" that an oracle has ordered
him to find for his daughter, Lavinia. In order to effect this union,
Latinus must dismiss Lavinia's already established fiancé, Turnus,
Prince of the Rutuli. There follows some strenuous palace intrigue,
with Latinus ranged against his wife, Amata, and her favorite,
Turnus, now understandably indignant. Aeneas maintains a dignified aloofness; of Lavinia's own feelings we hear not a word. A
trivial incident sets off armed conflict: Italian farmers, long accustomed to peace, dust off rusty armor and weapons, or seize
makeshifts—axes, knives, and even fire-hardened stakes. Latinus
retires in sullen dignity to his palace, leaving the command to
Turnus; Aeneas and his Trojans retreat to their newly built camp.
Here young Ascanius-Iulus, Aeneas's son, is left in command while
Aeneas himself slips up the Tiber to Pallanteum, the city of King
Evander, an exile from Arcadia, who has settled on the future site
of Rome itself. Aeneas enlists Evander's help against Turnus;
Evander gladly sends his son, Pallas, and a company of cavalry; he
also helps Aeneas to make an alliance with the neighboring Etrus-
cans, who have just driven out their cruel and tyrannical king,
Mezentius, only to see him given asylum by Turnus.

In the absence of Aeneas, Turnus attacks the Trojan camp and
nearly succeeds in capturing it. The timely return of Aeneas, with
his new-found allies, saves the day. From here on, the story is one
of battles, both mass and individual. Turnus and Aeneas are care-

fully kept from meeting, but each dispatch one after another of the enemy. They all, both Trojans and Italians, fight bravely, honorably, and skillfully; when slaughter unworthy of a gentleman must be performed—when, for example, the princess Camilla, half elfin-maid, half Amazon, must be killed—the task is assigned to some man of lesser breed, in Camilla's case to the coarse and brutal Arruns, an Etruscan of indeterminate rank and stature, and he himself does not long survive his ugly act. Camilla's death is the key to Aeneas' final victory: Turnus, counting on Aeneas' unfamiliarity with the terrain, has prepared to ambush him and a large task force of his men in a narrow defile through which they are planning to pass; he has Aeneas trapped and would most surely have defeated him, but at the crucial moment, word comes to Turnus of Camilla's death and of the rout of her cavalry: the bulk of the Trojan army was sweeping across the plain to Latium. Turnus has to leave his ambush and rush back to defend the city, and Aeneas passes through the defile in safety.

Now there is wild confusion in Latium. An angry debate arises between Drances, a sleazy character who wishes to appease Aeneas, and Turnus, who is determined to fight on; its outcome is the undertaking of Turnus to meet Aeneas in single combat. A truce is arranged, only to be violated by Tolumnius, a Latin, who shoots one of the Trojan soldiers. Again there is general conflict; in the end, Turnus and Aeneas meet. Turnus fights as bravely as any Hector, but the outcome has already been ordained. In a curious final scene, Aeneas is about to spare the wounded Turnus when he notices that Turnus is wearing the sword-belt he had taken from Pallas after the duel in which Pallas had been killed by the Rutulan prince. The sight infuriates Aeneas; he kills Turnus, and our story is at an end.

This is only the central thread of the narrative; subjoined to it are dozens of subsidiary incidents and characters, all arranged with an eye to their intrinsic interest and importance and to their appropriate places in the total scheme. There are, for instance, the gods; principally Venus and Juno. Above them sits Jupiter, acting as a kind of umpire and master of ceremonies: he knows the rules of the game and how it must be played; he knows the right time for each critical move, and sees that it is made when it should be and in the proper manner. There are others too—Neptune, Apollo, Minerva, Iris, Mercury, Vulcan, Mars, and the rest, but they are hardly more than runners of divine errands and patchers-up of unfortunate mistakes. Far beyond and above all these gods, even above

Jupiter himself, is a vast power, to whom, for want of anything better, Vergil gives the name of *Fatum,* "Fate." It is this transcendent power, Fate, that has commanded Aeneas' journey and ordained his mission; it is from this source that Rome's destiny to rule the world and impose the law of peace is to spring; this is the source of the divine imperative that Aeneas and Rome must obey. Only once does the power emerge from behind the anonymity of *Fatum,* and that is when his message is delivered to Aeneas through the ghost of Anchises; here he is the "Spirit" *(Spiritus),* the "Mind" *(Mens)* that gives being to all creation and orders its ways—the ways of all things and of all men, and in particular the ways of Aeneas and of Rome. The picture is fearful, hesitant, and sketchy, but as far as it goes it is theologically accurate. The gods—Jupiter, Venus, Juno, and the rest—are merely anthropomorphic embodiments of the ways, means, and purposes of divine power, insofar as these are observed by the human mind but beyond its comprehension. The gods of the Greco-Roman pantheon served Vergil as a kind of theological shortcut, saving him from interminable explanations of the immediate causes that propelled Aeneas now this way and now that. Without this "divine machinery," as it has so often been called, Vergil could never have got through his story.

All of this, including the gods and *Fatum,* is on the purely narrative level. But Vergil must not only tell what happened, but must tell it in such a way that we correctly grasp its symbolic as well as its narrative meaning. The seven years of wandering, for example, may be viewed as a symbol of the early struggles that attend the founding of an empire. They present the mistakes that arise from ignorance or half-knowledge, the false moves made in pursuit of political will-o-the-wisps, the frustrations occasioned by natural disaster, the reverses suffered through confrontation by superior force; and beneath all of this they tell of the indefatigable persistence, the sense of destiny that keeps a rising nation on its path in spite of every setback. They show us that even a manifest destiny does not present itself at once and in full; it comes to a people a little at a time, and only after long action and even longer thought does it finally emerge in clear-cut, unmistakable form.

If Aeneas' travels tire us, it is because Vergil meant them to; if his decisions sometimes seem foolish and ill-founded, it is because Vergil wanted them that way. For all of these things are part of the "why" and the "how" of the early growth of empire: empire grows because good men are determined that it shall, and in spite of mistakes, defeats, fears, disasters, and frustrations. When the symbolic import of Vergil's account of the seven years of wandering is placed beside the narrative account, we see that the latter had to be as it is. It is neither too long nor too short, neither too detailed nor too general. For Vergil's purposes it is exactly right.

The same analysis may be made of all the other episodes in the *Aeneid*; in every instance the result will be the same. The symbol, once discovered and read, will reveal the import, intent, and meaning of the poem, and will show why the narrative had to be as the poet has written it. Both on the narrative and the symbolic level, the poem is made to move from beginning to end through carefully selected and fitted aspects of a single proposition: *Tantae molis erat Romanam condere gentem,* "Such matter it was to found our Roman race." It begins with Aeneas and his company of refugees tired, discouraged, bewildered, their only certainties being further fighting and suffering. Symbolically, they are the Roman nation at the earliest beginning, facing enormous odds and uncertain of her course, sure only of opposition, of discouraging setbacks, and of their own determination to move on. At the end of the poem Aeneas and his Trojans have found Italy and know what the divine will wants of them; they are firmly based, but that is all. The vast bulk of the task still lies ahead: more weariness, discouragement, and bewilderment, more fighting and suffering. Symbolically, they are now the Roman Empire and nation, a people whose aspirations are firmly based on divine will, and whose first problems of organization have been settled—but again, that is all. The great task of "imposing the law of peace" on all men and for all time has just begun.

The *Aeneid* is a complex poem, as much more complex than Homer's *Iliad* or *Odyssey* as the world of the first century B. C. was more complex than Homer's, and as Roman society, Roman government and law, the Roman people themselves, with their attitudes and philosophies, were more sophisticated and more complex than their Greek counterparts. The Greek had a profound understanding of the importance of liberty, both of the individual and of the state; his philosophy and his world reflect his respect for man as a single, independent person. The Roman saw man more clearly in his collective existence, in his role as part of a smoothly functioning organization; if this meant the honing down of some of the rougher, craggier parts of man's individuality, the Roman was quite willing to accept this as a compromise for the common weal. Further than this, however, he did not choose to go; the Roman was no more fond of regimentation than the Greek, and, as his history shows, on occasion after occasion stoutly, and sometimes even violently, insisted on his right to respect as one man within the corporate organization.

Whether the Roman's familiarity with and affection for an orderly corporate existence led him to embrace the doctrine of the brotherhood of all mankind as a philosophical justification of attitudes he already possessed, or whether it was his innate feeling of brotherhood that led him to like and respect corporate existence, can scarcely now be determined. Certainly the Stoic idea that all men were brothers and equally part of the divine mind, struck him at once as congenial to his natural character and inclinations; he found himself liking a philosophy that claimed for all men the right to integrity of personality, but at the same time laid high value on his active, and above all orderly, participation in the difficult art of living together in a world that even then seemed crowded.

Out of these men, their complex world, their complex attitudes and philosophies, grew the concept of the Roman Empire, rooted in the idea that only through law and order—and specifically *corporate* law and order—could a world full of individuals be led to that mutual respect, if not affection, and to those necessary compromises in freedom both individual and corporate, by which alone peace, which is essential to the full development of a man and of men, could be achieved. We may, if we like, question the sincerity of this ideal; we may not question its reality, its practicality, and the fact that it did bring about several centuries of peace.

In the empire the Roman of course is to be leader, not to say commander; others must learn to yield to his superior sense of law and order and organization, for he has his job to do, and it was abundantly clear that no one else knew how to do it. He never expected to be regarded as infallible; in fact, he was intensely, not to say painfully aware of his mistakes, and enormously sensitive to the occasional acts of cruelty and injustice that he had perpetrated as he brought a recalcitrant world under what he deemed to be sensible control. He neither relished nor claimed the role of Messiah; he did claim that, for all his mistakes, he seemed to be blessed with an aptitude for rule and with the ability to bring men under one sheltering tent of government with a minimum of interference with individual differences and a maximum allowance of freedom.

In telling the story of this imperial ideal, the *Aeneid* necessarily adopted certain presuppositions. There were many of these, but two are particularly prominent and need to be kept constantly in mind for an understanding of Vergil's poem. The first is that since the poem is the story of an ideal, the world in which it is portrayed as taking place not only need not be, but probably should not be, a naturalistic world, for to set the ideal in the realm of the real creates problems which the practical statesman must face, but which only get in the way of the truth the poet wishes to tell. The world of the *Aeneid* is not a realistic world, and Vergil is careful to let us know this at that very beginning of the poem, for the storm in which the Trojans are involved as the story begins is unlike any storm ever seen by man; an examination of its meteorology will reveal a wild congeries of winds blowing from all four quarters of the compass at once. As if that were not enough, we must accept the picture of a Neptune thrusting his indignant head out of the waves, sending the misbehaving winds summarily to their petty king, and calming the seas by riding across them in his magical chariot.

Like the figure of Neptune himself, the winds are picturesque but unrealistic; they warn us not to expect real nature in Vergil's poem, and not to waste time in speculation as to the part nature is to play in the development of the Roman Empire. The warring winds and Neptune the peacemaker are important as symbols of the incomprehensible and violent resistance, and the irrational, frequently unexpected, and often unintentional assistance, that were to mold the course which the Trojans, that is to say, the Roman Empire, were to pursue.

As if to put a period to this unnatural nature, Vergil has Aeneas's battered fleet find refuge in a perfect harbor, the like of which no man has ever seen. Its delineaments are simple enough: a bay, across the mouth of which stretches an island, rendering the waters inside peaceful and quiet; so far, we do no violence to nature. But Vergil goes on to say that the waters in this natural harbor are so quiet that ships can be left to lie there without the need of anchor or mooring, a haven such as no mariner is ever likely to come across.

Strange, too, is the backdrop of this magical harbor: a mountain rises behind it, at its base a cave with springs of living water and natural seats, "the home of the Nymphs"; this does not stretch our imagination greatly, but Vergil moves on to tell us that the flora covering this mountain is upside down: at its base grow the dark conifers—pines and firs; up toward its top grow deciduous trees. Vergil knew perfectly well what he was doing. He was creating a natural world for his poem in which all the problems created by nature as such are irrelevant. It is the story that is important, not the background against which it is portrayed; the latter is brought to the fore by the poet only when he needs it for some mechanical or symbolic purpose. Because it is unrealistic, the poet may manipulate it as he will, to make it provide whatever natural setting he may need for any particular phase of the action of his poem. Vergil means that in the building of a world empire, nature is to be assumed; we know we must cope with it, we know its unpredictability and the troubles it may cause; we know that in the working out of the actualities of empire, nature is bound to play a significant and sometimes even a decisive part; in presenting the picture of the imperial ideal, we may simply disregard the realities of nature as taken for granted.

The second basic assumption Vergil requires us to make involves a moral polarity that is no more related to the realities of the world than was his Nature. Vergil knew as well as any man that morality is not simple, but involves extremely complex and intricately entangled questions of right and wrong; he knew too that, in the end, the principles of morality must be accepted as an act of faith; at the very best, man can hope that he is right in his moral judgments. This would have been clear enough to a Roman, and particularly to a Roman of Vergil's questing and sensitive mind, because his culture possessed no god-given sanctions for morality: the gods of the Greco-Roman pantheon, whatever else they may teach, do not give lessons in right and wrong; they lay down no Ten Commandments; they do not deign to explain God's moral law, if indeed they had any such to explain.

The ethnic morality of Rome was based on the *mos maiorum*, the "ways of our ancestors." The principle worked reasonably well as long as Rome was a small, close-knit society of farmers and soldiers, a relatively primitive social organization in which tabus were simply phrased, readily recognized, and easily enforced. But as Rome expanded in power and physical extent, as she reached out to become acquainted with other peoples and other ways of life, the old farmer-soldier morality lost its cogency.

Although the relatively poor and uneducated country people—the *pagani*—clung to the old morality for a long time, the same could not be said of the educated upper classes. As early as the mid-second century B. C. they had begun to see the parochial nature of the *mos maiorum*, and by the end of the first century B. C. had come to regard the old morality with nothing more than a tolerant smile. Into its place had stepped a plethora of moral systems, the chief of

them based on the ethical teachings of certain Hellenistic philosophers, but most of them resting on nothing more profound or more
altruistic than mildly enlightened self-interest. The two chief philosophical systems, the Stoic and the Epicurean, offered men no very
clear-cut answers to their moral questions; the Stoic ideal of the
"sage," who possessed only virtues and had no shadow of a vice,
presented to the Roman a moral perfection that was unattainable
and close to ridiculous. For the most part he adopted instead, as
guiding principles, the long list of "preferable activities" which the
Stoic philosophers had held as "harmless," and which, to the practi-
cal-minded Roman, seemed at least to offer some kind of guideline
to a decent and useful life. Thus, it was better to be kind than un-
kind, generous than selfish, public-spirited than self-centered, openhanded than miserly, etc. And it had always to be remembered that
"circumstances alter cases"; in effect, every action of a man had to
be judged and weighed on its own merits, in light of the general
circumstances in which it was performed—a tedious, time-consuming,
and in the end unsatisfactory way of distinguishing right from
wrong, partly because one could never be sure that he had got all
the pertinent circumstances firmly in mind, and partly because in
the end, no matter what he decided, he was only doing what was
"preferable" rather than what was truly good.

As for the Epicureans, they had come so close to establishing a
purely mechanistic system that their relatively stern morality comes
as something of a surprise; the personal integrity and purity of
individual Epicureans, to say nothing of their saintly founder himself, has always been cause for remark. The average Epicurean was
probably good simply because he found that it felt good to be good,
kind, generous, etc. etc.; to feel good was to experience pleasure,
and pleasure, according to the founder, was the single true guiding
principle of human behavior. The complex chains of reasoning by
which the Epicurean justified his moral position and the remarkable
twist of logic by which he proved the viability of free choice in an
otherwise mechanistic system, need not concern us here; to the
Roman the basic principle that "pleasure" was "good" was offensive;
it flew in the face of the *mos maiorum*, it seemed to be refuted by
countless actions of grand old Roman heroes who in the course of
performing uncontestably good acts had suffered and died, and
in the end it sounded entirely too much like an injunction to
self-indulgence.

This farrago of tradition, philosophical principle, and enlightened—or sometimes unenlightened—self-interest had left the
intelligent Roman of Vergil's day with little to stand on in the way

of sound and convincing moral principle. He could hardly have failed to be convinced that morality was relative, and that, in the realm of human conduct, absolute standards, or even consistently enforced rules, were neither defensible nor practical.

Certainly a sensitive and intelligent man like Vergil could not have failed to sense and appreciate the moral situation in which he found himself; he knew how hard, if not how impossible it would be to establish any man or men, any system or group of systems, as either infallibly right or infallibly wrong. Yet if he was to present the Roman Empire as an ideal form of government, he must show that it was not only useful, sensible, and practical, but morally right. No relative set of standards would do; either Rome was right in establishing her rule over the world, or she was wrong; either it was possible to find moral sanction for her imperialistic policy or else it must be dismissed as wicked and indefensible.

An ideal that was sometimes right and sometimes wrong, wavering between the moral and the immoral, would never do. Somehow, the poet must show that the ideal to be embodied in his poem was supported and sanctioned in such a way that its moral rightness was not open to question. It is only the ideal itself that must remain absolute; in the implementation of it there was ample room for errors of fact, of judgment, even for sheer blindness and stupidity; only deliberate evil intent need be excluded.

When we examine the moral structure of the *Aeneid,* we find that the poet left the bewildered moral stance of his generation behind; he did not deny its existence; he simply did not include it in his poem. He knew that, like the vagaries of nature, man's actual morality was a force that must be reckoned with in the practical working out of a world government, but he saw clearly enough that if he were to attempt to include in his poem the variable and various morality of his day, the *Aeneid* would become a shambles. "Realistic" morality had no more place in a poem like the *Aeneid* than "realistic" nature; as the poet assumes a manageable nature for his background, so he must contrive a morality that, however unrealistic it might be, would provide him with a firm moral base on which to construct his picture of a political ideal.

Nowhere in the accepted ethical systems of his day could Vergil find such a base; he elected therefore to move out into the realm of religious mysticism, in the hope that there he might find an absolute which would be understandable, or at least palatable, to his readers. The sources of his mystic view of the world need not concern us here; it is patent that he drew on Stoics, Pythagoreans, Platonists and in all probability on some of the mystic writings of the Near East, to all of which he added his own vision and imagination.

One thing is fairly clear: that Vergil was searching for an absolute imperative of some sort, the only kind of imperative upon which an absolute standard of morality could be erected; like a veritable Roman Moses, though with far less self-assurance than the old Hebrew prophet, he was looking for his own Mount Sinai, for some reasonable facsimile of the Tables of the Law. He never found it; he only groped uncertainly and unsteadily toward an absolute which was to him a moral and historical necessity, but which in the end remained beyond his ability to conceive or picture. The source of his categorical imperative Vergil never clearly understood; at best it remained a mystic Something, a power only partially definable in the standard terminology of philosophy, a power mystically sensed rather than precisely realized, but accepted by a process that came very close to religious faith. It is from this power that the rightness of the Roman Empire is derived; in the *Aeneid* itself, it is from this power that Aeneas gets his categorical imperative for the voyage to the "Westland," there to found the nation that will take as its mission the just and compassionate government of a world.

It is in this world of mystic power and absolute imperative that the story of the *Aeneid* moves, a world in which there is indeed a clear-cut difference between right and wrong: the "right" is that which moves in accord with the "power" and its "imperative"; the wrong is that which does not. To borrow a simple phrase from the old revival hymn, there are those who are "on the Lord's side" and those who are not. This is the ultimate test, and no other standard of rightness or wrongness is really operative at all; those "on the Lord's side" are frequently no better, in the ordinary sense of the word, than those on the other side. Both sides make mistakes; both sides are guilty of unethical conduct; both sides are guilty of blindness, foolishness, and cruelty. But throughout the *Aeneid* the distinction is clearly kept between those who are working out the divine imperative and those who are not; those who are, are right, and win; those who are not, are wrong, and lose. There are both lovable and hateful characters on both sides, for this is how people are. But Vergil's mystic Power looks always toward ultimate good, and to that end is willing to accept the efforts of imperfect men, and to bless them, whatever their defects.

In the simplified moral world of the *Aeneid*, the good always wins out in the end, in spite of all odds and obstacles. Here, "on the Lord's side," are the Trojans, and particularly Aeneas; they show that they are right by their love, loyalty, orderliness, decency, piety, and sheer physical power. It is in this sense that Aeneas is characterized by that troublesome Latin adjective, *pius*; he is not particularly "pious," but he is blessed with an inborn sense of what the right must be, and all his effort is directed toward its accomplishment. He fumbles and falters; he nearly succumbs to temptation, he commits outrageous blunders, he is even guilty of impulsive and unnecessary acts of bloodshed, but still he is driven indefatigably on toward the realization, in this world, of a supramundane imperative. To this imperative, no matter how many times he may deviate from it, he invariably returns.

By contrast, those who are not "on the Lord's side" are all those, whether divine or human, who oppose that imperative. They may be great and powerful figures, like the goddess Juno; they may be tragic figures, whose sufferings enlist our sympathy, like Dido; they may be good but tired old kings like Latinus, or fiery patriots like Turnus; they may range all the way from the elfin purity of Camilla to the pure evil of Allecto, from brave and proud Amata to brave but foolhardy Lausus—no matter, they are opposing the divine imperative, and are therefore in the wrong.

The first book of the *Aeneid* is largely occupied with the setting of this natural and moral scene. It is at once made clear that the poem will operate in a world in which nature appears only when her help is needed, and only in such form as will bring the story onward. The moral scene is set at once by the opposition between Juno and Venus, with the balance between them maintained by Jupiter, who, in Vergil's poem, is as flat and colorless as a mere umpire must be.*

On the human level, the moral polarity between those who are "on the Lord's side" and those who are not, is set by the opposing

---

*I have never been able to understand how it could have been imagined that Jupiter was the supreme power in the *Aeneid*. It is clear that he is somebody's mere appointee; he says only what he has been directed to say by the Scroll of Fate; he intervenes in the action only when things get out of hand and need to be set in proper balance once more; he decides nothing, least of all the outcome of the final battle between Turnus and Aeneas: this is settled for him by the scales on which he places the weights representing the two men; Aeneas's weight proves the heavier not because Jupiter has willed it so but because this is the moment at which the divine imperative requires that it be so. Of the three important deities in the *Aeneid*—Jupiter, Juno, and Venus—he is easily the least important and certainly the least interesting.

figures of Aeneas and Dido, he the brave and battered hero, she, the unhappy fugitive, victim of cruelty and deception. Aeneas had fought ten years to defend his native city; after all others had died or given up, he had continued the battle until Troy was literally nothing but a heap of ashes. He had then led the frightened remnant of his people through all kinds of miseries and trials, and in spite of everything, in spite of the fact that he knew there were yet more trials ahead, was still calm, dignified and undaunted. Dido, when widowed by her brother's murder of her husband, had sought not justice, but revenge; she had gathered about her the dissident and subversive of the population of Tyre, had stolen the state treasure, and with her crowd of followers had sailed to the shores of North Africa. There, by a piece of trickery, she had cheated the local ruler out of far more land than he had intended to give her; now, with her misbegotten wealth, she was building not a rugged city of refugees and pioneers, but a gorgeous metropolis with temples, parks, theaters, and public buildings.

The contrast between a courage coupled with endurance, magnanimity, and loyalty, as against courage coupled with deceit, pusillanimity, and a certain ostentatiousness, is not to be missed. Aeneas has his weaknesses, as shown, for example, by his self-pity during the storm. He is not perfect, but his goodness outshines his faults. Of Dido, the opposite is true. She has dignity; she has a compassion born of her own sufferings, she is generous and hospitable, but the moral base from which she operates is not a sound one: everywhere she has turned, everywhere the world has met her, it has been in a climate where something has been decidedly wrong; try though she may, she seems unable to do things right. Vergil does not ask us to love Aeneas; he most certainly does not ask us to hate Dido; he only asks us to observe the moral polarity which the two characters create. We know from now on that whoever is with Aeneas is right, and whoever is against him is wrong, not because he is Aeneas, not even because he is the symbol of Rome, but because the task that he is attempting to carry out is imposed on him by the divine will and the divine imperative.

This is the natural world, and this the moral climate in which the story of the *Aeneid* is to be read and understood; as far as absolute truth is concerned, Vergil makes no more case for the one than for the other; he asks only to be allowed to play out the story of the *Aeneid* against this setting. It is our eternal privilege, which he would be the first to recognize, to question the validity of both setting and story, but like any literary man, he hopes that we will read his story before we begin our questioning. In point of fact, he asks no more—and quantitatively far less—than Dante, with his Catholic Christianity, and Milton, with his Protestantism, were later to ask of their readers.

Out of this basic moral polarity grow a whole host of other lesser polarities, some of them, like the basic pair, mutually exclusive, but becoming less and less so and growing closer and closer together as the poem moves on to the expression of its true lesson, that is to say, the true reason for which the poem was written at all. Troy, for example, may not be accounted wrong, because Troy was the source and ancestor of Rome; at the same time, Troy is not Rome; it is instead a kind of Eastern despotism, well stocked with heroic figures like Hector and Priam and Aeneas, rich and powerful, so proof against the united power of the Greek world that it held out against Agamemnon's armies for ten years. Its weakness, the element that ultimately caused its fall, was its trust in human decency, its mercy and its generosity. The crocodile tears of Sinon found their way to the Trojan heart: blinded by their feelings of pity for this poor maltreated renegade, they were unable to see the absurdity of his assertion that the Greeks had set up the wooden horse on the plain in front of Troy in full awareness of the warning that if the horse were to be brought into the city it would spell defeat for the Greeks themselves.

In spite of heroism, too, the moral position of Troy was open to question; her conflict with the Greek world had begun with a violation of the laws of hospitality by Paris, when, as the guest of Menelaus, he abducted his wife Helen. The destruction of Troy, the burning of the city, the killing and enslavement of her population, were a tragedy, but a necessary one, for without the death of Troy, Rome could never have lived. Her death was a fearful price in greatness and goodness, summed up and symbolized in the slaughter of helpless old Priam by bloodthirsty Neoptolemus. Aeneas is the child of that death; purged of almost all of Troy's weaknesses, Aeneas is to found a city that will stand at the other end of the world from Troy; it will be "west" as Troy was "east," proud as she was proud, but strong where she was weak, ruled by law where she was ruled by kings, frugal where she was profligate; above all, where Troy was a single people, strong only in their solidarity, Rome was to be a nation hospitable to all sorts and conditions of men, united in their Latin speech and in their respect for the toga, garment that for the Roman symbolized his country almost as the flag does ours, a nation by its very polyglot character suited to rule a world.

As the story of the *Aeneid* proceeds, Aeneas breaks, one by one, the bonds that hold him to his former home. First to go is the bond of the soldier; as Aeneas lies asleep, unaware that the Greeks by the ruse of the wooden horse have already entered the city, the ghost of Hector appears to him, warns him that Troy is falling, and orders him to escape while there is yet time. The episode shows in unmistakable fashion how carefully and precisely Vergil has drawn up the symbolism of the *Aeneid*; in life, Hector was Aeneas's military superior, but now he is dead; his ghost, bloodied, and worn with grief, is the symbol of a military power that is now no more than a "ghost." His pitiful order to Aeneas to run for his life could only have been uttered by the ghost of the indefatigable warrior we know from the *Iliad*. Troy as a military power is dead; Aeneas, so to speak, has been released from his soldier's oath; he need not deem it necessary to fight on.

But Aeneas does not obey Hector's command; his personal safety—even the safety of Troy's "holy objects" which Hector has told him to take with him—are of less concern to him than his deep-seated loyalty to Troy; this commands him to fight on until there is nothing left with which and for which to fight. In disobeying the injunction of Hector's ghost Aeneas breaks the first bond that held him to Troy; the "chain of command," so to speak, between subordinate and commander-in-chief. Aeneas is no longer a soldier subject to discipline; he is his own man. Furthermore, he gives voice to a new kind of soldier's loyalty, tied not to a physical thing or to a discipline, but to an ideal: he fights on until loyalty itself has no further meaning.

Shortly thereafter occurs the second break between Aeneas and Troy; a city that had stood as a great power for centuries crumbles to ashes. Her streets are choked with the dead, filled with the screams of the dying and the survivors; there is nothing left but terror and death in a thousand forms. Until the last flicker of life dies out, Aeneas fights on, but in the end sees that he must leave. Carrying his old father Anchises on his shoulders, leading his son Ascanius-Iulus by the hand, and trailed by his faithful wife Creusa, he makes his way to a place of safety outside the city. Troy the city is gone; Aeneas no longer has any *place* to claim his loyalty. At the end of Book II, in a passage curiously reminiscent of the Psalmist, Vergil has his hero "lift up his eyes unto the hills" (*Aeneid* 2.804).

In the course of the destruction of the physical city, a further incident symbolizes the break that is taking place between Aeneas and Troy. This is the death of Priam himself. As Hector had symbolized the military might of Troy, Priam represents its civil side, its government and its law. In the person of Priam, an old and tired system of government reaches its termination; after him, there can be no more Oriental despots, however great, just, magnanimous, and surrounded by splendors. The figure of the poor old king, foolishly strapping on his armor and attempting feebly to defend himself against the young Neoptolemus, accurately depicts the demise, tragic but necessary, of an outmoded way of life and government.

Before we reach the end of Book II, two further examples of the separation between Aeneas and Troy remain to be examined. Hector's ghostly command, the burning of the city itself, and the death of Priam destroy what one might call the public link between Aeneas and his former home: he no longer has an army, a government, or a city. One important link still remains, that of the family, the personal bond between Aeneas, his wife, his father, and his son. All three are unquestionably Trojan, all three represent strong links between Aeneas and his past. Here Vergil faces a dilemma, for the solidarity of the family, the strong coherent line between father and son, son and grandson, must not be allowed to be destroyed; this was one "Trojan" quality and tradition that must be carried into the Roman way of life. No Roman was ever lightly to part with his paterfamilias or his son.

It was typically Roman, if not Trojan, that the wife, Creusa, should stand as the symbol of the break between Aeneas and his Trojan family. As the four made their way out of the city, Creusa somehow became separated from the others and was lost. It is characteristic of the affection and respect which Vergil, throughout the *Aeneid*, accords to women that he did not simply have Creusa killed, whether by a stray Greek soldier or by the collapse of a building or in some other equally imaginable way. It is equally characteristic of this same attitude that he has Aeneas, at the risk of his life and of his whole enterprise, rush back into the city and attempt to find his wife. At last she appears to him in a kind of vision, "bigger than lifesize" and assures him that he need not be concerned for her: it was not fated that she was to leave Troy with him, and he may at least comfort himself with the assurance that she will not be led in chains to become the slave of some Greek tyrant's wife.

We are never really told what happened to Creusa; the fact that she appears "larger than life" suggests that her death was no ordinary one, for in general the Romans thought of the dead as preserving for all eternity exactly the shape, size and appearance

that they had had at the moment of death. The implication is that
she has been translated, that she passed from this life to the next
without passing through the agony of death. Vergil does not say
this; he suggests only, as Sophocles did in the case of Oedipus, that
the manner of her departure from the world was not ordinary.
Thus subtly and delicately Vergil breaks the family bond between
Aeneas and Troy; it is broken as kindly and gently as could be, and
Aeneas's inevitable grief is softened by the assurance that his beloved
wife has in some strange way been especially blessed. Nonetheless
the bond is no longer there.*

Old Anchises we keep; in fact we find him in at least nominal
command of the party until his death in Sicily at the end of the
seven years of wandering. He is the revered paterfamilias, and
Aeneas's respect for him and deference to his wishes symbolize one
aspect of the old Trojan character that the Roman did well to
preserve. As for young Iulus, he was a mere boy when he left Troy,
a Trojan by blood but as yet not deeply imbued with Trojan
institutions and traditions; a mere child, he must be led out of Troy
by the hand of his father. More than that, his name has been
changed from Ilus, reminiscent of Ilium, to Iulus, a name with a
distinct Roman-Italian ring. Finally, it is the very head of this child
that gives the signal to Aeneas to leave Troy behind and seek for
another home: Aeneas stands in doubt, wondering whether to leave
his father, wife, and son, and go out to fight still more, or rather to
attempt to rescue himself and them. Creusa demands that he take
them with him either to live or to die. At this moment a mystic fire
appears on the head of Iulus; his frantic parents try to extinguish
it, but the flame burns on, and in miraculous fashion does no harm.
Anchises is sure that this is a heavenly sign of some kind; he turns
his eyes toward heaven and prays Jupiter to confirm his interpretation. At this point occurs the famous "thunder on the left," and a
comet streaks through the sky; it is now certain that the departure
of Aeneas and his family has been blessed by heaven. Thus fire is
revealed as a two-faced symbol: the old fire, the natural fire,
destroyed the old city; the new fire, the mystic fire, the fire that
sheds light but does no harm, marks Iulus as the founder of the
new city, and commands Aeneas to see that the prophecy is fulfilled.

---

*It is of course necessary for the story that Aeneas have no wife when
he arrives in Italy, for he must marry Lavinia, the daughter of King
Latinus. All this proves is that Creusa must somehow be got out of
the way; it in no way dictates the manner of her removal.

Thus enjoined and comforted, Aeneas and his band of refugees set sail from Troy for that "Westland" that has been so ambiguously and categorically declared to be their objective. Aeneas has broken very nearly every meaningful tie with the old, and by the miracle of the mystic fire has been commanded to turn his face resolutely toward the next generation, toward his son, who is to be the real founder of the Roman nation. Aeneas is the intermediary; he stands between two generations, that of old Anchises, his father, and the boy Iulus, his son. For the former he has done all that can be done; for the latter he has a journey to make and a city to build.

But the influence of the old in the person of Anchises is not yet at an end, for he too sails with the company when they leave Troy—in fact, as we have remarked, he is the paterfamilias with whom titular command still rests. It is he who is consulted for sailing directions, he who is asked to interpret signs; it is only after he has egregiously misinterpreted the oracle that directed the company to seek out their "ancient mother" that he is allowed to fade into the background; in this instance, as Anchises himself admits, he, like many an old man, has confused two stories and hence has wrongly directed the party to seek their "ancient mother" on the island of Crete.

From here on we hear very little of Anchises; he was, to be sure, paterfamilias; he was also incontrovertibly Trojan, a representative of that old order and old city, the sole remaining function of which was to serve as a point of departure both literally and metaphorically for the new city, Rome. Respect for the old, the "filial piety" that every Roman expected from his son, must be shown to Anchises; he must be allowed to teach all that he is capable of teaching and to remain in command as long as it is at all possible to keep him there. When he has done his best to help the company find the right direction, and has failed, he is allowed to slip into that oblivion which is the privilege of the old, and we hear virtually nothing more of him until his death is mentioned, almost as an obiter dictum, at the end of Book III.

Aeneas speaks of the death of his father with love and sorrow, but we are entitled also to read into his remarks a certain feeling of relief that he was now his own master, and that the old man, after all those years of loving and faithful service, has been granted the rest that is his due. It is a strange fact, not often noticed by students of the *Aeneid*, that when in Book V Aeneas stops once more in Sicily and seizes the occasion to perform elaborate funeral games in honor of Anchises, he does so quite by accident: he had not intended to stop there at all, but had turned aside solely on the advice of the pilot Palinurus, who informed him that the fleet was making no headway against an adverse wind, and that it might be wiser to make for the nearby port of Drepanum until the weather proved more favorable. When Aeneas and his party land, they are greeted with somewhat strained cordiality by old Acestes, who really had not expected to see them again; Aeneas, to make the best of an awkward situation, decrees the games in honor of his father.

Anchises, like Moses, only sees the promised land: as the fleet sails westward from Epirus, he is granted a brief glimpse of the eastern coast of Italy. His death symbolizes the final break of the tie between Aeneas and the people and race of Troy; from here on Aeneas is only nominally a Trojan; he is so by blood but he is incipiently Roman in character, personality, and action. From here on, Troy is only a memory, honored, revered, and loved, but like every important physical aspect of its existence, passed into history and not to be resurrected. When Anchises appears again, as he does on two other occasions in the *Aeneid*, it is in the form of a ghost, who speaks no longer as a mere man, a tired old prince of Troy, but as one who now has entered on a new life and is in converse with the divine.

The sole bond between Aeneas, his company, and Troy, are now the ships on which they sail, for these, as we later learn, were built of timbers cut from a sacred grove on Mt. Ida in the Troad. For the most part, these ships are taken for granted; they are no more than quite normal vehicles of transport. But when Aeneas and his company finally reach Italy, build their camp, establish their alliances, and come into full-blown conflict with Turnus and his Rutuli, the ships themselves, moored along the shores of the Tiber, come under attack by Turnus and his men, who threaten to set them afire. At this point, Jupiter, in response to an ancient promise given to Cybele, from whose grove the timbers had come, permits her to metamorphose the ships into sea-nymphs, and to Turnus's understandable amazement they dive under the waves and disappear.

This Miracle of the Ships is a troublesome incident, for in spite of all rationalization, it seems very nearly grotesque, and too naive for an epic as sophisticated as Vergil's. The poet himself explains that the tale is indeed hard to believe, but it is an old one and therefore must be accepted. In any event, grotesque, naive, or what not, the metamorphosis of the ships does signalize the break-

ing at long last of the final tie with Troy: the ships, built of
Trojan timbers, are gone, and with them the last possible link
between Rome and Troy. Aeneas and his company may never "go
east" again.

One of the best-loved and most dramatic of the figures of the
*Aeneid* is also its most controversial. This is Dido, Queen of
Carthage, whose passion for Aeneas very nearly diverts him from his
fated path. Many have wondered why the story was included at all.
There is good evidence that the story of Dido formed part of earlier
epics by Naevius and Ennius and that it was part of the Roman
tradition and in the nature of things could not have been discarded
by Vergil, even if he had wished to do so. It is clear enough that
Dido represents Carthage, and the ultimate quarrel and separation
of Dido and Aeneas symbolizes the decisive enmity between the two
nations that could end only in the destruction of one or the other.
That Aeneas should have stopped at Carthage is entirely defensible,
both on the grounds of tradition and of symbolism; that, having
stopped there, he should have left Dido, is inevitable. But one may
still legitimately wonder why the meeting between them had to
turn into a love story—if indeed it may be so styled, one-sided as it
was.

Here again, tradition played its part; Vergil is harking back to
some of the stories of passion that formed part of the Greek tradition, and primarily to the story of Medea and Jason, which had
been so dramatically narrated by Apollonius of Rhodes in his epic,
the *Argonautica*. The traditions of Greek tragedy and the story
told by Apollonius may account for some of the features of Vergil's
tale; they still do not show why Vergil found it necessary to make
it a love story. Vergil may have wished to show that his hero Aeneas,
like any good Roman, was a normal male with the normal interest
in women: after all, it had been seven years, and this is a long time
for a man! When Aeneas discovered that the beautiful queen herself was far from averse to love, who was he to repel her?

Perhaps a more important consideration is the fact that
throughout the *Aeneid* women play important and often highly
strategic parts; we have already seen the key position occupied by
Creusa; Aeneas's guide to and through the Underworld will be the
Sibyl, priestess of Apollo. Later on, Amata, Queen of Latium, the
princess Lavinia, and above all the elfin-warrior Camilla, will appear as major factors in Aeneas's story. And of course over the
whole tale hang the two goddesses, Venus and Juno, both of them
intensely female-feminine, in spite of their position as divine figures.
For that matter, it is the "conversion" of Juno, her willingness to

accept Aeneas and his mission, and the abandonment of her ill-will toward him, that enables him to win his final victory. It is hardly too much to say that women, their thoughts and feelings, are vital factors in the development of Aeneas's story; at every critical point, it is a woman, or women, who give the action a definitive turn.

Why Vergil should have chosen to give this important role to women can remain only a matter of speculation, but one cannot help thinking of the role played by women in the actual historical development of Rome. There was Lucretia, for example, whose rape by Tarquin the Proud triggered the revolution that established the Roman Republic; there were such semi-mythological figures as Verginia, Claudia, and Cloelia; there was the historic Cornelia, and in Vergil's own day the empress Livia. And in all the history of Rome, scarcely a single figure came closer to revolutionizing the course of Roman history than Cleopatra, Queen of Egypt, for whom the Romans felt very much the same strange combination of revulsion, fear, and affection that Vergil asks us to feel for Dido. Furthermore, as he tells Dido's story, she becomes the pattern of the woman scorned, and her resultant fury stands as a picturesque and compelling symbol of the deep animosity that arose between Rome and Carthage in historical times. For so deep a feeling, only the fury attendant upon scorned love—so much stronger and more violent than broken friendship or the abrogation of a contractual relation—could stand as an adequate symbol.

But in introducing the love element, Vergil created a difficult problem for himself, for he must allow his hero to engage in an intimate relation with a woman and then extricate himself from it without tarnishing his own reputation and without debasing either himself or her. The problem was complicated further by the fact that ancient love literature occupied itself almost exclusively with one of two types of love affairs. The first involved an ephemeral relation between a young man and a young woman, presumably of inferior social status, whom the young man, in the normal course of events, never expected to marry. The relation may have been passionate, but it was too shallow to serve as Vergil's model. The other had to do with the passions of mythological, even divine, figures, whose suprahuman status exempted them from the ordinary rules of human conduct, and whose stories were set in a half-real never-never land lost in the mists of the past.

But neither Dido nor Aeneas is such a figure; she is no Medea, he, no Jason; the tattered passions of the one and the easy perfidy of the other were not for them. The story of Jason and Medea may have many implications, both human and moral, but it hardly explains history and is at best only semihistorical. Aeneas and Dido may not be quite as real, historically speaking, as were Lucretia and Cornelia, Fabius and Caesar, but they were both, by tradition, part of Rome's past, and they stand in a rectilinear relation to Roman history. What they do and how they feel has significance not just in the broad human sense but in the specifically historical.

For all these reasons, the standard love literature of antiquity provided Vergil with few answers to his problem. If he could not make Aeneas and Dido a latter-day Jason and Medea, he most certainly could not make of them a Pamphilus and Glycerium or an Ovid and Corinna. The union between them must in some sense be honorable and yet susceptible of being broken off; there must be love between them, but Aeneas, at least, must give his love in such a way that it may be withdrawn with propriety if not with entire rectitude. The Roman must behave toward the Carthaginian with restraint, dignity, and a measure of human decency, but in view of the well-known perfidy of the Carthaginians themselves, he will be excused if circumstances compel him to break his word. The moral differences between Dido and Aeneas have already been pointed out; in Book iv of the *Aeneid* these differences are made even more marked in order to render the union between them a bond that will be blessed and yet unblessed, resting on a love that is somehow not love, a relation which is unbalanced because the obligation is on one side and the passion on the other, in which one party demands that gratitude be expressed in love, and the other that passion be restrained by reason.

That this is hardly sound basis for marriage or for any kind of genuine love is painfully obvious; Dido and Aeneas may be matched, but they are not a match. The contrast between the two is brought out in a piece of imagery that at the time seems almost incidental: on the morning when the two are about to go forth on the famous hunt, Aeneas appears at the appointed hour, dressed simply and unpretentiously, a modest and unassuming man whose only mark of distinction is the radiance which his mother Venus has shed about him; all silver, white, and gold, all unaffected strength and manliness, he is the pattern of those who are "on the Lord's side." As for Dido, she starts off on the wrong foot by being late for the appointment; her men are all there, her richly caparisoned horse is there, snorting and stamping, impatient to be gone; Aeneas and his company are all present; everything is ready, but no Dido! Finally she appears, dressed not as we would expect for the hunt, not in the simple garb that Venus had told us was

customary for Tyrian girls on such occasions, but in gorgeous
robes of scarlet and purple, tiara'd, loaded with jewels, splendid
but barbaric. Her misplaced elegance symbolizes the combination
of poor judgment and pride, verging on arrogance, which is to
characterize those who constitute the obstacles in Aeneas's way,
those who are not "on the Lord's side."

And to drive the point home, Vergil makes of their union
during the thunderstorm a kind of anti-wedding. It is initiated by
a black and terrifying thundercloud, dark as night—this in dia-
metric opposition to Roman marriage, which normally took place
at noon when the sun was brightest. Instead of passing through
the streets in joyous procession, the "bride" and "groom" rush
madly through the woods to the cave, while thunder roars and
lightning flashes and from the mountain peaks come the ululations
of the nymphs:

> That was the day, the first of death and first
> of evil. Repute, appearance, nothing moved
> the Queen; she laid no plan to hide her love,
> but called it marriage, with this word veiled her shame.
> (4.169–72)

Nothing could make clearer how wrong the position of Dido
is. She has broken her oath to Sychaeus, her dead husband; she
has tried even to deceive herself; she has accepted as valid a union
which she knew was wrong. Essentially, Dido is the *mulier pere-
grina*, having affinities with Helen, Medea, and Cleopatra; being
totally un-Roman, she cannot rise to the heights of Roman morality
or earn the rights of a Roman lady. She says she is Aeneas's wife,
but we know that she is not, for when the very arrangements were
made, the wily Venus had tricked a Juno so intent on harrassing
Aeneas that she had become careless; when the two laid their plot,
Juno said:

> "With your consent,
> I'll join them in marriage and name her 'lawful wife.'
> Their wedding this shall be." No adverse word
> spoke Venus, but nodded; such tactics made her smile.
> (4.125–28)

The point is, of course, that Venus had not given her consent, and
Juno had failed to notice the omission.

To us this may seem like an unconscionable legalism on

Vergil's part; to a Roman, far more familiar with the niceties of the law and legal language than we, the point would have been abundantly clear. Furthermore, Dido's insistence that the relation was a marriage, and her tacit demand that Aeneas show gratitude for her rescue of him and his men by acting as her consort, serve to palliate, although certainly not entirely to explain or excuse Aeneas's conduct. As a Roman gentleman, he must show gratitude for kindness and hospitality, and since the queen herself demanded that this gratitude be expressed by his acceptance of the position of prince consort, Aeneas may be pardoned for entering into what was, at least technically, an extramarital relation. It should be particularly noted that nowhere in Book IV is Aeneas's reaction toward Dido's proposal—if we may call it this—made clear; he appears at worst to be accepting the inevitable. He was no Hippolytus, to turn the deaf ear of self-righteousness to a kind and beautiful woman who was offering him her hospitality and her love.

The clearest thing about the contrast between Dido and Aeneas is its lack of clarity; Dido is not a vile temptress but a beautiful and courageous woman, and a great queen. Still, she is in the wrong, for she has broken her oath to Sychaeus and has allowed passion to lead her into a union which she knew was unblessed. On his side, Aeneas is no cold and sexless half-man, and is anything but unaware of his obligations to the lady who had saved his life. As the same time, he is careful to hold himself aloof; he utters no word of love or passion; he accepts, with all the graciousness of which he is capable, the love that is being offered to him, but he does not take the initiative himself, and as soon as he sees that the time has come to pursue his God-given mission, he obeys the great imperative, and in spite of his feelings leaves Dido and Carthage.

Thus Aeneas is incontrovertibly in the right, but there still remain certain shadows over his conduct which Vergil makes no attempt to dispel. Aeneas was no fool; he certainly knew that the union between himself and Dido was not blessed; he knew too that it could not last; Jupiter's warning to him to be on his way only served to speed a departure which Aeneas knew perfectly well was some day inevitable. No matter how we may attempt to gloss it over, the fact remains that Aeneas did deceive Dido into thinking that he reciprocated her passion and that he intended to stay with her. Even if we may excuse his awkward and clumsy farewell speech (331–61) as no worse than the gentleman's attempt to solve that perennial and insoluble problem of breaking off a love affair with a lady against her will, the fact remains that Aeneas did attempt to gather his men and prepare his fleet for departure without letting Dido know; his excuse that he would try to seek an appropriate time for telling her of his intentions is so shallow as to be ludicrous.

Neither of the pair is entirely in the clear from the moral point of view, but there is still no question as to which one is *essentially* in the right and which *essentially* in the wrong. Aeneas may be an imperfect vessel—and as the symbol of empire he must be so, for no empire, least of all the Roman, was ever free of imperfections—but he never falters in attempting to do the right as he sees it; the worst that can be said of his conduct with Dido was that seeing himself presented with circumstances which were virtually bound to produce unbecoming and possibly even dishonest conduct on his part, he made the best of the situation and tried both to accept it and later to escape from it, with as little damage to himself, his son, his company, and Dido, as he could.

With Dido, the opposite seems to be true. Everything she does goes wrong; her broken oath, her passion for Aeneas, her chicanery with witchcraft, her phrenetic recourse to suicide, and above all her final pitiful attempt to blame the whole affair on Anna—a pathetic Roman version of Adam's "the woman . . . gave me of the tree, and I did eat" (*Gen.* 3:12)—all put her in the wrong; every sign, every omen, every prophecy point to her as the source of evil. In the end she becomes literally deranged, and thus loses every possibility of winning back Aeneas; she is haunted and accursed, for all her beauty and dignity a symbol of the evil attendant upon uncivilized and uncontrolled passion, and of the moral wrong involved in sacrifice of principle for expedient aims. Her story ends as it began, in misery, sacrilege, death, and deception; for all this—and here we must grant sincere tribute to Vergil's superb artistry—she remains an inspiring figure, a truly great woman of the stature of a Helen or a Cleopatra, and while the story of her death as Vergil tells it may smack of over-empurpled operatic melodrama, we can at least understand why men of an earlier day found her a great tragic figure, whose death moved St. Augustine to tears.

Whether or not we are still able to be moved by Dido's death, we have little difficulty in seeing her as the symbol of the great conflict, expressed in three long wars, that very nearly destroyed Rome before her power even over so much as the western end of the Mediterranean had been consolidated. Dido is Carthage; Aeneas's near union—the mistake that came so close to costing him his mission—may well find its historical parallel in the "unholy alliance" entered into by Rome and Carthage at the end of the First Punic War, when the two powers virtually agreed to share the Western Mediterranean between them. Her death is the death of Carthage; her dying curse the symbolic representation and justification of the eternal enmity that was to exist between Rome and her rival. The Dido incident is symbolic of the dangers of alliances with inappropriate powers, particularly those of the Orient, whose ideals of government and society were incompatible with those of Rome. It is also symbolic of the danger that Rome was to face from women, and specifically of course from Cleopatra, whose feminine charm, vast wealth and power, and adroit diplomacy, came very close to accomplishing what Carthage had failed to do.

All this is reasonably obvious, but one aspect of the incident is often forgotten. Dido, for all her faults, excites our sympathy; she may be wrong, but she remains a great, heroic, beautiful, and courageous woman, whose death can only occasion sorrow. She symbolizes an aspect of the growth of empire to which few Romans ever gave expression and of which in general they may have been quite unaware. The growth of an empire, however nobly motivated, however disinterestedly pursued, even by God's own elect, exacts a price, sometimes a terrible one. Nations and governments must die in agony in order that a transcendent power may be established, and the agony is no less the real for being shortsighted, wrongheaded, or even downright evil.

Nor was the price in these instances paid entirely by the nations that were vanquished and destroyed; there was a levy on the victor too, who could rarely claim to have accomplished his objective without departing from the stern moral code to which, on the surface of things, he had devoted himself. Inevitably one thinks of the destruction of Corinth in 146 B. C. by Mummius, in what can only be described as a petulant and arrogant, not to say barbaric and cruel act. It accomplished the final subjugation of Greece to Rome, its immediate objective, but if Corinth and its people paid a price, so did the Romans, for this vile act was forever on their consciences and they never allowed themselves to forget it. There can be little doubt that similar cruel and barbarous acts were perpetrated by the Romans in many instances, particularly against the relatively uncivilized peoples with whom they came into conflict out nearer the edges of their Empire; we shall never know how many great peoples, with what noble national aspirations, were forced to give way to Rome's superior power and to her overriding imperial ideal.

Of all of this, Dido may be seen as a symbol, and in Vergil's sympathy for her we may see reflected a sympathy, which he shares almost alone with Tacitus, for the nations whose power and individuality Rome found it necessary to crush. That Vergil himself was keenly conscious and perhaps deeply disturbed by this as by other imperfections, not only of the Empire but of the emperor himself, seems quite clear; what we can never know now is the degree to which Vergil's poetic animadversions were given more than a passing glance by his contemporary readers.

There is one other incident which deserves special attention before we go on to the strategic Book vi. Book v, for the most part, is occupied with a series of incidents that come very close to comic relief, the cheerful, lighthearted games in honor of Anchises, described with all the reportorial skill at the poet's command, and culminating in the *ludus Troiae*, in itself hardly more than a gymkhana display by the boys of Troy. But it sets a definite period to the story of Troy, which has now become nothing but a game, a *ludus*, to be performed by young boys in honor of the boyhood, one might say, of their nation. The war that raged about Troy for ten years and ended in the destruction of the city is now only a memory, to be celebrated by the elaborate ceremonial dance of cavalry units, engaging in the some sort of formalized, patterned horseback riding still much loved by the Italians.

The most important feature of the *ludus Troiae* is the emergence of young Ascanius as leader, who for the first time emerges from the boyhood that has so far kept him in the background. Now it is he who leads the boys through their cavalry maneuvers and their display of horsemanship, proudly riding at their head to the loud cheers of Aeneas and the rest of the Trojan company. Nor is this the end of the emergence of young Ascanius from obscurity. Almost immediately after the conclusion of the games in honor of Anchises, the disaffection of a certain number of the Trojans, who have grown weary of travel, shipboard life, and eternal camping-out at one site after another, finds its expression in the revolt of the women—instigated as usual by Juno—who determine to express their protest, and compel the whole company to yield to their will, by destroying the means of further travel: they will burn the ships. News of the fire is brought to the Trojans, still assembled about the tomb of Anchises; Ascanius, still flushed with his success as leader of the gymkhana, still astride his horse, gallops off to the camp where the ships are moored. Ripping off his helmet and throwing it to the ground, he reveals himself to the frantic women as "your Ascanius." He cries out that their act is no less than treason, and the women, shamed by this reminder and by the fact that it has taken a mere boy to show them their error, scatter to the woods and caves to hide themselves in shame.

The episode of the burning of the ships has a double significance. First, it brings Ascanius to our attention as he takes his first step from the status of Trojan boy toward that of national Roman leader. Second, the revolt of the women and the disaffected occasions a purging of the Trojan company: those who had grown weak and tired, those whose courage and resolve have faltered, are left behind to form a harmless little colony under the kingship of Acestes. Instructed by the vision of Anchises in a dream, Aeneas marshals for the last stage of the journey to Italy only those who are best and strongest, the *fortissima corda*, who alone will be able to cope with the rough and muscular enemy who will oppose their settling in Italy. The symbolism is quite clear. When the "story of Troy," that is to say the early days of the development of empire, are complete, a new leader will emerge, trained in the old school but ready to take decisive action in new and unfamiliar ways. There will be those who will be tired, discouraged, and disaffected; they will be treated with kindness and justice, but will be gently and firmly thrust aside. Only the strongest and bravest are worthy to be participants in the new order, the kind who can meet, battle down, and as we later see, win over and join with others as tough and muscular as themselves.

The company are now ready to set sail for their ultimate goal, Italy and the Tiber, but as the ghost of Anchises has directed, Aeneas must first go down into the Underworld, there to receive his final orders and the clarification of his mission. This descent into the Underworld was a profoundly religious act, a journey into the very presence of God, and Vergil ends Book v with an incident that is intended to give a religious tone to the narrative. Venus begs Neptune not to interfere with the passage of the Trojans from Sicily to Italy; Neptune replies in a curious speech in which he reminds Venus that although, in his guise as Poseidon, he had been generally less than favorable to the Trojans during the ten years of the war at Troy, he had yet done a number of things to help them: he had built the walls of Troy, but for all his anger at the Trojans, had never destroyed them; he had saved Aeneas once from Achilles (*Iliad* 20.156–339), and it was he who had stopped the storm which at the beginning of the *Aeneid* had threatened to destroy Aeneas's fleet.

But before he may be completely reconciled to Aeneas and his Trojans, he will demand a sacrifice of them, for divine dignity and propriety must be preserved. He must have "one soul" to pay for the many, and it must be a good man, an important man, so that the sacrifice will have real meaning. He is paid his due, for as the fleet sails on through the night toward Italy, Palinurus, admiral and pilot, falls asleep at the helm and falls overboard to become a literal offering and sacrifice to the god of the sea. The symbolic meaning of this precious sacrifice is scarcely to be missed; any Roman could have named a dozen great historical figures, who voluntarily or involuntarily gave their lives for Roman victory. As for the story itself, godhead has now entered it in a decisive and immediate way; Vergil's picture of the corpse of Palinurus lying on some "alien strand," a sacrifice for the welfare of his fellows, prepares us for Aeneas's descent into the Underworld.

From the beginning of the *Aeneid*, it has been clear that Aeneas and his Trojans, in their quest for the Westland, are following a divine imperative; theirs is not a mere venture in colonization but a mission divinely ordered and inspired. Thus far, the imperative has been expressed only in the ways conventional for ancient paganism; that is to say, through dreams, oracles, and individuals with special access to the divine intent, e.g. Celaeno the Harpy, and Helenus. The directions, as was usual in such cases, were always obscure and unclear, or, although accurate enough in general outline, omitted to mention some of the most serious obstacles that the party would face; Helenus, for example, fails to mention the impending diversion of the Trojans to Carthage.

Furthermore, the directives have been expressed in terms of immediate aims and general goals: the Trojans are first to go West; after they have fumbled for some time, divine will finally defines the West as Italy. They are told that when they reach Italy they will establish a rule that is to last for all time. This is all very well, but it is in no sense extraordinary; these were the sorts of prophecies and directives that the ancient world had long since learned to accept from the gods. There was nothing transcendent, nothing superior, nothing to give the reader the impression that Aeneas's mission was somehow especially blessed, that it was in some manner raised above the conquests of a Croesus, a Xerxes, or an Alexander. These men too, after all, had been directed by the gods to do various things, and Alexander, by an adroit piece of religious diplomacy, had even managed to gain for himself the unique position of "son of Jupiter Ammon," and thus enjoyed the divine blessing in a degree somewhat above his fellows. But Croesus failed, Xerxes failed, and Alexander died, each without ever accomplishing his objective; oracles, prophets, even the figure of Zeus Ammon himself, failed to raise these men to any special status or to give to their imperial aspirations any more than quite ordinary blessing.

Clearly, this will not do for Aeneas, for the justification of his mission, and thereby of the mission of Rome herself, must rest on something more substantial than the shadowy talk of prophecy and the pompous pronunciamentos of the gods. We have heard all these before, and have learned to what degree they are to be trusted. If Aeneas is to receive a divine imperative more cogent than any hitherto delivered to man, if Rome's imperial mission is to be justified on grounds of something more substantial than the standard gobbledegook of ancient paganism, Aeneas—and in his person, Rome—must be brought into contact with the Ultimate Divine, or as we so easily express it, God. We have already seen how conscious Vergil is of the existence of God, even though he has as yet found no name for him other than *Fatum*, and has warned us in the very opening words of the *Aeneid* that it is this power that drove Aeneas forth from Troy to Italy—he is *fato profugus*.

Vergil's sense of the reality of this transcendent power is clear from the beginning of the *Aeneid*. It is His power, His law, His justice that are to motivate Aeneas and Rome. As for the Power himself, he is the "unimaginable You" of E. E. Cummings; his nature is beyond our comprehension, and his ways are beyond our power to reason and to understand. Aeneas and Rome stand before Him as Job did before the God of Israel, suffering, bewildered, and possessed only of the conviction that their will must bow to God's. This mystic concept of God is in direct, not to say violent, contrast with the literalism and legalism of Greco-Roman paganism, which gave man no more than the vague hope that he might bargain with the gods and by appropriate sacrifice win them over to his side. It is even in contrast to much orthodox Christianity, for it lacks the personal element, and shows no hint of the love of God that is "wider than the measure of man's mind." This is the Divine Power that directs Aeneas and Rome, and only from this Power can the authentic divine imperative, in full guise and without prevarication, proceed. The problem that Vergil now faces is that of establishing direct and unmistakable contact between Aeneas and this Power.

In Book v, Aeneas had learned, from the ghost of Anchises in a dream, that he must visit the Underworld; the death of Palinurus is a signpost pointing the way that Aeneas is to go, cast adrift, alone, and helpless on an "unknown strand." His only companion will be the mad priestess, the Sibyl, an impersonal, disinterested guide, whose performance has no shred of sympathy or affection; she is a technical expert, nothing more. The basic inspiration for this episode is Book XI of Homer's *Odyssey*, in which Odysseus consults the shades of the Underworld to find out how he is to get home, but the resemblance between the two episodes is entirely superficial, for Vergil's Realm of the Dead, with its heroic proportions and spectacular personalities, is a far cry from Homer's gibbering ghosts.

The precious sacrifice and logicaly indefensible death of Palinurus, "the innocent who died for many," introduce into the *Aeneid* an atmosphere of mysticism, of the incomprehensible nature of the divine, which the poet develops as he attempts to bring his hero into direct contact with it. Almost at once, Aeneas is informed by the Sibyl that the only approach to God is through prayer, that the doors of his temple will not open until prayer in proper form has been made to Him. Aeneas responds with a prayer to Apollo, which reminds the god of his previous services to the Trojans, suggests that it is now appropriate that he should allow and encourage the Trojans to find their home in Italy, and finally promises that once they are established in Italy he will set up a temple of Apollo and will grant particular distinctions to the Sibyl herself.

Aeneas's prayer, with its reminder to the god of his proper duty and its promise of due reward for services performed, is the purest paganism, and bears all the marks of the bargaining which was characteristic of Greco-Roman religion. Almost immediately comes the prophet's reply; Apollo inspires the Sibyl to utter once more a prophecy of the arrival and settlement of the Trojans in Italy, of the difficulties they will face, and of the quarters from which they may expect help. From the point of view of the ancient pagan, the agreement with God has now been drawn up and ratified; the details of its terms are not entirely clear: its references to "a second Achilles, he too the son of a goddess," to a "foreign wife" who is once again to cause trouble for the Trojans, and above all to the quite unexpected help "from a Greek city" leave Aeneas understandably mystified but not resentful, since he realizes that this is truly the language of religion.

Now Aeneas is permitted to take the first step from orthodox paganism, with its bargainings and its legalisms, into the mystic region of the divine imperative. His first task, he is told, is to find and pluck the Golden Bough, which he must carry to the Under-world as a gift to its queen, Proserpina. Much has been written and speculated about the nature of the Golden Bough, but Vergil tells us all that he wants us to know about it, and all that is truly pertinent to his purposes. The bough is in fact Vergil's attempt to express the idea of vital and substantial ambiguity; it grows on a tree like any other branch and must be pulled from the tree as any other branch would be. Thus it belongs to the world of physical nature, the world in which man himself moves. At the same time, it possesses a supernatural character, shown in the first instance by its being of gold and also by its power of self-regeneration, for as soon as a bough is plucked, another grows at once in its place. Finally and most uniquely, it can be separated from its tree only by the man "whom the fates have called"; no other force, not even the most violent, can separate it. It thus becomes the symbol of life, life which exists both in this world and in the other, in the world of man and in the world of God; it is at the same time natural and supranatural. Aeneas is instructed to pluck this bough and to carry it with him in his hands; it is, so to speak, his pass-port from this world to the next. It will be shown to Charon and thus secure passage for Aeneas and the Sibyl across Acheron, and finally it will be placed on the threshold of the Elysian Fields, where Aeneas by the mediation of the ghost of Anchises comes as close as he may to the presence of Divinity itself.

However, before Aeneas may hope to obtain the Golden Bough, he and his followers must cleanse themselves of sin insofar as it is possible for them to do this by their own power.* The impurity, or "sin," in this instance turns out to be the unburied body of "a friend": the presence of the body is uncleanly, and until it has been buried, the Trojans are in a state of impurity; not only is the

---

*Discussion of this particular point inevitably involves an anachronism, since "sin" is a Jewish-Christian idea totally unfamiliar to ancient paganism and not at all clear even to the ancient philosophers. The "sin" of the Trojans might be more properly described as a stain or impurity, particularly when we consider that its presence is due not to some voluntary transgression of divine law on the part of the Trojans, but entirely to an accident of which Aeneas and his im-mediate company are not even aware. The only respect in which this impurity resembles sin lies in the fact that its presence is an obstacle to the natural-supranatural Element, the possession of which alone can ensure contact with divinity; or, to put it negatively, as Vergil has done, such contact can be made only in the absence of impurity.

presence of the dead itself a pollution, but failure to bury it constitutes violation of one of the most fundamental laws of ancient
religion. This type of stain, man can himself remove; the burial of
Misenus—in fact as we see at once, the mere *intent* of the act of
burial—gives Aeneas the ritual purity which he must have before he
may approach the Element.

It is while Aeneas is in the process of cutting timber for
Misenus's funeral pyre that he is led to the Golden Bough; as he is
passing through the woods, two doves appear, who are recognized
by Aeneas as "his mother's birds." They become his guides and lead
him to the tree where the Golden Bough is growing. Presumably,
Aeneas would have found the bough without the help of the doves;
they only facilitate the discovery. Nor do they come in answer to
a request from Aeneas or as the fulfillment of any other obligation,
divine or human. Their presence, to borrow a Christian term, is an
act of grace, given freely and out of nothing more than goodwill.

Proof that Aeneas is indeed of the "elect" is offered by his
successful plucking of the bough, but at this point Vergil introduces
a curious and very puzzling note. The Sibyl had declared that if
the individual who approached the bough were one of the elect,
he would be able to pluck it from the tree with ease, yet when
Aeneas tries to pull off the bough, it comes only reluctantly; as
Vergil puts it, it "hangs back" *(cunctantem)* as if unwilling to be
separated.

This apparent inconsistency has puzzled readers of Vergil,
probably from the very beginning. In the fourth century A. D. the
scholar Servius, obviously aware that this passage was giving
trouble, attempted to explain it by saying that the reason the bough
hung back was because it was of gold, a material not easily broken.
Other suggestions have been made, but none of them really solves
the apparent contradiction between the bough's "reluctance" and
the Sibyl's statement that if he who plucked it were of the elect, it
would come away easily.

It may be that we are simply working too hard at this passage,
and that Vergil meant nothing more than that the branch showed
the natural resistance to being wrenched off that would have been
shown by any branch, golden or otherwise; when the Sibyl said that
the branch would come off "willingly and with ease" she did not
mean to say that it would simply drop off at a touch but that, being
a natural object at least in part of its being, it would require no
more than normal effort to wrench it free.

At the risk of overrefining Vergil's imagery, it might be suggested that the reluctance of the bough is one more indication of its ambiguous character: as a supranatural element, it must yield itself readily into the hands of the elect, but as a natural tree-born bough, it is bound to resist any separation from its tree. In a sense, it is like Aeneas himself; as one of the elect, he is to be granted the supranatural privilege of visiting the Underworld while he is yet alive, and of being entrusted with a divine mission, the like of which has never before been granted to any man. At the same time, Aeneas is very much a human being with human frailties and imperfections, a natural being possessed of flaws like all other natural beings. It is certainly in this character that Aeneas stands as the symbol of the Roman Empire, which showed the same ambiguous character: blessed by God, His vessel and emissary, it was as prone to weakness and error as any human institution must be.

Rites for Misenus are now performed. Aeneas and his company are ritually cleansed of the pollution which death and the failure to bury the dead had fastened upon them. Aeneas is now ready for the actual descent. First he must make appropriate prayer and sacrifice; in other words, he must do those things which he, as a mere human being, still can do to place himself in touch with the Underworld and its powers. In orthodox pagan fashion, Aeneas sacrifices black animals, at night, at the altars. At the conclusion of the sacrifices, comes the first pale light of dawn, and with it the signs of the presence of queen of the Underworld: the groaning and quaking of the earth, the howling of dogs in the darkness. At this sign, Aeneas and the Sibyl enter the cave that leads to the Underworld.

Vergil's geography and demography of the Underworld are part of the apparatus of mysticism, no more to be taken literally than the other external features of the poem; but in this case they represent not constants to be manipulated at will, but rather support for the divinity into whose presence Aeneas is about to be ushered. It is a strange world in which nothing goes quite as we would expect. Charon is an old man, but his old age is "unripe and green"; he is like death, deathless. The host of the dead waiting to cross Acheron into Hades fall into two groups, those who have received ritual burial, and those who have not. The unburied are driven summarily away from the riverbank; they wander about for a hundred years and only then may they so much as look at the waters they have longed for (*stagna exoptata,* 330). This seems natural enough, but a strange element is thrust in when we are told that even those who have been properly buried do not cross Acheron in any recognizable order; they all stand there with arms outstretched "in love of the farther shore," but Charon seems to make his choice entirely at random; some he accepts, others he drives away. Presumably, somehow, the inscrutable will of God operates to direct Charon; a similar principle appears to underlie Dante's picture of the angelic boatman who chooses, in similar inscrutable fashion, the souls whom he will transport from Purgatory to Paradise (*Purgatory* 2.91–102).

The overriding power of God's will and purposes is clearly illustrated by the story of Palinurus, who makes the mistake of asking Aeneas to help him cross Acheron before his appointed time and before he has received proper burial. The Sibyl thrusts him angrily aside with the injunction: "Think not to change the laws of God by prayer!" (6.376). For his comfort, she then reminds him that ultimately he will be buried and will be allowed to cross, but that in the meantime he must not expect, no matter what his merits, to be released from the obligation to follow the Right Way, whether or not he sees any reason for it and whether or not he can understand God's purposes in setting it up. A handful of dust or sand may seem a trivial thing, but God's law says that man must have this before he may cross to the other world. It is not for us to ask the reason for the injunction.

Here the mystic air of Vergil's account deepens perceptively, for the God of whom he is speaking is no Jupiter, no Venus, no Juno, deities whose behavior was often unpredictable and unreasonable, but for which motives of jealousy, revenge, or sheer ill-will could readily be assigned. The power that forbids Palinurus the right to cross Acheron acts out of no such motives but for reasons which men have no right to know or even to seek. It is impossible here not to be reminded again of Job's predicament and of Bildad's indignant words to him: "Doth God pervert judgment? or doth the Almighty pervert justice?" (*Job* 8.3), and of Jesus's parable of the wedding guest (*Mat.* 22.1 ff.) in which the unfortunate man, although virtually dragged by force to the wedding party, is "cast into outer darkness" because of his failure to have on a wedding garment. Vergil seems to have a curious foretaste of the importance of decorum in the pursuit of the Right Way, and of the realization that man must accept this decorum whether he sees a reason for it or not, simply on grounds that God does not pervert justice.

Finally, after Aeneas in the company of the Sibyl, has passed through the outer circles of Hell and has gone past Phlegethon, where it flows around the triple walls that imprison the utterly damned, he is conducted to the gates of Elysium. But before he may enter this realm of the blessed, he must purify himself of any stain he might have contracted merely by skirting the region of the damned and hearing an account of them from the Sibyl; accordingly he sprinkles himself with fresh water and then places the Golden Bough, the Element, at the threshold of the palace of Proserpina. The link between human and divine has now been established; Aeneas is in contact with divinity and may expect to receive, in full and unmistakable terms, the mission that he has been enjoined to perform.

In some ways, what follows here is the strangest part of the *Aeneid*. It is of the utmost importance, if the divinely commanded nature of Aeneas's (and Rome's) mission is to be established in the mind of the reader, that Aeneas be brought into direct contact with divine power. When he places the Golden Bough at the threshold of Proserpina's palace, he seems in fact about to establish such contact; we almost expect him to enter the palace and there face Proserpina and Pluto themselves. But it is at once apparent why he does not do so; to have had the gods of the dead, however exalted and ennobled the poet might have made them, hand down the injunction on which was to be based the *life* of Aeneas and of Rome, would have been a strange contradiction indeed.

Still, it would have been direct contact with divine power, at least of a sort. But in place of what we might have expected, Aeneas performs a perfunctory and hasty act of purification, drops the Golden Bough at the door, and immediately turns away to follow the Sibyl into a region where he will meet not God but the ghosts of the great, the wise, and the good, and of Anchises himself. Ghosts, to be sure, do possess, in Roman religious thought, a kind of divine character: the *Di Manes* were among those deities whom the Roman thought it wise to placate by appropriate prayer and offering on regular occasions. Yet on the face of it they seem unlikely as vessels of a divine imperative. Perhaps because of our reading of the Bible and of Dante's *Divine Comedy* and Milton's *Paradise Lost*, we expect a voice to come out of the clouds, or for Aeneas in some other way to face divine power itself.

Yet it is almost as if Vergil shied away from such contact, as if overpowered by the thought of the presence of divinity, or perhaps as if feeling himself inadequate to present divinity in a convincing way. The best that Vergil can have his hero do is to hear, from the ghost of Anchises, a mystic-philosophical definition. There is, says Anchises, a universal, indwelling, and vivifying spirit which gives being and life to all things everywhere; there is a mind, an intelligence, equally all-pervasive, that guides and motivates every act of everything that exists. From this mind-spirit, come the "fiery seeds" that give life and intelligence to all animate creatures, including man, but since the flesh is antithetical to mind-spirit, man (and of course all other animals) finds himself only partially able to realize the life and intelligence that have been placed in him: mind-spirit is dulled and stained by terrestrial flesh.

At death, the life of mind-spirit continues; passing through a kind of primitive purgatory, it is cleansed of the stains of the flesh and then moves on to Elysium, where, after dwelling for a thousand years, God calls it back to drink the waters of forgetfulness (*Lethe*), and grants it a desire once more to return to the flesh.

This definition is as close as Aeneas ever comes to the presence of divine power. Anchises does not even assert that he has been especially appointed to deliver this definition and the accompanying imperative to Aeneas. Anchises's ghost seems in no way different from the ghosts of the other heroes in Elysium; he seems to have been chosen—if "chosen" is the right word—for this task solely because he was Aeneas's father; otherwise, we gather, any of the spirits of the dead might have told Aeneas just as much. But the implication is nonetheless clear: God is indeed a spirit, the source of all being and all wisdom, universally indwelling in all forms of existence, and especially in all forms of animate being, and it is from this mind-spirit, this God, this Fate *(Fatum)* that the imperative is to come to Aeneas and to Rome.

This is the Indwelling God, the Universal Intelligence, that governs and moves the world, that gives to man all the nobility and intelligence of which he, as a mere terrestrial creature, is capable, and then at the conclusion of this earthly life purges him of its stains, grants him a thousand years of unalloyed joy, and then hails him back to Lethe and to this world once more. As a disembodied, purified spirit, Anchises has been granted this knowledge of God; Aeneas by following the Right Way, by presenting the Element, the Golden Bough, and under the guidance of the priestess, the Sibyl, has been permitted, though still clothed in the polluting flesh, to hear and learn what otherwise only the disembodied spirits of the dead may hear and learn.

It is characteristic of the ancients that at this critical point in the narrative, when the poet wished to bring his hero into the presence of God, he should have elected to do so not by means of a mystical, pictorial symbol, as Dante was later to do *(Paradise* c. 33) but instead by means of a philosophical definition as precise and very nearly as dry as a dictionary entry. Vergil, as if uneasy of the presence of divinity, keeps Aeneas at one remove from God himself. It is worthy of note that no divine personage, other than the ferryman Charon, appears in Vergil's account of the Underworld and of Aeneas's visit there. Clearly, the anthropomorphic deities of Greco-Roman religion would not serve Vergil's purpose; the God whose "kingdom on earth" Aeneas and Rome were to establish, transcended any quasi-human shape, however beautiful and noble, and it was beyond Vergil's theology, and perhaps also beyond his poetic art, to reduce a divinity of these proportions to plastic form. His God is in very fact the God of the philosophers (and one probably might add, of poets like Aeschylus, Sophocles and Euripides) for whose delineation a cold definition was the best that the ancient intellectual-poet could come up with.

This passage (6.724 ff.) introduces the keystone of the whole *Aeneid,* structurally, symbolically, and from the point of view of narrative. We—and Aeneas—are confronted as best the poet can manage it with the reality of God himself; we then pass on to the implementation of His will, presented here in a long Parade of Heroes, the "children of Dardanus" who by building the Roman Empire are to carry out the mission that divine will has imposed upon them. A long, sonorous catalog of names begins with Aeneas's own son by Lavinia, Aeneas Silvius, King of Alba, and passes rapidly down through the history and geography of Italy and Rome to the figure of Augustus himself:

> "child of godhead. He'll rebuild
> a Golden Age in Latium, land where once
> Saturn was king. Past India, past the Moor,
> he'll spread his rule to zones beyond the stars,
> beyond the Ecliptic, where Atlas carries heaven,
> and bears on his back the spinning, star-tricked wheel."
> (6.792–97)

Within this keystone of the whole poem, Augustus himself is the key figure, holding a central position in the great parade, which now continues with its list of heroes and places known and loved by every Roman. The keystone passage concludes with the lines that have sometimes been styled "the whole duty of Rome":

"Others will forge the bronze to softer breath,
no doubt, and bring the sculptured stone to life,
show greater eloquence, and with their rule
map out the skies and tell the rising stars;
you, Roman, remember: govern! Rule the world!
These are your arts! Make peace man's way of life;
Spare the humble but strike the braggart down."
(6.847–53)

Here at last is Aeneas's full imperative; here it is clearly shown how Aeneas is to fit into the long series of events that will culminate in the Roman Empire; here, symbol, history, and narrative are all brought together and capped with the imperative for which Aeneas has been seeking.

The parade of the heroes is a pageant of success and victory without a discordant note; one by one, the heroes of Roman history prove God's blessing upon their mission by their unbroken series of triumphs. The passage must have been deeply moving to any Roman patriot, and must have filled him with a sense of the glory of his history and the assurance of his God-blessed future. Yet all at once, Vergil drops from the tone of joyous triumph to that of sombre warning. The last figure in the parade is that of the young Marcellus, nephew of the Emperor Augustus and intended as his heir and successor; his death at the age of twenty in 23 B. C. had been a source of bitter disappointment and sorrow, not only to the emperor himself, but to the Roman people as a whole. For all the other figures in the parade, there have been victories and achievements; for this one concluding figure there will be only grief. Thus Rome is warned that even the executors of a divinely blessed mission, even the proponents of a law under which all men alike will be partners in justice, must not expect that their path will be one of uninterrupted triumph, or their rule untainted by error, disappointment, and disaster. Aeneas is a great hero, but he too at times can be frail; Rome was a great empire, but she too was subject to frailty. These weaknesses and deficiencies of humanity, both Aeneas and Rome must understand and accept; otherwise they will be guilty of hybris, the one form of misconduct which the gods could not tolerate. As every Roman knew, hybris was the surest road to disaster: the man or the nation who imagined that their enormous virtues somehow set them above the rest of humankind, and even raised them to the level of infallibility and perfect peace that only the gods might

enjoy, was doomed to imminent and spectacular downfall. Aeneas
and Rome both will be great only insofar as they evince that humility which springs from acceptance of the fact of human imperfection.

The second half of the *Aeneid*, at least in modern times, has
never been quite so popular as the first half, and the reasons are not
far to seek. For the first half of the poem is cosmic and general in
its purport; it applies in the immediate instance to Rome, but its
figures and events are equally applicable to almost any nation—and
how many of these there have been!—that, in the name of justice
and the equality of all mankind, has attempted to extend and
establish a rule of law beyond its own borders. By contrast, the
second half of the *Aeneid* is specifically national; its prevailing
elements are patriotism, national legend, and national pride, all of
these expressed in terms of the lands and people of Italy and Rome.
To be sure, the symbolism of Books VII–XII is as transcendent
as is that of Books I–VI, but because of the heavy overlay of
Italian-Roman names and places, the broader symbolism of this
part of the poem is not quite so obvious or so easy to grasp. To
Vergil himself, as he specifically states it, the second half of the
*Aeneid* was his "greater task" (*maius opus*, 7.45); for the poet, the
first six books have done no more than lay a foundation and define
an imperative; it was left to the later books to show, both in narrative and in symbol, the working out of that imperative and the
building of the structure for which the foundation had been laid.
In a sense, Vergil attempts to do what Walt Whitman was later to
attempt to do for America: to find and express the poetry indige-
nous to his own land and people, the poetry that lay in their very
names, and above all the poetry of her national character.

After warning us that his story will be one of war, of battle-
line, of kings "whose courage was their doom" and "of Tuscan
bands, of all the Westland forced to fight" the poet drops at once
into the lower and less frantic key of peace, for Italy is indeed the
land of peace, the *Saturnia tellus*, of which Vergil had sung somewhat earlier in the *Georgics* (2.173 ff.). Our immediate introduction
is through King Latinus "a king grown old in years of peaceful
reign" (7.46). His line of descent goes back through Faunus, whom
every Roman knew as a comfortable bumpkin god, patron of wood-
lot and pastureland, to Picus, very nearly a totem figure, changed
by Circe, whose love he had slighted, into a woodpecker; and
through Picus to Saturn, the ruling god of the Golden Age, the age
of perfect peace. Latinus's palace is a rustic hall, shadowed by tall

trees, and redolent of the simplicity of an earlier day; his people, the Latins, "the children of Saturn" (203) are just:

> but not by bond or law;
> rather, by nature and god's timeless code.
> (203–4)

So long unfamiliar are the Latins with war that when a foolish and quite trivial incident sets off armed conflict between the Trojans and the Latins, the simple peasants rush onto the field with any weapon their rummaging could turn up: fire-hardened stakes, clubs, and axes. Only when full-scale war breaks out do we find the Italians marching out with full accoutrement of spears, shields, swords, and body-armor. And with characteristically Roman restraint, the armies do not march until hostilities have been provoked by the other side, in this case by the Trojans, for it has been Ascanius whose innocent shooting of a pet stag had sent the peasantry pell-mell into battle, and in the battle it was the Trojans who had drawn first blood by killing Almo, a peasant boy, and Galaesus, "the justest man who lived in Italy, and her richest lord" (536–37). Even then, the Italians commit no overt act of formal warfare until, in good legal fashion, they have formally declared war on the invaders—and even here, so devoted to peace is King Latinus, that he cannot bring himself to perform the validating act of the declaration, the opening of the doors of the temple of Bellona, with the result that this act must be performed by the goddess Juno herself.

But it would be a serious mistake to imagine that, peaceful though they may be, the Italians are not good warriors. Anchises had correctly interpreted the omen of the horses (3.537–43): they were symbols of agriculture but also of war; they pull the wagon, they also pull the chariot. In reading the second half of the *Aeneid*, we must always be conscious that we are meeting a series of peoples, all of whom are to be lineal ancestors of Rome and the Romans; Latins, Rutulans, Etruscans, the long list of Italian peoples described in Book VII (647–817), even Greeks—for we presently learn that it is Greek-Arcadian exiles who have settled on the future site of Rome itself (8.102–83)—are all to contribute their racial stock to the "conjoint people" who are to be the Romans, themselves a miniature of the worldwide brotherhood of man which was to be part of their imperial ideal. For the purposes of the *Aeneid*, it is important that none of these peoples shall be shown as pusillanimous or inadequate to the role they are assigned to play, whether it be in the peaceful life of the farmer or the necessarily harsh and bloody work of the soldier.

The best description of the peoples of Italy is put in the mouth of a certain Numanus Remulus, a Rutulan prince, brother-in-law of Turnus, who challenges Ascanius and is killed by him:

> "We're a tough race! We take our newborn babes
> to the rivers and toughen them in the ice-cold wave.
> For the hunt, our boys will beat the woods all night;
> cavalry drill and archery are their games.
> Our men love hardship and the frugal life;
> they hoe their fields or shake a world with war.
> We always wear the steel; a lance reversed
> is our ox-goad. Old age is slow to come
> and never weakens our spirit or slacks our strength.
> Our white heads don the helmet; what we need,
> we take; for pleasure, we bring in fresh spoil."
> (9.603–13)

These are the Italians, these are the stout, brave, audacious farmer-soldiers who together with the Trojans are to form the base of the racial stock of Rome.

The Trojans are an ancient and civilized people; they are also brave warriors. The contest between them and the local peoples of Italy is a contest between two people, different in background and culture, but equal in valor and skill in war. There are no cowards or traitors on either side; defeats, no matter on which side they occur, are caused by errors in judgment, largely those occasioned by excessive zeal. The Trojans have the edge over their opponents in civilization and discipline, yet on two occasions they come very close to being defeated: when Pandarus and Bitias, in an act of ill-considered bravado, open the gates of the Trojan camp, Turnus and his men fight their way inside and might well have won the day except that Jupiter intervened, and Turnus was compelled to seek escape by jumping into the Tiber. And Aeneas himself is guilty of a military blunder that would scarcely have been made by the humblest Roman centurion (although, to be sure, it was later to be made by a pair of Roman generals). In the course of the final battle before the walls of Laurentum, Aeneas elects to try to out-flank the Latins by sending a contingent of men through a nearby pass in the hills, a stratagem in itself perfectly sound, but one which would never be adopted by a thoughtful commander without first checking to make certain that the pass was free of hostile forces.

This Aeneas neglects to do, and in point of fact, the very hills overlooking the pass through which Aeneas was to send his men had been occupied by Turnus and his men, who were prepared for just such a ruse on the part of the Trojans. Except for an accident of war, the Trojans would have been as certainly and ignominiously defeated as the Romans were later to be at Cannae by Hannibal; just as Aeneas and his men are about to pass under the escarpments where Turnus and his men are lying in wait for them, word is brought to Turnus of the death of his lieutenant Camilla and the rout of her cavalry on the plain before Laurentum. Turnus has no recourse but to abandon his position and rush back to rally the army in defense of the city. Only because of this accident does Aeneas get through the pass in safety.

As for the many individual battlefield duels that take place between Trojans and Italians, it would be difficult to assign superiority to either side; the individual heroes on both sides fight skillfully, bravely, and in full accord with the ancient laws of war, and if this included some taunting and boasting it cannot be said that either side had an edge on the other. The only instance of treachery occurs in Book xi, when the Etruscan Arruns stalks and kills Camilla by throwing a spear at her when her attention is diverted by the gorgeous robes of Chloreus, warrior and priest of Cybele; alone of all the fighters in the story, she dies without a fair fight, without a chance to face her assailant. Curiously enough, for all that Camilla was a deadly fighter, no one is pleased by Arruns's act; he himself runs off in shame, and when Camilla's patron and protector, the goddess Opis, finally kills Arruns, his companions leave him to groan and die alone on the field.

On the moral side too, the scales are close to being evenly balanced. We have already seen that the Trojans, as the emissaries of divine power, have been kept from the beginning as near to moral rectitude as is possible for mere human agents; the native Italians are no worse than they. It would indeed be difficult to place the onus of moral weakness on the side of men who were, after all, fighting to defend their homeland against an invader. It is true that the scales are tipped in favor of the Trojans, simply because they are "on the Lord's side"; this gives them a moral advantage that the other side cannot match. It is also true that they came to Italy not of their own free will but in answer to a divine imperative, and that their first act upon landing had been to extend the hand of friendship and goodwill to King Latinus and his people. They had been forced to go to war by the misguided loyalty of Queen Amata toward her favorite Turnus, and by Turnus's own equally misguided patriotism. The point on all counts is that all these peoples are to be forebears of the Romans; they must be shown in every respect, even in respect of their occasional weaknesses, to be worthy of participation in Rome's ultimate mission of law, order, brotherhood, and universal peace.

Critics have often experienced great difficulty in fitting Turnus into this scheme. He has been described as mad, bloodthirsty, fool-hardy, and cruel; he has even been designated, perhaps by those who have read neither *Paradise Lost* nor the *Aeneid* with real care, as the counterpart of Milton's Satan. But if Turnus is viewed dis-passionately, he emerges as a strong and vivid personality, a brave and skillful fighter and tactician, a natural-born leader of men, and the only patriot in the land with fire enough in his heart and on his tongue to rally his somewhat listless compatriots against the invading foreigner. When—in a dream, of course—he is approached by the fury Allecto in the guise of the doddering old priestess Calybe, and scolded by her for not paying sufficient attention to the activities of the invaders, he attempts at first patiently to reassure her, and with just that shade of impatience that a busy and preoc-cupied general might properly show under such circumstances, suggests that the poor old soul had better go back to her dusting and cleaning in Juno's temple and leave men like himself to worry about war. He is driven nearly out of his mind with terror when he discovers who the poor old priestess really is; it is scarcely strange if at this point he "rages, bloodthirsty, murderous, mad for war, ruled by his anger" (7.461–62). It is no more than natural that at this moment, so violently reminded of his duty as prince of Italy, he rushes to King Latinus, tears up the treaty the king had made with the Trojans, and commands his lieutenants to take up arms, defend Italy, and repel the enemy. What else, at this point, could an honest patriot do? His madness, if madness it is, is only momen-tary; he sets immediately about the task of arming and organizing his armies, and when he finds King Latinus stubborn, and to his (Turnus's) way of thinking, weak and irresolute, he accepts the supreme command himself.

The splendid general, clad in gorgeous armor, who strides onto the field at the head of his troops (7.783–802) is neither madman nor foolish misguided boy; rather, he is precisely the latter-day Achilles whose opposition the Sibyl had warned Aeneas to expect

(6.89). If, as we like to say, all things had been equal, Turnus might
have won the war, and Aeneas would have needed to feel no shame
at having been defeated by such a man; but of course Turnus cannot win, for he and his Italians are opposing the divine imperative:

> . . . the young men . . .
> . . . joined the demand for war—
> unholy war, by omens, by God's fate
> forbidden! (7.580–84)

Turnus is hot-blooded and passionate, of this there can be no
doubt; Vergil has drawn the picture with frightening clarity. But
he is not ill-tempered or deranged. He marshals his troops and
plans his campaign with care and sound military sense; it is sheer
genius that made him appoint Camilla his lieutenant, for among
his subordinate commanders, she was the only one who demonstrated anything like his own brilliance; the others were the merest
military time-servers, perhaps best characterized by the figure of
Messapus, a kind of indestructible old warrior who does his duty
and does it well, but who certainly shows no talent for military
leadership. The only other outstanding general is Mezentius, the
Etruscan, a much-maligned character whose personal bravery is
beyond question, but whose egocentricity disqualified him for military responsibility.

In a series of difficult and bruising encounters, Turnus keeps
his head very well; he has been criticized for losing his temper
when, after appearing before the walls of the Trojan camp with
his troops, not a single Trojan dares come out to meet him (9.47–
66). His anger and his taunts on this occasion are quite understandable; as far as he can see, the Trojans are too cowardly to
stand up and fight; to a soldier with any pretensions to skill and
courage, this is deadly insult: he is not in the habit of wasting his
time and military resources on cowards. There is also an element
of frustration present: Turnus knows that unless he can meet the
Trojans in open battle there is no way in which he can drive them
from the country.

In the end he makes a very sensible decision; he decides to
move around back of the camp and burn the Trojan ships which
are pulled up to the shore of the Tiber. This stratagem, he believes,
will have a double effect; it will at once destroy the Trojans' last
means of retreat, and at the same time compel them to leave their
camp and face him in open battle. That the stratagem does not

quite succeed is not Turnus's fault; once again, the gods intervene, and apparently before Turnus's own eyes, the goddess Cybele turns the ships into dolphins who dive under the surface and swim away.

This weird transmogrification, almost a parody of the translation of Creusa at the end of Book II, amazes and frightens the Rutulans; even sturdy old Messapus is stopped in his tracks with terror. But not Turnus. He recognizes the miracle as divine intervention, but encourages his men with the thought that the loss of the ships has cut off the Trojans' retreat as effectively as the burning of them would have done; he reminds them too that though the Trojans may be blessed by divine favor, he has divine support on his side too. And with justifiable scorn he reminds the Trojans that he and his Italians are ready to face them in fair open fight, and will not have to resort to ruses, as the Greeks did, to conquer them. If there is in this speech a certain note of desperation and bravado, it is hardly more than is to be expected from a leader who recognizes the signs of ultimate defeat—in this case, the miracle, with its clear indication of divine favor—but is nonetheless determined to fight on.

Turnus has also been accused of a lack of chivalry in his duel with young Pallas, son of King Evander, commander of the Arcadian troops whom Evander has sent to assist Aeneas. In particular, his conduct here has been contrasted unfavorably with that of Aeneas in the parallel contest between Aeneas and Lausus. While it is true that Aeneas is somewhat more chivalrous and generous than Turnus, in that he not only turns the body of Lausus over to his friends, but actually picks the body up and carries it across to them, still a careful examination of the Turnus-Pallas duel will reveal that Turnus was in no way guilty of misconduct. It will be recalled that there had been a long history of enmity between the people of Turnus and the Arcadian colony on the future site of Rome (cp. 8.146–47); when Turnus sees that his man Lausus is engaged in a desperate battle with Pallas, he very naturally takes this occasion to intervene, brushing Lausus aside and taking arms against Pallas himself. The fight between them is an uneven one, of course; Pallas is a raw young soldier, while Turnus is an experienced and skillful fighter; nonetheless the duel is perfectly fair and in accord with the ancient laws of war; to be sure, Turnus takes savage pleasure in dispatching the son of another foreign interloper, but again this is no more than one would expect from a fiery patriot of Turnus's type. He too, as Aeneas later was to do, gives back the body of his slain enemy to his own people.

Turnus's act is less chivalrous than Aeneas's in two respects: first, he sends the body back with a taunt:

> "Tell Evander this:
> I send him Pallas dead; this much he earned."
> (10.491–92)

The remark seems needlessly cruel, but we must not forget that, as has already been hinted, there has been a long history of enmity between the Arcadian settlement on the Tiber and the Rutulan people. Turnus's words can scarcely be classified as ill-tempered or gratuitously savage.

Turnus's second unchivalrous act is his stripping of the baldric from Pallas's dead body. As it turns out, it was a fatal act, for at the very end of the *Aeneid* it is Turnus's possession of the baldric that is the immediate cause of his death at the hand of Aeneas. Yet the act of taking the baldric was in itself entirely in accord with the ancient laws of war; the victor in any such duel was always entitled to strip the body of his fallen enemy; in point of fact, Turnus is generous, for he takes nothing from the dead Pallas except the baldric. He could just as well have taken all of the young man's accoutrements. The tragedy in this act lies in the fact that Turnus acts perfectly honorably in perpetrating it; it turns out to have been a mistake, but neither he nor anyone else had any reason to think so at the time. Nor would the reader have thought so except for Vergil's warning (501–5) to the effect that man never knows the future or how far to push his luck; the day will come, says he, when Turnus will loath the sight of that baldric.

It is in fact a little odd that Vergil finds it necessary again and again to inject into his account of the acts of Turnus the charge that he is mad and driven wild by bloodlust. It is necessary, of course, for the preservation of the appropriate moral tone of the poem, that Turnus be shown morally inferior to Aeneas, yet a dispassionate examination of the acts of Turnus shows few if any signs of motivation other than fierce loyalty and patriotism, or in the case of the battle scenes, of sound judgment and courage. Vergil's constant interjection of these pejorative terms sounds suspiciously like a deliberate coloring of the narrative to keep Turnus in his proper place in the reader's mind; magnificent figure though he is, a fully worthy prince of Italy, he must never be allowed to rise above the stature of a Hector, and his ultimate defeat and demise must be carefully justified. In the end Turnus is made to stand utterly alone; people curse him, and the war in which they see he has involved them; he is scolded by the miserable quisling Drances; he consoles himself with the thought that some still support him—chiefly, one gathers, his soldiers—and above him still looms the "great name" (11.223) of Queen Amata.

Turnus's defeat and death are no less tragic and no less pathetic than the defeat and death of Hector in the *Iliad*. In fact, Turnus is pursued by a series of niggling and deadly misadventures such as never befell the Trojan hero. Rushing out to face Aeneas in single combat, he mistakenly picks up the wrong sword; his own, an invulnerable weapon made for his father by the god Vulcan, he had dutifully laid aside during the truce (12.735 ff.); in the confusion that followed after the breaking of the truce by Tolumnius (12.257 ff.), Turnus picks up an ordinary sword, which shatters with his first blow on Aeneas's armor. To be sure, he gets his own sword later, but by then the battle is lost; his championing deity, Juno, at last succumbs to Jupiter's rehearsal of the decrees of fate, and with the proviso that Rome must never be a Troy reborn, agrees to withdraw all opposition to Aeneas and his Trojans.

Now Turnus must face cruel humiliation: Jupiter sends the *Dira*, a tiny bird that flies in Turnus's face, fluttering and squeaking. His sister, the goddess Juturna, who had been assisting him thus far, recognizes the *Dira* for what it is: the final sign of the gods' disapproval; she too leaves Turnus alone on the field. Like a man in a dream Turnus tries to carry on the fight with arms and limbs that seem too heavy to move. Aeneas at last wounds him, and he falls; lying on the ground, he pleads, in the name of Aeneas's father Anchises and his own father Daunus, for mercy if only this may be. For a moment, Aeneas hesitates, but then he catches sight of the baldric of Pallas, and in a violent access of affection for his fallen young friend and guilt at having failed to protect him, Aeneas plunges his sword into Turnus's breast.

The point is that Turnus is an entirely worthy antagonist of Aeneas; his skill and bravery on the battlefield are beyond question, his judgment is sound, his motivation is honorable and perfectly sincere. As a symbol, he represents the opposite of Aeneas himself. Aeneas stands for Rome and her empire, the gathering under one governmental roof of all the peoples of the world in a kind of international brotherhood for peace and justice; Turnus represents the spirit of national pride, the conviction of the value of national identity and singularity, in short, the very force that the Romans again and again were destined to have to overcome in the establishment of their world rule. Turnus is Greece, he is Egypt, he is Gaul, he is Germany, he is Britain; we are not to hate or despise him, instead we are to honor him for what he is and what he stands for, but to remember that for all his virtues and all the goodness that he represents—qualities that make his descendants worthy participants in the building of a great world power—he is unfortunately in the wrong, for he is opposing the divine imperative and divine will and attempting to block a divine mission; in short, he is not "on the Lord's side."

The same must be said for Turnus's two most important associates and subordinates, Mezentius and Camilla. Both are rather puzzling figures; when we first meet Mezentius he is introduced as an Etruscan blasphemer ("scorner of gods," *contemptor divum*); later (8.481–95) he is depicted as a hideous and bloodthirsty tyrant whose people finally drive him out of their country because of his barbarities. Yet his final part in the narrative (10.689–908) shows us no such man, but rather a proud and capable general and warrior, intransigently individualistic and stoutly independent, but far from devoid of normal human feelings and even, strangely enough, possessed of a degree of tenderness. He and his son Lausus are as close as father and son ever could be; the son fights defending the wounded father; the father, after his son is killed, goes out in spite of his wound to avenge his son's death, only to be killed himself.

The account of the final battle between Mezentius and Aeneas is one of the few genuine duels of the whole poem, an interesting account of a battle, the like of which must have been repeated many times in the course of Roman history, between a man on horseback and a foot soldier. Mezentius's horsemanship is magnificent, but Aeneas's circling tactics are no less so, and the outcome shows clearly that in such a duel the man on foot has the advantage, for he has two targets to attack instead of one: unable effectively to disable Mezentius himself, Aeneas attacks the horse and kills him, leaving Mezentius helpless on the ground, pinned under the horse's body. And when Aeneas starts another one of his rather fatuous taunts over a fallen enemy, Mezentius cuts him short, reminds him that this is a war, not a parley, confesses the obvious fact of his defeat, and tells Aeneas to get on with the killing.

It is impossible not to admire Mezentius; he is in many ways a minor Turnus, differing chiefly in that where Turnus is intensely patriotic, Mezentius is devoted only to himself and his immediate family. He loves his son; in a fashion that the modern reader can only find very touching, he loves his horse; he is strong, courageous,

self-reliant, able, intelligent, a skilled fighter. His weakness is that
he has no feeling of community and no true moral sense. His
strength is all self-derived; he is brave because cowardice is undignified and weak. A splendid figure of a man, he stands as a
symbol of many such people that the Romans must have encountered
and conquered in the course of the building of their Empire.

As for Camilla, she is a strange combination of elfin-like
delicacy, normal femininity, and a violent, bloodthirsty battle lust
that puts most of her male compatriots to shame. So light-footed
that, as Vergil says, she could run across a field of grain without
even bending the grainheads, so beautiful that the women of
Latium pray that their sons may have wives as lovely as she, so
normally female that the gorgeous finery of Chloreus can distract
her attention from the battlefield, there is yet no man who can face
her in open battle and defeat her; one after another, in the goriest
fashion, she dispatches her opponents, and meets her death only
when Arruns resorts to trickery. Like Mezentius, she represents in
symbolic form some of the peoples that Rome met and conquered,
peoples about whom the Romans themselves felt a kind of primitiv-
istic sentimentality, the beautiful, unsophisticated people of the
forests, capable of great sweetness and tenderness but equally capable of bloodthirsty cruelty. Along with Mezentius and Turnus
himself, Camilla stands as an appealing representative of the many
nations and peoples who met Rome in conflict, were defeated, and
absorbed by the conqueror. The profound sympathy and respect
with which these three characters are treated by Vergil show an
understanding, almost unique among Roman writers, of the tragedies that accompany the spread of an empire, however much
divinely directed.

As a poetic expression of empire, the *Aeneid* remains unsurpassed. All the necessary elements in the building of world power
are present: the sacrifice of national identity for the high adventure
of world conquest and world rule, the need for a conviction of
divine blessing on imperial aspiration, a conviction so deep and so
overriding as to render at least tolerable the tragic acts of destruction and suppression that are an inevitable part of its realization,
the acceptance of human weakness and of defeat, error, disaster,
deceit, fear, and frustration as inevitable concomitants of the growth
of any human power, even one divinely blessed, and finally the
realization that world power like this can never be realized except
under the leadership of one devoted and inspired man, whose
patriotism embraces not only his own people but the peoples of the

world, and who has the courage, the vision, the patience, and the wisdom to recognize and accept all the elements that must go into the building of a world power. In the poem itself, Aeneas is this man; in history, he is the emperor Augustus, whose magnificent figure, clad in gleaming armor and surrounded by the military and naval power of Rome—a scene depicted for us in Book VIII of the *Aeneid*—unites history and poetry to culminate and conclude the great Parade of Heroes that began in Book VI, and in Book VIII reaches its end and logical conclusion. In Augustus, the "whole duty of Rome" has been fulfilled.

# CHAPTER XIV

# The Elegists: Tibullus, Propertius, and Ovid

To move from Vergil and a monumental epic like the *Aeneid* to the poetry of the Roman elegists is to move from the heroic to the ordinary, from the broad sweep of time to the immediate moment, from the national-imperial to the intensely personal. The three extant Roman elegists, Tibullus, Propertius, and Ovid, are as different one from the other as well may be, but they bear in common the conviction that they are men whose minds, hearts, and views are intrinsically valuable and worthy of literary expression.

The world of ideas within which this egocentricity revolves is very limited; it is concerned almost entirely with love, and ventures into other realms only in the search for illustrative and supportive material or in response to the prick of conscience or some external pressure. For the elegist, love is life itself; the two are synonymous; the one is meaningless without the other. It must be understood that this is true only of the world of the poems themselves; we do not now know, nor is there any way to discover, to what degree the world of the elegy reflects the actual experiences of its practitioners, and it is unlikely that even if more were known about the lives, personalities, and activities of the elegists, this would throw more than quite casual illumination on the poems they write. In general, they tell us all we need to know; they set up their world of poetry for us and expect us to accept it as a constant in their writing. It is patent, for example, that any normal man must have more concerns than love; the quickest glance at a more catholic poet like Catullus reveals a poetic world of far wider spectrum. But to the elegists, love is the whole story; to win his lady and keep her, and to record the various experiences that befall them, is the poet's entire preoccupation.

The term "elegy" may be a little misleading, for an elegy today is normally a poem of lament, or at least is likely to embody rather sober and solemn thoughts. In actual fact, our conception of the elegy represents a curious reversion to its original state, for as far as we can now tell, it did indeed begin as a poem of lament, a dirge, a poem of death and sorrow. Its early history is quite obscure, but it seems to have originated with the Greek poets of Asia Minor. Tradition has it that the elegy was sung to the accompaniment of the flute, in contrast to the lyric, which was accompanied by the lyre, and that in fact it owes its peculiar metrical form to the exigencies of flute-playing. The meter of elegy, the elegiac distich, consists of one line of dactylic hexameter followed by a modified form of this same line that contains within it two stops, or "rests," as they would be called in music. This line, styled a dactylic pentameter, provided the flute-player with two points at which he could draw breath—a pretty tale, and probably fanciful, but as good an explanation as any for the meter of the elegy.

Beginning, then, as a song of lament, the elegiac form was quickly taken up and used as a vehicle for more varied types of poetic expression. We early find it in the guise of patriotic song, e.g. in the elegies of Tyrtaeus (c. 640 B. C.) and Solon (639–559 B. C.). It became too, so far as we can tell, the recognized and regular vehicle for convivial song—that informal type of composition that the Greeks indulged in for postprandial entertainment. The elegiac distich appears to have been an easily handled meter, readily adaptable to impromptu composition and as such very handy for the slightly inebriated dinner-guest.

But love and wine have always been companions, and it was not long before elegy slipped over into the realm of love, and it is here in fact that it finds its first extended expression. We hear the names of a number of Greek elegists, but perhaps the best known of them is Mimnermus (c. 630 B. C.), who is reported to have written a series of elegies about his mistress, whom he calls Nanno. Only fragments of his work exist; they reveal a fairly lighthearted poet who takes neither himself nor his love too seriously, but does strike the note that was later, with the Romans, to become the key-note of the elegy:

> What life is there, what joy, without Aphrodite the
>   Golden?
> I'd want to die when such things no longer interest me.
>   (frg. 1.1–2)

We are told, although the evidence is very fragmentary, that the early Greek elegists were less personal than their Roman followers, that in common with most Greek writers they tended to take a more objective view of their women and their experiences with them. Whether this is really true, or has simply become a handy cliché of literary history need not concern us here, and in any event the documentation is inconclusive. Suffice it to say that the Greeks apparently did develop a body of love elegy which began with the seventh century and continued to accumulate down into Roman times; it was certainly still being practiced when the first Roman elegists came on the scene.

Again because the Greek elegy is extant only in such scanty fragments, it is impossible to say just what was the relation between Greek and Roman elegy. Probably the most important name among the later Greek elegists was Callimachus (c. 310 B. C.), the chief custodian of the library of the Ptolemies at Alexandria. Propertius (e.g. 4.1.64) boasts that he was the Roman Callimachus; if we had more of Callimachus's work we would be better able to tell to what degree the boast was substantiated, and to what degree it was no more than the usual Roman pose, the sort of thing that we see reflected, for example, in Horace's boast that he "brought Aeolic song into Italy."

We can be certain that Greek elegy contributed its metrical structure to its Roman counterpart, although the use of the flute as an accompaniment had long since fallen into disuse. We may be reasonably certain that the general erotic atmosphere of the elegy, the centrality of the world of love, also owes its presence to Greek influences. And at least one poetico-rhetorical device can be definitely traced to the Greeks; this is the *exemplum*, the citation by the poet of experiences and sentiments paralleling his own and derived from mythology. We know that the scholars of Alexandria, among whom Callimachus must be included, were much interested in Greek mythology and made it their business to track down and record varying versions of the old tales so well known to the Hellenic world from the days of Homer. A secondary development of this interest was the aetiological elegy in which the poet took a given myth as his subject and attempted to trace it to its origin. Callimachus wrote a number of this type, and Propertius in his later days wrote several such aetiologies, apparently with Callimachus as his model.

In a large degree, these are matters of the mechanics of poetry writing and tell us very little about its spirit. It may well be that the Roman elegists borrowed no more from their Greek predecessors than did any other Roman poets from their Greek counterparts. Metrical form and genre, general background, mechanical devices of poetry and rhetoric—all these the Roman learned from his Greek master. The rest was his own.

Apart from a few clumsily executed verses of the second century B. C., the first Roman writer who certainly set his hand to the composition of elegy was Catullus. His position in the rank of the elegists has been attacked, to be sure, by many critics, who feel that his work in this genre is too different from that of the Augustans to ensure him a place here. The fact remains that he did compose a great many poems in elegiac meter, among them at least four fairly long ones, two of which (67 and 68) are emphatically erotic, although each of them deals with love in a very different way. Sixty-seven, with its story of cuckoldry, involves Catullus only as a bystander; 68, however, is the poet's long and very nearly tortured description of one of the aspects of his love for Lesbia; as such, it certainly counts as erotic-subjective elegy, and the differences between it and the work of the later elegists probably is to be attributed to the difference between the loves they celebrate rather than to any startling differences in the genre itself.

It is nevertheless true that the type of elegy represented by Catullus in 68, with its highly elaborate contrapuntal form and its curious, not to say clumsy, mélange of Greek and Roman symbolism, found no imitators or followers in later periods. Instead, we generally, and probably quite correctly, begin our account of Roman erotic-subjective elegy with the somewhat shadowy figure of Cornelius Gallus (70–27 B. C.). Of his work we possess less than one line, but we know that his influence was great. We have already seen Vergil's tribute to him in the tenth *Eclogue*; we know that he composed a series of elegies about a woman whom he called Lycoris. But, paradoxically, we know more about him as a man and civil servant than as a poet. A close friend of the emperor Augustus, he was appointed by him procurator of Egypt, certainly one of the most arduous, ticklish, and strategic governmental positions in the emperor's command. What possessed the otherwise usually astute Augustus to hand a job of this kind to a poet is quite beyond comprehension, and the succeeding debacle of the unfortunate Gallus was hardly more than to be expected. The job proved entirely too much for him; he was accused of incompetence and peculation, and removed from his post in disgrace, whereupon he committed suicide.

Quintilian, writing in the second century A. D., says that Gallus's style was rough. This is all we know of him; his name remains at the head of the list of Roman elegists simply because, as far as we know, he was the first of them.

With Tibullus (Albius Tibullus, c. 55–19 B. C.) we are on firm ground in the elegy for the first time. As is usually the case with ancient authors, little is really known about him; tradition has it that he was the son of a wealthy man who had lost his estates in some manner now unknown—possibly in the proscriptions following the battle of Philippi. In his poems he speaks of himself as poor *(pauper)*, yet at the same time tells of the pleasant and comfortable country estate on which he spent his life. He was a member of the salon that rivalled Maecenas's, the circle of Messalla; it may well be that his patron saw to his financial needs, as Maecenas did for Vergil and Horace. In one of his *Odes* (1.33) and in one of his *Epistles* (1.4), Horace refers to a certain "Albius" who, in spite of a number of small discrepancies, has often been asserted to be the poet Tibullus. Horace's poems depict a rather melancholy man, given to self-pity and hypochondria. There is nothing in Tibullus's writings that would definitely rule out the identification, but there is equally nothing in them to establish it beyond doubt. In any event, the figure of the poet as we find it in the poems is a poetical rather than an autobiographical creation, who receives more illumination from the poems themselves than from Horace's accounts of his friend Albius; it is doubtful that Tibullus's "real" life, even if we knew it for certain, would shed much light on the poet-lover of the elegies. This latter figure is clearly enough defined. He is a gentle soul, somewhat languorous, softly affectionate toward his friends, great and small, dominated by his mistress of the moment, sentimental about his farm, and possessed of a strong nostalgia for the fast-disappearing godlets of field, stream, and forest.

In his elegies, Tibullus celebrates his love for two different women; in the earlier poems, Delia is named as his lady, in the later, Nemesis. Both names are, as usual, poetic pseudonyms; we are told that Delia's real name was Plania; of Nemesis we know nothing. The two women are scarcely more than names; we learn virtually nothing about them from the poems; any other names than the ones Tibullus uses for them would have been suitable, provided only that they scanned. Of the two, Delia is the more appealing; Nemesis seems to have been a bit grasping. But as in the case of Catullus and, for that matter, of all the elegists, it is the figure of the poet-lover that emerges with the greater clarity. As with his confreres, the only life that really concerns Tibullus is his own.

About the elegies of Tibullus there is indubitably a certain monotony. That he writes of love in every poem is no more than we should expect; that he should append to this central preoccupation an absorbing interest in two other subjects, hatred of war and the joys of country life, is perhaps a little less to be expected. No matter whom the poet is addressing, whether it be Delia, Nemesis, the boy Marathus, or important friends like Messalla and Cornutus, Tibullus somehow manages nearly always to get these three subjects into the poem. As for his handling of love, we find here none of the passionate soul-searching of a Catullus, none of his anguished questing, and equally none of his ebullient joy. Absent too is the casual good humor of Horace, who enjoyed the pose of the lover, and found casual relations with women amusing enough, but never let himself be carried away. Tibullus is, in fact, a sentimentalist; love in a cottage is his ideal:

> How sweet it is to lie abed and hear the angry winds, to
> hold my lady to my tender breast; or, when wintry
> Auster pours his icy waters, to drop peacefully asleep,
> helped by the rain.
> (1.1.45–48)

This is the poet's ideal of love; this is how he wants his Delia, and later his Nemesis, to think of love. That his view is totally egotistic is painfully patent, for the lines demand a total subjection on the part of the lady to the lover's whims and desires. More elaborate but in the same vein are the concluding lines of the third *Elegy*:

> But, Delia, I pray you, remain chaste. Let chastity be holy to you and let an old lady, your ever-watchful guardian, sit by your side. Let her tell you old wives' tales, and when the lamp is lighted, unwind the long threads from her full distaff. And all about you let your maids be intent upon their heavy tasks and, bit by bit, as sleep wearies them, let fall their work. Then may I come all of a sudden; no one must give news of me before! No, I would seem sent from heaven to your side! Then, just as you are, your long hair all confusion, your foot bare, run, run, Delia, to meet me. This is my prayer; may bright Aurora bring on her rosy steeds a shining dawn like this to me!
> (1.3.83–94)

The lines—and there are many like them in tone if not in specific subject—breathe an atmosphere unlike any we are likely to find until we reach the Romantics of a far later age.

But if love is Tibullus's primary preoccupation, he is almost equally absorbed in his two other topics, hatred of war, and the joys of country life. In part, Tibullus's hatred of war is one more expression of the egotism of the elegist; war is an uncomfortable, ugly business, utterly foreign to his gentle, pensive nature:

> Who was it who first forged the fearful sword? How savage he was, how truly a man of steel! That was the birthday of murder and battle for humankind; on that day a shorter road was opened to dread Death.
> (1.10.1–4)

Besides, war commits the ultimate malfeasance, for its draws the lover away from his lady, and since love is the elegist's life, this is tantamount to sacrilege:

> He was a man of steel, who, when he could have had you, thought rather, the fool, to chase after spoils and the sword.
> (1.2.65–66)

In most instances, this hatred of war, however strongly expressed, becomes scarcely more than a transition to war's opposite, the peace of the countryside. Tibullus regularly effects the transition between war and peace by means of the mythical Golden Age;

> In those days the stout ox never submitted to the yoke, and the mouth of the horse was not tamed to take the bit; no house had doors; there was no stone stationed in the field to mark fixed boundaries to plots of land. The very oak tree gave honey, and of their own accord, sheep offered milk-filled udders to carefree men. There was no battle-line, no quarrel, no war, and the village smith, with his heartless art, had not yet forged the sword.
> (1.3.41–48)

Consonant with this pensive dream of a period that never was, is Tibullus's view of country life. Succumbing to the romantic fallacy of primitivism, he sees in the country the simplicity, sincerity, naturalness, beauty, and purity that constitute his dream of human life. The dream is of course the purest sentimentality and the purest egotism, for the poet is totally disregarding the realities

of farm life, its backbreaking labor, its earthy uncouthness, its insecurity; instead, he sees in country life only the reflection of the
poetic personality which he has chosen to set into his poems. Even
when he protests his love for the farmer's tasks, it is with the easy
assurance of the landed gentry, who in actuality turn over such
work to their underlings:

> Oh, now, now, let me be content to live on little, and not be
> forever surrendered to endless journeying; let me rather avoid
> the hot rising of the Dogstar under the shade of a tree where
> streams of water pass by. And let me not be ashamed from time
> to time to hold the hoe, or with the goad to drive the sluggish
> oxen, never weary of bringing home in my arms a lamb or kid
> its mother has forgotten.
>
> (1.1.25–32)

If one may be allowed to doubt the poet's genuine pleasure in
playing farm-boy, it may at least be said that the pictures he draws
of farm life are taken from the realities of Italy and not from some
hazy dream of a nonexistent Arcadia. And love of the countryside,
too, leads Tibullus to describe in loving and apparently accurate
detail some of the simple rustic religious festivals that had persisted
in the country; Tibullus's delight in these rites and ceremonies, his
genuine affection for simple rustic gods, comes close to preserving
for us some of the genuine religious feeling that the Roman pagan
must have known. In the first elegy of Book II, Tibullus describes
a rustic festival which might well be called "The Blessing of the
Fields"; as if it were a veritable Sabbath, everything and everybody
on the farm is commanded to take a day of rest and prayer: the
land itself, the plowman, the oxen, the housemaids. All who attend
the prayers must be ritually pure: they must not have had sexual
intercourse the night before, they must don clean clothes and wash
in fresh water. After the prayers and the sacrifices, they may all turn
to the wine-cups, the singing, and the dancing. Priapus, Pales, Ceres,
Bacchus—these are Tibullus's gods; the love that he lavishes on
them has a strong admixture of nostalgia and melancholy; one gets
the distinct impression that this poet-cum-farmer-cum-priest is honoring gods who have become scarcely more than myths, whose
statues, shrines, and rites are maintained out of respect for ancient
tradition but have ceased to have any real meaning to the educated
and the thoughtful. The peasantry still love them; it is as if the
sophisticated poet were attempting to translate their earthy love

into terms of beauty and sensitivity that he and his like might yet appreciate.

Tibullus was described by Quintilian (10.1.93) as "polished and fastidious" *(tersus atque elegans)*. The epithets are well deserved, for this dreamy, sentimental poet has written some of the smoothest and most euphonious Latin that has come down to us. Not only is his language impeccable and his taste well-nigh perfect; his poems are constructed with infinite delicacy and care. His three favorite subjects, love, hatred of war, the joys of country life, are brought together in smoothly flowing poems, where every transition is deft and unobtrusive, every part of the poetic fabric balanced precisely against every other part, the sentences not too long nor too short, the imagery not too vivid nor too subdued, the whole possessed of just enough variety to maintain interest. He is a poet whose poems should be read one or two at a time, never more than that; his comfortable sweetness and prevailing tone of peace, goodwill and harmony provide a pleasant respite from the passions and agonies of greater writers. He is a Sabbath among the Augustans, and one such in the progression is enough.

To move from Tibullus to Propertius is to migrate from country to city, from dreamy idyll to passionate reality, from peace to turmoil. Sextus Propertius (c. 50–c. 16 B. C.) was born in Umbria, probably at Assisi. He seems to have come from landed gentry, as did Tibullus and Vergil before him; of his family we hear only of his mother and possibly of a sister; it appears that his estates were confiscated like Vergil's in the year 41 after the battle of Philippi. He is said to have gone to Rome, where he began the study of law, but soon gave it up and turned to poetry. Like Tibullus, he is an egotist—or, if we prefer, a "personal" poet—who writes almost exclusively about himself and his own ideas and feelings, and again like Tibullus, these thoughts and feelings are almost exclusively concerned with love.

In his poems, although there are clear references to many women, only one name appears as central to the poet's interests. This is Cynthia, the lady whose real name, we are told, was Hostia. Her name suggests membership in a Roman family of some standing and antiquity, but in the poems her station is that of the usual freedwoman; her relationship with Propertius is spoken of as deep and sincerely passionate, but never more than temporary. It was certainly not a prelude to marriage, much less a part of it. Cynthia is thought to have died in 18 B. C.; at any rate, the seventh elegy of Book IV is a beautiful tribute paid to her after her death.

According to tradition, it was Propertius's first published work, now commonly called *Cynthia monobiblos* (Book I), that brought him to public attention and eventually to the circle of Maecenas, who became his patron. Propertius later produced at least three more books of poems; as he grew in maturity and years, he tended to turn more and more away from exclusive devotion to erotic subjects and toward themes of a more national and patriotic character. There is some evidence that he was under pressure to do so from the emperor Augustus and from Maecenas; Propertius's reaction to this pressure—if pressure it was—is similar to Horace's; he protests his inability to handle such exalted subjects in the style that befits them and asserts again and again the essential simplicity of his muse.*

Like Horace, Propertius persisted to the end in his refusal to attempt artistic expression of the patriotic ideal as such. Horace honors Rome by honoring some of her great men; Propertius finds his solution in a somewhat different way, turning instead to the aetiological poem, a form which he derived from his studies of Callimachus; as the Greek scholar had committed to verse the results of his studies of the myths of Greece, so Propertius now expresses his devotion to Rome and her empire by creating poetic versions of some of the myths of Italy and Rome. As with Horace, this interest remained always secondary; we dare not say that he found it uninteresting and composed the poems solely as the result of pressure; we may only say that these products of his poetic imagination and art are less appealing than his more immediately personal effusions.

One device of the Alexandrians persists throughout Propertius's work; this is the *exemplum*, the mythological parallel for whatever erotic or emotional experience is occupying the poet's mind at the moment. In poem after poem, these *exempla* appear, most of them drawn from a mythology that was familiar to the ancient if not to us, but some of them employing names and references that even Propertius's contemporaries may have found unfamiliar. Sometimes the story is developed at some length; for example in the first elegy in Book I, Propertius, speaking of his own lack of success in love, contrasts his experience with that of Milanion, who won his Atalanta not by the usual lover's words and services but by displaying his manliness in the hunt and by fighting off his rival, the centaur Hylaeus. But in the second elegy in Book I, the *exempla*

*See footnote, p. 240.

are reduced to scarcely more than a list of names, as the poet cites heroine after heroine from ancient mythology who, unlike his foolish Cynthia, attracted and won their lovers without recourse to artificial adornment. Propertius does not often overuse this device, and if we are unfamiliar with the recondite forms which his excursions into mythology sometimes take, we can always enjoy, as most of us now do with Milton, the pleasing sound-patterns created by euphonious names.

Devices of this sort are, however, hardly more than poetic ornamentation, and at least in theory could be turned to good use in almost any kind of poetry. Their very nearly exclusive appearance in the literature of love is probably a poetic accident. Of far greater interest is the actual content of Propertius's elegies. Like Tibullus, he is primarily a poet of love, but his devotion to this subject is vastly more passionate and all-inclusive than was Tibullus's. Not only is love the poet's life; only his part in that love is of any interest to him; the girl in the case exists only for his pleasure and satisfaction: her feelings are of little interest to him, except insofar as they may affect his own attitude toward her and his own feelings of happiness and well-being. If he gives her gifts, it is that she may be more complaisant; if he plays the part of her slave, it is not because he has exalted her to so high a position in his thoughts that the role of mere slave seems appropriate; rather he seeks by this self-abnegation to impress her with his devotion and place her under obligation to reciprocate by entertaining him with her singing, her dancing, her sparkling conversation and, of course, her bed.

The love that is Propertius's life is not something that is built up by mutual devotion and selflessness; it is totally man-centered, not because he thinks of himself as more important than the girl, but because he knows how he feels, and finds himself eternally fascinated by the problem of expressing these feelings in poetry; the feelings of the girl were no doubt very much in his mind but do not find their way into his verse, perhaps because they were beyond his comprehension and his powers of expression.

The love of a poet like Propertius is in the realest of senses a "literary" love, which may have had only the most tenuous relation —and in some instances no relation whatever—to the day-to-day life of the poet. Propertius creates a "world" in his poems; in this world, whatever he says about it is true; whatever feelings he describes, are true; whatever he says he experiences, these are true experiences; whatever persons he portrays, these persons are true. With their *reality* or *actuality*—whether these events, as we say, "really occurred," whether these persons, again as we say, "really were"—should not form part of our poetic judgment.

But even poetic worlds must have some fixed characteristics, some clear-cut landmarks that will provide the poet with elements that he and his readers may take for granted, that we may reasonably expect to find in almost any literary love affair, and that will act, as it were, like the constants in a mathematical problem.

This was certainly true of the love affair as we find it in the poems of Propertius. In his poems, as in those of Tibullus and Ovid, certain events and assumptions are canonical, and we know that sooner or later they will occur or be stated. First and fundamental is the assumption that the love affair occurs outside marriage, and is, in fact, adulterous. This assumption has a long history behind it, and the various steps and stages by which it developed can no longer be determined with precision.

In whatever way this canon of adultery developed, in the elegy it is a fixed assumption: the love of the elegists is spoken of as if it were adulterous, as if the lady in question were the wife of someone and were being tempted to play her husband false by offering herself to his rival. But by a further convention, the whole drama of elegiac love is played outside the realm of legal marriage; in point of fact, the woman in question is assumed to be either a slave or a freedwoman, and as such would be debarred from legal marriage with anyone. She cannot therefore have a true legal husband and, lacking one, she can scarcely engage in adultery. But we are asked to pretend that she is indeed married, that the lover who, so to speak, semipermanently cohabits with her is indeed her husband, and that she is subject to constant temptation to play this husband false with an adulterous lover. The "adultery" of elegy thus emerges as pure fiction—a prose, a conceit, a convention.

As for Propertius, he plays the part now of the "husband," now of the "lover," depending on the immediate circumstances. At one point he finds himself accepted as husband and his adulterous rivals are locked out:

Others were pounding in vain on her door, and were crying out "Lady! Lady!" But my girl was deaf, and pillowed her head by mine.
(2.14.21–22)

On another occasion it was he who was the shut-out lover and someone else has won a place by Cynthia's side:

Now for the first time I am alone, and am learning how long are the nights (I have no choice!) and am a burden to my own ears.
(1.12.13–14)

With this conventional pseudo-adultery as a base, Propertius's story of love proceeds along a path that is marked at strategic points by conventional episodes and ideas. At one point (2.5), Cynthia and Propertius have separated in anger. He accuses her of disgraceful conduct about which the whole city of Rome is gossiping. He will find himself another girl, he says, who will not have such heartless ways *(duri mores)* and goes on to warn her that she is more likely than he to suffer from this unfortunate incident: she may be angry now, but she will shed a tear when she suddenly realizes that the love that had lasted so long is now gone. And she should remember, too, that even poets have ways of punishing waywardness like hers: "I'll not tear the clothing from your lying body; I'll not lose my temper and break through your locked door; I'll not, in a moment of fury, tear out your braided hair or gouge you with a thumb—I wouldn't dare!" (2.5.21–24). Such conduct is for the boor. And what will the poet do? Naturally, he will write:

No, sir! I'll write words that all your life's years will not wash out: Cynthia: beauty: power; Cynthia: words: lies!
(2.5.27–28)

In another poem Propertius again depicts the lovers separated; this time he has Cynthia complaining that a rival woman has bewitched Propertius with potions, with the rhombus-wheel, with the innards of toads, the bones of snakes, the feather of a screech-owl picked up in a graveyard, and a bit of ribbon filched from someone's coffin (3.6.25–30). But she will get back at him, for she has been dreaming, and her dreams tell her that the bed where Propertius and his current love are lying will be festooned in cobwebs, and "Venus herself will sleep through the nights they spend together" *(ibid.* 33–34). On another occasion, the two have quarreled and another man has taken the poet's place:

But you could not go without a lover for a single night (indecent creature!), you could not live alone for a single day!
(2.9.19–20)

Is this my reward, says the poet, for the tears and the prayers that saved you once from death? Where was this pet lover of yours then? But when women get angry, they turn completely faithless and ungrateful. By contrast, the poet, whose self-righteousness in the matter is a bit trying, swears by all the stars in heaven that nothing was ever dearer to him than Cynthia: "Even now you shall be so, though you have come to hate me. And no other lady shall make her mark upon my bed: alone shall I be, since I may not be yours!" (2.9.41–46).

But the poet's arsenal of song would soon be exhausted if he could write only of quarrels and anger. Inevitably the two are brought together again, and for the poet this is a moment of triumph:

> Here is my victory, greater than a Parthia brought to heel!
> here are my spoils, here, my kings, here my triumphal car.
> Great are the gifts, Cytherea, that I shall nail to your column;
> and there my name shall be, and under it these words: "Lady,
> at your temple door, Propertius has offered these spoils, when,
> through all one night, he was a lover once more!"
> (2.14.23–28)

The joys of that night may have formed the subject of the poem that immediately follows this one (2.15), for here the poet describes the lovemaking of the pair: they talked and talked by the light of the lamp, then put the lamp out, and came to each other's arms; she teased the poet by offering him her breasts to caress, and then, on a sudden impulse, covered her body with her gown. He pretended to sleep, but she kissed his eyes open and jokingly accused him of being unresponsive. They embraced, they kissed, she bared her body for him, for "to make love blindly is to spoil love."

The poem is, in fact, a masterpiece; few writers have succeeded in describing lovemaking without becoming coarse; somehow this poem, in spite of the intimacy of its details, successfully represents the ineffable sweetness that is the essence of physical love.

That lovers should quarrel, and then be reconciled, seems so natural a part of a love affair as scarcely to need special comment: we expect this to happen; we would be disappointed if it did not. Less readily anticipated is the incident of illness; but in fact, the love affair of elegy would not be considered complete if the girl did not fall ill. On one occasion we find the poet worrying over Cynthia's illness:

Jupiter, my lady is ill! Have mercy! She is so lovely; if she should die, that will be a crime to lay at your door!
(2.28.1–2)

How could this have happened? Had Cynthia, by pride in her own beauty, offended Venus? Had she forgotten her prayers to Juno? Had she been so foolish as to say that the eyes of Pallas were not beautiful?

O you lovely creatures, you have never learned to hold your tongues! You have boasted of your beauty: here lies the guilt that has brought you to this!
(2.28.13–14)

Nevertheless, the poet urges Cynthia to be patient; he quotes his inevitable *exempla* from mythology to encourage her, and reminds her that, if she should not recover, she will be the greatest beauty to grace heaven. But she must be patient:

Now, as best you can, in pain though you may be, be patient with your lot; this day may be cruel, but it will pass; God may be cruel, but He will change.
(2.28.31–32)

In the end, of course, the girl recovers, for her death would put an abrupt period to the love affair. The lover has at least made it clear that if Cynthia is to die, he will die with her (2.28.35–40). And, in the end, his appeal to Jupiter and Persephone rescues her from the death that had seemed so imminent, and the incident ends with Propertius reminding the girl that she should now in gratitude dance before the altar of Diana and offer a novena of prayer to Isis (2.28.59–62).

One might remark, in this connection, that novenas of this kind were viewed with more enthusiasm by the poet on this occasion than on some others. In another poem, he complains bitterly of those ten long nights during which Cynthia, saying her prayers to Isis, as, we gather, she did once a year, has promised to remain chaste: Isis must indeed be a heartless creature to keep a passionate pair apart for so long! (2.33.5–6). She had plenty of dusky disciples in Egypt, and Rome was a long way off: why did she have to come there at all (*ibid.* 15–16)? We'll chase you out of Rome, says he; the Nile

and the Tiber were never good friends (*ibid.* 19–20). And he ends
with a promise to Cynthia:

> But, my girl, who have made your peace at the cost of such
> pain to me, once we're free of these nights, let's travel the path
> three times!
> (*ibid.* 21–22)

And if the lover's devotion to his sweetheart is shown by his
prayers for her recovery when she is ill, it is shown even more
signally by the self-abasement—really an inverted form of egotism—
with which he views his part in the love affair. Only when he has
lowered himself to the position of the merest slave, does he really
know what love is; Propertius had known many a woman, but it
was only when Cynthia made him her captive that he came to know
the true nature and meaning of love:

> Cynthia was the first who took me prisoner with her eyes;
> before that no passion had so much as touched me. On that
> day she bent to the ground the gaze of pride I had so long
> maintained, and Love put his foot upon my neck and forced
> me down.
> (1.1.1–4)

From then on, his life became a round of misery and frustration
from which he sought to escape, but without success; from that day
on, he saw nothing but years of pain stretching before him. Eventually, his humility won him his lady; like a true slave, he found life
bearable only in the discharge of the commands imposed upon him
by his *domina*; in the end, he comes to view his slavery as comfortable and merciful: even her beauty and fame have not so strong
a hold upon him (2.20.19–20). He becomes accustomed to the slavery
that she imposes upon him, and resists every attempt on the part of
his friends to wean him away from it. When Bassus, by singing the
praises of many women, tries to get Propertius to diversify his interests, he has this to say:

> Bassus, why do you keep singing the praises of woman after
> woman to me, trying to change me and get me to leave the
> lady who rules my life? Why, for what remains of my years,
> do you not permit me rather to live in the slavery to which I
> have become accustomed?
> (1.4.1–4)

But such feelings of gentle resignation are relatively rare; more often the poet indulges in self-pity, complaining of the heartlessness and cruelty with which the lady persists in treating the man who has devoted his life to her:

> Oh, what a fool I was for all those many years, through which, you fair criminal, I put up with you and that house of yours. Have you ever thought of me as a free man? Or will you, forever and ever, continue to hurl proud insult at my head? Is it thus, then, Propertius, that, in the first years of life, you shall die? Well, *die*! and let her take joy at your demise! Let her chase my ghost, pursue my shade, dance upon my tomb, kick my bones!
> (2.8.13–20)

As this last passage suggests, Propertius seems to think of death as the only possible escape from the servitude to which he has committed himself. His friends have suggested travel, on the perhaps perverted theory that absence will make the heart grow *less* fond (1.1.29–30); the poet himself, at one point, in a style that must seem a little fatuous, suggests that he might cure his passion by going to Athens to enroll in the university and study philosophy and rhetoric (3.21.25–28); in the intervals of solemn study, he could visit the museums and rest his aching heart by looking at paintings and statuary (*ibid.* 29–30); perhaps the passage of years and the miles of ocean that separate him from Cynthia may serve to lessen the pain for which his heart can find no words (*ibid.* 31–32). And if this does not work, and he does in fact die, it will at least be an honorable death: he will not have crumpled in the ugly service of love (*ibid.* 33).

Propertius delights in thoughts of his own death. With gentle hand and many a tear, shed partly in his own honor, and partly in pity for those who, some day, will be deprived of his fresh young voice, and his warm, passionate heart, he turns over the poor little handful of dust which he must some day himself become. At one point he declares that it is not so much death itself that terrifies him, as the thought that, in the hour of his death and burial, Cynthia may not be at his side (1.19.1–2). But wherever he shall be, he will be called "Cynthia's ghost" (*ibid.* 11) and no matter how many of the glorious heroines of past history may come to dance for him, none will be lovelier than Cynthia herself, and no matter how old she may live to be, her bones will be dear to him, and perhaps a little illogically, he will shed a tear for her (*ibid.* 13–18).

At another point, he elaborates in affectionate detail on the kind of death he hopes to have:

> So then, whenever death shall close my eyes, hear the order of burial that I would have you follow. Let there be no long parade of statues of my ancestors on that day, no trumpet to sound vain sorrow at my death; I'd not have my couch piled with pillows and plated with ivory, nor have my corpse rest in Orient splendor. Give me no train of thurifers: I want the simple prayers of a poor man's death. My procession will be long enough if my three little volumes make it up—volumes I will give to Persephone as the best I have. But do you, Cynthia, bare your breast and rake it with your nails until it bleeds; then follow me, and grow never too faint to utter my name. Place that last kiss on my ice-cold lips, and use a whole vial of Syrian perfume to anoint me! Then when the flame, that has turned me to ashes, has died down, let a modest jar collect my ghost; dig a slight trench, and plant a laurel above it to roof with its shade the spot where the dead man lies; and let there be two verses: "Who rests here now, mere ugly dust, was once the slave of a single love."
> (2.13.17–36)

On still another occasion (1.17), the poet thinks of himself as shipwrecked on a lonely shore: what a fool he was to try to cross a forbidding sea! If he is to die here, how will Cynthia be able to stand it? They may have quarreled, but will she be able to hear the news of his death without shedding a tear? Will she not be even a little sorry that she won't be there to gather his bones and dust into her lap? How much better if he had stayed at home, put up with his girl's petulance, and died where both he and she might have the advantage of her grief and her ministrations! The figure of the shipwrecked sailor singing his sad complaint to the seabirds, and the equally sentimental figure of the poet lost in the wildwood, tearfully carving his beloved's name in the bark of a tree (1.18.21–22) are very nearly as standard a part of the apparatus of the ancient literary love affair as are the illness of the girl and the death of the lover himself. These are canonical experiences; these are the milestones, the distinct points around which the story of the love affair is woven.

But there was one incident that was mandatory; at any rate, it recurs with a kind of inevitability in nearly every collection of love poems that we have from antiquity, and even sometimes in the more oblique forms of the love story as they appear, for example, in the comedy. This is the *vigilatio ad clausas fores*, the watch by the closed door. In origin, apparently an outgrowth of the Greek *komos*, the drunken revel through the streets, the watch by the closed door early became a standard erotic incident. Taken over by the Romans from the Greeks, it was given even greater prominence in the literary love affair, and in fact acquired a centrality that it never had with the Greek writers. The ancient love poet—and in this respect Propertius is about as typical of their kind as may well be—invariably thought of love as an unhappy experience; washed with tears from beginning to end, it had only its occasional moments of gaiety. Of this kind of love, the *vigilatio ad clausas fores* becomes the perfect symbol. The lover, usually drunk and with his garland over one ear, comes through the streets to the door of his beloved, where he knocks and demands admission. She, either because she is occupied with some other man, or because she finds herself uneasy about his condition, refuses him admission. Hereupon, he sings a sad ditty of the sorrows and disappointments of love, throws himself prostrate at the lady's threshold, kisses her doorstep, bathes it with his tears, and remains there through the night, buffeted by the cold winter wind and soaked with the rain, until cockcrow at last releases him from his misery. He then pulls himself together and wanders wearily home.

In Propertius, this standard incident takes a rather strange form. Every one of Propertius's other love elegies is personal in the highest degree; the poet himself is protagonist in every scene and chief speaker of every sentiment that the lover has to utter. If there was ever a "personal" poet, it is he; he insists that we stand beside him with every line that he writes.

To this general rule, Propertius's song of the *vigilatio* provides a startling exception. In this poem (1.16) the door itself is introduced as the speaker, and when it retails the song of the shut-out lover (17–44), it is a song that could have been sung by any man; both the singer and the girl to whom his song is addressed—or, better, about whom he speaks, for the song is addressed to the door —are anonymous and impersonal: they could have been anybody. It is possible that Propertius was again thinking of himself as the singer of the song and of Cynthia as the lady behind the locked door; certainly he did so on many another occasion. But if this is indeed the case, it is the only poem in which Propertius was able to write about himself and Cynthia in an objective and impersonal way. It is rather more likely that Propertius's paraclausithyron—for this is the name we find Plutarch giving to this "song at the locked door"—was given this impersonal quality precisely because, for this once, he wanted his poem to speak in general, rather than in specific terms, because he wanted it to stand in a symbolic way for the totality of that literary love affair about which not only he but many another poet had written so many poems. It is a poem that, in symbolic language and through a set of symbolic experiences, tells the whole story of the love affair as the elegists conceived it. The search for love, the plea for acceptance, the proffering of gifts, both those of financial value and those love verses that were the peculiar benevolence of the lover-poet, the servile humility, rejection and disappointment, pain and sorrow, anger, long-suffering endurance, ultimate rejection of the girl by the lover himself, and finally, those occasional moments of joy when the lover found himself admitted to house and bed—all of these elements are neatly presented and symbolized by the various parts of the paraclausithyron. The lover comes to his beloved's door, he begs to be admitted and accepted, he offers gifts—flowers, wine, verses—he sings his song of sorrow and devotion, and sometimes even writes it on the door itself, he prostrates himself in the humble position of the slave; he finds himself rejected by the girl, he suffers disappointment, pain, and sorrow, he even on occasion turns to anger (symbolized by his kicking, pounding, or burning the door); he endures the hard threshold and beating of the elements; his ultimate gathering of himself together and walking off home symbolizes his own rejection of the love he had thought he wanted. Of course, when, upon his knocking, the door does open a crack—just wide enough to let in his emaciated form—and he is admitted to lie beside his lady, and to hear outside the door the cries of those who did *not* get in, he knows at last that true joy that is the thing for which he lives. Propertius's paraclausithyron contains all these elements; it is, so to speak, a summary of the literary love affair; it is the keystone of Propertius's poetic arch, the central general statement of the love of which all his other love elegies are immediate and particular manifestations. Perhaps this is why Propertius's paraclausithyron has this curiously impersonal character; it was not that he wished to represent himself and Cynthia in an oblique and indirect way, but rather that for once he wished to remove himself and Cynthia from the scene, and to present in an objective guise those elements which he felt were essential to love as he wished to write of it.

Where, in this welter of the poet's own feelings, is Cynthia herself? She seems a strangely shadowy figure; if we consider the matter, we discover that we know very little about her, even after we have read all the poems. That, to Propertius at least, she was beautiful, goes without saying; the loves of literature are always beautiful. He tells us once that she was blonde *(candida)*, that her complexion was like roses floating in a bowl of milk (2.3.12), that she let her hair hang *de more* over her smooth shoulders, and that her eyes were bright as twin torches—every one of these bits of description completely conventional, for which parallels are abundant both in other Latin and in Greek love poetry. All that emerges is a standard prettiness quite without individuality. As for her other accomplishments, she could dance and sing; she could even write poetry, which, so Propertius claims, might rival the works of Corinna (Propertius at least does not claim that she rivaled Sappho). In point of fact, the best descriptions we get of Cynthia are in a moment of fury when she caught Propertius with two rival women, and with screams of rage drove them from the house (4.8); from this, we learn that she was at least normally female. Again, after her death, Propertius draws a vivid and touching, if somewhat gruesome, picture of her with her burned clothing, her scorched flesh, and the melted ring on her finger (4.7).

The fact is that Propertius did not love women; he loved himself; but even such self-centered men on occasion rise to poetic greatness. Once in a while, the poet lets out a line or two to show that even if he could not understand the love of a woman, he could understand her loveliness. In a poem that begins on a note of frivolity, and concentrates for the most part on the painful and frightening effects of love upon the lover ("Whosoever he was who painted Love a boy, don't you think that he had the hands of a miracle-worker?"), Propertius has incorporated lines that are his sincere tribute to the loveliness of woman. Speaking again, as he so loved to do, of his death, the poet ends by saying:

[and after I am gone] who will there be to sing songs like these (this foolish Muse of mine is your great glory)—to sing of the hair and the fingers and deep dark eyes of a girl, and tell how softly her feet are wont to fall?
(2.12.21–24)

From a fairly early point in his career Propertius was subjected to persuasion, if not pressure, from the emperor and Maecenas, to turn to the writing of more serious poems. Scattered indications of this pressure and persuasion are to be found throughout Books II and III of the elegies, in each case accompanied by the poet's *recusatio*, which takes much the form that it took in Horace's odes. The poet writes a relatively short passage, in which he gracefully acknowledges the achievements of the emperor (e.g. 2.1, 10; 3.1, 9), then returns to the intellectual, emotional, and artistic problems that really interest him, and in the expression of which he feels at home.

However, the emperor's pressure was not without its effect on Propertius's poetry; chiefly, it seems to have compelled the poet to write a more imaginative type of love elegy. *Cynthia monobiblos* no doubt remains Propertius's best-known and best-loved and appreciated volume of poems; the intensity of their feeling and their spontaneity of style, have properly earned them a place among the great love poems of the Western world. But as the poet grew older and his view of himself and of the world widened, we find not only a greater smoothness and concinnity of style and versification in the poems, but also a reaching out to more varied forms of experience and imagery.

In the love elegies as such, this broadening culminates in two poems that must be regarded as among Propertius's masterpieces, 4.7, and 4.11. The former of these is the poet's sensitively executed tribute to Cynthia after her death, a poem in which the poet displays as he never had before the true depth and extent of the feeling that he had for Cynthia; if any poem in all the elegies demonstrates that for all Propertius's egotism and self-centeredness he really loved his lady, this is that poem. Only after she was gone, apparently, did the poet realize his loss. As for the *Eleventh Elegy*, sometimes styled the "Queen of the Elegies," it is a remarkable tribute to married love, once again in the form of a eulogy of the dead; in it, the dead Cornelia, speaking from beyond the grave, comforts and encourages her bereaved husband, Paulus, with thoughts not of the joys of eternal life but of the deep affection they two had shared. She speaks of their children, and turning to them, reminds them to be patient with their father in his grief, to comfort and stand by him if he chooses not to marry again, but, if he does, to accept their stepmother with love and goodwill. In some ways this seems a strange poem for Propertius to have written; it is hard not to couple it with the *Seventh Elegy* and to see in it in some degree the sorrows of the poet himself for the love that he might have known if he and Cynthia too might have been husband and wife.

In the end, whether as a result of continued pressure from the emperor and Maecenas or as the outgrowth of his own broadening poetic interests, Propertius, like Horace, turned to the expression of national ideals and accomplishments in forms that did at last present him with an artistic problem that he found worthy of his attentions. Horace, as we saw, at this point turned to the celebration of the personal greatness of members of the imperial family; Propertius turns rather to Roman mythology, and even to the early history of Rome; much as Vergil did, Propertius (4.1) imagines himself as standing in the streets of Rome and pointing out to a visiting stranger the landmarks of Roman greatness that he sees all around him. Complementing this is 4.6, with its account of the dedication of the Palatine temple of Apollo, to which is appended a long account of the military victories of Augustus. These poems may with entire right be placed alongside Vergil's great Parade of the Heroes in Book VI of the *Aeneid* and his description of the shield of Aeneas in Book VIII, and with the several poems in Book IV of Horace's *Odes*. It seems fair enough to say that Propertius, no more than Horace or Vergil, ended up by weakly giving in to pressure and insincerely praising men and deeds for which they had in fact little respect; on the contrary, like the two other poets, Propertius's "change"—if change it was—came about because the poet not only grew in admiration for the emperor and for Rome's imperial designs and ambitions, but also because at long last he discovered poetic forms which would enable him to embody his admiration in artistically satisfying forms.

This is perhaps more obvious in the poems devoted directly to Roman mythology. Here the poet's love and admiration of his native country are not expressed in so many words but are left as a conclusion for the reader to draw from the grand old tales that the poet so gracefully relates. We have a poem on Vertumnus (4.2), a discussion of why this strange god was called the "god of turning"— since this is what his name appears to mean. Another poem (4.9) is on the story of Hercules and Cacus, where it must be admitted Propertius produces a less interesting version than Vergil's. Like 4.2, 4.10 is a study of the name of a deity, in this case Jupiter Feretrius, and a poetic investigation into the reason for his being popularly known as "Jupiter, the Tray-god." Finally, the poem on Tarpeia (4.4) gives the poet an opportunity to add an elegiac twist to this famous old story: as the original version had it, Tarpeia betrayed Rome out of greedy desire for the golden ornaments that

Tatius, King of the Sabines, wore; in Propertius's version, characteristically she does so because she has fallen in love with the Sabine king.

Propertius, like Horace, is the despair of the translator, although for a somewhat different reason. It is not that the Propertian elegy is so intricately and elaborately constructed, as are the odes of Horace, and thus finds its innate structural excellence and beauty beyond the powers of the English language to represent it; in Propertius's case, it is rather the brilliantly unorthodox fashion in which he handles the Latin language, in the subtlety with which he expresses ideas through mere strategic juxtaposition of grammatically unrelated words, and in the cavalier imbalance and irregularity of his verse and sentence structure. Like that of any truly great poet, his poetic artistry is unique and inimitable. Ezra Pound found Propertius's elegies fascinating; he at least understood what the poet was trying to do—understood, too, how well he had succeeded in doing it. In Ezra Pound's *Homage to Sextus Propertius* (*Personae*, New York, New Directions, 1926, pp. 205–30) is to be found at once the best representation in English of the Propertian style and manner and one of the finest tributes ever paid by one poet to another.

Last of the Roman elegists was Ovid (Publius Ovidius Naso, 43 B. C.–18 A. D.), a poet of enormous talents, who eventually became better known for his nonelegiac poems than for his elegies: his great work, the one that assured his reputation in his own day and made him in later ages the most widely read, studied, and imitated of all the Roman poets, even including Vergil, was his *Metamorphoses*, a sort of mytho-historical epic in fifteen books of dactylic hexameters. Ovid was born at Sulmo, about 90 miles from Rome, of a family of some standing, although not of the aristocracy. We are told that Ovid's father intended him to follow a career in the law, the only one, in fact, that was considered entirely respectable for a well-born Roman. For most of his preparatory studies in this field, Ovid had little taste; but for rhetoric, the molding of speech into interesting and provocative patterns, he felt a great attraction, so great, we are told, that he even enjoyed the generally detested school exercise of preparing set speeches on formal topics.

Ovid's rhetorical studies, together with his witty proclivities, and his quick and facile genius, are no doubt responsible for much of the brilliance of his poetry and for his signal genius as a storyteller. The *Metamorphoses* is one long series of neatly spun tales, carefully dovetailed one into another. It is no wonder that this was later to become the favorite storybook of the Western world. But stories are scarcely less prevalent in Ovid's other poetical works; no matter what he is writing, he cannot resist a good yarn.

We are told that after some schooling in Athens and Asia Minor and Sicily, Ovid returned to Rome and actually entered on a career as an advocate and government official. But he found the work uncongenial:

> My body was not patient nor my mind fit for labor. Ambition to me was a nuisance, and I ran away from it.
> (*Tristia* 4.10.37–38)

Fortunately for the young poet, it was not necessary for him to work for a living, since his family fortune was quite adequate to take care of all his needs. He turned instead to the one thing that really interested him, the writing of poetry. In his autobiographical poem, *Tristia* 4.10, he tells us that he wrote verses without even meaning to, and that verse flowed out of him even when he was trying to write prose. There is no reason to doubt the truth of these statements; the character of his poetry amply substantiates them; we have seen few other poets who wrote with such easy skill.

Ovid's first published work, the collection of elegies known as the *Amores,* earned him immediate popularity. It was succeeded by a series of such compositions, the most famous of which was the *Art of Love.* This latter, a witty and rather cynical discussion of sex, rather than of love, seems harmless enough to the modern reader, yet it apparently incurred the displeasure of the emperor for its immoral teachings, and, at least according to the poet himself, was the chief reason for his being sent into exile in the year 8 A. D.

Ovid's exile remains one of the puzzles of ancient biography and history; the excuse that the *Ars amatoria* was a naughty book seems a very feeble one in view of the anything but puritanical writings of other Roman authors and of the tolerance of Roman society in general for sexual liberties. All that Ovid himself has to offer beyond his naughty verses is the mysterious statement that he had "seen too much." What he saw, he does not say, and we shall probably never know what it was. In any event, the upshot of all of this was the banishment of the poet to a wretched frontier town, Tomi, on the shores of the Black Sea. Here he spent the remaining ten years of his life, bored and miserable, writing dull and melancholy poems of self-pity, and hoping to the last for pardon from the emperor. Augustus died without granting the pardon; his dour successor, Tiberius, was even less inclined to be forgiving. The weary and homesick poet finally died at Tomi in 18 A. D.

It is patent that Ovid was a voluminous writer. Even though much of his verse is lost we still have extant a long list of works from his hand: the *Amores* in 3 books, the *Heroides*, the *Art of Love* in 3 books, the *Remedy of Love, On Cosmetics*, the *Metamorphoses* in 15 books, the *Fasti* in 6 books, the *Tristia (Poems of Lament)* in 5 books, the *Ibis*, the *Halieutica (On Fishing)*, and the *Letters from Pontus* in 4 books. Of greatest interest to the modern reader are the *Amores*, the *Ars amatoria*, and the *Metamorphoses*; these are in fact the works of Ovid that have had the most marked and lasting influence on later literature.

It is in the three books of *Amores* that Ovid shows himself most closely in line with his two predecessors, Propertius and Tibullus. His attitude, however, toward the literary love affair is quite different from theirs; while his stance is as personal as theirs, his involvement with the lady of whom he writes—a certain Corinna—is of a very different nature. It is almost wrong to say that Ovid was ever "involved" in the literary love affair at all; even when he writes in the first person of his amorous escapades, it sounds more as if he were merely playing a part on the stage, or even better, were standing in the wings and amusing himself by observing himself in the role of the unhappy lover. All the clichés of the standard literary love affair are there; the life of love, as we saw it in the poems of Propertius is represented in Ovid's poems, personality by personality, and scene by scene; yet it is impossible to take the poet seriously or to think that he would ever have allowed himself, even on the pages of a poem, to become so deeply involved with anyone else.

The solemn sorrows of the elegiac lover become in Ovid's hands the foolish divagations of not very sensible men. In *Amores* 1.2, for example, Ovid professes to feel the restlessness brought on by the sting of love, and debates with himself whether to give in to it or struggle against it:

What should I say this means? My bed feels so hard and my blankets won't stay in place! I've not slept a wink all night, and Oh, how long that night was! I've tossed and turned till I ache to my weary bones. Why! I think I would know if it was love that was troubling me. Or has he sneaked up on me,

cleverly concealed his strategy, and inflicted his wound? That must be it! His little arrows are fixed in my heart; Love, the barbarian, has captured my breast, and now is ruler there! Am I to yield, or am I, by struggling, to set the whole thing on fire? I'd better yield: a burden borne graciously weighs less.
(*Amores* 1.2.1–10)

Again, in what looks suspiciously like a daring satirization of the emperor Augustus's attempts to restore the old Roman military spirit, Ovid playfully compares the sufferings of the lover with the hardships of the soldier:

Every lover is a soldier, and Cupid has his camp, too. Believe me, Atticus, every lover is a soldier! The years fit for soldiering also go well with love; the old soldier is ugly; the love of an old man is ugly. The heart that generals look for in a brave soldier, a pretty girl also looks for in the man at her side. Both watch through the night; they sleep on the bare ground; the lover stands watch at his lady's door, the soldier at his general's. The long march is the soldier's job; send away the girl, and the lover, bursting with energy, will follow her, world without end.
(*Amores* 1.9.1–10)

The poem ends on a note that, with its savagely barbed puns, must have tickled the dissidents of the day and infuriated the Augustan imperialists:

I myself was a lazy fellow, born to sloth and ease; my hammock in the shade had turned me soft. Then I fell in love with a beautiful girl. That woke me from my lethargy! That sent me to the camp to earn my soldier's pay! That's why you see me so nimble now and so busy at nocturnal battling. You want to stop being a slugabed? Fall in love!
(*ibid.* 41–46)

The modern reader may perhaps catch the pun in "nimble" (*agilis*); the even sharper pun involved in "nocturnal battling" (*nocturna bella*) will pass unnoticed unless we recall that one of the Latin words for a "battle" (*rixa*) is also the recognized term for sexual intercourse.

In actuality, Ovid's *Amores*, together with his better known

*Art of Love* and its companion piece, the *Remedy of Love*, scarcely deserve the name of love poetry at all. They need only be laid beside the poems of Propertius and Tibullus to show wherein the difference lies: for all their limitations and their colossal egotism Propertius and Tibullus write about love; Ovid writes about sex. The fact that critics have commonly expressed doubts about the reality of the girl, Corinna, whose name figures largely in Ovid's poetry, suggests that, unlike Propertius's Cynthia or Tibullus's Delia—to say nothing of Catullus's Lesbia—Ovid's Corinna had little cogency or reality outside of bed.

The book called the *Heroides (Letters of the Heroines)* is of a piece with these earlier works. Ovid has composed a series of fictitious poetic epistles from deserted heroines to their faithless lovers; the characters are largely drawn from Greek tragedy and epic; we have a letter from Penelope to Ulysses, from Medea to Jason, from Ariadne to Theseus, from Phaedra to Hippolytus, and so on. There is also one Roman letter, from Dido to Aeneas. Although these letters may perhaps be said to embody Congreve's famous maxim, "Heaven has no wrath like love to anger turned nor Hell a fury like a woman scorned," they can scarcely be said to express a great deal more than that. Their pleas are little speeches embodying all the tricks and devices of the rhetorical schools, clever and amusing, especially to one who, like any educated Roman, could contrast Ovid's treatment of these famous women with their originals in tragedy and epic. In spite of all the posturing and weeping of these heroines, we feel that they are no more than a bit grieved and hurt, and that in time they will get over it. The women of these letters have lost not a lover, but a bed-companion.

The schoolmaster Quintilian, writing in the second century A. D., tells us that Ovid wrote a tragedy, the *Medea*, in which, says Quintilian, "he showed how great a poet he might have become if he had chosen to regulate rather than to indulge his genius." Quintilian was an earnest man, with little sense of humor; it could be anticipated that he would never appreciate the gaiety and the irony of Ovid's erotic poems, and would have turned with some relief to a work that, at least to him, seemed to be serious in intent.

Unfortunately, Ovid's *Medea* is lost, but one is forced to wonder whether Quintilian had ever read Ovid's greatest and most extensive poetic effort, his *Metamorphoses*. This is indeed a serious poem, not lacking in humor and irony, for Ovid could scarcely have written anything without these notes, but predominantly serious in purpose and executed with a skill, grace, and human understanding that come only to the poet who has let himself become deeply involved in an artistically meaningful project.

The *Metamorphoses* has often wrongfully been regarded simply as a collection of short stories; it is not that, but rather an epic in fifteen books, a kind of mythological history of the development of the world, from its beginning in chaos up to the times of the emperor Augustus. In the poem, Ovid views this history as a series of changes—hence the name *Metamorphoses*—from the first great change of chaos into cosmic order, up to the translation of Julius Caesar into a constellation and the change of Rome from the discord and bloodshed of the civil wars to the ordered, peaceful, and prosperous world of Augustus.

In telling the story of these changes, Ovid manages to introduce into his poem an amazing number of myths, most of which are true "changes," e.g. of Io into a heifer, of Daphne into a tree, of Echo into a rock and voice, of Narcissus into a flower, of Niobe into a waterfall, etc., etc. To anyone at all familiar with ancient mythology, it is a constant delight to read the *Metamorphoses* and to run across these ancient stories here told in a setting that could scarcely have been excelled by any other poet of antiquity.

Originally, these stories had religious significance, sometimes quite profound; as we may imagine, Ovid is little if at all interested in this aspect of his tales, but sees them primarily as stories, as vehicles for a narrative art in which he was unsurpassed. It is sometimes tempting to think that it was his fascination with narrative that prompted him to bring into his poem stories that, strictly speaking, are not changes, e.g. the story of the rape of Proserpina, yet this is probably quibbling; in any event he weaves all these tales so gracefully into the thread of his narrative that we scarcely stop to question their appropriateness.

In the end, Ovid produces a wonderful catalogue of myths, the most complete and most entertaining collection that has survived from antiquity. In the most ingenious fashion, story is woven into story, so that we seem to glide imperceptibly from one to the next, always guided by some titillating device: a contest in song, a description of tapestry, a tale told by a soldier or a returning traveler, bedtime stories told by mothers to their children, stories told by lovers, etc., etc. The mood of the stories also varies; a frivolous tale will be balanced by one on a serious note, the comic by the tragic, the idyllic by the horrible. In every one of the fifteen books these elements are combined in different ways and in different order.

The poem begins on a serious note with a description of the birth of the world from chaos, that reads not unlike the opening of Genesis:

> Before there was sea and land and the heavens that cover all things, there was only one face of nature in all the world; men have called it Chaos. It was a crude and disordered mass; there was nothing but lifeless weight and a heap, gathered in one place, of the elements of things not joined in useful union.
> (*Metamorphoses* 1.5–9)

From this beginning Ovid passes on to a description of the creation of the earth out of chaos, the creation of man "in the image of the gods" (*ibid.* 83); we are taken through the four ages, the Golden, the Silver, the Bronze, and the Iron. The real body of the work then begins with the story of the Deluge and of Deucalion and Pyrrha, the pair who, according to ancient pagan mythology, survived the flood, and for their piety were given the right to create a new race of men, "from the bones of their great mother" (*ibid.* 383).

It is perhaps characteristic of Ovid that, after this solemn introductory story, he should turn at once to a love escapade, the tale of Apollo and Daphne, Apollo's "first love"; she was saved from his amorous demands by her father, the river-god Peneus, who changed her into a tree, the laurel, forever after sacred to Apollo. Perhaps the most notable thing about this story, apart from the grace and poetic skill with which it is told, is its total lack of religious reverence: in Ovid's hands, the god Apollo—and the same is to be true of virtually every other deity who appears in the poem —becomes no more than a self-centered youth, not many degrees above the fatuous *iuvenis* of the Roman comedy, and showing very few traits of divinity beyond the presumed possession of supernatural powers.

Perhaps best known of the love stories in the *Metamorphoses* is the tale of Pyramus and Thisbe, whom Shakespeare has made doubly famous: their story is in a very real sense the original of the tragedy of *Romeo and Juliet,* and it appears in its own right in broad caricature in *Midsummer Night's Dream.* Nor was Ovid himself above caricature; his account of the love of Polyphemus for Galatea makes great sport of the hopeless passion of the ugly one-eyed Cyclops for the beautiful sea-nymph. In the story of Narcissus,

Ovid treats the theme of self-love, and deftly turns this aberration into a lighthearted and playful tale.

But of all the stories in the *Metamorphoses*, probably the best-known and best-loved is the sentimental Darby-and-Joan tale of Baucis and Philemon:

In the hills of Phrygia a beech stands neighbor to an oak, both surrounded by a modest wall. I myself saw the place, for Pittheus, son of Pelops, sent me once to the lands his father had ruled. Not far from the spot is a lake, once habitable land, but now water, thronged with gulls and swamp-birds. Along came Jupiter in mortal guise, and with his father came Mercury, grandson of Atlas, bearer of the caduceus, with his wings laid aside. They went to a thousand houses looking for room and rest; a thousand houses were tightly locked. But at last one took them in, a small place thatched with straw and reeds, but decent: old Baucis and, of years like hers, Philemon, were married in that house in the days of their youth, and in that house they grew old. They were poor, but by accepting their poverty and bearing it without resentment they made its burden light. There was no point in asking there for masters and slaves; they two were the whole house, they two gave orders and obeyed them. And so, when the dwellers in heaven had come to that frugal home, and bent their heads to enter under the low lintel, old Philemon bade them take their rest on the bench he put out for them, a bench that busy Baucis covered with rough cloth. She stirred the warm ashes on the hearth, blew up yesterday's fire, and fed it with leaves and dry bark; and, puffing as an old lady will, brought out the flames; she pulled down kindling and dry sticks from the roof and broke them up and pushed them under a little brazen pot. Her husband had gathered vegetables in their well-watered garden; these he stripped of their leaves. With a two-pronged fork, she lifted down a black side of bacon from the sooty ceiling, and from that carefully saved slab she cut off a tiny part and sank the slice in the bubbling waters. Meanwhile they passed the hours with conversation; they shook out the mattress stuffed with river sedge, that lay on the bedstead with its willow-wood feet; they covered it with blankets which they had never used except on holidays; and the cloth itself was old and cheap—quite the right thing for a wickerware couch. The gods took their places.

The old lady tucked up her skirts, and with shaking hand set out the table—but one of the three legs of the table was short; a potsherd evened it up. After they had thus removed the slant, they scrubbed the level table with green mint. They set out a dish of mottled, natural olives, and autumn berries preserved in jellied wine-lees, and lettuce and radishes, and a mound of new cheese, and eggs gently turned in ashes not too hot—all of this on pottery plates. After them came a wine-bowl of the same precious metal, and cups made of beechwood coated on the inside with yellow beeswax. In a minute or two the hearth-fire brought them hot dishes, and once again the wine came back—a wine not precisely aged—and pushed to one side made room for dessert. Here were nuts and figs and shriveled dates and plums and apples, sweetsmelling in broad baskets, and grapes gathered from the purpling vine. In the middle, a white honeycomb, and above all these dishes beamed kindly faces and the poor man's zealous goodwill. Meantime, the old folk noticed that the mixing-bowl so often emptied was filling up of its own accord, and the wine kept coming in! Baucis and Philemon were frightened and thunderstruck at this miracle. They lifted their hands and began to pray, begging pardon for their simple unadorned feast. They had one gander, guardian of their little farm; this they made ready to slaughter to the gods of hospitality. But the gander was swift on the wing; he wearied the couple, lamed with years, and long eluded them; at last they saw him take refuge at the feet of the gods themselves. The gods forbade his sacrifice, and said, "We are gods. Your impious neighborhood will pay deserved penalty," said they. "But you will be exempted from this suffering. Only leave your house and match your steps to ours; come with us to the highlands!" They both obeyed and leaning on staffs they trudged along and left their footsteps on the long slope. At last they were as far from the top as a single arrow-shot; they turned their gaze about and saw that all else was sunk under water; only their house still remained. Even as they were marveling at this, and shedding a tear for the death of their neighbors, the old house, too small even for its two owners, changed into a temple. Columns grew up under the roof-tree; the thatch shone yellow with gold; the floor was paved with marble; the doors were decorated with reliefs, and the whole house looked like gold. Then the son of Saturn, with a smile on his face, said, "Good sir, and you, lady, worthy of your good

husband, tell me honestly what you would like to have!"
Philemon whispered a word or two with Baucis and then revealed to the heavenly beings their common request: "We ask
to become priest and priestess, and to have custody of your
shrine; and since we have lived our years in peace, let a single
hour take off the two of us; let me never see the tomb of my
wife, let her never have to bury me!" His prayers were answered; they became custodians of the temple as long as their
life lasted. One day when they were weakened with the passage
of the years, and standing before the sacred steps were telling
tales of what had happened there, Baucis saw Philemon put
out leaves; Philemon, who was older, saw Baucis put out leaves.
And now, as the treetop grew up over their two faces, while yet
they might, they exchanged words, and with one voice said,
"Goodbye, dear spouse"; at that very minute the bark covered
and hid their faces. Even today, the inhabitant of Bithynia
points out those twin trees with their trunks side by side. I
heard this story from old men who told no lies—and there was
no reason why they should wish to deceive me; yes, I saw
garlands hanging on those branches, and as I placed a fresh one
there, I said, "God loved them: call them holy! They wor-
shipped God; now let us worship them!"
(*Metamorphoses* 8.620–724)

Here for once Ovid has left his wit and cleverness behind, and with
affection and gentle humor has presented sympathetically the laud-
able qualities of humility, piety, loyalty, and contentment.

It would be impossible in a treatment such as this to examine
even any large number of the stories incorporated into the *Metamorphoses*. And although the poem undoubtedly has epic structure,
it will certainly always be loved as it has been in the past for the
individual stories themselves, which for all the neatness with which
they are incorporated into the total structure, can still be extracted
and enjoyed one at a time. Not as great in any sense as Vergil's
*Aeneid*, the *Metamorphoses* remains a beautiful, graceful, and
utterly charming tapestry of stories, and an invaluable source book
of ancient Greek and Roman mythology.

Ovid's other works never enjoyed the popularity of his love
poems and his *Metamorphoses*. Most learned of his works, and
again a valuable source book for the mythology of Rome, is the
*Fasti*. Ovid originally planned twelve books, one for each month of
the Roman year, but his work on the poems was interrupted by

his exile, and as a result only the first six books were completed. The plan is a simple one; Ovid follows the days of the year in logical order and describes and discusses the ceremonies, stories, and myths that are appropriate to each day. He returns here to the elegiac form, and in fact much of the *Fasti* resembles very closely some of the aetiological poems of Propertius's fourth book. As poetry, the *Fasti* leaves a good deal to be desired; it shows little of Ovid's customary wit and grace and sounds at times suspiciously like a duty performance—a kind of concession to the pressure that no doubt had been placed upon him as it was upon Propertius and Horace, to write "more serious" poems. To the student of ancient religion, the *Fasti* is invaluable for its description of Roman cult and ritual; perhaps it is not too much to say that, at least from time to time, the work reveals a certain degree of true religious feeling.

After Ovid was exiled to Tomi, he gave himself over to lament and self-pity. But we must not blame him too harshly for this; he had certainly lost all that meant anything to him: the life of Rome, his friends, his family, and his ever-loyal wife. The work of his years of exile, as we might expect, is filled with bitterness and sadness; the two collections called the *Tristia* (*Poems of Lament*) and the *Epistulae ex Ponto* (*Letters from Pontus*) are collections of elegies more interesting now for the historical and biographical information they give us than as poetry. One of the *Tristia* (4.10) gives us an autobiography of the poet—one of the few such that we have from antiquity. The rest of the poems are mostly pleas for intercession to friends who had remained faithful to him and ill-tempered reproofs to those whose faith and loyalty the poet questioned. There are also a few pitifully hopeful panegyrics on the emperor Augustus, and later on his successor Tiberius, and a long defense of Ovid's writings (*Tristia* 2), and a kind of apology for his shortcomings. These two collections make dreary reading and reflect all too accurately the misery of their author.

The influence of Ovid is an enormous subject. It began almost immediately; a popular best seller in his own day, his poems were widespread throughout the Empire, where they continued to be read on down through the Middle Ages. Ovid was the favorite author of the period of chivalry. His works live again in the *Romance of the Rose*, in Chaucer, Boccaccio, Petrarch, and the whole circle of Italian writers and painters—for the *Metamorphoses* in particular provided many a subject for the artists of the Renaissance. Later, Ovid was to influence Ariosto, Erasmus, Goethe,

Ronsard, La Fontaine, Molière, Spenser, Shakespeare, Milton, Congreve, Byron; and early American literature has preserved a retelling of some of his stories by Nathaniel Hawthorne *(Tanglewood Tales).* Neither great nor profound, with none of the historical vision or human sympathy of Vergil, he remains one of the most skillful writers of verse and tellers of tales that the Western world has ever known.

# CHAPTER XV

# Augustan Prose: Livy

By the end of the Augustan Age, the Roman poetic effort had reached its culmination. It had begun with Andronicus's translation of the *Odyssey* in the third century B. C.; now it came very nearly to a conclusion with the death of Ovid. Roman Comedy had reached its height in the second century B. C. in the works of Plautus and Terence; tragedy, such as it was, seems to have reached its flowering at about the same time. Roman lyric saw its greatest representatives in Catullus and Horace, didactic in Lucretius, elegy in Tibullus, Propertius, and Ovid, epic in Vergil. Lucilius and Horace between them brought the verse-essay—the satire—to its broadest and most polished expression. Skillful and accomplished poets were still to come: Martial in epigram and Juvenal in satire, but for all their indubitable genius and unquestioned skill, they were never to display those unique qualities of human sympathy combined with artistic skill that characterized the greatest poetry of the Romans. The work of Ovid, in fact, was symptomatic of the change, not entirely for the good, that was to come over Roman poetry after the Augustan Age. The pointed wit, the display of sheer verbal virtuosity, in which Ovid took such delight, and which formed no small part of his excellence as a poet, began in the next generation their decline to the superficially clever, sensational, and bombastic, and Roman poetry fell prey to the makers of point, the phrase-balancers, and the purveyors of shock and novelty.

As for Roman prose, it had probably reached its apogee with the works of Cicero, who, as we have seen, constituted in himself an ideal of Latin prose writing which forever after became standard among the writers of Latin prose. The norm that he established was the base from which all subsequent writers of prose worked, and while Rome was yet to produce many great prose artists, each with his distinctive and highly individualistic style, there were none who could truly be said to have surpassed the master.

Oratory had been the great prose accomplishment of the last years of the Roman Republic; the Augustan Age produced not one orator of the stature of Cicero or even of any of his lesser rivals. It is a truism that oratory flourishes on controversy, particularly political controversy; in this, the Republic had been rich, but the Empire was correspondingly poor. Although the emperor Augustus allowed a good deal of freedom to his loyal opposition, nonetheless there were clear limits beyond which it was not advisable for political speakers to go.

As for philosophical prose, Cicero again seems to have brought it to such a peak of perfection that none cared to attempt to follow him. We hear of no major philosophical writer during the age of Augustus; in fact, none of any stature was to appear until the age of Nero, when Seneca published his disquisitions on Roman Stoicism.

In actual fact, Roman poetry in the age of Augustus so tends to overshadow prose, that we very nearly forget the presence in Rome of one of her two greatest historians, and one among several of her greatest stylists, the historian Livy. Titus Livius (59 B. C.–17 A. D.) was born at Patavium (modern Padua) in northern Italy. According to tradition, the peoples of this section were famous for their zealous patriotism and their sternly maintained standards of virtue. It is probably no coincidence, either, that at least two of Rome's most original and most sensitive poetic geniuses, Catullus and Vergil, came from this same part of Italy; the people there seem to have been possessed of a remarkable gift for literary expression.

As is usual with ancient authors, we know little of Livy's life. It appears that he had his early training at his northern home, and subsequently came to Rome, where he set up as a professor of rhetoric. He also had a taste for philosophy; we know that he wrote a number of short treatises, now lost, on this subject. He also wrote a manual of rhetoric addressed to his son. It was shortly after 27 B. C. that Livy began his great life's work, a history of Rome from the founding of the city down to his own day. This enormous undertaking occupied him for the rest of his life, and as portions of his history were written and published, they were greeted with great interest.

Livy seems to have led a long, successful, and tranquil life. He was always in favor at the emperor's court, and was a personal friend of Augustus himself, a fact which is a tribute to the emperor's sympathetic goodwill to men of literary gifts, for Livy was an enthusiastic republican who spoke of the great heroes of the last days of the Republic in laudatory terms. Livy, in fact, viewed his great history as the account of Rome's rise to greatness and subsequent decline, a decline which he felt was still going on in his own day. Livy, like Horace and Vergil, has been accused of making a sycophantic accommodation to the new order, of having, like them, "sold out" to a system that was antagonistic to his expressed ideals. The accusation is doubtless as false in Livy's case as in those others; like them, he undoubtedly found himself viewing with enormous relief the end of thirteen years of civil war and the establishment of a stable and decent regime.

Livy's history (Latin, *Ab urbe condita*) was written, as the author himself says in his preface, "to record the achievement of the Roman people from the founding of the city." In its original form, Livy's *History* had 142 books; extant are Books I–X, and XXI–XLV. In addition, for all the books except 136 and 137, we have short synopses *(periochae)*, which were written about the fourth century A. D. and give us at least a brief indication of the material that was included in the books now lost. Books I–XV, of which I–X are still extant, treated of the beginnings of Rome and her history up to the time of the conflict with Carthage; Books XV–XXX, of which XXI–XXX are extant, treated of the wars with Carthage; Books XXX–XLV treat of the expansion of Roman power in the wars with Macedonia and the East, and bring us up to the battle of Pydna, 167 B. C., in which the Roman general Aemilius Paullus accomplished the final subjugation of Greece.

In composing his history, Livy reverted to an older form of historical writing; abandoning the episodic scheme, he returned to the annalistic, by which each year is treated as a unit. In choosing it, Livy was probably influenced, at least in part, by the ancient tradition of the Roman priestly records and the records of the actions taken by the Roman Senate; these would naturally have been kept in year-by-year fashion. The annalistic plan has manifest faults, the most obvious of which is its tendency to break up episodes that stretch over several years, so that if we are to see the continuity of a longer episode, we must piece together for ourselves the portions of the episode that occur in individual years. On the other hand, the annalistic plan, by showing in a single scene, so to speak, all of the component parts and influences of a single phase of an episode, does perhaps give the reader a better look into historical cause and effect. It is nonetheless true that it sometimes causes the author to allow small matters to usurp more space than should be given them; sometimes, too, as the author draws closer to his own age, he tends to expand unduly and to make the modern part of his history far exceed the earlier portions in sheer bulk. Thus we see that in Livy's history, Book I covers nearly two centuries; Books II–X two more, Books XXI–XLV only fifty years—but these were very momentous years, comprising the conflict with Carthage, the conquering of that power, and the subjugation of Greece. The last twenty-three books covered the events from 43 B. C. to 9 B. C., a mere thirty-four years.

In discussing a historian, it is inevitable that question should be raised concerning his sources. In Livy's case, these are practically all what we should now call secondary, i.e. other historians. Many of the writers whom Livy mentions are now no more than names to us; none of them, with the single exception of Polybius, is extant to us in more than fragments. Unlike a modern historian, Livy did not view himself as a social scientist, but rather as a literary man engaged in the composition of a work of art; for his purposes, as long as his source presented a reasonable and logical account and one that was not violently contradicted by other sources, he was inclined to accept and use it without further critical examination.

The imprecise fashion in which Livy handles these sources is clearly indicated by the fact that from time to time he simply says that a given account was found "in certain authors," not even bothering to give their names. As far as we can determine, he did very little with primary source-material, e.g. treaties, laws, inscriptions, coins, and the like. Again this must never be attributed to any willful neglect on Livy's part or to any lack of a "correct" historiographical method; it is patent that he writes his history much in the manner of other ancient historians, that he learned his lessons in historiography from them, and that it would never have occurred to him to write history in any other way. We cannot find that he made any serious evaluation of one author against another; such critical principle as he has, other than that of logic and reason, is simply that of nose-counting: reading all the accounts of an incident available to him, he follows the interpretation supported by the majority. He has no hesitation at permitting his own personal feelings to show through: a loyal Roman, he tends to gloss over Rome's defeats and magnify her victories, even when this leads him to some fairly tortuous explaining, for example when he is writing of the period during which Rome was virtually a vassal state of the Etruscans. Livy is also an aristocrat, and tends to favor the aristocratic Senate against the common people, an attitude not unnatural in the case of a man who had come to admire the law and order imposed by the new imperial regime.

It would scarcely be fair, however, to say that Livy distorts the facts. He does recognize that Rome has been at fault. Some of her defeats, for example the defeat inflicted by Hannibal at Lake Trasimenus, form the most brilliantly written parts of his history. Nor is he blind to senatorial weaknesses and faults; in telling the old story of Verginia, it is clear to see that Livy's sympathies are with the plebeian father and his daughter, and against the cruel and unprincipled aristocrat Appius. Probably his greatest fault is his tendency to embellish an incident into a good story, to create an interesting bit of narrative, rather than to look behind an incident for its possibly more prosaic causes.

It would be wrong, however, to condemn Livy for historiographical shortcomings that are more properly viewed as the result of the predilections of his times. To the Roman, history was something more than a record; it was above everything else a literary form, a type of literature, and required submission to the same canons as those that governed any other literary type. Since the ancient was convinced that all worthwhile literature must offer instruction, it was required that history too have a didactic purpose; since it was expected that literature would provide the reader with delight, it was required that history be interesting. Like any other work of literary art, it must have a central unified theme to which all other portions of the work were subordinated and to which they would lead. It must be properly embellished both in matter and in style; the historian was expected to insert stories, anecdotes, orations, in order to help delineate famous characters and bring action to life. By sheer power of his imagination he was expected to set before his readers the original setting of an incident, the things that were said, the behavior and expression of a speaker, as well as his words, and the reactions of his hearers to what he said. The historian's style must be smooth and graceful; he must never lapse into bare exposition of dull facts.

These were the prime requisites for the writing of history; if in addition a man could be an objective historian like Thucydides, this was all very well, but such scientific precision was not demanded. What was demanded was that history tell a story, tell it well, and tell it with a purpose, in Livy's case, the purpose of moral betterment. It was Livy's hope that by showing how Rome had fallen away from the qualities that had made her great, he might yet bring her back to the path of moral rectitude. In Livy's historical drama, Rome is the protagonist; her rise to greatness and her decline, and the hope of better things for her future, form his central theme.

It is in developing this theme that Livy shows his true greatness. One impressive incident follows another in his account, each of them illustrating some side of the Roman character as well as narrating historical fact. Even the young boys Romulus and Remus must be made to show some old Roman trait: "The boys . . . had no sooner become young men than they began—yet without neglecting their duties in stable and pasture—to explore the uplands for game" (1.4.8). The fact that they were good boys, who did their chores before they ran off to hunt, adds nothing to history as such, but in Livy's history it is an essential note, for it shows one reason why the Romans are a great people and encourages the careless and forgetful Romans of his own day to strive once again after the moral ideals that the two boys represented in such simple form.

Again, in telling of the rape of the Sabine women, Livy deliberately inserts a note of national pride, for he has the Romans effect peace between themselves and their forced brides by reminding the women that they were to unite with these new husbands of theirs in Roman citizenship and in the privilege of producing Roman children. The story of Verginia, besides recounting an incident of the quarrel between patricians and plebeians, serves to illustrate the chastity of Roman women and the fierceness with which their men protected it. All of these stories Livy tells with the vividness of an eyewitness; how much of his detail he derived from his sources we can no longer say, but it is reasonably certain that most of the descriptive material is his own. Certainly the psychological element, the ascription of motive and meaning, is his; his own, too, are the inserted speeches which he puts into the mouths of his characters.

These inserted speeches were in no sense peculiar to Livy; they had been a regular feature of Greek and Roman historiography from the beginning, and no ancient historian is without them. They serve three purposes, first, to illustrate character, second, to enliven the narrative, third, and perhaps most important, to explain motives and causes. They are frankly anachronistic, and do not pretend to be the actual words of the speaker. In many cases, these words would not have been known; even where they were available in published form, they would have been used by the historian merely as a basis for the speech which he himself composed. Livy's speeches were greatly admired in antiquity; those that we find in the extant parts of his history are lively and dramatic. Furthermore, by composing equally convincing speeches on both sides of a given question, Livy is enabled to attain a kind of objectivity, although it is usually clear on which side of the argument he himself stands. It must always be recalled that his purpose was never to distort or to prejudice, but rather to guide and teach. We may sometimes quarrel with the factual precision of Livy's accounts; it is rarely possible to deny the moral truth of what he says, or to quarrel with its artistry.

The modern reader, unappreciative as he is of the rhetorical arts, is unlikely to be deeply stirred by Livy's speeches, but his narrative skill still remains a source of delight. In fact, unburdened as Livy is by the need to be clever and witty, his narrative art excells even that of Ovid; as keenly aware as was that poet of the pictorial values commonly considered to be the prerogative of poetry, Livy adds to these a sense of earnestness and a feeling for personal and national grandeur which other ancient writers rarely attain. It would be hard, for example, to surpass Livy's account of the taking of Rome by the Gauls in the fourth century B. C.; he tells how the Romans had withdrawn to the citadel in the center of their town, leaving behind them deserted streets, empty houses, and in the vestibules of the palaces of the nobles, the old men sitting silent and immovable in their chairs, each holding in his hand his staff of office, far too proud to retreat, and waiting for the death they knew was to come:

> The Gauls found their lust for combat cooled by the night which had intervened. At no point in the battle had they been pushed to desperate exertions, nor had they now to carry the capital city by assault. It was therefore without rancor or excitement that they entered Rome, on the following day, by the Colline Gate (which lay wide open), and made their way to the Forum, gazing about them at the temples of the gods and at the Citadel, which alone presented some show of war. Thence, after leaving a moderate guard to prevent any attack upon their scattered forces from Citadel or Capitol, they dispersed in quest of booty through streets where there was none to meet them, some rushing in a body into whatever houses were nearest, while others sought out the most remote, as

though supposing that only those would be intact and full of plunder. But being frightened out of these by their very solitude, lest the enemy should by some ruse entrap them as they wandered apart, they came trooping back to the Forum and the places near it. There they found the dwellings of the plebeians fastened up, but the halls of the nobles open; and they hesitated almost more to enter the open houses than the shut—so nearly akin to religious awe was the feeling as they beheld seated in the vestibules beings who, besides that their ornaments and apparel were more splendid than belonged to man, seemed also, in their majesty of countenance and in the gravity of their expression most like to gods.

While they stood reverentially before them, as if they had been images, it is related that a Gaul stroked the beard of one of them, Marcus Papirius—which he wore long as they all did then—whereat the Roman struck him over the head with his ivory mace, and, provoking his anger, was the first to be slain; after that the rest were massacred where they sat; and when the nobles had been murdered, there was no mercy then shown to anyone; the houses were ransacked, and after being emptied were given to the flame.

(Livy 5.41.4–10, translation of B. O. Foster)

Behind the incident as Livy has related it lies historical truth —the truth that the city was indeed invaded, captured, and sacked by the Gauls in 390 B. C., and that some of the population, at any rate, had elected rather to die than to suffer the dishonor and discomfort of a siege in the Capitol. The rest of the narrative is Livy's, and it is designed to tell the truth that he wished his Roman readers to apprehend: the truth of Roman greatness and courage in the face of disaster. It is an important part of Livy's aim to arouse in his readers pride in Roman character and accomplishment, and thus to encourage them to renew these half-forgotten qualities.

Told with equal skill is the story of Horatius at the bridge, an incident, part myth, part history, from the attempted invasion of Rome by the Etruscan king, Lars Porsena:

The Sublician Bridge well-nigh afforded a passage to the enemy, had there not been one man, Horatius Cocles, . . . who, happening to be posted on guard at the bridge, saw the Janiculum taken by sudden assault, and that the enemy were pouring down from thence in full speed, and that his own party, in terror and confusion, were abandoning their arms and ranks; laying hold of them one by one, standing in their way, appealing to the faith of gods and men, he declared, "that their flight would avail them nothing if they deserted their post; if they passed the bridge and left it behind them, there would soon be more of the enemy in the Palatium and Capitol than in the Janiculum; for that reason he advised and charged them to demolish the bridge, by their sword, by fire, or by any means whatever; that he would stand the shock of the enemy as far as could be done by one man." He then advanced to the first entrance of the bridge, and being easily distinguished from those who showed their backs in retreating from the fight, facing about to engage the foe hand to hand, by his surprising bravery he terrified the enemy. Two, indeed, a sense of shame kept with him, Sp. Lartius and T. Herminius, men eminent from their birth, and for their gallant exploits. With them he for a short time stood the first storm of the danger, and the severest brunt of the battle. But as they who demolished the bridge called upon them to retire, he obliged them also to withdraw to a place of safety on a small portion of the bridge still left. Then casting his stern eyes round all the officers of the Etrurians in a threatening manner, he sometimes challenged them singly, sometimes reproached them all: "The slaves of haughty tyrants, who, regardless of their own freedom, came to oppress the liberties of others." They hesitated for a considerable time, looking round one at the other, to commence the fight; shame then put the army in motion, and the shout being raised, they hurled their weapons from all sides on their single adversary; and when they all stuck in the shield held before him, and he with no less obstinacy kept possession of the bridge with firm step, they now endeavored to thrust him down from it by one push, when at once the crash of the falling bridge, at the same time a shout of the Romans raised for joy at having completed their purpose, checked their ardor with sudden panic. Then Cocles says, "Holy father Tiber, I pray that thou wouldst receive these arms, and this thy soldier, in thy propitious stream." Armed as he was, he leaped into the Tiber, and amid showers of darts hurled on him, swam across safe to his party, having dared an act which is likely to obtain more fame than credit with posterity.

(Livy 2.10, translation of B. O. Foster)

Livy's history is full of brilliantly described incidents of this sort, some brief, some extended to great length, as for example in his account of Hannibal's invasion of Italy (Books xxi–xxii). The extant books show an amazing consistency in style and manner; in spite of the enormous length of his work, the historian seems never to have flagged in his enthusiasm or to have failed in his art. Livy's history was very popular in his day, and its popularity never diminished until the Middle Ages when it disappeared from sight. Recovered at the time of the Renaissance, the extant portions remain an invaluable source of information about Rome and the Romans and a delight to all lovers of good narrative and skillful literary style.

The figure of Livy looms so large in Augustan prose that we easily forget the presence in that age of other prose writers, none of whom, it must be admitted, attained to anything like the stature of the historian himself. Still we should at least be aware of such writers as Pompeius Trogus (fl. c. 27 B. C.–14 A. D.) whose *Philippic History (Historiae Philippicae)*, in forty-four books, is extant in an epitome made by Justin, a writer of the second or third century A. D. Trogus's history covered Greece and all the nations of the Near and Middle East, including Persia and Parthia, and gave an account of the early rise of Rome. Somewhat better known is Vitruvius (fl. c. 59–23 B. C.), architect and engineer, who served with Caesar and also under the emperor Augustus. His work, *On Architecture (De architectura)*, written in his old age, includes not only matters relating to buildings, but also a discussion of water supply and of various mechanical contrivances such as clocks. Marcus Verrius Flaccus (fl. 27 B. C.–c. 15 A. D.) was probably the most famous teacher of the age of Augustus, and held the position of tutor to the emperor's grandsons, Gaius and Lucius. His life's work was a lexicon of the Latin language, in which particular attention was paid to archaic and unusual words. The original work has been lost; it was abridged by Festus in the third century A. D.; the second half of Festus's work is extant in mutilated form. The whole of the Festus abridgment was further abridged by Paulus Diaconus, of the eighth century A. D. This last named work is extant. Finally, mention should be made of Lucius Annaeus Seneca (55 B. C.–c. 40 A. D.), the first and oldest of that illustrious family to make a name for himself in Rome. The Senecas came from Corduba in Spain; this first of the family to appear in Rome is called Seneca the Rhetorician, to distinguish him from his even more famous son, **Seneca the Philosopher**. The elder Seneca was primarily an orator and teacher of oratory. In his old age, his sons urged him to write of his experiences. In response to their request, he sketched from memory his ideas of how various Greek and Latin orators and rhetoricians had handled a vast variety of subjects. His book, the *Controversiae et suasoriae,* is of interest now chiefly for the anecdotes which the elder Seneca incorporated into his accounts.

# CHAPTER XVI

# Augustus to Nero: Seneca the Younger

The life of Seneca the Elder bridges the period from the end of the Roman Republic, through the age of Augustus, and on into the reigns of Tiberius, Caligula, and Claudius, with his greatest period of literary activity falling in the reigns of the last two. After the brilliance of the age of Augustus, these succeeding years seem dull and drab, for apart from Seneca himself, not a single really major figure appears during them. Two minor poets have come down from the age of Tiberius (14–37 A. D.); these are Marcus Manilius, whose *Astronomica*, in five books, is more famous for having been edited by the great A. E. Housman than for its poetic qualities. Rather more interesting is Phaedrus, a Macedonian freedman, whose charming versions of Aesopic animal-fable, liberally embellished with ideas of his own, make pleasant, if rather unsubstantial reading. The prose writers are uniformly dull and second rate. Valerius Maximus, whose encyclopedia, published about 31 A. D., was dedicated to the emperor Tiberius, remains an important if somewhat haphazard source of information about the ancient world, and Velleius Paterculus, whose *Histories*, in two books, gives a brief sketch of Roman history up to 30 A. D., is an important source of information about the growth and culmination of the Roman Empire. Velleius has sometimes been admired for his supposed objectivity; on the whole, however, the work is dull and of little interest to any but the professional historian. Perhaps slightly more interesting is the treatise of Cornelius Celsus *On Medicine*, this being the only extant part of his *Encyclopedia*. The work scarcely qualifies as literature, nor was it intended as such. It remains a valuable source book for the history of medicine.

The unhappy and dour Tiberius was succeeded by mad Caligula and he in turn by Claudius, a man, strangely enough, of scholarly interests, who had the throne thrust upon him much against his will. He was not unintelligent, and the earlier part of his reign was successful enough; in his later years, however, he came under the influence of unprincipled women, particularly the empress Messalina, and came to his end—tradition has it by being served a toadstool by his loving wife, Agrippina—in an atmosphere of corruption and ill will.

If Tiberius was ill-adapted to encourage literary pursuits, Caligula and Claudius were even less so, and the periods of their reigns were as barren of important names as was that of Tiberius himself. Perhaps best known is the historian Curtius Rufus, whose history of Alexander the Great, in ten books (of which III–X are extant), is not without interest, although it scarcely qualifies as distinguished historical writing. We also hear of a certain Aufidius Bassus, who wrote a history of the German campaigns undertaken during the reign of Tiberius, and another historical treatise covering the period from the death of Caesar to about the year 31 A.D. Neither of these works is extant, but we know from citations by later authors that Aufidius Bassus was much admired in antiquity. We do have the *Geography* of Pomponius Mela, a work in three books which describes the coastlines of the Mediterranean. This book was written during the reign of Claudius. Bridging the period from the reign of Claudius to that of Nero is the satirist Persius (A. Persius Flaccus, 34–62 A.D.), whose six books of satires have the dubious distinction of being among the most difficult Latin extant. Persius belongs in the tradition begun by Lucilius and continued by Horace, and later brought to its culmination by Juvenal, but his work is so mannered and so heavily larded with contemporary allusions, and its contents are so thin and meagre, that it is rarely read except by professional classicists in search of odd words, strange locutions, and an occasional bit of curious information.

The age of Nero began in an atmosphere of good cheer and hope. Claudius's last days had been sheer misery; with his death in 54, the Roman world heaved a sigh of relief. The young Nero was handsome, charming, a devotee of art, music, and literature; moreover, he was ably advised by the gruff and able old general, Afranius Burrus, and by the younger Seneca, a thoughtful humanitarian and devout Stoic, now in his sixties. Behind all of them, to be sure, lurked the sinister figure of the emperor's mother, Agrippina the Younger, but in the beginning, at least, she was checked by Burrus and Seneca from exercising too complete domination of her young son.

The first five years of Nero's reign were always accounted among the most prosperous and happiest of the empire. On the borders there was relative peace; internally the Mediterranean was prosperous; Roman rule had proved itself beneficial and in general not too oppressive. The capital itself, under the emperor's patronage, strove to become the cultural as well as the political capital of the world; Nero instituted a number of musical and literary festivals, in many of which he himself performed.

Unfortunately, Seneca and Burrus began to lose their power as the influence of Agrippina increased, and by the year 65 A. D. there was great unrest. Six years before, in 59, Nero in a particularly revolting incident had caused the murder of his mother; it had soon become clear that in spite of her basically evil nature, she had exercised at least some restraint over her son; with her death, even this was gone. Nero proceeded to demonstrate all too clearly that he did not himself have the faculties and qualities required of the throne; in many ways an adolescent who had never grown up, he began frantically to turn this way and that, seeking somehow to keep his hold on his post. In 65, a conspiracy under the leadership of Calpurnius Piso was formed with the intent of removing Nero from the throne, forcibly, if necessary. Unfortunately, the conspiracy was detected, and its leaders put to death. Implicated along with the conspirators were important individuals like Seneca and his nephew, the poet Lucan, who may or may not have been involved, but were caught up in the net that brought in the actual conspirators.

With the death of these conspirators, Rome was left without reliable leadership; Nero turned more and more to the advice of the infamous Tigellinus. For three years more, Rome labored under Nero's rule, but in 68 the armies under Galba revolted and Nero was forced to leave Rome. The story is that he attempted to commit suicide, but could not find the courage to do so and had to be assisted by a slave. His story is a pitiful one, rendered the more so because he had the poor judgment to make a literary man, the historian Tacitus, his enemy, for Tacitus's account has blackened his name almost beyond recognition. He was probably not as bad as Tacitus portrays him or as we have commonly come to think. He was blamed, for example, for the great fire that destroyed a large part of the city; we forget that Rome, being built largely of tinder and matchsticks, was periodically subject to such devastating fires, and this was by no means the first or the last. It was typical of Nero's frantic loss of self-confidence that when the populace began to blame him for the fire, he had to find a scapegoat, and settled on that strange new sect, the Christians, several hundred of whom he is reputed to have crucified and burned to death as supposed arsonists. This hideous act, frightful enough in itself, has been augmented by the indignation of organized Christianity; altogether we may adjudge Nero a most unfortunate man who should never have been an emperor and probably never wanted to be one, and once in the office, found himself totally inadequate to the administration of it.

One figure inevitably stands out among all the rest; this is Seneca the Younger (4 B. C.–65 A. D.) often called Seneca the Philosopher. His lifetime spans the reigns of Augustus, Tiberius, Caligula, and Claudius, as well as a large part of that of Nero; it is during the reign of Claudius that he first came to prominence in governmental circles. Like the rest of his family, Seneca the Younger was born in Spain in the city of Corduba. He was one of three brothers; of the other two, Novatus was to become famous as the "Gallio" before whom St. Paul appeared in Achaea in 51–52; the other, Mela, gained no fame in his own right, but was the father of the poet Lucan. Seneca had his education in Rome, where he found himself particularly drawn to the study of rhetoric and philosophy; literary criticism he felt was inclined to be trivial and pedantic. His rhetorical studies had great influence on his style, which was always terse and epigrammatic. In philosophy, he found himself deeply attracted by Roman Stoicism, a version of the older philosophy which had disposed of most of the impasses that were inherent in the original doctrines, and had come to be primarily a practical guide to the good life. Chief emphasis, in Seneca's eyes, was on self-discipline, the simple life, and constant self-examination, for the purpose of attaining the self-sufficiency which to the Stoic was indispensable to the good and happy life. Seneca took this philosophy very seriously; in fact he so zealously followed a regimen of physical discipline that he fell ill and found it necessary to travel abroad to recover his well-being.

Returning to Rome about the year 31, Seneca entered government service and became quaestor; he also practiced law successfully —in fact, so successfully that he incurred the jealousy of the emperor Caligula (37–41) and was very nearly executed by him. Seneca was also successful as a businessman, and became very rich, this in spite of the Stoic doctrine that wealth was a matter of indifference. It is said that in reply to all charges of hypocrisy, he remarked that he possessed his wealth but was not possessed by it. On the accession of the emperor Claudius, Seneca found himself in favor with the emperor's two nieces, Julia and Agrippina, and until they were displaced in the emperor's favor by Messalina, he was able to continue successfully with his career in government office. Messalina, however, hated him, and managed to get him exiled by trumping up a charge against him of carrying on an intrigue with Julia.

Seneca was exiled to Corsica for eight years (41–49), where he was scarcely any happier than Ovid had been at Tomi. But his Stoic philosophy stood him in good stead, and he managed to face tedium and boredom with some equanimity; he kept himself busy by writing treatises on the geography and ethnology of Corsica. During this time he also composed a philosophical work, the *Consolatio ad Helviam*, a work in which, in a way that seems very odd to us, he consoled his mother for her loss of him. He also wrote a similar *Consolatio* to the freedman, Polybius, one of the emperor's secretaries, on the death of Polybius's brother. This was quite clearly an attempt to win the intercession of Polybius with the emperor; it revealed one of the strangest aspects of Seneca's character: he could scarcely have thought very highly of the unprincipled Polybius, yet in this work he was able to flatter him in fulsome terms, apparently without feeling the slightest twinge of conscience.

After the death of Messalina, Seneca was recalled through the influence of Agrippina, who had now married her uncle, Claudius. He was appointed tutor to Nero, and as we have seen, on the death of Claudius, he and Burrus together exercised a salutary influence on the young man. Here again, Seneca revealed the strange ability to soothe his conscience, for when Nero had his mother murdered, it was Seneca who composed the speech in Nero's defense which the emperor delivered to the Senate. We have already seen how the death of Burrus and the rise in power of Tigellinus undermined Seneca's influence with the emperor, and led ultimately to his being implicated in the conspiracy of 65. On this occasion, like most of the other conspirators, he was offered the choice of execution or suicide, and in the true spirit of the philosophic aristocrat, chose the latter course.

Seneca's character has always been considered fair game by his critics; he has been called a hypocrite and a shameful toady of the emperor; it has been pointed out that in his philosophical writings he scorns power, yet apparently did everything he could to obtain power, and that he preached the scorning of wealth, yet became one of the wealthiest men of his day. It is impossible entirely to counter these charges, for in a certain sense they are true. In spite of all apology, whether from Seneca himself or from his defenders, Seneca, the politician, statesman, and businessman, remains a different person from Seneca the philosopher. Only by the most agile defense can his philosophical principles be made to square with his practical life. He is, in fact, one of our best examples of the fact that the "self" of a man's writings need not be taken as a reflection of the "self" in actual life, that it is not really fair to compare the one with the other, or to interpret the one in the light of the other. Seneca's writings reveal principles of generosity, kindness, courage, justice, and sheer moral strength that have inspired many generations of men; human experience has amply demonstrated the truth of his teachings. Whether he himself lived up to them or not is, and must continue to be, a purely academic question.

The sheer bulk of the extant works of Seneca is quite impressive. There are twelve philosophical dialogues, of which the best known are probably those *On the Happy Life (De vita beata)* and *On Peace of Mind (De tranquilitate animi)*. To these should be added the one hundred and twenty-four *Moral Epistles (Epistulae morales)*, which are really brief philosophical essays cast in the form of letters. In addition to these, we have *Natural Investigations (Naturales quaestiones)* in seven books, nine tragedies—incidentally nearly the only complete examples we have of Roman work in this genre—and finally a strange satire, the *Apocolocyntosis Claudii* or *How Claudius Turned into a Pumpkin*, a satirization of the deification of that unhappy emperor. There is also another tragedy, the *Octavia*, which has been sometimes ascribed to Seneca and is usually included in the corpus of his works, but which has now come to be regarded as not by him.

In considering Seneca's philosophical works, it is entirely appropriate to place the essays and the epistles in a single body, for they differ primarily in length; their content is entirely similar, and the epistolary form is no more than a bow to convention. In both the essays and the letters, Seneca's aim is to produce treatises on Stoic ethics, which he hopes will encourage the cultivation of philosophy as a guide to the good and happy life. He is frankly what we would now call a popularizer, although at Rome, of course, the populace to which his books were directed was the educated aristocracy; he would have had no interest whatever in disseminating his works among the common people, even if they

had had the education necessary for their appreciation and understanding.

Seneca is not interested in philosophical speculation; in spite
of all he says, he is a preacher rather than a teacher; he does not
argue; he exhorts. The principle, for example, that all things should
be pursued in moderation is responsible for the following section
of Seneca's essay *On Peace of Mind*:

> A gentleman may with perfect propriety spend his money on
> the pursuit of learning, but even this is defensible only if it is
> kept within limits. What is the point of those countless
> volumes, those rooms full of books? Why! Their owner, in all
> his life, has scarce so much as read their titles! When you are
> trying to learn, a thousand faces only get in your way; they
> do not teach you. It is much better to devote your whole self
> to a few authors than to flit through a lot of them. Forty
> thousand volumes were reduced to ashes at Alexandria. Some
> people may praise that library as the finest monument a king's
> wealth ever had—Livy, for example, says that it was "a splendid
> memorial to royal culture and scholarship." That was no
> "culture," no "scholarship"; it was conspicuous educational
> waste. In fact, I would not even call it educational, for those
> books had been purchased not for education but for ostenta-
> tion. I am reminded of our ignorant citizenry to whom books
> are books, even if they be of the most vulgar character; they
> want them not as the instruments of education but as orna-
> ments for their drawing-rooms. Buy books, then, but buy for
> need, not for show. "But this," you say, "is a more honorable
> way to spend your money than to throw it away on bronzes
> and paintings." All excess is vicious, anywhere and everywhere.
> What defense can you offer for the man who is always on the
> hunt for citron and ivory bookcases, always looking for the
> works of authors nobody ever heard of, or who were failures,
> who sits there among his thousands of volumes and yawns his
> head off, who has no real interest in his books beyond their
> titles and their covers? Go to the homes of men totally devoid
> of intellectual curiosity and there you will see the world's
> whole supply of orations and histories, bookshelves from floor
> to ceiling. Nowadays they put libraries even in their baths: "a
> nice, shiny, decoration; no house should be without one!" I
> should be quite willing to excuse all this if it were due to an

excess of zeal for education; but actually all those expensive illustrated editions—the works of sainted intellects—have been purchased for show and decoration."
(*De Tranquilitate animi* 9.4–7)

The passage is quite typical of Seneca's thought, which consists very largely of the embellishment of ancient saws such as "Nothing too much" and "Know thyself" with bits of flashier wisdom drawn from the tenets of Neo-Stoicism. Seneca, no more than Cicero before him, was a systematic philosopher; like Cicero, he gathers wherever he wants whatever will suit his immediate purpose. Although he is in form and by conviction a Neo-Stoic, yet he constantly alludes to the teachings of Zeno's chief rival, Epicurus, of whom he invariably speaks with deepest respect. Seneca's work indicates clearly enough what had happened to philosophy in his day; it had been transmogrified from an intellectual pursuit of knowledge and wisdom into a set of practical rules for the happy and successful life. The process had already been begun by Cicero himself, whose two little essays, *On Friendship* and *On Old Age*, clearly exemplified this more practical approach to the problem of human behavior. With Seneca, the work is all on this level, or perhaps an even humbler one, for Cicero still argues, while Seneca merely exhorts.

Neo-Stoicism, of which Seneca affords the chief example from the period of Nero, was a product of many forces, chief among which we may list the growing insecurity of the wealthy and educated classes at Rome, who saw their ancient ranks being infiltrated by newcomers from the provinces—like the Senecas themselves, in fact—and who were entirely too subject to the sudden needs or even whims of all-powerful emperors, who on the slightest provocation could strip them of their wealth and position either for their own or for public purposes. Where tradition, ancestral custom, and the honor that attaches to great names had once protected them in their positions, they now found themselves exposed to attack on all sides, and found in philosophy an intellectual and perhaps even an emotional bulwark against the troubles of the world.

This flight to philosophy, if it may be so called, was augmented by the decay of the Roman state religion, which for many years had been very thin in content, but by the age of Nero had degenerated into a public show, continued by inertia, tradition, superstition, and the need to amuse the populace. Long before Seneca's day, educated Romans had ceased to take much stock in the Olympic deities; even the uneducated common people had tended to turn away from the great Greco-Roman pantheon to the little gods of house and field, with whom they felt on surer footing. The old Roman state religion had virtually no ethical content in its own right, for the gods, as we well know, were morally rather sad scapegraces, but it had at least served as a support for tradition, for the *mos maiorum*, which in fact provided the only real moral sanctions of which Roman life was aware. World power, enormous wealth, greater sophistication, and the infusion into the body of Roman citizenry of peoples from all over the world had weakened the hold of the *mos maiorum*; with the concurrent loss of any true religious feeling in the state cult, the educated Roman was left without any intellectual and spiritual base.

This was the vacuum into which the Christian religion was later to make its way, but in Seneca's time the new cult was far too little known and had yet to extend its influence beyond the lowest social classes. For Seneca, and for men like him, the only possible recourse was to philosophy of some type. Of the two philosophies current in Rome at the time, Epicureanism and Stoicism, Stoicism easily won out, for it not only upheld moral principles very similar to those the Romans had long known as part of the *mos maiorum*, but in addition it had a strong theological element, a sense of dependency upon God and his goodness, which did much to supply the religiosity so patently absent from the state cult. The Stoicism that we find in Seneca's writings lays great emphasis upon the soul, upon God as man's helper and guide, and upon the strength and satisfaction to be derived from the contemplation of eternal truth. Typical of the religious feeling that pervades Seneca's philosophical writings is this passage from one of the *Moral Epistles*:

> I declare to you, Lucilius: a holy spirit dwells within us, the watchful observer of all we do, both good and bad. As it is treated by us, so does it treat us in return. Truly, no man can be good without God: could anyone rise above his fortune unless with God's help? The counsel that He gives is noble and upright. In every single good man "there dwells a god; we know not what god it is."
> (*Epistulae morales* 41.2)

In view of sentiments like these, we can well understand why Julius Kanus, when condemned to death by the emperor Caligula, spent his last hours in the company of his "philosopher." Seneca too is supposed to have spent his last hours in this way.

In other ways too, Neo-Stoicism had come to be more in

harmony with Roman character. The original doctrine of Zeno had taught that since virtue was an absolute, only the man who was absolutely good could be good at all. This patently made human goodness an impossibility—a fact which the early Stoics were quite willing to admit. To the Roman, such a doctrine was absurd: even if he found it possible to accept it as a kind of theoretical proposition, he found in it no help for the problems of this life. He turned instead to a second doctrine of Stoicism, whereby all activities other than the purely virtuous were classed as "indifferent," and these in turn were divided into the "preferable" and the "less preferable." The indifferent activities were those which in themselves neither led to or from either virtue or vice—in other words, activities that were inherently neutral, so to speak. Some of these did however move in the direction of virtue, and others did not; the good Stoic was directed always to choose the former.

On this basis Neo-Stoicism erected a moral code which, to the practical Roman mind, made sense. If there was no hope that he, as a mere human being, could ever attain to true, perfect virtue, he could at least move in that general direction by electing to pursue those activities which were classed as "preferable." His practical mind could not see why, for all the iron-bound logic of the old Stoics, it was not better to have some goodness than none, not better to have more goodness than less. Since God was by definition good, and since in every man there was an indwelling spirit of God, man did best when he ordered his life as nearly as he could in consonance with that good which God directs. Furthermore, the sidetracking of the doctrine of the perfect Stoic sage, the man of perfect virtue, allowed men free play in the experience and expression of normal human impulses and feelings; they were not required to be unfeeling themselves or to reject sympathy with the feelings of others.

The central problem for the Neo-Stoics of the age of Nero was human happiness, the desire for peace, tranquility, and security; this Seneca attempts to teach by showing that human happiness cannot depend on externals of any kind, such as health, wealth, power, and the like, but must come from within the man himself. On the positive side, by living as far as he can in harmony with God-Nature-the Good, by engaging in study and other activities that will help to clarify and strengthen his comprehension of the Good, he will build in himself a strong Self, capable of withstanding all external vicissitudes, of whatever kind. Negatively, he will learn to reject all things, persons, and influences that may, either immediately or ultimately, tend to weaken his self-dependence. He will strive always to practice wisdom, justice, courage, and temperance, not in the expectation that he will become perfect in any of them, but in the conviction that however short he may fall of the ideal, it will always be better to have made some progress, always be better at least to have tried. Because love of others enriches the power of the self, he will love other men and cherish them all as his brothers, remembering that in every man there is an "indwelling Spirit" just like his own that makes all men equally akin to and part of God himself.

Probably most representative of Seneca's philosophic thought is his essay, *On Peace of Mind (De tranquilitate animi)*. After a preliminary section in which Seneca's interlocutor, Serenus, speaks of the troubles and difficulties under which he labors, and asks for Seneca's help for a better life, Seneca reassures him by asserting that Serenus has, on his own, nearly reached the end of his difficulties; he offers to help him through the last stages of distress. Then, having asserted that peace of mind was the one sure source of goodness and happiness in life, he offers his definition of the quality they seek:

> Let us then try to find out how the soul may pursue its course with ever even keel, and breeze ever favorable, how it may be the answer to its own prayer, contemplate its own lot with joy, and never know an interruption in that happiness, but be forever calm and unshaken, never frenetic, never depressed—this will be "peace of mind."
> *(De tranquilitate animi* 2.4)

One of the greatest enemies of peace of mind is boredom; the philosopher must combat it by engaging in the active life:

> You ask by what means we may combat boredom. To quote Athenodorus: "It will be best to keep one's self occupied in business, law, and politics. Some people pass their days in sunbathing, exercising, and swimming; athletes find it most helpful to spend the greater share of their time in developing their muscular strength—in fact, they make this their sole aim in life. Similarly you who are preparing yourselves for the hurlyburly of public life will find it best always to be busy. Any man who proposes to make himself useful to his fellow men and fellow citizens will find that he gets training and acquires

experience when he throws himself into the midst of life's
duties, carrying out civic and private responsibilities to the
limit of his powers." (*id.* 3.1)

But a man cannot be forever working; he must have his
leisure hours. These he should spend in the study of philosophy,
for this will not only bring him relaxation but also will strengthen
his soul for the trials of life. The true philosopher too will make
friends, for they are life's most valuable acquisition; the man who
turns entirely in upon himself will find that he has not become
self-sufficient but only lonely. A man must have an aim in life, for
the aimless life is futile and meaningless; at the same time he must
also learn to mingle pleasure with work; a life of unrelieved toil is
nearly as dull and ineffective as its opposite.

There is no doubting the common sense in this philosophy, no
doubting that it sounds very much like the popular "philosophies
of life" of our own day. Much of it seems to foreshadow eventual
Christian ethic; here and there, it displays the directness and
simplicity of the Gospel. However, its lack of a personal deity, its
lack of any hint of the love of God, and finally, its total reliance
upon the reasoning faculty for the soundness of its doctrines, in the
end render it dry and bloodless, an unprofitable synthesis having
neither the fervor of true religion nor the clarity of a genuinely
complete and consistent philosophy.

The rest of Seneca's philosophical works, although they vary
somewhat in immediate subject, deal pretty much with these same
propositions; everywhere, the emphasis is upon self-control, moderation, public service, and inner strength and self-sufficiency. Probably
it is just as well that the age of Nero produced such a thinker; we
cannot now tell how wide Seneca's influence may have been; probably, like most Roman authors, he appealed to and was read by
only members of the educated elite. But at least among them his
work and his thought remained a force for goodness which the age
of Nero no doubt sadly needed.

It is symptomatic of the broad interests which Seneca recommends to men as one of the means to a serene and happy life, that
he should have written on science. He would have considered his
*Investigations into Nature* (*Naturales quaestiones*) no more than an
extension of his normal philosophic interests, for after all, one of
the first questions asked by philosophers concerns the nature of
Being in all its forms, and it is to this subject that Seneca's book
is dedicated. Writing long before the day of specialization, long

too before the day of objective and empirical methods, his work is bookish, at second and third hand, and woefully imprecise to our way of thinking. He divides it into three large sections, the first dealing with celestial phenomena, the second with a combination of celestial and terrestrial phenomena, and finally a section dealing entirely with this earth. The book is rarely read now except as a curiosity in the history of science, and as showing us the status of scientific knowledge in Seneca's day. Whatever its defects, it remained, along with Pliny's *Natural History*, one of the most important source books for natural history during the Middle Ages.

It is a curious accident of literary history that of all the enormous mass of Roman tragedies that were written throughout the Roman period, only the nine tragedies by Seneca (plus the Ps.-Senecan *Octavia*) should have survived intact from antiquity. Like most Romans, Seneca found in Euripides his favorite model; four of his plays, *The Mad Hercules (Hercules furens), The Women of Troy (Troades), Medea*, and *Phaedra*, are adapted from Euripides's work. The *Oedipus* and the *Hercules on Oeta (Hercules Oetaeus)* are on models by Sophocles. The *Agamemnon* is modeled after Aeschylus's play of that name, and the *Phoenician Women (Phoenissae)* seems to have been based on a combination of all three of the great tragic authors. For one play, the *Thyestes*, we can find no extant model.

Seneca's relation to his Greek originals seems to have been at least as free as was that of Plautus and Terence in the field of comedy. The most cursory comparison, for example, of Seneca's *Medea* with Euripides's original will show that Seneca has taken from Euripides the plot, the general subject, and a rough outline of the action, plus a few passages translated almost verbatim. But Seneca's play is emphatically not Euripides's; in fact, one may hazard a guess that the Greek playwright would not have cared to own authorship of Seneca's version. Euripides appeals to us largely because of his sensitive penetration into human character and psychology; the characters in his plays are, for all their antiquity, intensely real, and in the guise of problems drawn from a long-dead mythology, they have much to say about human action and interaction. Seneca's plays by contrast present us with a series of stiff, highly formalized characters; if they did not wear the mask—assuming that the plays ever were produced on the stage—they most certainly should have, for they act and speak as if they had been born with masks on. They do not lack eloquence; in this respect, at least, Seneca is a great master, and many individual speeches are

models of rhetorical dialogue. But while in Euripides's Medea and
Jason, Phaedra and Hippolytus, we may see people we ourselves
have known, we will look far before we find anything in our
experience that even remotely resembles the Senecan characters.
There is very real question whether his plays ever were intended
to be produced on the stage; some have thought so; others have
contended that they were intended merely for recitation in oratorio
style. Their long speeches and almost total absence of action would
probably try the patience of any modern theatre audience; even in
oratorio-style reading, their excessive bravura, overblown sententiousness, and sheer bombast often bring them critically close to the
fine line that separates the sublime from the ridiculous.

Some of the differences between Seneca and Euripides may
serve to show some of the ways in which Seneca's versions varied
from their originals. Euripides's Medea, for example, in spite of
her black arts and her savagery, remains a full-blooded woman
whose love for Jason was deep and sincere, who sacrificed everything for him only to see herself roughly brushed aside when Jason
found her no longer useful to his political ambition. Her revenge
on him was bloody, to be sure, but if we remember the virtually
prehistoric setting in which the story is laid, it is not entirely out
of line. In Seneca's version, Medea is no longer a woman; she is
plainly and simply a witch. She is so bombastic, bloodthirsty, and
barbaric that we feel little sympathy for her, even though Jason is,
on his side, as bad as she. Her opening speech sets the tone of the
play:

> "Ye Jupiter and Juno, patrons of wedlock; thou Lucina, keeper
> of the conjugal couch; thou Minerva, who didst teach Tiphys
> to bridle a novel craft that would master the seas; thou Nep-
> tune, savage lord of Ocean's depths; thou Sun, who dost
> apportion bright light to the globe; thou triform Hecate, whose
> radiance serves as accomplice to silent sacraments—ye deities
> by whom Jason swore to me, yea, and ye deities whom Medea
> hath better right to invoke: thou Chaos of endless night; ye
> realms opposed to the upper world; ye impious ghosts; thou
> Pluto, lord of the gloomy demesne; thou Proserpina, ravished
> with more honorable intentions than was I—all you I invoke,
> but not for blessing. Attend, ye goddesses who avenge crime;
> attend, your unkempt hair foul serpents, your bloody hands
> grasping the ominous torch. Attend now in such dread pres-
> ence as once ye showed when ye stood posted at my bridal.

Make your gifts death for the new bride, death for the father-
in-law and the royal stock."
(*Medea* 1–18, translation of Moses Hadas.)

After this, it is not hard to conjecture what is to come. In
Euripides's play, Medea kills her children after they have been
sentenced to exile; we tend, in spite of the bloodiness of the act, to
sympathize with her because she knows that if she does not kill
them they will face a life of slavery, torture, and misery. In Seneca's
play, she kills her children only after she discovers how deeply
Jason loves them; the act is one of pure cruelty and bloodiness;
there is in it no mother-love, only a desire to give pain to Jason.

The other plays are of a piece with this one. The prevailing
note is one of death and horror. Murderous acts are represented as
occurring on the stage; Hercules kills his wife and his children
there, Medea her children, and Jocasta commits suicide before the
eyes of the audience. We come to expect not only witches like
Medea but wizards like the seer Tiresias, a bowdlerized version of
the grand old prophet of Sophocles's plays; we are presented with
ghosts like that of Thyestes at the opening of the *Agamemnon*. It is
probably no more than natural that the types of character and
action which Seneca chooses to develop in his plays should have
found themselves expressed in the language of melodrama, horror,
bombast, and pseudo-realism. Thus we see Medea, in a passionate
moment, declaiming in mythological terms; we see a nurse who
talks like a proverb book; we see a Theseus putting together the
rags of flesh of Hippolytus like a jigsaw puzzle. Yet on occasion this
same bombastic rhetoric can produce a moving and impressive, if
somewhat unnatural exchange:

*Medea:* Fortune fears the brave, the cowardly, crushes.
*Nurse:* Valor is admirable when it has a place.
*M:* It is impossible that valor should ever have no place.
*N:* No hope points a path in your prostrate position.
*M:* Who has nothing to hope should despair of nothing.
*N:* The Colchians have deserted you, your husband is gone, of
   all your resources nothing is left.
*M:* Medea is left. Here you see sea and land, steel and fire and
   gods and thunderbolts.
*N:* A king is to fear.
*M:* My father was a king.
*N:* Are you not afraid of soldiery?

*M:* No! Though they sprouted from earth.
*N:* You will die!
*M:* So I desire.
*N:* Flee!
*M:* I have regretted flight.
*N:* Medea—
*M:* —will I prove myself.
*N:* You are a mother.
*M:* You see by whom.
*N:* Then do you hesitate to fly?
*M:* I shall fly but first take my revenge.
(*Medea* 159–76, translation of Moses Hadas)

To deliver sententious lines like these with a straight face would be difficult for a modern performer, yet one can find little in the sentiment expressed in individual lines with which to disagree: their keynote of unflinching courage is expressed with considerable force.

When Seneca turns frankly to the exposition of philosophic ideas through his plays, he is at his best, for his sententious speeches lend themselves well to the pronouncement of his tenets, the sufficiency of virtue for happiness, the need for self-reliance, and the folly of dependence on externals. There is little of this sort of thing in the Greek originals; it may be a trifle dull and undramatic but it is indubitably Roman:

> "Let him who will stand in power upon the perilous heights of the royal court. As for me, let me be satisfied with sweet peace. A lowly place be mine, there to enjoy untroubled calm throughout life. Let the public know me not; let my life flow by in silence. So, when my days have passed by without acclaim, may I die an old man of the common people. Upon him death lies heavy, who, known too well to every man, dies to himself unknown."
> (*Thyestes* 391–403)

It seems strange to us, though it would not have seemed so to earlier centuries, that Senecan tragedy should have had so wide an influence. Yet the truth is that the whole course of continental European drama was largely determined by his plays; in default of the original Greek sources, it was Seneca's Latin plays that became the models for Renaissance tragedy. In France, Seneca's influence is to be seen in the work of Corneille and Racine. In England, his tragedies were very popular in the time of Queen Elizabeth; his mingling of drama and moral reflection appealed to the people of that day. Fortunately for English drama, a strict following of the Senecan pattern was obviated by Shakespeare, who, although he knew Seneca well and draws much from him, nonetheless, by his own invincible originality, made the English stage independent of the continental tradition. Even so, there is much Senecan material to be seen in English drama, for example in plays like Kyd's *Spanish Tragedy* and Webster's *Duchess of Malfi*. Ben Jonson is probably the last representative of the Senecan tradition; with his *Catiline* and *Sejanus*, Senecan influence virtually comes to its end in England.

# CHAPTER XVII

# Lucan and Petronius

The Senecas were a truly remarkable family; not one of them, once they had moved from Spain, failed to achieve some measure of prominence and even of power. Least known of Seneca's brothers was Annaeus Mela, whose chief claim to distinction is his son, Marcus Annaeus Lucanus (39–65 A.D.). This young man, whom we know as Lucan, came to Rome as a child, where he received the traditional Roman education in philosophy, law, and rhetoric. We are told that like his uncle Seneca he excelled in rhetorical practice, and that his declamations were brilliant. He was a bright and attractive young fellow, considered by his friends and his teachers to be a man of great promise. Perhaps he was a little too attractive and was given a little too much praise, for one of his greatest weaknesses was his self-contentment. In the early days of Nero's reign, Lucan was a great friend of the emperor, with whom he used to engage in contests of verse-writing; his first literary triumph occurred in 60 A.D. when he won a prize with his recital of a poem he had written called *In Praise of Nero (Laudes Neronis)*. Unfortunately, although Nero admired poetic genius at a distance, he found himself uncomfortable in its immediate presence, and the friendship between himself and Lucan did not last long. In one way or another—whether with justification or not, we do not now know —Lucan became implicated in the conspiracy of Piso of 65. His death was something less than glorious; in an attempt to gain pardon for himself, he turned state's evidence on various of his friends, and even on his own parents. In this, his conduct was distinctly in contrast to that of a slave girl, Epicharis, who really did know the names of the conspirators, but although put to the torture, died without betraying her friends.

In antiquity Lucan was credited with thirteen different works, but of these only one, the *Civil War (Bellum civile)* or *Pharsalia*, in ten books, is now extant. This poem represents a radical departure from previous Roman epic, for unlike any of the earlier Roman poets of whom we have any knowledge, Lucan dispenses entirely with divine machinery: no gods appear in the poem in any form. Radical too is Lucan's departure from the mythological, semi-historical theme that had been Vergil's choice; instead, Lucan turns to the kind of theme that Vergil himself apparently considered and rejected, that is to say, straight history. Lucan's epic tells the story of the civil war between Pompey and Caesar, beginning with Caesar's famous crossing of the Rubicon and continuing on through his conquest of Italy, the battle of Pharsalus itself, the defeat and death of Pompey, and finally the war in North Africa against the remaining Pompeian forces under Cato the Younger. The last book deals with Caesar's campaign in Egypt; it is weak and poorly organized, and was never finished by the poet.

It is clear that in writing his epic, Lucan intended Pompey to be his hero and Caesar to appear as the adversary. The modern reader generally finds it hard to accept this juxtaposition, for in spite of all the poet's efforts, Pompey is weak, and only in his death and in Caesar's grief over it does he achieve anything like heroic stature. The fate of Pompey in Lucan's poem is proof of the inadvisability of choosing a historical subject for epic poetry, for although Pompey had many great qualities, particularly as a general, he was an inept politician, an uninspired statesman, and a pompous, self-righteous man, whom even Cicero, his stoutest apologist, could never quite stomach. Lucan attempts to gloss over Pompey's faults and to put him in a favorable light, but Caesar emerges as the greater of the two: Lucan's attempt to transform Caesar's genius and magnanimity into raw ambition never quite comes off; inevitably, the greatness of the man shines through the poet's attempt to blacken his character.

Some have thought that the real hero of the poem is Cato the Younger. In the century or so since his death, a legend had arisen around this man whom we see, in Cicero's *Letters*, stiff, cold, utterly unsympathetic, unbending and self-righteous. His suicide after the battle of Utica, in which he purportedly took his own life rather than compromise his Stoic principles by accepting the leadership of Caesar, had invested his name with a mystic aura, and made him into a kind of national hero, a legendary embodiment of all that the Romans fancied was noble, righteous, and patriotic in their tradition. In Lucan's hands, Cato emerges as a somewhat more sympathetic character than he does in Cicero's frank descriptions of him, but the poet is never quite able to rescue him from the pompousness with which he was cursed. Like some of Seneca's heroes, Lucan's Cato is so solemnly virtuous that we find it hard to believe him, and inevitably see him approaching close again to that tenuous line between the ridiculous and the sublime:

> Such was the character, such the inflexible rule of austere Cato—to observe moderation and hold fast to the limit, to follow nature, to give his life for his country, to believe that he was born to serve the whole world and not himself. To him, it was a feast to banish hunger; it was a lordly palace to fend off hard weather with a roof over his head; it was fine raiment to draw over his limbs the rough toga which is a Roman's dress in time of peace. In his view the sole purpose of love was off-spring; for the State he became a husband and father; he worshipped justice and practiced uncompromising virtue; he re-served his kindness for the whole people; and there was no act of Cato's life where selfish pleasure crept in and claimed a share.
> (*Pharsalia* 2.380–91, translation of J. D. Duff)

But in spite of Lucan's noble efforts, Cato never achieves the stature of heroism for which the author designed him. That place, in spite of the poet's best efforts, must go to Caesar, who for all his faults, so vividly portrayed, emerges as the one character in the poem with true heroic stature.

Lucan's poem begins in a way, again, that is hard to accept. We can come to terms with invocations to Muses or gods or goddesses, for although we have lost any vestige of religious feeling about them, we can still read them as poetic figures. Lucan chooses to begin his poem instead with an invocation—or rather, dedication—to Nero. One wonders if even Lucan could have been deaf to the ugly irony of the following lines, especially when we remember how truly great poets like Vergil and Horace felt about the horrors of civil war:

> Let Pharsalia heap her awful plains with dead; let the shade of the Carthaginian be glutted with carnage; let the last battle be

joined at fatal Munda; and though to these be added the fam-
ine of Perusia, the horrors of Mutina, the ships overwhelmed
near stormy Leucas and the war against slaves hard by the
flames of Aetna, yet Rome owes much to civil war, because
what was done was done for you, Caesar.
(*ibid.* 1.38–45, translation of Duff)

"Caesar"—by whom of course Nero is meant—is urged to look ahead
to his deification and to decide what royal perquisite and function
he will assume, for of course all the gods will give way to him.
Further, the poet expresses the hope that when Nero chooses his
place in the heavens, it will be near the center, not at either extreme, for if he should choose one of the latter, his weight might
overset the universe (*ibid.* 56–58).

After this fulsome introduction, the work follows the progress
of the civil war chronologically, but with many long digressions, a
good number of which sound suspiciously like padding. The poem
seems less like a poem than like a versified declamation, a piece of
display oratory, in which individual episodes or scenes may hold
our attention, and an occasional bit of realism may give us a delightful shudder, as for example when a soldier, struck in the eye
by an arrow, "stamps on the weapon and on his eye, too" (6.219).
Lucan, like his uncle Seneca, is also fond of necromancy, magic,
ghosts, and the like: when word is received at Rome of the advance
of Caesar's troops upon the city, the heavens are filled with enough
weird and abnormal phenomena, and earth with enough monsters,
to foretell a century of disasters. New stars and comets appear in
the sky; out of a clear sky lightning strikes the Capitol; the sun
turns dark at midday; Aetna erupts; Charybdis churns up blood;
the fire on Vesta's altar goes out; the statues of gods, great and
small, break out in sweat; animals speak; women bear misshapen
monsters, and the ghost of Sulla walks (1.522–83).

As with Seneca again, Lucan shows his greatest strength in the
composition of highly rhetorical speeches. At the shrine of Zeus
Ammon, the general Labienus advises Cato to consult the god as to
the outcome of the war, but Cato replies:

"What question do you bid me ask, Labienus? Whether I would
rather fall in battle, a free man, than witness a tyranny?
Whether it makes no difference if life be long or short? Whether
violence can ever hurt the good, or Fortune threatens in vain
when Virtue is her antagonist? Whether the noble purpose is

enough, and virtue becomes no more virtuous by success? I can answer these questions, and the oracle will never fix the truth deeper in my heart. We men are all inseparable from the gods, and, even if the oracle be dumb, all our actions are predetermined by Heaven. The gods have no need to speak; for the Creator told us once for all at our birth whatever we are permitted to know. Did he choose these barren sands, that a few might hear his voice? Did he bury truth in this desert? Has he any dwelling-place save earth and sea, the air of heaven, and virtuous hearts? Why seek we further for deities? What we see is God; every motion we make is God also. Men who doubt and are ever uncertain of future events—let *them* cry out for prophets: I draw my assurance from no oracle but from the sureness of death. The timid and the brave must fall alike; the god has said this, and it is enough!"
(9.566–84, translation of J. D. Duff)

Modern critics have tended to condemn Lucan as tasteless and uninspired, and his *Pharsalia* is today—as someone has said about Milton's *Paradise Lost*—more talked about than read. In earlier ages, however, for example, in eighteenth-century England, it was not only popular, but its author was considered an even greater poet than Vergil. Lucan must be given credit for picturesque and striking language, but above all for his attempt to re-infuse a somewhat wilted Roman literature with the spirit of life. As Vergil had correctly seen, the historical theme is not a good one for epic, for history will not subject itself without violence to the artistic exigencies of poetry; nevertheless, Lucan was right in seeing that Roman literature could not go on forever writing about mythological fantasy, about ancient never-never lands and never-never histories, but if it was to have any real meaning it must somehow bring itself back to reality and actuality. His choice of a historical subject for his epic was courageous enough in itself; even more courageous was his deliberate abandonment of the handy divine machinery that had been of such help to Vergil, and his choice of what was very nearly a contemporary subject—for not much more than a century had elapsed since the end of the Civil War. His attempt to make philosophy and science serve as the divine machinery had once served is less than successful; the philosophic portions of the poem seem pompous, forced, and insincere, and require entirely too much argument; the scientific—and pseudo-scientific—episodes are too long and detailed, and get in the way of narrative progress.

Lucan also failed to notice that if he was to write about real men and real history, he must write about them in "real" language and not in the high-flown, artificial style of the rhetorical schools. For this linguistic adventure, unfortunately, he did not have the courage or the genius. He remains a bright young man, but nothing much more than that, and was never quite equal to the task he had set for himself. He saw that task, its nature and significance, clearly enough, but he never became enough of a poet to say what needed to be said.

That there was good reason for Lucan's rebellion against the shallowness of contemporary literature is clear from the works of Calpurnius Siculus (54–68 A. D.). His seven *Eclogues* show all too clearly how futile it is to attempt to recapture the spirit of an earlier age. Their dependence upon the *Eclogues* of Vergil is everywhere apparent, but they never come within reaching distance of Vergil's poems. Their versification is smooth; the lines are pretty, pleasant, and sometimes coy, but they have a picture-postcard quality that rarely rises above the level of casual doggerel. Calpurnius's praise of Nero (*Eclogue* 1) has been dismissed as foolish flattery; actually, if we place it alongside Lucan's tribute to that emperor, Calpurnius may even emerge as the more sincere, if not the better poet. His lines reflect, as do Lucan's, the enthusiasm that attended the accession of Nero to the throne. The seventh *Eclogue*, again, gives a brief but interesting picture of the amphitheatre of Nero and of the games that were held there (7.23–72). Nonetheless, it is impossible to give Calpurnius more than a passing glance and to acknowledge his existence; his poems are mere poetic lace and ribbons that tell us nothing except that their author knew and loved Vergil's *Eclogues,* and could turn a hexameter with skill and grace.

It is an odd happenstance that the age which produced so little in the way of great poetry should have produced one of the greatest masters of Latin prose—but it should be immediately added that the master was far from orthodox, and handled the Latin language in ways that must have made the burgeoning school of Neo-Ciceronians shudder. Variously known as Gaius or Lucius Petronius, and with the cognomen *Arbiter* regularly added with quite uncertain justification to his name, Petronius (fl. 54–66 A. D.) emerges with a wonderful freshness from the dull and unimaginative literature of his day, and indeed from the mass of works produced throughout the Roman period. For his work is utterly unlike that of any other Roman author; totally unpretentious, and without any attempt to walk the Olympian heights of a Vergil or a Cicero, Petronius's single known work, the *Satyricon*, has all the urbanity of Horace at his most urbane, all the lustiness of Catullus at his most earthy, all the satire—and better put, at that—of Lucilius, and all the bubbling warmth and good Italian humor of Plautus, all of this expressed for once in a wondrously convincing literary version—or rather, versions, for there are many kinds—of the Latin language as it actually came from the lips of living Romans. Even more than the beautifully informal Latin of Cicero's *Letters*, even more than the occasionally self-conscious stage version of Plautus, Petronius gives us the speech of the common man of Italy, of the Latin that must in fact have been heard on the streets of Naples or of Rome. Add to all this an ability to spin a yarn that is even more brilliant than Ovid's, and we have a Roman writer whose only near analogue in English must be Chaucer, and whose latter-day blood brother can only be Mark Twain.

Almost nothing is known for certain about Petronius. Tacitus in his *Annals* (16.18–19) gives an account of a certain Gaius Petronius, who, he says, was an artist in *la dolce vita*, and because of his skill and sophistication in the arts of luxurious living, became Nero's *elegantiae arbiter*—a phrase that has been thought by many to account for the cognomen later assigned to Petronius. Of this Gaius Petronius, Tacitus says further that he was highly successful in government service and served with distinction as governor of Bithynia and as consul at Rome. In the end, so runs Tacitus's account, Petronius incurred the jealousy of Tigellinus, and upon learning that he had been condemned to death, took the usual recourse of suicide. Tacitus says that he spent his last hours not in philosophic speculation or in serious contemplation of the problems of eternity, but in gay banqueting and cheerful conversation with his friends. He cut the arteries in his wrists, but prolonged the process of dying by alternately opening and closing the wounds; when he felt that death was near, he dictated a record of all of Nero's escapades of which he had known, signed it, sealed it, and gave it to his attendants to be delivered to the emperor in lieu of the usual flattering testimonial.

Whether this Petronius is the Petronius of the *Satyricon*, we do not, and probably never shall, know. Tacitus makes no mention of any book by his Petronius; the impudent final statement that Petronius composed and sent to Nero could scarcely have been the *Satyricon*. On the other hand there is nothing in the character of the *Satyricon* itself that would be out of harmony with the man whom Tacitus describes; if that Petronius did write a book, it could well have been the *Satyricon,* and in default of any more precise information, it is probably best to allow the traditional association to stand.

The original length, scope, and even the story of the *Satyricon* are not known. We have extant today only portions of Books xv and xvi; we do not know how many more books were included in the entire work. There may have been as many as thirty or thirty-five. Many attempts have been made to reconstruct the probable course of the whole story, most of these being based on the theory that the *Satyricon* was a kind of parody of the *Odyssey;* as the *Odyssey,* so they say, is the story of the expiation of the wrath of the god Poseidon, so the *Satyricon* is the story of the expiation of the wrath of Priapus. All that can be said for certain is that the story involved a good deal of travel from one part of Italy to another, and, to judge from the extant fragments, the journey itself provided a kind of scaffolding upon which were hung countless ancillary incidents involving adventures in the various towns at which the characters in the story stopped.

Judging again from the extant fragments, the individual stories seem to have been strung together in somewhat haphazard fashion, and to have singularly small pretense to any kind of unified theme. It may be that the story originally was put together much as is Mark Twain's *Huckleberry Finn,* with the various travels of the characters having something of the same function as does the Mississippi River in Twain's story. But in fact this is all conjecture, and until further fragments turn up we would probably do best to content ourselves with the approximately one hundred twenty pages that are still available to us. Much the largest portion of these pages is the episode now known as "The Banquet of Trimalchio" *(Cena Trimalchionis);* the rest consists of short pieces, many of them embodying entire incidents, and nearly all of them from those portions of the original that followed the banquet.

We do not even know why the *Satyricon* was so called. It is not strictly speaking a satire, although it might with some justification be assigned to the type called *Menippean Satire*—that prose-verse medley which seems so much to have fascinated the scholar Varro and in all probability was the model for Seneca's *Apocolocyntosis Claudii.* In form, the *Satyricon* could scarcely be classed as a novel, since it lacks the unified theme and study of character development that are considered essential to that form. Some have assigned it to the special type of novel called picaresque, of which Cervantes's

*Don Quixote* is the outstanding example; in actuality, the most
that can be said with any certainty is that the *Satyricon* took a
single set of characters, who stay virtually unchanged from beginning to end, and put them through various adventures in various
places; also involved are a large number of incidental characters
who are brought in when needed and discarded when their function has been fulfilled. The technique is essentially a very simple
one; there was little need for a unifying theme other than that
supplied by the central set of characters; their personalities and
their anticipated reactions to any given situation, plus the inherent
interest in the various incidents themselves, would have been
sufficient to maintain the reader's interest through the long narrative.

The central set of characters consists of three persons, Encolpius, Ascyltus, and their young slave Giton; a pompous professor
named Agamemnon appears in the opening fragment, and apart
from the rich array of characters present at Trimalchio's banquet,
to whom we shall presently advert in more detail, there are slave-
girls, prostitutes, witches, pimps, homosexuals, pickpockets and
sundry other types: thieves, soldiers, and even a somewhat moth-
eaten poet.

The extant portion of the work begins with a discussion of
education between Encolpius and Agamemnon; in terms that sound
startlingly modern, Encolpius claims that the training in the
schools is artificial and meaningless and has no connection with
reality: "No, I tell you, we don't educate our children at school; we
stultify them and send them out into the world half-baked. Why?
Because we keep them utterly ignorant of real life. The common
experience is something they never see or hear" (*Satyricon* 1.3, trs.
of W. Arrowsmith). In reply, Agamemnon maintains that the profes-
sors are doing the best they can with the stupid students that are
sent to them, and claims that in the end it is really the parents who
are to blame.

The story then slips on to a brawl in the Forum and from
there to a number of erotic scenes, one between Ascyltus and Giton,
and another involving the pseudo-marriage of young Giton and a
little girl, who are ceremonially put to bed and then observed by
the adult company through a slit in the door. The *Satyricon* is
liberally peppered with erotic scenes of this kind, most of them
brief if titilating sexual encounters of one sort or another; only one
of them is drawn out to any length; this is the long series of incidents near the end of the extant portion of the book (126 ff.)

revolving around Encolpius's sudden impotence and the attempts of various interested parties to revive his virility.

Inevitably, our interest centers on the longest piece of connected narrative, the so-called "Banquet of Trimalchio" (26–78). Trimalchio himself is a wealthy freedman, a self-made man who started in the gutter and is now so enormously wealthy that his holdings are organized into provinces, with overseers who submit daily reports on the lands and activities entrusted to their care. The scene of the banquet is in Campania, possibly in Naples itself; the characters who appear at the banquet—except of course for the two supercilious young travelers, Ascyltus and Encolpius, their slave Giton, and Professor Agamemnon—are of a piece with the host himself, all of them freedmen, businessmen of one sort and another, some successful, some down on their luck.

The dinner itself is fantastic, with a long series of elaborate dishes, all of them pretending to be something other than what they really are. At one point, for example, eggs are passed around to the company; when Ascyltus opened his, he was about to throw it away because he thought it had already "gone to chick." His neighbor warned him not to discard it but to look more closely; sure enough, the egg turned out to be a confection made of pastry, and the "chick" a neatly roasted little bird. On another occasion, a whole roast pig is brought in and placed on the table; Trimalchio looks at it and shouts out that the stupid cook had forgotten to "draw" the pig before he roasted it. He commands the cook to be brought in and orders him to disembowel the pig at once; this, the chef does; whereupon out of the pig's belly tumble long strings of sausages and puddings.

More interesting than the food and the elaborate dancing and singing with which it is served, are the guests themselves and their conversation, the latter delivered in a wide variety of Latin *patois*, each accurately revealing the social position, trade, and education of the speaker. Petronius has given us here the only examples we have of the actual unvarnished Latin of the streets; it is as rich, colorful, and ebullient as its modern Italian counterpart. In English, one turns once again to Mark Twain, who in *Huckleberry Finn* and *Tom Sawyer* has given us a similar and equally skillful version of American English of the mid-nineteenth century. To render Petronius's Latin into English is an impossibility; the following piece, the reply of a certain Hermeros to Ascyltus's scornful observations on Trimalchio's menu, will perhaps give an idea of the general flavor of these conversations:

"Still cackling, are you? Who the hell are you to snicker?
Where'd your daddy buy you? Think you're made out of gold,
eh? So that's it, you're a Roman knight? That makes me a
king's son. Then why was I a slave? Because I wanted to be.
Because I'd rather be a Roman slave than a taxpaying savage.
And as I live and breathe, I hope no man thinks I'm funny. I
walk like a free man. I don't owe any man a thing. I've never
been hauled into court. That's right: no man ever had to tell
me to pay up. I bought a few plots of land and a nice bit of
silver plate. I feed twenty stomachs, not counting the dog. I
bought my wife's freedom so no man could put his dirty paws
on her. I paid a good two hundred for my own freedom. Right
now, I'm on the board for the emperor's worship and I hope
when I die, I won't have to blush for anything. But you're so
damn busy sneering at us, you don't look at your own behind.
You see the lice on us, but not the ticks on yourself. Nobody
but you thinks we're funny. Look at your old professor there:
he appreciates us. Bah, you're still sucking tit; you're limp
leather, limper, no damn better. Oh, you're rich, are you? Then
cram down two lunches; bolt two suppers, sonny. As for me, I'd
rather have my credit than all your cash. Whoever had to dun
me twice? Forty years, boy and man, I spent as a slave, but no
one could tell now whether I was slave or free. . . . I did
everything I could to please my master. He was a good man, a
real gentleman, whose fingernail was worth more than your
whole carcass. . . ."
(*Satyricon* 57.4–10, trs. of W. Arrowsmith)

Hermeros is quite characteristic of all the guests; he is coarse
but utterly honest, a hard-working businessman with a sound sense
of values. It is worth noting that in this speech he does not protest
against slavery, for this is an institution he accepts as normal, and
to which he quite willingly grants its due. His protest rather is
against the social values of the day, that proclaim silly, lazy, unpro-
ductive creatures like Encolpius and Ascyltus superior to solid citizens like himself. In point of fact, that is the whole tone of the
social criticism of the *Satyricon*; characters like Hermeros, Habin-
nas, and the others are indubitably amusing, and their rich, vulgar
speech is productive of much laughter in and of itself. Nevertheless,
the contrast between Trimalchio and his friends and the silly
heroes of the story is painfully obvious; there can be no question in

our minds, and there probably was none in Petronius's, as to where the real merit lay.

Interspersed with bits like these are stories like Niceros's tale of the werewolf (61–62) and Trimalchio's own story about the un- breakable glass bottle:

> "But, you know, there was once a workman who invented a little glass bottle that wouldn't break. Well, he got in to see the emperor with this bottle as a present. Then he asked the emperor to hand it back to him and managed to drop it on the floor on purpose. Well, the emperor just about died. But the workman picked the bottle back up from the floor and, believe it or not, it was dented just a little, as though it were made of bronze. He pulled a little hammer out of his pocket and tapped it back into shape. Well, by this time he thought he had Jupiter by the balls, especially when the emperor asked him if anyone else was in on the secret. But you know what happened? When the workman told him that nobody else knew, the emperor ordered his head chopped off. Said that if the secret ever got out, gold would be as cheap as dirt."
> (51, trs. of W. Arrowsmith)

Most famous of all, perhaps, is the story of the Widow of Ephesus, from the later part of the *Satyricon*—the tale of that lady, who, while mourning her dead husband was happily seduced by a soldier who had been set to guard the bodies of some crucified thieves. So enamored of her soldier-lover did the virtuous widow become, that when the body of one of the thieves was stolen from its cross, and the soldier thus put in serious jeopardy for failure to perform his duty, she allowed him to hang her husband's corpse on the cross in its place (*Satyricon* 111–12).

But the list of unforgettable tales and incidents is almost in- exhaustible. We think of our first meeting with Trimalchio, when we find him playing a ball game, in which he demonstrates his delicate taste by refusing to pick up any ball that had touched the ground and instead has a fresh one supplied him by a slave. We are amused at his ostentation when, a silver dish falling to the floor, he ordered a slave to "sweep it up with the rest of the trash." His learning is deliciously faked ("I've got two libraries, one Greek and one Latin") as he proves by such monstrous distortions of mythology as having Cassandra kill her children, Daedalus shut

Niobe up in the Trojan horse, etc., etc. His utter vulgarity is perhaps never so eloquently demonstrated as when, near the end of the banquet, he has his will brought in and read, and then commands the whole company to shed tears over his demise.

But although we may laugh at these and at many other incidents, we are bound to realize that Trimalchio and his freedman friends are solid, genuine, honest people, rich and full-blooded, and far from lacking in kindness and love for their neighbors. In these healthy, humble characters, we see the strong base on which the Roman Empire was built, the latter-day, polyglot, multiracial representatives of the very kind of empire that the *Aeneid* had both predicted and demanded. The contrast between Petronius's solid citizens and the cynical, shallow sensualists of upper Roman society whom we meet on the pages of Suetonius, Tacitus, and Juvenal, and with whom Petronius himself can have been only too well acquainted, is painfully obvious.

Only one other writer of the age of Nero perhaps deserves at least brief attention. This is Lucius Junius Columella, whose book on farming *(De agricultura)* was completed about the year 65 A. D. and forms one more of the corpus of agricultural works that began with Cato and continued through Varro and Vergil's *Georgics.* Columella's work belongs with Varro's rather than with Cato's; like Varro's, it is a bookish treatise, and while it gives us many interesting sidelights on farming in Roman antiquity, it is not written with sufficient imagination to interest the lover of literature or with sufficient realism to interest the farmer.

# CHAPTER XVIII

# Martial, Statius, and Quintilian

The death of Nero in 68 was followed by the year of the three emperors, Galba, Otho, and Vitellius, a period of considerable political unrest. Vitellius was succeeded in 69 by the first of the Flavian emperors, Vespasian. He was a rather harsh and stern man, but his rough, practical wisdom was a great relief after the years of governmental insanity that had preceded his accession. Neither Vespasian nor his successor Titus showed any particular interest in literature, but their successor Domitian, who came to the throne in 81 A. D., openly fostered literary effort and established two new literary contests in addition to the one already established under Nero. The reign of Domitian was scarcely a happy one, for the emperor was arrogant, ill-tempered, and treacherous. Nevertheless the Flavians must be credited with augmenting the stature and dignity of the imperial civil service, and with opening that branch of government work, previously pretty much relegated to unprincipled freedmen, to gentlemen of the stamp of Tacitus and Pliny the Younger.

During the reign of Vespasian (69–79) no major poets make themselves known. Mention should perhaps be made of Silius Italicus, the longest-lived of the Roman poets (25–101 A. D.), who, to judge from the references to him in Pliny's letters, was a man of enormous personal charm—in fact, a delightful, wealthy poetaster, who fancied that he had a gift for epic, and in consequence composed a clumsy and fulsome poem in seventeen books, called the *Punica*, a versified history of the war with Hannibal. The poem is not without purple passages of some merit, but on the whole it is tiresome, and seldom read today even by professional classicists.

Worthy also of at least a moment's notice is the poet Valerius Flaccus (fl. 70–90 A. D.) whose *Argonautica*, in eight books, relates a part of the story of Jason and Medea. Like most of the verse of the post-Augustan age, it is skillfully executed and not without charm, but falls a good many degrees short of greatness. It is of interest now chiefly to literary historians, who like to compare it with the Greek version of Apollonius of Rhodes (third century, B. C.).

Very nearly the same is true of prose, although a number of men who later made their mark—e.g. Quintilian, Tacitus, and Pliny the Younger—were at least beginning to emerge at this time. Easily the most prominent prose-writer of the period was Pliny the Elder (Gaius Plinius Secundus, c. 23–79 A. D.). This enormously energetic man, born at the city of Novum Comum in the Po Valley, came early to Rome and spent a life in vigorous pursuit of public service, and in indefatigable study. He served in the army in Germany and became an expert on cavalry; he was equally at home in the navy; in fact, he was in command of the Roman fleet at Cape Misenum when Mt. Vesuvius erupted in 79 A. D. He immediately cast off and sailed across the bay of Naples on a mission half of mercy, half of scientific curiosity, for he was at least as anxious to observe this strange phenomenon as he was to rescue the unhappy inhabitants of the towns located around the base of Mt. Vesuvius. Unfortunately, he suffered from asthma, and the combination of fatigue and sulphurous gases from the eruption caused his death.

The elder Pliny was an omnivorous reader; he is said to have claimed that he had never read a book from which he did not derive some profit. And he seems to have stopped reading only when he was asleep, for on one occasion he roundly scolded his nephew, Pliny the Younger, for walking from place to place in Rome, when he might have ridden in a litter and used the time in reading. He not only read everything he could lay hands on; he also took notes on his reading; his nephew tells us that at his death he left 160 papyrus rolls full of his notes "on both sides."

The list of his works (preserved for us by Pliny the Younger, *Epistles* 3.5) shows a breadth of interest unequalled at Rome since the days of the scholar Varro. Pliny wrote a book on *Throwing the Javelin from Horseback (De iaculatione equestri)*, on *Oratory (Studiosus)*, on *Dubious Usage (Dubii sermonis L. VIII)*; he also wrote a biography of the poet Pomponius Secundus, a history of the wars in Germany (in twenty books) *(Bellorum Germaniae L. XX)*, and a history in thirty-one books of his own period—a book with the curious title *From Where Aufidius Bassus Left Off (A fine*

*Aufidi Bassi).* (Bassus had written a history, now lost, from the death of Caesar to the fall of Sejanus in 31 A. D.)

All of these works have been lost, but Pliny's greatest single effort, his *Natural History (Naturalis historia)*, is extant in its entirety. This enormous work, in thirty-seven books, was not quite finished at the time of Pliny's death, and was edited and published by his nephew. It is the most complete account we have from antiquity of the state of science in the days of the early Empire. In subject matter it ranges from a mathematical, physical description of the universe, through geography, ethnology, anthropology, zoology, botany, pharmacology, mineralogy, and metallurgy. Pliny shares the usual ancient predilection for book-knowledge in the scientific field; his information is patently at second hand, and it is clear that he had no acquaintance whatever with laboratory and empirical methods. It is easy for us now to see where Pliny failed, and to be amused at his naive combination of scientific fact, superstition, and sheer gossip; still, we may be reasonably certain that a man of his habits was careful to be as accurate as he could be, and that in his own day, he qualified as a scientific expert and polymath. His work has little stylistic merit and can scarcely qualify as literature, yet it remains one of the great landmarks of the history of Western science, and its influence through the Middle Ages, when it was virtually the only available source of scientific knowledge, was enormous.

The reign of Domitian (81–96 A. D.) was a far from happy period for the Romans. The emperor himself was stern and strait-laced, stuffy about his own importance, and insistent upon the observation of the formalities (he insisted, for example, that the Romans wear the clumsy, hot toga to the games of the Circus, although for years they had been accustomed to wearing a lighter, less cumbersome dress, the *synthesis*). Alone of the emperors, he liked to be called Lord *(Dominus)*; as a military commander, he was close to a disaster; it was during his reign that the Roman armies suffered at the hands of the Dacians one of the worst defeats of their history, yet Domitian insisted on claiming this as a victory.

It is not surprising then if, although a number of younger men were beginning to acquire the strength and skill that later made them famous, there appeared in the age of Domitian himself almost no great names other than that of the epigrammatist Martial. Marcus Valerius Martialis (c. 38–c. 104 A. D.) was born in the little town of Bilbilis in Spain. About the age of twenty-six he came to Rome, where he appears to have attached himself to the Senecas,

Spaniards like himself, as patrons. Although we have little or none of the work that Martial produced during this earlier period of his life, it is fairly clear that, unlike most Roman youths, he did not attempt a career in the law but was a poet from the beginning.

How he lived in those early years, especially after the death of Seneca and Lucan in 65, we do not know; if his later epigrams are any evidence, he managed to survive somewhat in the fashion of the comic *parasitus,* by attaching himself to the households of wealthy men and making himself welcome there by his wit. Again, to judge from the epigrams (a shaky source of information about the poet in any event and particularly in Martial's case, since throughout his poems he adopts a comic-satiric version of the *pauper poeta* of poetic tradition), he never managed to acquire much money, and his assiduous attendance upon his wealthy patrons brought him very little income indeed. He did have a small farm at Nomentum—so small, he says, that it could hide under the wing of a cricket. In Rome, he lived three flights up in a squalid, tumble-down apartment.

One of the curious facts about this man is that, to all appearances, he was the first poet of the Western world to derive any appreciable income from the sale of his books; in the course of his epigrams, here and there he inserts what would today be called advertisements, telling where and at what price various editions of his poems could be purchased. There is some evidence, again from the poems, that Martial's epigrams may have been among the first books in the Western world to be published in the codex form, like a modern bound book, instead of in the customary papyrus roll. Martial's activity as a poet seems to stretch from approximately 80 A. D. until his death about 104. He left Rome in 98 and retired to his home town of Bilbilis. Pliny, in one of his letters, tells us somewhat self-consciously that Martial could not have made the trip except for his (Pliny's) supplying him with the necessary funds. His last book of epigrams was sent to Rome from Bilbilis, and it appears that he died soon thereafter.

The extant epigrams of Martial comprise fourteen books, traditionally preceded by a short volume called the *Book of Epigrams* or *Book of the Spectacles* (*Liber spectaculorum*), a collection of epigrams centering mostly around the dedication of the Flavian Amphitheatre in 80 A. D. This great building, now known as the Colosseum, had been built by Vespasian and Titus on the site of Nero's infamous Golden House, an enormous palace, the building of which had dispossessed many Roman citizens, and had been one of the many causes of Nero's unpopularity. The little *Book of the Spectacles* is not without its merit, particularly as giving us a number of interesting pictures of some of the "acts" of animal-baiting and gladiatorial combat that took place in the Roman arena, but it is on the whole a stiff and artificial performance, with all the ring of a duty-job.

This apparent artificiality is in direct contrast to the rest of Martial's work, for he is almost never again mannered or artificial. He represents, in fact, a voice of protest against the mannered and artificial literature of his day and complains bitterly of so-called poets who spent their time rehashing and redoing Theseus and Oedipus and Agamemnon and the Seven against Thebes—themes so threadbare by this time that it was virtually impossible even for a great poet to breathe any life into them. Martial, of course, makes no attempt to do so; he scornfully brushes all such pseudo-literature aside, and insists that poetry, to have any meaning, must be derived from real life: he boasts that his pages "have the taste of man" (*hominem pagina nostra sapit*, 10.4.10). In consonance with this doctrine, Martial reveals Rome as he saw it, its amusing features, its vices, its follies, sycophancy, prudery, and hypocrisy. Incidentally, he also gives us many pictures of the realia of Rome: its public buildings, homes, both tenements and palaces, shops, the games of the Circus, and so on. He draws for us pictures of generous friends, delightful small children, scholars, doctors, lawyers, drunkards, fools, perverts, in short, virtually every sort of character one might expect to find in a rich and cosmopolitan city. Martial may be excelled as a poet by some of the other voices of Rome; no other single writer gives us so complete a picture of the life of the city itself; even apart from their indubitable charm and wit, Martial's epigrams provide us with invaluable information about Rome, and his descriptions of the streets and buildings are so accurate that they have been of real assistance to archaeologists in locating important finds.

In one respect in particular Martial is most noteworthy; although he uncovers much immorality, perversion, and even downright ugliness, he never suggests the need for reform; he never regrets or bewails what he sees; on the contrary, he seems to take keen delight in every aspect of life. Martial is one of the most objective observers of mankind that Rome produced; he seems to have no axe to grind, but merely to find the world full of interest and humor. Only one aspect of life arouses his anger and opposition, and this is sham, hypocrisy, pretense, trickery. His feelings in this matter take many forms of expression; the following epigram may perhaps sum up his attitude:

> Faustinus, since the day when the *Lex Julia* found new birth among our people and Decency was commanded to enter our homes, this is less than the thirtieth, or certainly not more than the thirtieth day, and Telesilla is already marrying her tenth husband. A woman who marries that often is not marrying; she is committing legal adultery. I find an out-and-out whore less offensive!
> (*Epigrams* 6.7)

But Martial is not only famous for his pictures of Roman life and his merciless attacks on sham; he is also responsible for giving to the epigram its final form, the form in which it was ever after to be known in Western literature. Previous to this time, the epigram had been simply a short poem, usually satiric, but not necessarily so, usually involving, as a short poem necessarily must, some very simple, single idea. It was Martial who gave to the epigram its distinctive feature of point, particularly what one might call re-served point: the poem begins in an innocent way and proceeds to describe a situation or a person in language that appears to be heading in some quite innocuous direction; then in the last line—or even better, in the last word—the whole point or aim of the poem is reversed, and we are shown that the supposedly innocuous situation and the poet's supposedly harmless comment on it, were no more than build-up and background for the sting of satirical laughter.

Except for a very few serious epigrams, nearly every one of Martial's poems is constructed in this fashion, and his delight in the cleverness with which he is able to deliver the final sting is quite palpable. We gather that a certain Linus had offended Martial:

> You ask me, Linus, what yield I get from my farm at Nomentum? This is the yield my farm brings me: Linus, I don't see you. (2.38)

Again:
> Paula wants very much to marry me, but I don't want to marry Paula: she's old as the hills. I wouldn't mind, if she were older. (10.8)

But not all of Martial's epigrams are as unkindly pointed as these; his poems can be full of warmth and affection, as for example when he writes of the happy marriage, now in its fifteenth year, of Calenus and Sulpicia—years, he says, which Calenus counts as his whole life, for he only counts as "life" the days that he has spent as a husband. Martial writes too with great tenderness of a slave-boy named Alcimus, whose death "in his years of growth" brought the poet great sorrow (1.88); he writes another poem to honor another friend, Rufus Camonius, who had died in his twenties; Martial, who could not be present at the young man's funeral, asks him to accept these few verses as "a pinch of incense from an absent friend" (6.85). He speaks warmly, too, of his namesake, Julius Martial, and of another friend, Quintus Ovidius, whose birthday, he says, is dearer to him than his own, because that day gave him a friend (9.52). But probably the most famous of his songs of sorrow is his epitaph for the little girl Erotion:

> Mother, and sire, to you do I commend
> Tiny Erotion, who must now descend
> A child, among the shadows, and appear
> Before Hell's bandog and Hell's gondolier.
> Of six whole winters she had felt the cold,
> But lacked six days of being six years old.
> Now she must come, all playful, to that place
> Where the great ancients sit with reverend face;
> Now lisping, as she used, of whence she came,
> Perchance she names and stumbles at my name.
> O'er these so fragile bones let there be laid
> A plaything for a turf, and for that maid
> That ran so lightly footed in her mirth
> Upon thy breast, lie lightly, Mother Earth!
> (5.34, trs. of Robert Louis Stevenson)

Martial, in fact, loved the whole world, everything and everybody in it. His affection extended even to nature, although he preferred nature in her more cultivated forms. Two of his finest epigrams, 3.58 and 4.64, describe in great detail the farm of Faustinus, with its grainfields, barnyard, vineyards, and company of busy slaves, and dwell with pleasure on the view from the estate of his friend, Julius Martial, on the Janiculum.

Martial is no philosopher; he is far more concerned with what men do and are than he is with what they ought to do or think.

From time to time (e.g. 1.15) he urges his friends to take life as it comes and to enjoy each day without too much thought for the future; on another occasion, in rather simple, unpretentious style, he suggests the things that to him make up the good life:

> The things that make a better, happier life, my dear dear Martial, are these: money not gained by toil but inherited; a farm not unproductive, a hearth where a fire ever burns; never a law-suit, rarely the toga, a mind at peace; the strength of a gentleman, a healthy body; prudence and honesty, friends like one's self; informal society, a simple table; a night not drunken but free of care; a bed not puritanical yet decent; sleep that makes the night short: wish to be what you are and ask for nothing more; neither fear nor pray for your last day.
> (10.47)

A delightfully uncomplicated soul, Martial is never bitter, rarely angry, generally full of goodwill and good humor, finding the world entirely too fascinating to be resentful even of its unpleasant features, and finding in every corner of Rome some scrap of life on which to exercise his endless fund of wit.

The only other poet produced in the age of Domitian who made much of a name for himself was Statius (Publius Papinius Statius, fl. 80–c. 95 A. D.). He came from Naples, and was the son of a schoolteacher and poet; in fact, his father had won prizes for his poetry both in Greece and in Italy. Statius began his poetic career with some acclaim, for he won a prize at the *Agon Albanus* for his panegyric on Domitian's campaigns in Germany and Dacia. His next attempt however, at the *Agon Capitolinus* in 94 A. D. was a failure, and he retired in disappointment to Naples. Statius's extant works consist of two epics, the *Thebaid*, in twelve books, and an *Achilleid*, in two, the latter either unfinished or perhaps intended only as a short epic (or "epyllion"); and besides these two, a volume of poems called the *Silvae*, in five books. This last-named collection consists of short poems mostly in lyric meters on a considerable variety of subjects, and addressed to a number of the poet's friends.

To our taste, Statius's poetry seems affected, shallow, and mannered. His two epics illustrate entirely too clearly the reason for Martial's bitter protest against this kind of writing: the subjects are worn-out and hackneyed, and all Statius's ingenuity cannot bring them to life again. However, Statius seems to have enjoyed a good deal of popularity in his own lifetime, and during the Middle

Ages he was considered one of Rome's great poets; in fact, by virtue of a medieval tradition to the effect that Statius had been converted to Christianity, we find him in Dante's *Divine Comedy* (*Purgatory* 21 ff.) on his way to a paradise that was denied his self-acknowledged master, Vergil, an honor that seems strangely anomalous, but only because it is hard for us, as it was not for Dante, to understand why Vergil should be denied this honor simply because he was born before the Christian era.

Almost equally undistinguished as a writer but of vast importance because of his position in the history of education is Quintilian (Marcus Fabius Quintilianus, c. 35–c. 100 A. D.). Quintilian, like Martial and the Senecas, was from Spain; he received his education at Rome, but returned to his homeland, where he made the acquaintance of the future emperor Galba, who was at the time proconsul in Spain. When Galba became emperor in 68, he took Quintilian to Rome with him and set him up as a public rhetorician —a professor of rhetoric, paid by the state. In spite of Galba's subsequent disgrace and death, Quintilian managed to survive into the reign of Domitian, and continued his career as a celebrated teacher. He was tutor to Domitian's two grandnephews, whom the emperor intended to succeed him; he is perhaps even better known as one of the teachers of Pliny the Younger.

Late in his life Quintilian published the one work that established his fame, his *Institutio oratoria* (c. 93 A. D.), a complete treatise on the training of the orator, from his learning of the alphabet to his mature studies in philosophy and literature. Much of what Quintilian writes is concerned with the now obsolete art of oratory, but the many passages that deal with educational theory and with literature contain matter that is still of interest. Quintilian seems to have been the first person to regard education itself as a specific art; he directed a great deal of time and energy toward discovering the best methods of teaching, especially for children. His insistence that children must be allowed to enjoy the learning process, that they must be consulted about their interests and praised for their successes has a curiously modern ring. We are bound to find congenial, too, his insistence on a thorough grounding in the liberal arts before the student should be allowed to specialize; Quintilian thought that only in this way could the young man become a good *man*, and only if he were a good man, could he be a great orator.

It is in discussing the proper reading for the young student of oratory that Quintilian produced the most interesting part of his long treatise. In Book x of the *Institutes* he gives us thumbnail sketches of those authors whom he thinks the young orator should include in his training. In a fashion that had long been standard among ancient thinkers, he dictates that the young man must begin with a thorough reading of Homer, and goes on from there to suggest those Greek writers whom he thinks most important. The list includes Pindar, Aristophanes, Sophocles, Euripides, Menander, Thucydides, Herodotus, and above all, Demosthenes. Among the Romans, his ideal is Cicero; it was in fact Quintilian himself who was largely responsible for the Neo-Ciceronian movement in Latin letters at this time. Among the poets, he has the highest praise for Vergil, whom he places second only to Homer. Lucretius, he calls "difficult"; Ovid he says, was "entirely too enamoured of his own brilliance"; Horace he characterizes as *verbis felicissime audax* ("bold and infinitely happy in his handling of words"); he quotes Varro as saying that "if the Muses had spoken Latin, they would have spoken Plautine Latin."

The *Institutes of Oratory* is the only genuine work of Quintilian that has survived; two corpuses of declamations sometimes attributed to him are no longer considered genuine. One might remark in passing that Quintilian's attempt to revive the style of Cicero, while it may have been salutary for a Latin style gone rather rough and uncouth, may also have been a sign of intellectual deterioration: when the leaders of a nation's thought begin to look backward for direction, it is all too likely that regression rather than progress will be the result.

With the death of Domitian in 96 A. D., and the accession of Nerva to the throne, a feeling of relaxation spread over the Empire; Nerva was old—he was to reign only two years—but he was a sensible, capable and honest man, with none of the smallness of mind that had characterized his predecessor. During his reign and that of his successor, Trajan (98–117), Rome not only reached her widest geographical extent but also experienced one of her most prosperous and effective periods; men felt released, as they had not in many years, from the suspicions and the hatreds of sometimes well-meaning but generally unprincipled rulers. A rediscovered tolerance for ideas and a newly found willingness to let greatness have its say resulted in the blossoming of what many consider to be the last flower of Roman culture, the last period in which the voices of Rome expressed Roman ideas and ideals, before the intellectual currents of Italy were submerged in the new culture of the Middle Ages.

# CHAPTER XIX

# Pliny the Younger and Tacitus

Most closely linked to the preceding age is probably Pliny the Younger (Gaius Plinius Caecilius Secundus, 61–c. 114 A. D.), for his career both as public servant and as writer extends from his quaestorship in the year 89 on through a round of public offices under Domitian and into highly responsible posts in the imperial civil service under Nerva and Trajan. Pliny came from the city of New Comum in the Po Valley, and was a member of an old and distinguished Italian family. Upon the death of his father, Pliny was adopted by his uncle, Gaius Plinius Secundus, "Pliny the Elder," and this indefatigable student and writer had an enormous influence over the young man. He studied both at Milan and at Rome, where he came under the influence of Quintilian, and from him absorbed the Ciceronianism which was ever afterward characteristic of his style of writing and speaking.

After early success as a pleader in the law courts, Pliny moved on into public service and held many important offices under Domitian; his infinite tact, courtesy, and discretion enabled him to escape the emperor's displeasure; yet it appears that Pliny too might have suffered from Domitian's ill will, if Domitian had not died when he did: after his death, papers were found in his desk that purported to incriminate Pliny.

But this tactful young gentleman found no difficulty in passing from the reign of Domitian into that of Nerva and Trajan; one after another he held offices of high responsibility and distinction. His final honor was his appointment to the governorship of Bithynia, c. 111–13 A. D., a tricky and dangerous post that demanded the greatest diplomatic ability. It is presumed that Pliny died in

Bithynia, or shortly after his return from there, in the year 114 A. D. An enormously wealthy man, he was noted for his philanthropic activities; in his home town of New Comum, he established a library, a fund for assistance to the children of poor but respectable families, and in his will endowed an annual banquet in his own honor for the entire population of the town. A kindly man, he had hosts of friends, both men and women, young and old; he was married three times, and was particularly devoted to his third wife Calpurnia.

Pliny led a comfortable, happy, and successful life. He found his niche in the Roman system and fitted it perfectly. With consummate skill, he threaded his way through the imperial bureaucracy, with which he found himself entirely content, even under Domitian. If at times he was discommoded or distressed by imperial repression or by the nefarious activities of malevolent enemies, he felt that his wise course was forbearance and patience rather than rebellion. However, he was far from weak-kneed; if he thought he was being unjustly attacked, he could reply with effective force.

Probably because of his uncle's influence, Pliny remained a zealous student throughout his life—in fact, he was in danger of becoming a bookish prig. He himself tells us in one of his letters (6.16.8) that when his uncle offered him the chance to go with him to investigate the eruption of Vesuvius, Pliny replied that he would "rather stay home and study." Like his uncle, he never ceased his reading and studying, and never lost his interest in education. He was a zealous supporter of culture, particularly in its literary form, and conscientiously attended the public readings, given by friends of his, of their newly completed works, even though these might be endlessly tedious. In short, Pliny was the perfect example of a Roman gentleman, polished, urbane, courteous, kind, generous, of a type scarcely possible except in an age like the one in which he lived, an age of general contentment, order, and prosperity. There was little question of distress or unrest, either domestic or foreign. To the people of Trajan's day, Rome seemed perfectly and solidly founded, and destined to last forever.

Like the Cicero whom he so greatly admired and emulated, Pliny has left us an amazingly complete record of his life and activities. There is one great difference: Cicero's records of himself are largely contained in his letters, which he never intended for publication; Pliny's are also contained in his letters, but they *were* intended for publication. They are, in fact, his epistolary autobiography, and he was entirely confident that they would establish his fame forever. Witness to the man's self-conscious preoccupation with himself and to his confidence in his own greatness are provided by the letter that he wrote to his friend Cornelius Priscus on the occasion of Martial's death. In the letter (3.21) he tells how he provided Martial with funds for his trip home to Spain; he then quotes a part of an epigram (10.19) which Martial had written about him, apparently precisely in the hope of some such donative, lines in which Martial praises Pliny for his endless studying and his genial hospitality; Pliny then makes the following comment:

> You see what he wrote about me. Don't you think I did right at that time in sending him off home with my warmest blessing? And right too, in that I now mourn his death as that of a very dear friend? After all, he gave me the best that he could, and would certainly have given me more had he been capable of it. But after all, what greater gift can be given to a man than distinction, praise, and everlasting life? **But, you say,** Martial's poems are not likely to live forever; perhaps not; still, he wrote them as if he expected them to live forever. (3.21.6)

It is quite clear that Pliny had no intention of allowing at least this little bit of Martial's poetry to fail of everlasting life; to that end, he quoted it in one of his letters, for which he patently and confidently expected eternity.

Pliny turned out to be not so bad a prophet, for his letters have survived down to our own day at least, and at times in the history of Western culture have had wide and deeply felt influence. The letters, 368 of them, have come down in a collection of ten books, the first nine of which were arranged and published by Pliny himself, although it is a little difficult now to determine the scheme on which Pliny based his arrangement. The tenth book, consisting entirely of correspondence between Pliny and the emperor Trajan, was published after his death, presumably by his wife. Pliny's inspiration in writing the letters was undoubtedly Cicero; their style represents a curious midpoint between the totally unselfconscious informality of Cicero's letters and the highly polished rhetoric of his orations and essays. Far more polished than Cicero's, they are much less spontaneous—many of them are clearly written for display purposes, or simply as essays on miscellaneous topics. The immediate result of this aim is a literary rather than a historical or biographical presentation of a given incident; nowhere,

for example, is Pliny himself allowed to appear in any other than
a favorable light. He is always the wise counselor, the warm friend,
the generous philanthropist, and, in all matters of contest, the spectacularly brilliant winner. We never see him as we see Cicero, so to
speak, in his shirtsleeves, but always on display and on his best
behavior. In spite of this fact, it is true that we know more about
Pliny as a man than about any other ancient Roman.

The fact that Pliny's letters are really little essays is apparent
at once; there is no formlessness, no conversational rambling, no
polite padding, no abrupt beginning or close. Every letter has its
introductory statement, its main body, containing the real subject,
and its formal, commonly epigrammatic, close. He begins a letter to
his friend Nepos with a sagacious observation:

> I seem to have observed that among the actions and sayings of
> both men and women, those that are most famous are not
> always the noblest.
> (3.16.1)

Pliny then continues with a number of stories about women who
showed both loyalty and courage toward their husbands when the
latter were suffering from disease, imprisonment, or imminent
death. Among these is the story of Arria, the wife of Paetus Thrasea,
who, when her husband was condemned to commit suicide, first
thrust the dagger into her own breast, then handed it to her husband with the famous words, "Paetus, it doesn't hurt." But Pliny
thinks that Arria showed even greater courage on an earlier occasion, when both Paetus and her son lay seriously ill, and it became
clear that the boy would not recover. In spite of her suffering and
sorrow, Arria concealed the state of the son's health from her suffering husband; even when the boy died, she took care of disposing of
the body without letting her husband know, and continued to come
to his room without a tear and with a smile on her face, reporting
that the boy was getting better. Pliny thinks that this latter example
is a greater sign of courage than the more famous story about the
dagger, and after this and several other stories, concludes:

> From this we may gather what I said in the beginning, that
> men's most famous acts are not always their noblest. (3.16.13)

Time and again, the letters begin and end on some such pithy note,
showing clearly enough that these letters were only such in name,
and that they were intended, like Seneca's, to be little essays.

The range of subject covered by the letters is wide. We get dozens of stories like those about Arria and Paetus, stories about Pliny's uncle, Pliny the Elder, an account of Pliny the Elder's writings and the manner of his life, a very touching letter on the death of Silius Italicus, showing that however miserable a poetaster he may have been, he was a man of inspiring character and of great courage. We get accounts of Pliny's encounters in the law courts with unscrupulous opponents such as Marcus Regulus (1.5). We are also given the results of Pliny's rather considerable scientific interests; he discusses in utter seriousness the genuineness of a ghost story (7.27); he attempts to unravel the mystery of the floating islands of Lake Vadimonis (8.20), and has given us in two letters (6.16, 20) our only surviving contemporary accounts of the eruption of Mt. Vesuvius in 79 A. D. These two letters, incidentally, were written to his friend, the historian Cornelius Tacitus, who when engaged on writing a history of this period asked Pliny, as a near eyewitness of the catastrophe, to describe for him what had happened. Pliny also appears in the letters as a patron of education and learning (4.13) and as a loving and devoted husband (6.7).

Throughout all these letters, the conscious assumption of roles on the part of the letter-writer is obvious, yet this pose should not mislead us as to the genuineness of the revelations that Pliny has made, or blind us to their importance as descriptive of the life of the aristocratic upper classes during one of the happiest periods of the Roman Empire. He tells us about the *recitationes,* the public readings of their own works by authors (1.13), and bewails the fact that he virtually alone seems to feel it incumbent on him always to attend such recitations when he was invited to them. He tells us about some of the ceremonies of Roman life, such as the assumption of the *toga virilis,* about funerals, the making of wills, about the home life of Romans, both in the city and in the country, about sports such as ball, swimming, riding, and hunting (he deeply disliked the bloody games of the Circus). He describes in great detail his vast country place at Laurentum (2.17); in all of this, Pliny is actually far more vivid than Cicero ever could have been, for Pliny has a set purpose to reveal these things and to show how he fitted into them; and his incessant study, however farfetched it may seem, produced in him the breadth of vision that comes to the well-read. Doubtless he owes a great deal of his humanity, timeliness, personal charm, tact, wit, and broad interests to those studies that he so assiduously followed throughout his life and which, if they could not make a genius of him, at least turned him out a cultivated and highly informative gentleman.

Book x of the letters, the correspondence between Pliny and the emperor Trajan, is of a rather different character. To all appearances, at least, these are genuine letters, written to the emperor when Pliny was governor of Bithynia; most of them ask for the emperor's ruling on various vexing problems. Probably most famous of them are the two that concern the early Christian church (10.96–97). Clearly, Pliny had been constantly harassed by complaints lodged with him against the Christians, in large part from petty tradesmen who made their living selling religious objects around the pagan temples. It would appear that the Christian sect had grown sufficiently so that this trade was being seriously interfered with: religious objects simply were not selling at the accustomed rate. Upon investigation, Pliny discovered that this strange group included both sexes and people of all ages, that, as far as he could tell, they were engaged in no harmful or antisocial activities, and were in general hard-working, sober citizens. He did discover that they were technically in violation of the law, since they constituted a "secret organization," and membership in any secret organization of whatever kind had been forbidden by imperial decree, on pain of death.

The reason for the decree was clear enough: Trajan was anxious to suppress subversive political groups in order to prevent them from undermining or disturbing Roman rule in the provinces. Since the purposes for which the Christians were organized were, clearly enough, anything but subversive, and since the membership was so miscellaneous and so innocuous, Pliny was much disturbed as to what he should do about them. He tells how he offered them every chance to disprove membership in the group; all that was required was that they offer a pinch of incense at the emperor's statue, for this, it was known, no Christian would do. He offered to dismiss the charges against them if they would "repent" and disclaim further membership in the group, though under the law, repentance was not normally regarded as excuse for illegal conduct. However, he found the Christians incomprehensibly stubborn; they flatly refused to do the simple things he asked of them, and under the law he found he had no recourse but to exact the death penalty. This troubled him greatly; a humane and kindly man, he did not like to put to death women, children, and old people. Every day, he complained to Trajan, he was in receipt of anonymous accusations against various individuals charging them with membership in this forbidden society. What should he do?

Trajan's reply is revelatory. He instructs Pliny not to take the initiative in investigation of the Christians, in other words, to leave them alone unless they were forced on his attention by formal accusation. Other than this, says the emperor, Pliny has proceeded in correct fashion. Only on one point does he roundly and deservedly castigate his conscientious governor: under no circumstances is he to accept anonymous accusations:

> But anonymous accusations which are lodged with you must not be considered as evidence in any criminal case, for this sets a very bad precedent and is inconsistent with the times in which we live. (10.97)

But it was in Pliny's friend Tacitus (Cornelius Tacitus, c. 55–c. 120 A. D.) that the age of Nerva and Trajan found its most brilliant literary figure. The precise date of his birth is not known; it is generally held that he was born during the reign of Nero. He held public office under the Flavian emperors, this in spite of his dislike for their harsh and oppressive rule. Under Domitian, whom he particularly detested, he held the offices of quaestor and praetor; after the latter, he appears to have left Rome on some foreign assignment for four years. He returned in 93, and for the remainder of Domitian's reign, stayed in retirement. Under Nerva, in 97 A. D. Tacitus held the office of consul; it is thought that he died early in the reign of the emperor Hadrian.

He was married to the daughter of Gaius Julius Agricola, one of the ablest and most trusted of Domitian's generals; in spite of this association, or perhaps because it gave him entirely too close an insight into the operations of Domitian's government, Tacitus conceived a bitter hatred for the Flavians, and from them extended his dislike to the whole imperial system, his particular bêtes noires being the Julio-Claudian emperors (Augustus–Nero). Even the freedom that came to Rome with the accession of Nerva and Trajan never succeeded in removing or palliating Tacitus's anti-imperial bias; it suffuses all his writings, and these in turn are probably responsible for our usual view of the first century of Roman imperial rule as an age of tyranny, oppression, and injustice, all accompanied by widespread debauchery.

Tacitus was an orator from the start, and gained early fame in the field, as we learn from the tributes of his friend Pliny. His earliest known published work was his *Dialogus de oratoribus*, a treatise on the decline of oratory; Tacitus's thesis is that under any stable government like that of the Roman Empire, oratory neces-

sarily declines, since men either need not or dare not speak openly
on highly controversial topics. The *Dialogus* is now primarily of
historical interest; it is set decisively apart from Tacitus's later work
by its Ciceronian style—for Tacitus too had been influenced by
Quintilian, whether or not he actually studied under him. Although
Tacitus uses Cicero's style with remarkable skill—more skill than
that of Pliny—the imitative character of this writing is all too
patent, and it is small wonder that a genius as original and independent as Tacitus soon moved on to develop the Latin style that
is so distinctly his own.

The date of publication of the *Dialogus* is not known for
certain; it was probably somewhere in the nineties A. D. It was
succeeded after some years by the *Agricola*, a biography of his father-
in-law, and by the *Germania*, both of which were published in 98.
The *Germania* is a study of the peoples, geography, and customs
of Germany, a country in which great interest was being felt in
Rome at this time, partly because of Trajan's campaigns in Northern Europe and partly because of his realization that Rome was
subject to potential danger from that quarter. Although Tacitus
doubtless got his information about Germany and the Germans at
second hand and never himself had direct contact with the people
or the country, it was inevitable that he should contrast their
vigorous barbarism with the habits of a Rome that was fast dropping into a state of over-civilization. It is probably wrong to think
that Tacitus in his *Germania* was attempting to draw a sort of
Utopia, a portrait of the "noble savage" with which to contrast his
effete compatriots; nonetheless, the difference between the Rome of
Tacitus's day and the Germany that he described is clear enough.
Because the *Germania* is so imprecisely and unscientifically docu-
mented, Tacitus's observations about the Germans must be taken
with some reservations; nevertheless, the work remains a valuable
source of information about the type of barbarian that was beginning to make himself felt along the borders of the empire.

The *Agricola* is one of the finest pieces of biographical literature that has come down to us from antiquity. It is filled with deep
respect for its capable, hard-working, and sincere hero; it displays
the qualities that we like to think of as distinctly Roman: stateli-
ness, dignity, and utter seriousness. Agricola himself emerges not
as a truly brilliant man, but nonetheless strong and resolute, able if
not imaginative, and far too loyal a citizen of Rome ever to reveal
the distrust he must have felt for his commander-in-chief, the
emperor Domitian. The bulk of the biography, and its most inter-

esting portions, deal with Agricola's command of the Roman armies in Britain, the chief incident of his tenure being an uprising of the Britons under the leadership of Calgacus.

Tacitus begins the work with a sardonic pseudo-apology for venturing to write about a good man, and continues with a bitter indictment of the age of Domitian:

> Great indeed are the proofs we have given of what we can endure. The antique times saw to the utmost bounds of freedom, we, of servitude; robbed by an inquisition of the common use of speech and hearing, we should have lost our very memory with our voice, if it were as much in our power to forget as to be dumb.
> (*Agricola* 2, translation of J. W. Mackail)

The passage continues with Tacitus's expression of gratitude and relief at the coming of the new era, even though the sorrow and bitterness of earlier years could not easily be forgotten; nonetheless, he does not expect to regret, however rude and untutored his voice may be, having composed a memorial to earlier servitude and a testimony to present happiness (*Agricola* 3).

The bulk of the biography, after a sketch of Agricola's early career, is concerned with his activities in Britain; much of the marching and countermarching of armies seems dull now, but the work reaches a high point in Tacitus's description of the battle of *Mons Graupius*—or one had rather say, in the two speeches that precede his description of the battle itself. Like the speeches of all ancient historians, these are the work of the writer and do not necessarily represent the words of the speaker; like the speeches in Livy's history, they are intended primarily as an expression of point of view, to show in a brilliant and dramatic way what the feelings of the two factions were on this occasion. Over the years, the Britons had come to be used to Roman rule, feeling that the peace and order it brought were sound compensation for loss of national identity and liberty. However, the peoples to the center and north of England, being less pacific than their more southerly neighbors, had banded together to rebel against Rome. Their leader was Calgacus; when the armies of Calgacus and those of Agricola had assembled at *Mons Graupius* and were preparing for battle, Calgacus addressed his Britons in a fiery speech which may well be regarded as the most eloquent expression of the feelings of at least one native people whose national aspirations had to be crushed and set aside if Rome were to accomplish her mission of world domin-ion. Calgacus's exhortations to the Britons to remember children, family, hearth and fireside, his excoriations of the Britons who had accepted Roman rule—all of this is more or less conventional—but at one point he rises to an eloquence that reduces Roman imperial ambition to raw aggression:

"These destroyers of the world, now that they find no more lands to include in their all-embracing devastations, are rum-maging the sea. If their enemy is rich, they are greedy, if poor, they are lustful for glory—men who have been satiated, not by the eastern, not by the western world. Alone of all mankind they lust with equal passion after rich and poor. They plunder, they slaughter, they seize power under lying names, and where they make a desert, they call it peace."
(*Agricola* 30)

Not since the figure of a Dido cruelly misused and a Turnus brought harshly and unjustly to his knees, had the imperial policy of Rome been so relentlessly castigated. To be sure, the words are put in the mouth of one of Rome's enemies, but we know—and the ancient reader knew, too—that it was Tacitus himself who was speaking, and the eloquence of his speech reveals all too clearly how resentful he was of an imperial policy for which he could find slight justifica-tion. All the eloquence of Agricola's counterbalancing oration can-not dispel the feeling that Rome has for once been unmasked, and the easy victory of the Romans over the Britons in the subsequent battle serves only to place a decent and honorable general, Agricola himself, in the unenviable position of being the instrumentality by which a cruel and oppressive rule was confirmed.

The point could scarcely have been lost upon Domitian him-self, under whose rule this campaign took place; it is no wonder that Tacitus delayed the publication of this biography until Domitian was safely in his grave. Throughout the work, Agricola himself is presented as able, just, loyal, modest, in obvious contrast to the age in which he lived. The book ends in a kind of peroration, in the noble abjuration of grief, and the decision to show respect for men like Agricola by emulation rather than by mourning.

From the point of view of style, the *Agricola* and the *Germania* both show the manner that we have come to think of as typically Tacitean, this in strong contrast to the Ciceronianism of the *Dialogus*. Tacitus's revolt against Neo-Ciceronianism is obvious; not only does he avoid carefully balanced and harmonious periodic sentences, with their parallel and meticulously complementary constructions, and their painstaking attention to rhythm and euphony; Tacitus goes deliberately to the opposite extreme. His sentences are not balanced, his constructions are not parallel or harmonious, he tends to brevity and terseness; as far as rhythm and euphony are concerned, it appears to be his deliberate intention to make his Latin rough and harsh. He is equally as far from Seneca's style, for he has no patience with the eternal neatness, pithiness, and sententiousness of Seneca's manner.

Tacitus's harshness has an almost abrasive quality; it is clear that he felt he had a harsh story to tell, and that he could tell it only in a style equally harsh. For Tacitus was convinced that Rome had fallen on evil days—in fact, that the whole concept of the Empire had begun with evil designs and evil men, and had continued on this downhill course all the way to his own day. He sees the history of the Roman Empire as the history of the moral, political, social, and economic downfall of a great people, whose chance for greatness was lost with the fall of the Republic, and whose every tentative attempt thereafter to recover from that fall had been thwarted and repressed by a series of tyrannical emperors.

Even in these two early works, the *Germania* and the *Agricola*, this attitude is patent; it becomes all the more so in his two masterpieces, the *Annals* and the *Histories*. These great works, really two parts of one long work, originally totaled thirty books. We now have extant, of the *Annals*, Books I–IV and the first portion of Book V, most of Book VI, the last portion of Book XI, Books XII–XV, and the first part of Book XVI. Of the *Histories*, we have Books I–IV and the first part of Book V. The *Annals* originally covered the period from the death of Augustus to the death of Nero; lost are the years 29–31 A. D. (during the reign of Tiberius), the whole of Caligula's reign, the first seven years of the reign of Claudius, and the last year of Nero's reign. The *Histories* originally covered the period from the accession of Galba in 68 to the death of Domitian in 96; the extant portion takes us only through the first three years of this period (68–71 A. D.). Tacitus began with the *Histories*, and originally planned to carry his story through the reigns of Nerva and Trajan, but when he had gotten as far as the death of Domitian, he abandoned this plan and went back to the death of Augustus, carrying the story of the *Annals* up to the beginning of the *Histories*.

Like Livy, Tacitus relied very largely on secondary sources, and in most instances does not even bother to give their names. He uses formulas such as, "certain writers say," or "I find in many historians." He mentions the history of the German wars written by Pliny the Elder; that he did at times at least attempt to go to primary sources is evidenced by his use of the orations of the emperor Tiberius and the memoirs of various other important people; we know too of his effort to get firsthand information about the eruption of Vesuvius from Pliny the Younger. It is probable too that he made fairly considerable use of the records of the Senate and the Roman courts. In the case of the *Histories*, Tacitus had his own observations on which to rely. In the end, like Livy, he is not highly critical; his criterion is usually "what seemed reasonable" under the circumstances, and his interpretation of "reasonableness" is heavily colored by his pro-republican, anti-imperial bias.

Again like all other ancient historians, Tacitus's aim is didactic; he claims at the outset of the *Annals* to be writing *sine ira et studio* ("without prejudice or special interest") yet we are never in any doubt as to the meaning that Tacitus wished us to derive from his account. If we are to believe his lesson, there had been no goodness in the leaders of Rome since the fall of the Republic, except in the cases of men who had failed, or who, like Agricola, had steeled themselves to carry out their patriotic duty in spite of their abhorrence of the power that imposed it. Tacitus's artistry manages to turn this grim tale into an endlessly fascinating account. It is no wonder that our concept of the Roman Empire as a period of wickedness, debauchery, cruelty, and immorality has been indelibly fastened upon our minds; largely because of what Tacitus has written we are very nearly incapable of ascribing anything good to the Roman imperial system.

It is obvious that Tacitus's history must be handled with great caution. He has often been accused of being a "magnificent liar," and of deliberately falsifying his account in order to feed his own prejudices. That he often tells untruths is all too clear; that he does so with deliberate intent to mislead is not so much so. The fact is that his views of the periods about which he writes are so colored by his prejudices that he misinterprets the truth even when he tells it; somehow, the emphasis gets placed on the wrong spot, the facts are interpreted in a prejudiced way, or the insinuation is made that the reported facts are false. In diabolically clever fashion, Tacitus often offsets indubitable fact by the introduction of reports, traditions, etc., all of these reported as mere gossip, but reported in such a way that they seem to disprove the facts. Perhaps it is true that Tacitus passionately believed he was telling the truth—so passionately that on occasion he forced himself to believe what he knew could not be true. His manner has perhaps been best summed up by Laurence Sterne, who, in *Tristram Shandy*, speaks of "the decisive manner of Tacitus, who outwits both himself and his reader."

Both the *Histories* and the *Annals* contain many egregious examples of Tacitus's helplessness in the face of his own strong feelings. For example, in his account of the death of the emperor Augustus, Tacitus, totally disregarding the political aspects of imperial deification, insists that Augustus had himself deified in order to set himself above all the other gods, and finishes the account with so bald an absurdity that one wonders whether Tacitus himself really could have believed it:

> Even in adopting Tiberius as his successor, he had not been moved by affection, or by care for the public good; but having sounded the depths of that proud and cruel nature he had sought to win glory for himself by contrast with an execrable successor. (*Annals* 1.10, trs. of G. G. Ramsay)

But it is probably Tiberius who has become the most famous example of Tacitus's art of defamation. In diabolically ingenious style, by occasionally admitting praise, Tacitus gives the impression that he is telling the truth dispassionately, yet he prejudices his reader immediately with his opening sentence:

> The opening crime of the new reign was the murder of Agrippa Postumus. (*Annals* 1.6, trs. of Ramsay)

Tacitus then tells how all the people rushed to swear allegiance to the new emperor, Tiberius, who, instead of administering the oath himself, allowed the consuls, Pompeius and Apuleius, to do so:

> For Tiberius left all initiative with the consuls, as though the old Republic were still standing, and as if he himself had not made up his mind to assume the empire: even the edict by which he summoned the senate he only put forth by virtue of the tribunician authority conferred on him in the lifetime of Augustus. (*Annals* 1.7, trs. of Ramsay)

It is perfectly possible that in this instance Tiberius acted with complete honesty; there is good evidence that he sincerely wished to restore republican government; his reluctance to assume the throne is well known. His action in the matter of summoning the Senate was, on the face of it, little other than honest concern not to exceed his legitimate powers. Yet it will be noticed that Tacitus reports this fact in such a way as to make it appear that the emperor was being hypocritical. Tacitus further insinuates that in assuming immediate control of the praetorian guard, Tiberius had shown that he intended to be a despot, and that his conciliatory words to the Senate were simply camouflage; yet it is entirely possible that Tiberius acted quickly and by virtue of powers already vested in him by Augustus, in order to make sure that the praetorian guard, notoriously hot-headed, did not get out of control, and that law and order were preserved.

Tacitus goes on to say that Tiberius showed a great deal of hesitation in all his actions and that he did so through fear of Germanicus, his nephew:

> His chief reason for this attitude was his fear of Germanicus. That prince had many legions under his command, and a vast force of allies; he was the darling of the people; and it might be that he would prefer possession to expectation. (*Annals* 1.7, trs. of Ramsay)

Tacitus makes us feel that Tiberius's "fear" proceeded either from jealousy or from a sense of guilt, a feeling that he had become emperor not in a legitimate way but "through the intrigues of a wife, or as the adopted son of a dotard." Yet as it transpires in later chapters of the *Annals*, Tiberius had good reason to be uneasy about Germanicus. He was a popular hero, a man of great personal charm, but in spite of all Tacitus's attempts to make a great general of him, he turns out to have been utterly incompetent, weak, and vacillating. When his troops on the Rhine mutinied, he was not even able to get them to stand in order while he spoke to them. When he found that he could not make himself heard, he melodramatically threatened to commit suicide; and when he found himself totally unable to stand against his men, he forged Tiberius's name to papers granting their demands. His most illustrious exploit, as Tacitus tells it, was a night raid against a village of drunken and defenseless Germans. That a man as weak and vain as Germanicus might indeed "prefer possession to expectation" of the throne was no more than a reasonable conjecture, and it was doubtless very wise of Tiberius to make certain that his adoptive father's will, to the effect that he, Tiberius himself, should take over the throne, be carried out before popular disaffection settled on Germanicus or some other such popular hero.

Throughout Tacitus's *Annals* and *Histories* we see the same tendencies, although he is perhaps less unfair to other emperors than to Tiberius. In almost no instance can he be accused of withholding the facts; the facts are there, recorded with precision and care, and yet in almost every instance again, they are so offset by gossip, rumor, and suggestion, by "what people said," or "what might be thought," that we almost inevitably accept the slanted version rather than the disinterested one. It is easy to condemn Tacitus for this technique, for in a modern historian it would never be tolerated. And it has in fact led to a distortion of our view of the Roman Empire: reading Tacitus's account, we wonder how we could ever have believed Vergil's idealism.

This may not be tribute to Tacitus as a historian, but it is certainly tribute to him as a writer, for never can it be denied that every page of his history is vivid and interesting. One dramatic incident follows another with skill and speed; one deft and devilish characterization succeeds another. His historical writing is like a vast spectacle, an enormous stage, constantly filled with changing faces, personalities, and actions. If we wish to learn the objective truth, we must learn to read between the lines, to discount Tacitus's prejudices, to accept the facts that he gives and to be cautious of the gossip, to discount his well-known prejudices and to balance his account with the more reliable evidence of inscriptions, coins, and other writers. But Tacitus never meant to be objective, any more than Livy did; to him, as to the earlier writer, history was a literary form, not a piece of social science, and its purpose was not so much to transmit historical fact as to reveal human and philosophical truth. Tacitus's historical work shows us the truth that arrogance, ambition, pride, and moral irresponsibility can end only in cultural decline and ultimate defeat. This is what he wanted men to learn from his historical work; in the unrivaled brilliance and profundity with which he presents this "lesson," lies his true greatness.

# CHAPTER XX

# Suetonius and Juvenal

We should probably not leave the age of Trajan without at least brief mention of Marcus Valerius Probus (fl. 96–105 A. D.), a scholar from Beirut, who was the first to bring Greek scholarly methods to the study of Latin literature. Probus was interested in establishing authentic texts for the great Roman writers, particularly those of an earlier age, whose works, published of course in manuscript form, had suffered over the years from the accumulated errors of transcription and sheer physical accident. Probus sought out older, better texts than those that were currently available; he set to work to emend their errors and to put them into readable form; he then added critical and interpretive notes of his own. He is known to have edited Vergil, Horace, Lucretius, Terence, and Persius, and may well have edited many another author; unfortunately his work has all been lost, but there can be no doubt that he should be given credit for having preserved good texts of the great Roman classics for succeeding generations.

The age of Nerva and Trajan slipped without disturbance into the reign of Hadrian (117–38 A. D.), who added vast geniality and personal charm to the excellent administrative ability of his predecessors. His rule, like theirs, was wise and just—perhaps the last one to be truly so, for after his death, the increasing threat of the barbarians along Rome's borders and increasing unrest at home soon weakened and ultimately destroyed the centuries-long peace and prosperity of a great empire. Although Hadrian may justly have been proud of his accomplishments as emperor, he would probably not be displeased to know that he has been best remembered in later ages for his delightful little poem, addressed to his soul as he lay dying:

Poor little soul, homeless, sweet-voiced, friend and guest of my body, where, where will you go now, poor little pale, cold, naked thing, and never again make me laugh as you used to do?*

Paradoxically, there is little likeness in the two most famous authors of this period, Suetonius and Juvenal. Gaius Suetonius Tranquillus (c. 75–140 A. D.) was a friend of Pliny the Younger, as we learn from Pliny's letters addressed to him; however, very little is known of his personal life. His father appears to have been an army officer; he is known to have been a friend of the emperor Hadrian and of his wife, the empress Sabina. He was Hadrian's private secretary and a member of his imperial council.

By profession, Suetonius was a historian and biographer, the author of two works, the *Lives of the Caesars* (*De vita Caesarum*), and *Lives of Famous Men* (*De viris illustribus*). The first of these two, dedicated to the praetorian prefect Septicius Clarus, was published between 119 and 121 A. D., and contains the lives of twelve of the Caesars, beginning with Julius and ending with Domitian. The second was originally published in five sections, dealing respectively with poets, orators, historians, philosophers, and grammarians. The last part, on the grammarians and rhetoricians, is preserved in incomplete form; we also have his biographies of Terence, Vergil, Horace, Lucan, Crispus (an otherwise obscure orator), and Pliny the Elder.

Of these writings, the *Lives of the Caesars* is much the best known; along with Tacitus's *Agricola* and Plutarch's far more famous *Lives*, they constitute the most important biographical material that has come down to us from antiquity, and for the first time in Roman literary history we have biographies that at least attempt to be honest and objective, and are not merely panegyrics. It is true that Suetonius is no more the social scientist than was Tacitus; it is equally true that Suetonius, again like Tacitus, had other than purely informational aims in mind. It cannot be said of him, however, that he had any single aim, or that he viewed his series of imperial biographies as a unified work with a single message. He is totally lacking in the profundity that characterized

*animula vagula blandula
hospes comesque corporis
quae nunc abibis in loca
pallidula rigida nudula
nec ut soles dabis iocos?

Tacitus; his aim seems to be nothing much more than to make each of the emperors an interesting person to read about.

To save himself trouble, and perhaps to enable his readers more easily to follow and remember his accounts, Suetonius devises a standard biographical form which he applies to each of the emperors in turn; the biographies are divided into sections dealing with birth, early life, public career, personal qualities, and death, a neat little system that makes the reading of an individual biography logical and informative, but gives to the group of them a certain repetitiousness. Suetonius is delighted with gossip and loves to report curiosities. He tells us, for example, that Nero was born "just as the sun rose, so that its beams touched him before they could well reach the earth," and that later when the empress Messalina hired two thugs to strangle the young Nero "it is said that they were frightened by a serpent that crept from under his cushion, and ran away. The tale was occasioned by finding on his couch, near the pillow, the skin of a snake, which by his mother's order, he wore for some time upon his right arm enclosed in a bracelet of gold" (*Nero* 6, trs. of Thomson and Forester). He reports of Augustus that he had on his chest and belly birthmarks in the shape of the constellation of the Great Bear, that he suffered from warts and skin rashes, and was troubled by weakness of the legs.

Details of this kind, in fact, seem to interest Suetonius rather more than sober and informative matters about public career, etc. The result is a series of lively if not too trustworthy accounts of the Caesars, written in a clumsy Latin which suffers considerably by comparison with the styles of Tacitus and Pliny. In spite of his many and manifest deficiencies, Suetonius remains an important source for our knowledge of the history of the first century of the Roman Empire; it is to Suetonius, for example, that we owe the famous saying that Nero "fiddled while Rome burned":

> . . . pretending to be disgusted with the old buildings and the narrow and winding streets, he set the city on fire so openly, that many of consular rank caught his own household servants on their property with tow and torches in their hands but durst not meddle with them. There being near the Golden House some granaries, the site of which he exceedingly coveted, they were battered as if with machines of war, and set on fire, the walls being built of stone. During six days and seven nights this terrible devastation continued, the people being

obliged to fly to the tombs and monuments for lodging and shelter. Meanwhile a vast number of stately buildings, the houses of generals celebrated in former times, and even then still decorated with the spoils of war, were laid in ashes; as well as the temples of the gods, which had been vowed and dedicated by the kings of Rome and afterwards in the Punic and Gallic wars: in short, everything that was remarkable and worthy to be seen which time had spared. This fire he beheld from a tower in the house of Maecenas, and "being greatly delighted" as he said "with the beautiful effects of the con-flagration," he sang a poem on the ruin of Troy, in the tragic dress he used on the stage.

(*Nero* 38, trs. of Thomson and Forester)

More charitable, and showing that Suetonius did have at least some sense of humor, is his reporting of the last words of the emperor Vespasian. Recalling the sanctimonious deification of a number of preceding emperors after their death, Vespasian is reported to have said, as he felt death coming upon him, "Dear me! I think I'm turning into a god!" (*Vespasian* 23). It is probably for gossipy tidbits of this sort that Suetonius has become best known and best liked; no great historian, biographer, or writer, he at least managed to preserve for us something of the interest and color that attended the lives of Rome's first twelve emperors.

Far outshining Suetonius in brilliance and in fact often considered one of the greatest writers of Rome is the satirist Juvenal (Decimus Junius Juvenalis, c. 60–c. 140 A. D.) Of this strange man very little is known; ancient accounts of his life are contradictory and confused; his writings sound like those of a disappointed, disgruntled and perhaps impoverished aristocrat, with an enormous sense of outraged dignity, in short, like the work of a man deeply conscious of his own goodness and bitterly resentful of having fallen upon evil days. There is no way to tell now to what degree this is merely a literary pose—a stance taken by the writer as part of his literary apparatus—or whether it represents, as we like to say, the "real" Juvenal. There is some indication that he may have served in the Roman army, possibly in some fairly responsible capacity; there is a persistent tradition to the effect that in his old age he was exiled to Egypt. From internal evidence it is clear that the last of his satires was published about the year 127 A. D. The five books of satires as we now have them seem to follow in chronological order up to that date, although it is impossible now to set any but a very approximate date—say, about the year 98—for the earliest publication.

Juvenal has been described, perhaps a bit rashly, as the greatest satirist of all time. Criteria of greatness in any literary field are entirely too imprecise and variable to make any such judgment; the satire in particular is subject to such vast variation in manner and content that no one of Western culture's many satirists may safely be judged to tower above all the others. Juvenal is a "strong" writer, vigorous, outspoken, and—considering that he was careful to write of the present in terms of the past—courageous. The sixteen satires, divided over the five books, can no longer be completely comprehended, since they are so heavily loaded with contemporary references, the point of many of which is now hopelessly lost. Even the professional classicist reads Juvenal with an elaborate commentary at his side, and finds it necessary constantly to refer to scholarly notes in order to ensure a reasonably correct interpretation of the poet's lines. In spite of this inevitable obscurity, Juvenal has always been widely read since his works were first published. Even if we can no longer get the point of all of his strictures, we can still enjoy and appreciate the depth and sharpness of his sabre-like attack, and his ability to sum up a point in a mordant phrase. "Bread and circuses," "a healthy mind in a healthy body," "virtue is praised, but left out in the cold": these and other famous sayings of Juvenal have passed into Western culture, where they have become proverbial.

As for the subjects of the satires, it could best be said that Juvenal liked virtually nothing that he saw, and was deeply outraged by most of it. To keep on the safe side, the dramatis personae of his satires are all long since dead; he makes no attacks upon living persons or actual circumstances. This had the immediate effect of securing his immunity from attack during his lifetime—or most of it—and also of giving to his satires a sort of timelessness that they possess in spite of their heavy overlarding of contemporary reference. Juvenal's hatred of the world and everybody in it was all-embracing:

> From the day when the rain-clouds lifted up the waters and Deucalion climbed that mountain in his ship to seek an oracle —that day when stones grew soft and warm with life, and Pyrrha showed maidens naked to men—all the doings of mankind, their prayers, their fears, their angers, and their pleasures,

their joys and goings to and fro, shall form the motley subject
of my page. For when was vice more rampant? When did the
maw of avarice gape wider? When was gambling so reckless?
(*Satires* 1.81–89, trs. of G. G. Ramsay, modified)

And again in that same satire:

When a soft eunuch takes to matrimony, and Maevia, with
spear in hand and breasts exposed, to pigsticking; when a
fellow under whose razor my stiff youthful beard used to grate,
challenges, with his single wealth, the whole nobility; when
a guttersnipe of the Nile like Crispinus—a slave-born denizen
of Canopus—hitches a Tyrian cloak onto his shoulder whilst
on his sweating finger he wears a summer ring of gold, unable
to endure the weight of a heavier gem—it is hard *not* to write
satire. (1.22–30, trs. of G. G. Ramsay)

Juvenal sees much of what Martial had seen a generation before him, but where Martial found the whole thing vastly amusing,
Juvenal is filled with anger and resentment. Juvenal sees in the
cosmopolitan character of Rome only a once-great city overwhelmed
by degenerate foreigners. He resents them all, but reserves his
particular indignation for the Greeks:

I cannot abide, my fellow-citizens, a Rome of Greeks. . . . Your
good country-boy now wears Greek running-sandals and wears
Greek medals on his Greek-perfumed neck . . . [the Greeks] all
make for the Esquiline, or the hill that takes its name from its
willows, all ready to worm their way into the houses of the
great and become their masters. Quick of wit and of unbounded
impudence, they are as ready of speech as Isaeus, and more
torrential. Say, what do you think that fellow there to be? He
has brought with him any character you please; grammarian,
orator, geometrician, painter, trainer, or rope-dancer; augur,
doctor or astrologer:—your hungry Greekling knows everything;
tell him to climb high heaven, he'll climb it. (*Satires* 3.60–78,
trs. of Ramsay, modified)

To all foreigners, and particularly to the Greeks, Juvenal ascribes the moral degeneration of the Rome of his day, the loss of all
the old Roman virtues, such as honor, trust, and above all dignity.

The Romans themselves have become a servile mob, whose only concern for their government, while they still could participate in it, was to sell their votes to the highest bidder; now that they can no longer participate, they have no interest except "bread and circuses" (10.81). Worse than that, the men of Rome have allowed themselves to be overwhelmed by a horde of women, who have forgotten how to be feminine and insist on pushing men out of their rightful places as lords and masters:

> If you are . . . devoted to one woman, then bow your head and submit your neck to the yoke. Never will you find a woman who spares the man who loves her; for though she be herself aflame, she delights to torment and plunder him. So the better the man, the more desireable he be as a husband, the less good will he get out of his wife. No present will you ever make if your wife forbids; nothing will you ever sell if she objects; nothing will you buy without her consent. She will arrange your friendships for you; she will turn your now aged friend from the door that saw the beginnings of his beard. Pandars and trainers can make their wills as they please, as also can the gentlemen of the arena, but you will have to write down among your heirs more than one rival of your own. (*Satires* 6.206–18, trs. of Ramsay)

In all this farrago—incidentally Juvenal's own term—there is scarcely a single note of hopefulness or even of goodwill. To Juvenal, nothing is right nor ever will be. The only hope he feels is that vice has now gone so far that it cannot go any farther; things can get no worse: now if ever is the time for the satirist to make his attack (*Satires* 1.146–50).

For any positive grounds on which the satirist is to base his attack, Juvenal is rather vague. He is happier in his role of being against things, and has few positive suggestions to make. The nearest he comes to this is in the closing passage of the *Tenth Satire*:

> Is there then nothing for which men shall pray? If you ask my counsel, you will leave it to the gods themselves to decide what is good for us, and what will be serviceable for our state; for, in place of what is pleasing, they will give us what is best. Man is dearer to them than he is to himself. Impelled by strong and blind desire, we ask for wife and offspring; but the gods know of what sort the sons, of what sort the wife, will be.

Nevertheless, that you may have something to pray for, and be able to offer to the shrines entrails and presaging sausages from a white porker, you should pray for a sound mind in a sound body; for a stout heart that has no fear of death, and deems length of days the least of nature's gifts; that can endure any kind of toil; that knows neither wrath nor desire, and thinks that the woes and hard labors of Hercules are better than the loves and banquets and the down cushions of Sardanapalus. What I commend to you, you can give to yourself; for it is assuredly through virtue that lies the one and only road to a life of peace. You should have no divinity, O Fortune, if men had any sense; it is we that make a goddess of you and place you in the skies. (*Satires* 10.346–66, trs. of Ramsay)

Juvenal's influence as a writer of satire has been widespread. His vigor, his clear-sighted if prejudiced vision, and his unparalleled ability to coin a cutting phrase, have made him the model of all satirists since his time. The eighteenth century in England particularly admired him; men like Swift and Pope, Addison and Steele, owe much to Juvenal. And the old Roman satirist is probably best-known to the general reader from the two imitations of his work produced by Samuel Johnson, whose *London, a Satire* is a deftly phrased if somewhat pompous imitation of Juvenal's *Third Satire;* his *Vanity of Human Wishes* gives a similar version of Juvenal's *Tenth Satire.*

# CHAPTER XXI

# Hadrian to the Antonines: Apuleius

Besides Suetonius and Juvenal, the age of Hadrian produced a number of other less well-known writers. Annius Florus (fl. c. 130 A. D.) composed a history called *The Wars of Rome (Bella Romana)* in two books. This work is a panegyric on the rise of Rome; the Roman people are its hero. It is divided into "ages," like the Ages of Man: childhood, the age of the kings, boyhood, the age of Italian conquest, manhood, the age of the consolidation of Roman power over the Mediterranean during the last years of the Republic and under the emperor Augustus. Characteristically, Florus allows for no old age; to him, the Empire represents a rejuvenation that culminated in the reign of Trajan. The work is not without its value as a historical document, but it should be obvious that its heavily biased point of view was bound to present an account something less than objective.

Also attributed to Florus, almost certainly falsely, is a lovely poem, the *Vigil of Venus (Pervigilium Veneris)*, a gay and charming tribute to that same Venus, the spirit of fresh creation, that centuries before had figured in the introduction to Lucretius's poem. The poem, in approximately ninety lines, gives a clear indication of its quality in its opening lines:

> Tomorrow love comes to the loveless, tomorrow lovers love again. Spring now is fresh and full of singing; in spring the world was born, in spring loves join hearts, in spring, the birds mate and the wood loosens her hair for her husband rain. Tomorrow among the trees' shadows, the Queen of loves weaves her bowers, plaited green with myrtle shoots, tomorrow Dione

reigns from high upon her throne. (*Pervigilium Veneris* 1–7, trs. of R. W. Postgate)

The poem continues in this vein, interrupted every few lines by the refrain, "Tomorrow love comes to the loveless, tomorrow lovers love again." In its grace, lightness, and charming flower-imagery, in its easy swinging metre, the *Pervigilium Veneris* seems almost to stand on the threshold of the Middle Ages, when Roman poetry, grown stale, heavy, repetitive, and imitative, was brought to fresh life by the poetic inspiration that rose from the people once again. Lovers of English literature will recognize in this poem the piece about which Walter Pater constructed his pretty tale, "Marius the Epicurean." As for its authorship, it is virtually certain that Florus did not write it; it had best remain anonymous.

Another writer, Marcus Cornelius Fronto (c. 100–175 A. D.) is represented by a body of letters, the correspondence between himself and the emperor Marcus Aurelius. The letters are almost entirely literary and rhetorical in content and character, and tell us very little about either Fronto or the emperor; perhaps the most significant fact about Fronto is that he was an African, the first of a number of such to come to Rome and to bring with them a new concept of the handling of the Latin language. Fronto was frankly an archaist; he vastly preferred Ennius and Lucretius to Vergil; he felt that Cato and the Gracchi were greater orators than Cicero, who he thought was much too restrained and inhibited in his manner of speaking. In this, Fronto represents a revolt from the Neo-Ciceronianism of Quintilian and Pliny, a revolt, too, from the classic, although not strictly speaking classical, style of Tacitus, and an attempt to revert to what he fancied was a more natural and rugged form of speech and writing. He did not have many imitators, but his insistence on the importance of high color in Latin style was an early indication of the coming of the "New Style" (*Oratio Novella*), a style so colorful, so full of sound-effects such as rhyme, alliteration, and assonance, as to be scarcely distinguishable from poetry. Fronto himself is no great stylist, but his teachings had considerable effect on the next generation of writers.

Aulus Gellius (born c. 130 A. D.) may also have been an African, although this is not entirely certain. He did study literature with Sulpicius Apollinaris of Carthage at Rome, and was a friend of Fronto. Gellius was an ambitious polymath of the pack rat variety, a collector of miscellaneous fact and fancy. His collections are embodied in the twenty books of his *Nights in Athens (Noctes*

*Atticae)* a long and rambling pseudo-encyclopedia covering virtually every subject of which the ancient world took cognizance:
philosophy, rhetoric, history, literature, philology, science, etc. etc.
Buried in this amorphous mass are many invaluable quotations from
early writers; in fact, Gellius is often our only source for the
scattered texts of some of the earliest writers of Rome. He also tells
many stories about famous figures from the Roman past. Much of
what he brings to us is waste material, but he still remains a valuable source for miscellaneous information about the ancient world.

Again not strictly literary are the *Institutes (Institutiones)* of
Gaius, of the second century A. D., our earliest and one of our most
valuable complete treatises on Roman jurisprudence. Little is
known of Gaius; even his name is only a praenomen, like a modern
"given" name; his family name is not known. Some five hundred
years later, when the emperor Justinian authorized his codification
of the Roman law, his jurists depended heavily on Gaius for their
information about the basic form of the Roman law.

As the Roman world moved on at the death of Hadrian into
the reigns of Antoninus Pius and Marcus Aurelius, it became in-
creasingly clear that the older culture had largely lost its creative
force. The archaism of Fronto and the dust-sifting of Gellius represent scarcely more than a frantic attempt to reach back and recover
something that had been irrevocably lost in the course of the centuries. A revival of Lucretius, a displacement of the *Aeneid* by
Ennius's *Annals,* could never bring back the Roman Republic or
the Roman Idea again. The "New Style," for all its indubitable
charm, was flamboyantly un-Roman—if by "Roman" we mean the
thought and manner of the first centuries B. C. and A. D. Latin, in
fact, came very close to being sidetracked as a literary vehicle and
failed to regain anything like its earlier vigor until it had developed
into the looser, freer, more colloquial form that we characterize as
medieval. Symptomatic of this decay is the fact that the emperor
Marcus Aurelius composed his *Meditations* not in his native Latin
but in Greek. A new force, too, was on the rise, bringing with it
ideas foreign to the Roman way of thinking. This was Christianity,
the force that was destined in the end to take over the Empire and
mold it into an entirely new form.

It is foolish to speculate as to which of the later writers should
be characterized as the "last" of the Romans. Some would end the
series with Tacitus and Juvenal; some would include Ausonius,
the poet of the fourth century, or even Prudentius, his counterpart
in the fifth century; some would go as far as Boethius, the poet-

philosopher of the latter part of the fifth and early part of the sixth century A. D. The choice is obviously an arbitrary one to be made solely on the basis of subjective feelings as to what constitutes or does not constitute the Roman point of view.

Still, any account of Roman literature is incomplete if it does not include the work of Lucius Apuleius, who was born about the year 125 A. D. at Madaura of Numidia, and thus represents another of those Africans whose influence was to be so strongly felt in Rome. Apuleius was educated at Carthage and later at Athens; he also practiced law in Rome, but later retired to Africa again, where he held an official post in the city of Carthage. A number of works by Apuleius have been preserved; the first of them, the *Apologia*, is a defense of himself against the charge that he had used witchcraft to win his wife; second, the *Florida*, which consists of excerpts from his declamations; third, a treatise on the *Divine Inspiration of Socrates (De daemone Socratis)*, a study of that special inspiration which Socrates claimed he possessed; fourth, a treatise on Plato and his doctrines, fifth, an Aristotelian treatise on the universe. None of these is as important as his great work, the *Metamorphoses*, commonly known as the *Golden Ass*, a prose narrative in eleven books.

The tale begins with its hero, Lucius, involved in a series of foolish and not very palatable adventures, which eventually find him in love with a slave girl, Fotis, whose mistress is a witch, who at night, by applying a certain salve to her body, transforms herself into an owl. Fotis brings Lucius to a place where he can observe this transformation; it so fascinates him that he asks Fotis to help him get hold of the magical ointment and transform himself into an owl too. After the mistress—whose name is Pamphile—has departed, Fotis lets Lucius into the room and leaves him there to go about the work of transformation. Unfortunately, Lucius is given the wrong ointment, and instead of being transformed into an owl, becomes a donkey. There he stands, more or less imprisoned, in Pamphile's room, when the house is ransacked by a gang of bandits, who take the ass Lucius off with them. The remainder of the story centers around Lucius's frantic efforts to regain his human shape; eventually he learns that only if he can eat some roses will he once again become a man. After a year's search, in which, time and again, the poor donkey is frustrated in his attempt to get hold of a few roses, he finds himself in a city in which a procession in honor of the goddess Isis is taking place. Part of the honor to Isis consists in scattering roses in her path; the donkey Lucius manages to get hold of some of these, eats them, and returns to his human form. "The Quest of the Rosepetals," as the story might well be called, forms only a thin thread upon which countless adventures are strung, much in the manner of Petronius's *Satyricon*. Probably the most famous part of Apuleius's story is the long episode of Cupid and Psyche, which occupies Books IV through VI of the narrative.

Curiously enough, this story, which is virtually central to the whole book, has no immediate connection with Lucius and his un-happy fate; the donkey hears the story when he is tied in a stable where the gang of bandits have imprisoned a young girl whom they have kidnaped. An old woman, a member of the gang, attempts to console the poor young lady by telling her a sort of ancient bedtime story. There was a king, she says, who had three beautiful daughters, the youngest of whom was so beautiful that the surrounding coun-tryside began to worship her as if she were the goddess of beauty herself. This, as might be expected, aroused the jealousy of the true goddess of beauty, Venus, and she sent her son, Cupid, to cause the lovely Psyche (for that was her name) to fall in love with some horrible monster. With this beginning, much of the rest of the story can easily be guessed. Cupid himself falls in love with Psyche, and with the help of an obliging West Wind, carries her off to a secret palace of his own, where he makes love to her. However, he never allows her to see him, but comes only at night; the rest of the time Psyche is waited on by attentive but invisible servants. She is sur-rounded with every luxury, and her sole unhappiness is that she cannot see the lover whose soft voice and gentle ways have made her nights so happy.

Eventually, in spite of all the attentions showered upon her, she becomes lonely, and asks her invisible lover to allow her to invite her sisters to see her. His consent is somewhat reluctantly granted, and again we have little difficulty in guessing what the outcome of the visits will be. The two sisters become violently jealous of Psyche, and in an attempt to cut her down to size, sug-gest a scheme whereby, after her mysterious lover is asleep, she may light a lamp and see who he is. She falls in with their scheme, and of course beholds not a hideous monster but the beautiful young Cupid at her side. Curious about his arrows, she fondles one and pricks herself with it, thereupon falling madly in love with Cupid herself. At the same time, a drop of hot oil from the burning lamp falls on Cupid's shoulder and wakes him. Realizing that Psyche has violated his one command, he now ousts her from his house. She wanders the world in utter misery, and finally, with supreme irony, appeals to the goddess Venus for help. Venus, as we have already guessed, is not disposed to help her, but sets her to tasks which are, on the face of it, impossible and quite likely to cause Psyche's death. By various magical interventions, she still manages to perform the tasks; in the end, she and Cupid are reconciled and reunited; Psyche becomes a goddess and Venus relinquishes her anger and jealousy.

This story has all the elements of the folk-tale: the three sisters, the invisible lover, the hopeless wanderings, the impossible tasks, and the strange mystico-magical ways in which all the problems presented by these persons and circumstances are solved. The structural relation of the story of Cupid and Psyche to the rest of the tale is not immediately apparent; nonetheless it should be noted that it forms a kind of apex to the whole: before the story of Cupid and Psyche, the tale is largely made up of witchcraft, fairy tale, and stories related on the basis of hearsay; the parts after Cupid and Psyche contain the actual experiences of Lucius the Ass, or of other characters in the story. The first part of the *Golden Ass* is largely whimsy; the part that comes after *Cupid and Psyche* is to a large degree realistic.

The style of the *Golden Ass* is utterly unlike anything else in Latin literature; highly florid, crammed with imagery, syntactically often abnormal to the point of obscurity—this in violent contrast, for example, to the easy rippling syntax of the only other long narrative extant from classical times, Petronius's *Satyricon*. The sentences are made up of short isometric members, often almost manacled to each other by patterns of alliteration, assonance, and rhyme. Although a vast amount of popular vocabulary is included in the work, it is about as artificial, strained, and unnatural as it is well possible for any literary language to be. It is in fact the "New Style" carried to its logical extreme. Apuleius, as far as we know, had few if any imitators; his story of Lucius the Ass, readable and delightful in spite of its tortured and artificial style, remains, along with Petronius's *Satyricon*, an important landmark in the development of Western European narrative prose.

It would be fatuous to call Apuleius the last voice of Rome, but equally fatuous to name any other man for that somewhat dubious distinction. There is much about Apuleius that seems utterly un-Roman, although it is not at all clear what we mean by "Roman" to begin with. But whatever influence Christianity may or may not have had upon the structure and soundness of the Roman Empire, it had vast influence upon Roman intellectual and cultural life. The concept of a god of love, whose sacrifice of his own life in a way that was reserved in the ancient world for slaves and the lowest kind of criminal, brought an entirely new concept to the world of the relation between man and man and between man and God. There was to be no more comfortable bargaining with deity, no more purchasing of divine favor, no more easy tolerance of all points of view, all gods, all religions, all moral systems. With Christian monotheism came the idea that only one way could be right, and this "right way" must be central to all man's thinking and acting. Corollary to this was the necessity of defining the "right way" with meticulous precision, for the slightest error or deviation could leave a man utterly cut off from the love of God. Small wonder under the circumstances that practically all the intellectual life of the Western world, from the time of Constantine on, came to be centered on religion, on religious problems, and on an endless tangle of theological definitions and theories. The new way was not without its brilliance and its fascination, and certainly not without its dependence on the old, at least in matters of language, style, and logical discourse. But the Roman Idea itself was reduced to a form as hollow as the meaningless constitutionalities, harking back to the days of the Republic, that were cautiously but cynically preserved by one imperial despot after another.

The Roman Idea and the literature that sprang from it had a colorful history at least five hundred years long, even if we begin with the arbitrary date, 240 B. C., and make no allowance for the years-long—perhaps centuries-long—tradition of oral literature that must have preceded that date. Rome's literature grew with the city and its power. Starting with scraps and bits of barnyard and fireside wisdom such as might well have suited a nation of farmers and soldiers, the literature was given an enormous impulse toward artistic excellence by the importation of the Greek New Comedy, which perhaps for the first time introduced the Italians to the concept of literary form. From then on, progress both in breadth and in depth was constant. Rome had no sooner begun to expand her political horizons beyond the Italian peninsula when simple nationalism began to be replaced by a concept of supra-nationalism which would unite all the peoples of the world under a single rule of law that was to insure peace and order without destroying individuality. Cato's *Origins* and Ennius's *Annals* gave the first coherent expression to this imperial ideal; and the comedies of Plautus and Terence might be said to have taught the Romans a new international ideal of literary expression, for their work indicated that literary excellence in Rome was best to be attained by a fusion of Greek form and Roman substance.

As Rome expanded in territory, she increased in wealth, and as her wealth increased so did the leisure of her educated classes, to read, to study, and to write. The last fifty years of the first century B. C. have been with justice considered the "Golden Age" of Latin literature, when in the full vigor of Roman political and economic power, Rome produced a flood of great literary minds; Catullus, Lucretius, Cicero, Caesar, Vergil, Horace, Livy, Ovid: these were the greatest of her writers, with Vergil himself the central intellect of the lot. One may almost go so far as to group around Vergil all the writers that Rome produced: to one side of him lie the questing, experimental minds of a nascent culture; immediately around him are the writers who, like himself, actively participated in the enjoyment and expression of Rome's literary powers at their full. After him come figures that, for all their individual greatness, were derivative and secondary; without exception, they lean on the work of their predecessors, from whose standards, as from a base, they work their individual ways to bodies of subject matter and forms of expression which show their individuality chiefly by their deviations from the base with which they began.

The Empire had scarcely been established under Augustus when it began to diffuse and to lose its Roman-Italian character. As the center of the world, political, economic, and cultural, Rome attracted to her governmental activities, her business world, and her intellectual circles a constantly widening coterie of foreigners— non-Italians of all sorts, from the provinces both east and west, and finally even from north and south. These immigrants contributed richly to the culture of Rome and her people; under their influence Rome became a truly cosmopolitan city and the Romans themselves true world-citizens. The ideal of Rome had already been expressed, better than any other man could express it, by Vergil; there was literally nothing more to be said on this subject. In any event, Rome, her people felt, could now be taken for granted, as an establishment destined to last for eternity. There was no need any further to explain, interpret, or justify it; it simply *was*, a foundation accepted by all civilized men everywhere.

Deprived then of a national-imperial base, and in another sense freed from it, the writers of the so-called "Silver Age" of Roman literature, turned to more intimate personal problems, as did Seneca, or to the depiction of the life around them, as did Petronius and Martial, or to the historical interpretation of what had gone before them, as did Tacitus, or toward a charming, but in the end tediously repetitive, handling of subjects that had long since lost their bloom and most of their meaning, as did Statius, Calpurnius, and a host of other lesser writers. In the end, we find Juvenal attacking a society grown smug and self-satisfied, but, as he himself probably never quite realized, long since gone past the point at which the sources of its self-satisfaction might have been refreshed and renewed. With writers like Apuleius, we come close to leaving reality behind, perhaps simply because reality had now come to be so much a matter of course, and to setting out into the realm of the imaginative, the magical, and the mystical—in short, into the realm of folk-tale and fantasy.

From here on, most of the important writers are Christians: Minucius Felix, Tertullian, Lactantius, Ausonius, Claudian, Namatianus, Augustine, all have a greatness distinctly their own, but it is not a greatness that would have impressed a Cicero, a Vergil, or a Tacitus. Rome was destined to live on as a government for several centuries; her language was to persist as a lingua franca for at least a thousand more years; the Christian tradition absorbed much of her culture and indeed used it as a base on which to construct its own peculiar literary edifice. The Renaissance brought a renewed interest in the ancient world and its literary monuments, and occasioned a revival and a renewal of all that Rome, and in part Greece, had stood for, as a base upon which the culture of modern Western Europe and America has come to stand.

# A Brief Bibliography of Translations
## and Supplemental Reading

### I
# General

Duff, J. Wight, *The Literary History of Rome from the Origins to the Close of the Golden Age*, 3rd ed. rev. by A. M. Duff, London, 1953.
——. *The Literary History of Rome from the Origins to the Close of the Golden Age*, New York, 1963.
——. *A Literary History of Rome in the Silver Age, from Tiberius to Hadrian*, 2nd ed. rev. by A. M. Duff, London, 1960.
Hadas, Moses, *Ancilla to Classical Reading*, New York, 1954.
——. *A History of Latin Literature*, New York, 1952.
Rose, H. J., *A Handbook of Latin Literature*, 2nd ed., London, 1949.

### II
# Individual Authors

ANDRONICUS

Warmington, E. H., *Remains of Old Latin*, 4 vols., Cambridge, 1953-59.

APULEIUS

Graves, R. (tr.), *The Golden Ass of Apuleius*, New York, 1956.
Haight, E. H., *Essays on the Greek Romances*, New York, 1943, Chap. 2.

CAESAR

Adcock, F. E., *Caesar as a Man of Letters*, Cambridge, 1956.
Buchan, J., *Julius Caesar*, London, 1932.
Holmes, T. R., *The Roman Republic and the Founder of the Empire*, New York, 1967.
Warner, R. (tr.), *War Commentaries of Caesar*, New York, 1960.

## CATO

Brehaut, E., *Marcus Porcius Cato on Farming,* New York, 1966.
Harrison, Fairfax [A Virginia Farmer], *Roman Farm Management,* New York, 1913.

## CATULLUS

Copley, F. O., (tr.), *Gaius Valerius Catullus: the Complete Poetry,* Ann Arbor, 1957.
Frank, T., *Catullus and Horace,* New York, 1928.
Gregory, H., (tr.), *C. Valerius Catullus, Poems,* London, 1956.
Harrington, K. P., *Catullus and His Influence,* New York, 1963.
Lindsay, J., (tr.), *Catullus, the Complete Poems,* London, 1948.
Quinn, K., *The Catullan Revolution,* Melbourne, 1959.
Swanson, R., (tr.), *Odi et Amo, the Complete Poetry of Catullus,* New York, 1959.

## CICERO

Boissier, G., *Cicero and His Friends,* New York, 1898.
Hadas, M., (tr.), *Basic Writings of Cicero,* New York, 1951.
Petersson, T., *Cicero, a Biography,* Berkeley, 1920.
Poteat, H. M., (tr.), *Cicero: Brutus, On the Nature of the Gods, On Divination, On Duties,* Chicago, 1950.
Rolfe, J. C., *Cicero and His Influence,* New York, 1963.
Sihler, E. G., *Cicero of Arpinum,* New Haven, 1914.
Wilkinson, L. P., (tr.), *Letters of Cicero,* London, 1949.

## ENNIUS

See *Andronicus:* Warmington.

## HORACE

See *Catullus:* Frank.
Butler, H. E., (tr.), *The Odes of Horace,* London, 1929.
Commager, S., *The Odes of Horace,* New Haven, 1962.
Fraenkel, E., *Horace,* Oxford, 1959.
Fiske, G. C., *Lucilius and Horace,* Madison, 1920.
Kraemer, C. J., (tr.), *Horace, Complete Works,* New York, 1936.
Michie, J., (tr.), *The Odes of Horace,* New York, 1963.
Rudd, N., *The Satires of Horace,* Cambridge, 1966.
Sedgwick, H. D., *Horace,* Cambridge, 1947.
Showerman, G. D., *Horace and His Influence,* New York, 1922.

## JUVENAL

Creekmore, H., (tr.), *The Satires of Juvenal,* New York, 1963.
Highet, G., *Juvenal the Satirist, a Study,* New York, 1961.
Humphries, R., (tr.), *The Satires of Juvenal,* Bloomington, 1958.
Mazzaro, J., (tr.), *Juvenal: Satires,* Ann Arbor, 1965.
Ramsay, G. G., (tr.), *Juvenal and Persius,* Cambridge, 1957.

L I V Y

Conway, R. S., *Harvard Lectures on the Virgilian Age,* Cambridge, 1928, Chap. 4.

Foster, B. O., Sage, E. T., Schlesinger, W. C., and Moore, F. G. (trs.), *Livy,* 15 vols., Cambridge, 1948–61.

Taine, H., *Essai sur Tite Live,* Paris, 1856.

Walsh, P. G., *Livy: His Historical Aims and Methods,* Cambridge, 1961.

L U C A N

Duff, J. D., (tr.), *Lucan,* Cambridge, 1957.

Graves, R., (tr.), *Lucan, Pharsalia,* London, 1957.

L U C I L I U S

See *Horace:* Fiske.

See *Andronicus:* Warmington, (tr.).

L U C R E T I U S

Bailey, C., (tr.), *Lucretius, On the Nature of Things,* Oxford, 1926.

Geer, R. M., (tr.), *Lucretius,* New York, 1965.

Hadzsitts, G. D., *Lucretius and His Influence,* New York, 1963.

Leonard, W. E., (tr.), *Lucretius, On the Nature of Things,* New York, 1950.

Santayana, G., *Three Philosophical Poets: Lucretius, Dante, Goethe,* New York, 1953.

Sikes, E. E., *Lucretius,* Cambridge, 1936.

M A R T I A L

Ker, W. C. A., (tr.), *Martial, Epigrams,* 2 vols., Cambridge, 1947–50.

Murray, P., (tr.), *Poems after Martial,* Middletown, 1967.

Nixon, P., *Martial and the Modern Epigram,* New York, 1927.

Whipple, T. K., *Martial and the English Epigram,* Berkeley, 1925.

N A E V I U S

See *Andronicus:* Warmington, (tr.).

O V I D

Fränkel, H., *Ovid, a Poet between Two Worlds,* Berkeley, 1945.

Gregory, H., (tr.), *Ovid, the Metamorphoses,* New York, 1958.

Humphries, R., (tr.), *Ovid: the Loves, the Art of Beauty, the Remedies of Love, and the Art of Love,* Bloomington, 1957.

———. *Ovid's Metamorphoses,* Bloomington, 1955.

Otis, Brooks, *Ovid as an Epic Poet,* Cambridge, 1966.

Rand, E. K., *Ovid and His Influence,* New York, 1963.

P E T R O N I U S

Arrowsmith, W., (tr.), *Petronius, the Satyricon,* Ann Arbor, 1959.

Bagnani, Gilbert, *Arbiter of Elegance; a Study of the Life and Works of C. Petronius,* Toronto, 1954.

**PLAUTUS**

Beare, W., *The Roman Stage,* London, 1950.
Copley, F. O., and Hadas, M., (trs.), *Roman Drama,* New York, 1965.
Duckworth, G. E., (tr.), *The Complete Roman Drama,* 2 vols., New York, 1942.
Duckworth, G. E., *The Nature of Roman Comedy,* Princeton, 1952.

**PLINY**

Melmoth-Hutchinson, (tr.), *Pliny, Letters,* 2 vols., Cambridge, 1958–61.
Sherwin-White, A. N., *The Letters of Pliny: a Historical and Social Commentary,* Oxford, 1966.

**PROPERTIUS**

Butler, H. E., (tr.), *Propertius,* Cambridge, 1952.
Carrier, C., (tr.), *Propertius: Poems,* Bloomington, 1963.

**QUINTILIAN**

Butler, H. E., (tr.), *Quintilian, the Institutio Oratoria,* 4 vols., Cambridge, 1953–63.
Gwynn, A. O., *Roman Education from Cicero to Quintilian,* New York, 1966.

**SENECA**

Basore, J. W., (tr.), *Seneca, Moral Essays,* 3 vols., Cambridge, 1951–58.
Charlton, H. B., *The Senecan Tradition in Renaissance Tragedy,* Manchester, 1946.
Gummere, R. M., (tr.), *Seneca, Epistulae Morales,* Cambridge, 1958.
Gummere, R. M., *Seneca the Philosopher and His Modern Message,* New York, 1963.
Tragedies: see *Plautus:* Copley and Hadas, Duckworth, (trs.).

**SUETONIUS**

Rolfe, J. C., (tr.), *Suetonius,* 2 vols., Cambridge, 1950–51.

**TACITUS**

Boissier, G., *Tacitus and Other Roman Studies,* New York, 1906.
Church-Brodribb-Hadas, (trs.), *Tacitus, the Complete Works,* New York, 1942.
Syme, R., *Tacitus,* Oxford, 1958.

**TERENCE**

Copley, F. O., (tr.), *The Comedies of Terence,* New York, 1967.
Graves, R. (ed., tr.), *The Comedies of Terence,* New York, 1962.
Norwood, G., *The Art of Terence,* Oxford, 1923.
See *Plautus:* Beare, Duckworth.

**TIBULLUS**

Postgate, J. P., *Tibullus, with Catullus and the Pervigilium Veneris,* Cambridge, 1966.

**VERGIL**

Bovie, S. P., (tr.), *Virgil, the Georgics,* Chicago, 1956.

Copley, F. O., (tr.), *Vergil, the Aeneid,* New York, 1965.

Humphries, R., (tr.), *Virgil, the Aeneid,* Boston, 1951.

Jackson Knight, W. F., (tr.), *Virgil, the Aeneid,* London, 1956.

Lewis, C. D., (tr.), *The Aeneid of Virgil,* New York, 1952.

———. *The Eclogues of Virgil,* London, 1963.

Lewis, C. S., *A Preface to Paradise Lost,* New York, 1942.

Lind, L. R., (tr.), *Vergil's Aeneid,* Bloomington, 1963.

Otis, Brooks, *Virgil, a Study in Civilized Poetry,* Oxford, 1964.

Putnam, M. C. J., *The Poetry of the Aeneid,* Cambridge, 1965.

Quinn, K., *Virgil's Aeneid, a Critical Description,* London (and Ann Arbor), 1968.

Rand, E. K., *The Mystical Art of Virgil,* Cambridge, 1931.

Rieu, E. V., (tr.), *Virgil, the Pastoral Poems,* London, 1954.

For additional bibliography of interest to the general reader, see the excellent lists published regularly by *Classical World* under the title "Inexpensive Books for Teaching the Classics" (most recent list, by Ursula Schoenheim, *C.W.* 62, 1969, pp. 173-86).

# Index of Proper Names

*(The names are alphabetized under the form most likely to be known to the general reader, or under the form actually used in the text.)*